Problems of American Society: Values in Conflict

Problems of American Society: Values in Conflict

THIRD EDITION

JOHN F. CUBER
The Ohio State University

•

ROBERT A. HARPER
Washington, D. C.

•

WILLIAM F. KENKEL
Iowa State College

New York: HENRY HOLT AND COMPANY

21630-0316
PRINTED IN THE UNITED STATES OF AMERICA

To the memory of
Richard C. Fuller

Preface

As stated in the Preface to the first edition, the idea that underlies this book was suggested by the late Professor Richard Fuller and other sociologists over a decade ago. Professor Fuller decried the tendency to make of the social-problems course an omnibus of facts and pronouncements on social problems and their remedies—a hodgepodge without explicit statements indicating how a social problem is defined and the role of the sociologist in the many-sided task of studying and treating it. It was Fuller's view—and we are in complete agreement with him—that values fostered by various persons and groups run at cross-purposes. *This does not deny that there are many causes of the problem conditions; rather it emphasizes that the societal condition becomes a problem condition coincident with the emergence of value clashes concerning it.* This point of view is explained more fully in the Introduction.

This third edition incorporates the efforts of a third author—in fact, practically all of the detailed work and a considerable amount of the over-all revision planning have been his. He belongs to the younger generation of sociologists and has a prime interest in social stratification.

Changes are of two types. First, newer statistics and other factual materials have been incorporated in the unending process of "bringing up to date" the substantive part of the book. This has occurred in virtually every chapter, and in some instances it has necessitated the addition not only of more recent statistical material, but also of new kinds of factual data to supplement or to supplant the earlier treatment. Second, there have occurred several alterations of subject matter. A new chapter on the vexing problem of maintaining national security in the context of

vii

traditional personal liberties has been added. The treatment of the problem of mental health is now confined to one chapter, chiefly by the reduction of attention to the less sociological aspects of the problem. Problems of older people are given much more attention, not so much because the problems are more acute than they were five years ago, but because we know more about them now. The former more diffuse treatment of "social class" has now become more sharply focused on the dynamic interplay of pressure groups.

We have tried to resist the temptation to "revise" by the process of addition. Even though the present volume is slightly longer than the second edition, there has been much culling and substituting, especially in Part 2, which constitutes the major part of the volume.

This is a book for students. It is written out of experience with students, their questions, their hopes, and their fears; it is projected toward their world—tomorrow.

Columbus, Ohio   J. F. C.
Washington, D. C.   R. A. H.
Ames, Iowa   W. F. K.

February 1, 1956

Contents

Part 3: *American Ideologies and Values*

Introduction · On Theory and Pedagogy for the Social Problems Course

Authors of textbooks are usually spurred to their unexciting task by the belief that they have conceived of some new need or of some unique approach which will improve the utility of the courses for which the book is intended. Sometimes the faith that the book is a contribution springs from new or modified concepts of a sociological-theoretical sort and sometimes from new or modified pedagogical notions. Often the adverse evaluation of a book results from a failure on the part of the author to make explicit the theoretical and pedagogical assumptions he makes, the purposes he has in mind, the kind of courses for which the book is intended, and how the book relates to the total course. This introduction is intended as an express statement of what this book purports to do and to be. It is also designed to make suggestions as to pedagogy and as to the relations of this book to other materials properly involved in a social problems course on the elementary college level.

Theoretical considerations. Social problems courses, generally speaking, suffer from a lack of sociological integration. They tend to be—or come to be—more or less of a hodgepodge of interesting but largely unrelated and theoretically undisciplined confabulations upon current events, with emphases upon the bizarre and the pathological. Students' interest, as a rule, runs higher than their learning as judged by more or less strict sociological criteria. Since social problems courses are usually taught in sociology departments and by sociologists, it would seem that the latter should reasonably be held responsible for the sociological character of the courses.

What is, however, the sociological (as distinct from some other) frame of reference for studying social problems? Probably at this time there are several frames of reference which can be called "sociological," and the treatment of values is a crucial difference among them. Certainly no consistent orientation to values can be found among the existing textbooks in social problems. Within a given book there is often reasonable consistency, but between books one can easily observe at least one fundamental and significant dichotomy. Some sociologists take a frank and unabashed position espousing or rationalizing some value or set of values. This makes the social problems course, for better or for worse, an undertaking of an ethical character. There is ample precedent for this type of an approach. The propriety of an implicit or explicit espousal of values in the elementary social problems book could be documented with a long list of sociological worthies including such honored names as Edward A. Ross, Charles Ellwood, John Gillen, Stuart Queen, and Cecil C. North, to mention only a few. The legitimacy of such an approach is by no means denied, although we would take issue with the assumption that this is the *only* approach, or necessarily the most acceptable approach, to the social problems course. Certainly, of course, someone has the right to advocate or recommend that this or that value position is better or worse than some other one. We, however, do not choose to accept that responsibility. There is another way to handle the value matter. Instead of *advocating* a value position, the sociologist may assume the role of treating values *as data*. For this point of view there is also precedent in the sociological tradition, although it seems not to be consistently exploited as the frame of reference in any of the existing textbooks for the over-all treatment of social problems on the elementary level. The *An American Dilemma* by Myrdal may well be regarded as representative of this point of view. The crux of Myrdal's hypothesis seems to be that the race problem in the

United States grows out of the incongruities of democratic values and authoritarian value survivals from a predemocratic system.

Existing textbooks in social problems can be roughly dichotomized on the basis of the above distinction between value espousal and value analysis. At least three factors, however, complicate the undertaking:

1. Current textbooks differ in the degree to which they make their value assumptions explicit. C. Wright Mills'[1] well-known article on the professional ideologies of social pathologists presents sharply, if not also caustically, some of the insidious penetration of value considerations into works whose authors disclaim their advocacy of, or even their assumption of, value positions. Thus it is probably possible to err, or at least to reach a difference of opinion, as to whether a given book actually advocates some value position or not.

2. It is also difficult to determine the value position of a work because of the indirectness of the value orientation. Sometimes the valuations of the author are once, twice, or thrice removed from the actual evaluation of data. This is found, for example, in the approach through such a frame of reference as the organization-disorganization hypothesis. In such instances the author frequently purports to be entirely objective and without bias in examining his data but, as Fuller[2] and others have pointed out, actually he employs his biases in the implicit or explicit conception of or evaluation of the disorganization process. Actually he reasons thus: Condition A, about which we are neutral, is an example of disorganization which is bad; therefore, Condition A is bad, not because we are biased, but because it conforms to the criteria of disorganization!

3. The dichotomy is also obscured to the degree to which the author dodges the question of defining social problems themselves. Are they those conditions which *he* thinks are problems, or which he thinks his *colleagues* think are problems, or those

[1] C. Wright Mills, "The Professional Ideology of Social Pathologists," *American Journal of Sociology*, Vol. 49 (1944), pp. 165-81.

[2] Richard C. Fuller, "The Problem of Teaching Social Problems," *American Journal of Sociology*, Vol. 44 (1939), pp. 415-35.

conditions which *the groups in the society* cause to become problems by forcing them into the level of conscious discussion?

What, then, is the frame of reference which we conceive as having greatest utility for an elementary textbook in social problems? The chosen frame of reference, of course, is not ours—except by adoption. It is the frame of reference formulated by the late Professor Richard Fuller of the University of Michigan. Fuller, himself, did not claim the theory solely as his own, but admitted intellectual dependency specifically upon Lawrence K. Frank and the late Willard Waller.

[In Fuller's own words,[3] the frame of reference is as follows:

> The phenomena which we commonly refer to as social problems have one thing in common: They represent a social condition which is regarded by a considerable number of individuals as undesirable, and hence these persons believe that something "ought to be done" about the situation. This means that our value-judgments derived from culture define given conditions as social problems. Second, value-judgments themselves are in most instances a formal cause of the condition which is regarded as undesirable. For instance, our pecuniary emphasis incites crimes for gain against private property, our profit mores prevent employers from continuing the employment of workers at a loss to themselves, our sacred worship of monogamous marriage compels the unwed mother to neglect her child. Third, value-judgments prevent people from agreeing on "solutions" because most of them are unwilling to forsake those values which are causal factors in the problem—for example, we are reluctant to abandon "conspicuous consumption" though it incites stealing among children; employers fear that collective bargaining will "put them out of business" by destroying profits; we dare not give the illegitimate child inheritance rights and the name of the father though we recognize that it is the stigma which makes the problem.]

The utility of the Fuller-Frank-Waller frame of reference seems to us to lie in several considerations.

1. It is consistent with the amoral position of the sociologist-analyst. The admonition not to engage in the propagandizing of particular value positions is a well-established one in the

---

[3] Fuller, *op. cit.*, p. 419. This and the following quotation reprinted by permission of The University of Chicago Press, publishers.

sociological tradition. It is held, by no means exclusively, for example, by positivists. [We feel that for our time, at least, the sociologist is better suited to the role of *interpreter of values* than to the role of *value advocate.*]

2. This frame of reference seems to be a good vehicle for the realistic study of value positions in regard to interest groups, classes, and other group advocates of points of view. Fuller illustrates this himself.

For example, a substantial number of Detroit citizens [1939] are becoming alarmed over the trailer-residence situation. It is a social problem to certain widely varied groups of individuals having very little in common. The health officials are concerned; and the school authorities see a threat to attendance standards. These groups are bringing pressure to eliminate or restrict trailer villages. Is this the urge of humanitarianism or is it the desire to perpetuate basic organizational mores pertaining to public health and education? Be that as it may, real estate operators, hotel owners, neighborhood residents, and taxpayers also want the homes on wheels banned from the community. Their motivations are pecuniary and spring from the profit mores—hence, they are organizational and definitely not humanitarian. These interest groups collide with another set of organizational mores articulated in the Coach Trailer Manufacturers' Association, which is a pressure group fighting those pressure groups which are trying to license, tax, and otherwise restrict trailer residences. Then there are the value motivations of those who live in trailers. They have a pressure group of their own in the Mobile Home Owners' Association of America. This organization contends that trailer homes are the solution to the housing problem with property and rental costs held beyond the means of most people by the organizational mores of capitalism. We even find humanitarian sentiments arrayed against other humanitarian sentiments, for example, our urge to let the trailer resident solve his housing problem in his own way is tempered by our fears for his health, morals, and the education of his children.

So the core of the social problem is a multi-sided conflict of interests with humanitarian interests joining forces with organizational interests to combat other humanitarian and organizational interests. The job of the sociologist is to isolate and define those conflicting value-judgments which are the *modus operandi* of the problem. He must chart the oppositions and cooperations between the warring pressure groups. He must lay bare the issues of policy which in their conflict deter the public in its solution of the problem. His findings should revitalize our theories of social control. After his spadework is done, he should be in a position to say to the social planners, "Attitudes and values being what they are today, you may (or may not, as the case may be) expect success with the program you have in mind"; or, "Before your plan will work you will have to change the attitudes and policies of this or that interest group."

This analysis in terms of what certain interest groups think they have to gain or lose can be applied with equal success to all our social problems. The discussions of what should be done about automobile fatalities turn on the interests of certain well-established pressure groups. Shall we require all drivers to carry public liability insurance, shall we place automatic governors on the speed of cars, shall we replace fines with jail sentences for offenders, shall we publish gory pictures of accident victims? Interested in these questions of policy are automobile clubs, tax-payers' associations, insurance companies, police officials, automobile manufacturers, citizens' safety councils, school officials, et cetera. Here is the area for sociological study of the patterns of discussion, conflict, and compromise which evolve in the natural history of the problem.

Likewise, in the theater of labor conflict we do not have a neat dichotomy of interest groups such as employers versus workers, but again a very complex alignment: big business against big business; big business against little business; big and little business against C.I.O.; big and little business against A.F. of L.; C.I.O. versus A.F. of L.; company unions versus independent unions; unaffiliated workers against union workers; citizens' vigilantes against union workers. Within the C.I.O. we have the communists, communist party opposition, socialists, middle-grounders, right-wingers, and what not; within the A.F. of L., similar if not as diverse factions.

It is with such concrete realities that the teacher of social problems must deal. *He need no longer hold himself out as an authority on everything* from technological unemployment to dementia praecox. To the contrary, his function will be that of demonstrating how various social philosophies, notions, and taboos pertain to these phenomena. *He need not be an expert on social problems but an expert on the sociology of social problems.*[4]

3. This frame of reference makes explicit the needed emphasis that problem areas may emerge in a society as a result

[4] Fuller, *op. cit.*, pp. 422-24. (The italics are the authors'.)

of changes in the value structure *per se*, and not simply as a residuum from biological or economic changes as has too long been inferred from the Ogburn cultural lag hypothesis and the social disorganization theory. The point is not that these earlier frames of reference denied the possibility of a more or less independent variable of values, but rather that their emphasis tended to direct attention away from such an important possibility.

4. Such a mode of treatment as that advocated by Fuller assists us in keeping data and theory in better perspective *for a sociological treatment* of social problems. Sociologists are not the only ones who study social problems. Nor are they the only ones who have a vital interest in the outcome. What seems to be needed, and what sociologists seem best able to perform in an ultimately practical way, is to exploit the role of understanding social problems *from the point of view of their relation to group-related values*, both instrumental and more ultimate. So long as we use this point of view, we seem less likely to get "bogged down" with reams of tables and charts on mere technological aspects of social problems. We do not mean to depreciate the technological aspect of social problems *on the professional level of research*. We do advocate keeping the *introductory* treatment of social problems on the level of such conceptions as "What are various groups really fighting for?" and "Why are they fighting for them?" and "What are the results of these value clashes?"

In this book we have probably taken some liberties with the Fuller-Frank-Waller frame of reference, which none of them would endorse. All that is claimed is that we have made an attempt, tempered somewhat by considerations of pedagogy and based upon our own and others' classroom experience, to write a somewhat encompassing interpretation of the main value currents of American life with respect to social problems and related conditions.

It will require no academic Sherlock Holmes to discover, despite the attempt to be fair to various value "sides," what are the authors' value positions on many matters. We have not assumed the obligation of "covering our tracks." But we have endeavored to remain primarily in the role of analysts.

Scope and pedagogy. Any general treatise on social problems is to some degree arbitrary as to items included and excluded, phases of the data emphasized more and less, and the order of treatment. This arbitrariness is unavoidable because of the vastness of the total data. Eclecticism, moreover, unavoidably involves some degree of personal predilection; thus the personal and professional judgments of the authors of this book are evident throughout. The book is so organized, however, that it can easily be adapted to the widely varying judgments of different teachers as to which problems should and should not be treated, which ones minimized and which ones emphasized. Accordingly, Parts 1 and 3 contain the essentials of theory, which, when adequately mastered by the student, should equip him to analyze meaningfully a somewhat wide variety of social problems in terms of our stated frame of reference. Should, then, some teacher prefer to include a treatment on the "social problems of war," which we omitted, he may do so at any point in Part 2, using any materials which he may find available and useful. Similarly, if he wishes to omit the problem of recreation and leisure, for example, he may do so without handicapping the student in his over-all understanding of the frame of reference and of its application to other social problems conditions. This, we think, might go far toward allowing a maximum of variation at the discretion of the teacher while maintaining a unity of theoretical sociology in line with the Fuller-Frank-Waller theme.

Part 1

A Framework
for Studying
Social Problems

· 1 · Orientation to the Study of Social Problems

The word "social" in the expression "social problems" makes it apparent that conditions so labeled affect people in a society. For this reason, it is not difficult to engender an interest in the study of social problems. Some conditions are discussed that touch directly and deeply the lives of the students analyzing the problems, and it is almost impossible not to imagine or discover that all problems of a society have *some* implication for each of its members. Throughout the study of social problems many new, and sometimes startling, facts will be met. "Red-hot arguments" among students will probably occur on numerous occasions to add to the zest of the course. But the study of social problems can also be *significant* as well as merely interesting. Too often students who study social problems fail to get as much out of the course as they might because there is a lack of vital meaning in the various activities and a lack of uniformity in the approaches to the problems studied. We believe that this book will provide the opportunity for the student to acquire a meaningful and useful point of view, that it will assist him in being an informed citizen with respect to his relation to social problems at least.

▶ FACTS AND MORE FACTS

Use and misuse of "facts." Judging by popular comment, there is great respect for "getting the facts," and the person who has them is purportedly much sought after. Facts are in demand

3

because they are supposed to give one knowledge, understanding, and insight into some area of life.

To be sure, facts are necessary but they are not worth much *in themselves*. Certainly facts alone do not give adequate understanding and may actually lead one to serious confusion and even error. The reason for this is that facts are only the raw materials of knowledge or understanding, as the bricks, lumber, and nails are the raw materials of a house. Facts, then, are basic but insufficient. What more is needed to complete one's understanding?

What do facts mean?   Facts must be interpreted in order to have meaning. Facts may be interpreted in more than one way. Let us take, for example, the fact that in more or less prosperous times there are around two million American wage earners who are unemployed. That means that nearly sixteen million man-hours of work are wasted each day and nearly four billion man-hours of unused skill and effort are lost during a so-called prosperous year. Now what does this set of facts mean? Obviously, it means different things to different people. To the unemployed workman, or to his wife or to his children, it means hunger, insecurity, and countless daily frustrations; to the employer trying to get a job done as cheaply as possible, it probably means getting work done for somewhat lower wages than would prevail if everyone were employed; to the social worker it means more clients; to the merchant it means more customers who are unable to pay their bills; to the courts it means people to be evicted for nonpayment of rent; and so on and on. Somewhat more profoundly, does an unemployed group of two million workers even during "good times" mean that we have a "good" or a "bad" economic system? Do these two million people "count"—or are they merely the price which some people have to pay in individual misery in order to keep an economic system going? Or does it mean simply that The Holy Bible is good prophecy because we note there that "Ye have the poor with you always"? Or does it mean that the threat of falling into the ranks of the unemployed is the spur which makes men work; we need the unemployed as a living example to the man who is tempted to be lazy that this too would be his fate. We could go on endlessly with the problem of interpretation, but our purpose has probably already been achieved —namely, to demonstrate that a simple statistical fact may mean many different things to different people or to the same person who considers it in several different contexts. What makes up these "different contexts" for interpreting facts? And what basically different contexts are there? These, and other similar questions we shall try to answer throughout this book.

Which interpretations of facts are the correct ones? Here, again, there is no easy answer, in fact there may be no answer possible. Correct *to whom?* Rich or poor? Old or young? The religious or the irreligious? Obviously, again, the legitimacy of using a term like "correct" is in serious doubt, unless one is so bigoted or so ignorant that he does not recognize the existence and the legitimacy of varying frames of reference for determining correctness. Only the naïve and the misinformed expect that there is only *one* correct interpretation possible; the wise man knows that there are several—maybe an infinite number—of correct ones. To be sure, all of us are not equally naïve in our assumptions of correctness, nor are we equally intolerant of the existence of interpretations opposing our own, but the interpretive horizons of all of us are to some degree at least limited by our knowledge of other facts and nonfactual understandings and intentions.

Isolated facts mean almost nothing. Any fact derives its significance from its relationship to other facts in the knowledge of the person. The fact of a normal reservoir of two million of unemployed men in the United States, *when added to other facts*, begins to take on meaning. Moreover some of the related matters which supply the perspectives to which we have referred, are not facts at all, but are, instead, pertinent ethical principles such as justice. Thus, many of the disagreements among us in regard to the significance of some fact which we all know arise from differences among us in regard to the number and kind of *other data* with which we are acquainted.

▶ THE IMPORTANCE OF A "POINT OF VIEW" OR A "FRAME OF REFERENCE"

As we have seen in the foregoing paragraphs, much depends upon the point of view from which factual matters are observed. We also must recognize that the given fact itself is only a valid fact from some one point of view. Suppose two men observe an arc from two sides of a room, thus.

Joe — — — — →) ← — — — — Jack

What, now, is the "fact": Is the arc convex or concave? It is neither, or both. From Joe's point of view it is concave; from Jack's it is convex. They could, with honesty, argue from now till doomsday as to which was "correct" regarding the "fact" of the nature of the arc.

The interpretation of social facts—especially those pertaining to social problems—is often like our illustration. We disagree as to the facts themselves, as well as to their meanings because we reason often from different points of view. Catholics often differ from non-Catholics regarding the divorce "facts"; Republicans disagree with Democrats, and both with Socialists, regarding the facts of wage rates and especially the interpretations thereof.

A sociological point of view. In this book we shall try to maintain what might be called a "sociological" point of view. The chief characteristic of the sociological point of view is the deliberate attempt to see both—or all—points of view from which the various persons and groups "see" social problems. Going back to our previous illustration of Joe and Jack and the arc, the point of view which we shall attempt to maintain is that of a somewhat detached observer who can understand why Joe argues that the arc is concave and why Jack argues that it is convex. But having the *perspective* which we do, we have a greater understanding, because we have the advantage of *all* of the various—or at least *several* of the various—points of view.

This objective, detached, sociological point of view is not easy to achieve. Anyone can get the point regarding the arc in the above illustration, but it is an oversimplification of the kind of objectivity on social problems which is readily attainable. Everyone can see that both Joe and Jack had good reason for his "view" because Joe and Jack are abstractions with which we do not identify ourselves. But if the illustrations were, instead, the points of view of Catholics and most non-Catholics on birth control, then it might be much less easy to recognize that there are two "good" sides because each one of us is already more or less committed to one view or another, and the other one seems not very tenable, "logical," "realistic." So it is with almost every social fact which we shall attempt to interpret or to evaluate.

▶ SOME BASIC UNDERSTANDINGS IN THE SOCIOLOGICAL POINT OF VIEW

The following are four of the underlying understandings which experience has shown are useful as a means to the effective achievement of an objective, unprejudiced point of view regarding social problems and the facts about them.

Dynamic society and static attitudes. "Times have changed" is a popular cliché. "Times" have always changed, but man seems almost always reluctant to accept the requirements which changing times impose upon him. While he admits now and then, usually somewhat grudgingly, that times have changed, man tends to act and to think as if times had *not* changed. This is quite natural, of course, because change in the system of human relationships brings need for other readjustment requiring time, energy, and inconvenience for the person who must fit his ways to the new order. And often by the time man has adjusted his ways and ideals to fit the so-called "new" state of affairs, he finds that he is already out of date because the world has changed again. Ceaseless, bewildering change seems to be largely uncontrollable and inherent in the nature of human society, especially of the kind of society which we have in America.

We often speak glibly of a social "system" or a social "order," implying by these words that there is a greater stability and permanence to human society than the facts warrant. There is, of course, a system and an order to human society, but it is a moving and dynamic system, not a static one.

Past uncontrollability of social change. It is now more or less generally recognized that the changing nature of society is closely related to the intermittent appearance and disappearance of "trouble spots" in human relationships, which we call "social problems." It appears to the layman, and sometimes also to the professional analyst of human affairs, that, if somehow we could stop the onward surge of social change, human life would be somewhat better because we would then eventually "catch up" in the solution of our problems.

History is replete with examples of societies which have passed long series of laws designed to prevent social change or to force persons to go back to some pre-existing modes of behavior or systems of human relationship. During the great business depression of the 1930's, when unemployment was rampant, it was suggested that we "declare a moratorium on invention"—that is, that we should prohibit the replacement of men by new machinery for the production of goods. But invariably all such efforts have been in vain, for no society has yet been able to stop the clock of change. It is doubtful, even, whether the clock can be slowed down to any appreciable extent or for long periods. In our time as in other times, there are those persons and groups who still try to accomplish the impossible: to establish a changeless, static system of human affairs. The futility of this undertaking having been so frequently and so decisively demonstrated, it would seem reasonable to expect that eventually some other orientation and interpretation of social change would develop. While there are signs that a more sophisticated understanding of the inevitability of change is becoming diffused in American society, there is also abundant evidence that there are many among us who have not yet learned this primary lesson of social science. There are those who still try to move sociological mountains by avalanches of words and frantic appeals to their political medicine men.

Understanding and rational adjustment, control, or direction of change. Understanding social change does not necessarily mean a supine acceptance of the blind and heartless forces of chance. One may seek to understand some universal phenomenon, like the weather, largely so that one can adjust to it with a minimum of effort and be able to secure the maximum attainment of one's wishes which the immutable circumstances will permit. Or one may seek to understand trends for the purpose of anticipating events before they happen. The accurate forecasting of weather, for example, makes it possible for fruit-growers to anticipate a frost, take precautions against it, and thus save a fair proportion of the crop which would have been destroyed completely if the grower did not know of the impending freeze until it was upon him.

Moreover, understanding may eventually make it possible to control and to direct social change more successfully than in the past. Thus, if and when we understand the factors responsible for automobile accidents, we may be able to control them in such a way as to reduce some of the casualties which annually result from automobile accidents. If we understand the factors which make for juvenile delinquency, we may find that we can control or eliminate some of them, and thus reduce the incidence of this national scourge. So with many others of our social problems.

Difficulties of understanding social change objectively. Understanding, however, is not easy, especially in a society as complex as ours. The facts and forces involved in social changes and social problems are so numerous, so subtle, and so inextricably interrelated that the task of understanding becomes an involved technical process. On the simplest level, understanding involves a knowledge of the magnitude and incidence of the problem and change involved. For some of our social problems we do not now know these fundamental data.

Far more difficult is the question of cause. The person who is relatively ignorant of sociological matters usually speaks quite glibly about the question of causality. He tends to base his conclusions on (1) *a priori* judgments—that is, what appears to be "logical," "reasonable," or "natural"; or (2) the observation of one or a few cases with which he is personally familiar. Scientific students of human behavior have long since demonstrated that both the *a priori* and the informal case methods are not only largely useless but often actually lead to serious error. The adequate understanding of the nature, cause, and treatment of social problems is a specialized technical task. Until such time as Americans more widely recognize this, we may reasonably expect to continue to be unable to cope effectively with our collective societal problems. It is as futile to entrust explanations of complex and technical societal questions to the well-intentioned efforts of the untrained layman as to entrust questions of medical diagnosis and treatment to a clergyman. Good intentions are no substitute for scientific knowledge.

▶ PREVIEW OF THIS BOOK

The purpose of this book is primarily to provide a basic point of view for the scientific understanding of social problems and, secondarily, to outline some of the basic social problems which currently exist in American society. We shall examine not only the nature and extent of the problems as far as these have been statistically determined, but shall also briefly treat some of our major findings concerning the causes of and factors involved in each of these problems, together with various evaluations of the proposals for handling them.

Before treating specific problems, however, we must first achieve at least three preliminary objectives:

1. We shall need to understand something of the nature of the emerging society within which the present generation is living. In other words, we must come to appreciate more accurately than most citizens do, some of the forms and directions which social change in America is taking and, if possible, the speed with which these changes are occurring.

2. We shall need to examine the idea of "social problem" itself. What makes some particular condition a social problem? Is it a problem simply because it is harmful? Harmful to whom? Suppose it is harmful to one class and not to

another, is it then a social problem? What determines whether or not a given condition is considered harmful?

3. Finally, before discussing any specific problem, we shall need to discuss the whole *concept of treatment* in general. Social problems are rarely "solved" or "cured" in the literal sense of these words. Often problems are only ameliorated. There are many different approaches to the treatment of problems, such as the approach "through the individual" over against the approach "through the group" or "through society more or less as a whole."

The next chapter is devoted primarily to the first of these three preliminary objectives. We turn, then, first to an examination of some of the important changing phases of American life.

SUGGESTED READINGS

Cuber, John F., *Sociology: A Synopsis of Principles*, New York, Appleton-Century-Crofts, 1955, Chap. 2. A considerably more detailed discussion of the sociological frame of reference than we have offered here. This material is not specially oriented to social *problems*, but is as applicable to understanding them as has been the discussion in this chapter.

Lee, Alfred M., and Elizabeth B. Lee, *Social Problems in America: A Source Book*, rev. ed., New York, Henry Holt and Co., 1955, Chap. 1. An excellent collection of excerpts designed to orient the student to the study of social problems.

Lemert, Edwin M., *Social Pathology*, New York, McGraw-Hill Book Co., 1951, Chap. 1. This chapter contains a critical examination of early viewpoints on social problems and a presentation of the author's own theory of "sociopathic behavior."

Nordskog, John E., and others, *Analyzing Social Problems*, New York, The Dryden Press, 1950, Chap. 1. A collection of six articles on the nature of social problems selected to illustrate the differences in approach to the study.

STUDY QUESTIONS

1. What is meant by the statement that "facts" are only the raw materials of knowledge or understanding?

2. Why is it that facts may be interpreted in more than one way? Illustrate with an example of your own how a given fact can be interpreted differently.

3. Why is a point of view or frame of reference necessary even to establish the validity of a fact?

4. What is meant by the "sociological point of view" with regard to the study of social problems? Illustrate with an example of your own why this point of view is not easy to achieve.

5. Discuss the possibility of slowing down or stopping social change. Can you think of a current illustration of an attempt to prevent social change?

6. Distinguish between understanding social change and blind acceptance of the results of change.

7. Illustrate with an example other than one used in the text how understanding of social change may make it possible to control and direct it.

8. What is meant by *a priori* judgments? Give an example of such a judgment that has led to error in understanding a given condition.

9. What are the dangers in using one's personal experiences with one or a few cases as a basis for studying social problems? Of what utility could such personal experiences be?

· 2 · Our Dynamic Society

There is no such thing as a static, never-changing society. In some eras and in some societies change may appear to be slight; in other times and in different societies change may be rapid, dramatic, and all-encompassing. It is, nevertheless, true that the fundamental lesson of human history is that human societies are dynamic. Even after one has studied a considerable amount of social history and has mastered the general proposition that human society is ever-changing, he may easily underestimate the true *extent* of the change through which he has lived or the many different aspects of his society which have been significantly modified.

The purpose of this chapter is to investigate the nature and extent of change in recent American society and to provide some interpretation of its meaning. We can, of course, fill in only a small fraction of the total picture, for so many phases of American society have been profoundly altered in the last half century or so that a library of books would be required to trace them all. Brief as our treatment necessarily is, it may help the student to appreciate the contrasts between yesterday and today, the problems of interpreting these changes, and the necessity of learning to think in terms of a dynamic society instead of a static one as the more naïve tend to do.

Inventions and innovations. When the typical layman thinks and talks of the "changes" that have taken place in his society, he frequently begins and ends with a cataloging of "wonderful inventions" and new "things" that we have produced. It is difficult to remain oblivious of the new material products of our culture and, lest we forget, we are constantly reminded that such "everyday conveniences" as telephones, radios, automobiles, and aircraft came into use within the lifetime of many living Americans. These and a host of other inventions and improvements *are* important and have had far-reaching effects. The very world in which we live, for example, has "shrunk," in the sense that the extent to which men are able to *participate* in that world has increased phenomenally. It has been estimated that there is at present no place on earth capable of constructing an airfield that is more than two or three days travel time away from any other similarly equipped spot.

All too frequently, however, we are prone to ignore the innovations that have taken place in nontechnological areas.[1]

During the past ten or fifteen years, the innovations that have had a major impact on the American economy were nearly all non-technological, were nearly all innovations in something else than product or process. First among them certainly stands the tremendous changes in distribution methods. Hardly less important, especially in its impact on productivity, has been the development of new concepts of business organization. There have been tremendous innovations in plant, store, and office architecture; similarly in respect to the management of worker and work, whether industrial engineering, human relations, or personnel management. Finally there is the emergence of new basic management tools, especially measurements and controls like budgets, cost accounting, production scheduling and inventory controls. . . . *In the long view of history, it is for social inventions—and not technical ones—that Americans may be best remembered.*

Drucker's outline of "social inventions" could, of course, be elaborated and greatly extended, and the resulting list of innovations and their impact would be impressive. The extension of the ballot to women, mass public education, and our attempts at racial equality, meager as they sometimes appear, represent but a few of the multitude of "new ideas" which we have witnessed in recent years.

Rural-urban population shift. Within the last 150 years this nation has evolved from a nation made up almost entirely of rural people to one in which over two thirds of the people live in

[1] Reprinted from Peter F. Drucker, "America's Next Twenty Years," Part I, *Harper's Magazine*, Vol. 210 (March 1955), p. 32, by permission.

cities. Even within the past 50 years we can notice profound changes: there are over three times the number of people living in cities as there were in 1900 and the proportion of urbanites has risen from almost 40 percent to 64 percent.

The enormity of the change that has taken place becomes even more evident when we consider the *size* of the cities in which millions of Americans live. Over 44 million people are living in metropolitan areas with populations of more than a million. Almost every third American lives in one of our 108 cities with a population over 100,000. By way of contrast, a scant 13 percent of our population lives on farms.

Changing occupational patterns. Coincident with the shift from rural to urban living has occurred a change in the occupa-

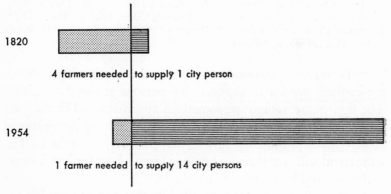

1820

4 farmers needed | to supply 1 city person

1954

1 farmer needed | to supply 14 city persons

Fig. 1. The number of farmers needed to supply city persons, 1820 and 1954. (Based on a press release of the U. S. Department of Agriculture.)

tions at which Americans work. Perhaps the most noticeable occupational change that has occurred since 1910 (Table 1) is the vast decrease in the number of farmers and farm laborers. An excellent insight can be obtained into one of the major factors in the decline in farming pursuits by examining the graph in Figure 1 on this page. To be sure, almost 150 years were required to make the radical shift, but nevertheless the required ratio of city persons to farmers has increased 56 times! It should be noted, however, that these figures do not refer to the *actual* number of

Table 1. Changing Occupational Composition of the United States *

Occupation	Percent in 1910	Percent in 1953	Direction and degree of change
Farmers	16.5	6.2	Reduced by over 60%
Farm laborers	14.5	4.9	Reduced by two thirds
Professionals	4.4	9.2	More than doubled
Proprietors and officials	6.5	10.2	Increased by 57%
Clerks, sales, and kindred workers	10.2	18.6	Increased by 82%
Skilled and semiskilled workers	26.4	33.9	Increased by 28%
Laborers	14.7	6.1	Reduced by 58%

* Data taken from *Abstract of the Fifteenth Census of the United States*, Washington, D. C., U. S. Government Printing Office, 1933, p. 306; and U. S. Bureau of the Census, *Statistical Abstract of the United States: 1955*. Washington, D. C., 1955, p. 207.

farmers and city persons, but rather to the relationship between the farmers *needed to support* city persons at the dates given. The figures are, moreover, somewhat approximate, but they are very useful to help one appreciate the extent of occupational change made possible by agricultural production methods. The same trend still continues and no one knows how far it can eventually go—and how soon!

Another dramatic occupational shift that has occurred is the increase in the proportion of professionals, proprietors, sales and clerical personnel, skilled and semiskilled workers, and the decrease in proportion of laborers of all types. In short, today's workers need more education and training than those of a half century ago. And with the present stress on mechanization, and, recently, automation, jobs in future years will probably require even more education and training than those of today.

Occupational shifts, finally, have not only affected the male breadwinner, but have also been evident in the increasing out-of-home employment of *married* women. Today about one out of **four** married women is gainfully employed outside the home, and, for the first time in our history, there are actually more married than single women in the labor force.

A more highly educated nation. Since the turn of the century significant changes have occurred in the educational attainments of Americans. In just about one generation, as a matter of fact, the proportion of college graduates has more than doubled, high school graduates have increased almost fourfold, and the relatively unschooled have shrunk by about 80 percent. Half of the people who in 1950 were between 25 and 29 years old, and presumably finished their schooling, had graduated from high school or had had additional education; half of those who were then 65 or over did not have much more than an eighth-grade education.

*Table 2. Educational Levels Attained by Persons 25-29 and 65 and Older, 1950 ***

Age	Percent completed less than 5 years	Percent completed 4 years high school	Percent completed 4 or more years college	Median grade in school completed
25-29	4.5	34.2	7.5	12.1
65 and over	22.0	9.6	3.4	8.2

* Computed from U. S. Bureau of the Census, *Statistical Abstracts of the United States: 1953*, Washington, D. C., 1953, p. 121.

As we noted previously, the occupational demand for better trained and educated personnel means that the nation must become even better educated. This is already reflected in present school enrollments and will become increasingly evident in the future. Whether the schools will be able to meet the demands placed on them is another matter. It is generally recognized that today both the professional staffs and physical plants of our elementary and secondary schools are grossly overtaxed. It is probable that this situation will become worse in the immediate future.

The college situation is said to be particularly acute. It has been estimated that in twenty years college enrollments will increase three- or fourfold and that a staggering nine to twelve million students will be in colleges and universities.[2] And even the highest estimate will represent but half of the college-age youths.

If, at first, it sounds incredible that such a high proportion of the nation's youths will be in college twenty years hence, we have but to recall the similar phenomenal change in educational attainment that has taken place within the lifetime of millions of Americans. Between 1900 and 1953 the proportion of youths 14 to 17 years old who were in school rose from 11 percent to almost 86 percent. Thus, we can now expect something approaching this growth in college attendance.

Impersonality of economic and other relationships. Today, relatively few people work at tasks which are of such a nature that the worker is able to see the exact product of his own labor in the form of goods or services produced. Nor can he usually, if ever, be held responsible by someone else, or by his own conscience, for inadequate effort or achievement. Instead, the great mass of Americans work at tasks which are highly specialized and for the most part far removed from the eventual consumer of the goods. Almost never does the consumer know who worked upon the goods he buys, nor does the worker know who consumes the product or service on which he works. This means that the rewards for work and skill must be evaluated almost solely in terms of wages received rather than in terms of pleasing the ultimate consumer and securing personal satisfaction from the job well done.

Likewise the consumer thinks of the product he buys quite impersonally, almost as if it had not been created by men at all. Worker and consumer are thus separated from each other by a chasm of impersonal and mechanized relationships which makes it impossible for either to see the other in any realistic sense. It is thought by many observers that the present problems of consumer-management-labor stem in considerable measure from the fact that none of the three really knows much, and therefore hardly cares, about the problems of the other.

[2] Drucker, *op. cit.*, p. 55.

Problem of social ethics. When we pointed out in the preceding discussion that no one really "cared" about the personal problems of others in the economic web, we perhaps committed a slight exaggeration and injustice. A more careful examination of the facts might not show that modern man is insensible to the plight of his fellows, *when he knows and understands them*, but that modern society is such that *it is difficult, if not impossible, even for a morally sensitive man or woman to see and appreciate many of the problems and points of view of men and women above and below him or her in the pyramid of occupational classes and jobs.* It is almost as if the person from each occupational class lives in another social world; about the "other" worlds, in their real and vital aspects, he knows but little. One may properly wonder whether the industrial manager who drives from the exclusive suburbs to his downtown factory through the neighborhoods of workingmen's homes knows less about what goes on inside those houses than these inhabitants know about the problems of the Cadillac-driving manager. No one has probably deliberately fostered this separatism, but it has occurred nevertheless, and now constitutes a fundamental and stubborn problem in the solution of economic problems many of which cut across class lines.

Large-scale labor organization. It is difficult to determine whether the recent rise of a strong and politically powerful labor union movement in America is cause or effect of this schism. It is quite probable that it may be both. Labor originally organized largely in order to be able to make a better wage bargain with employers who had in many cases a near monopoly on employment and the setting of wage rates. The employers tried by every means (both fair and foul) to break the trade union movement and for a time were successful. This further antagonized the workers and intensified their hostility toward employers as a class. Eventually stronger and stronger unions grew up until at present some persons believe that unionism constitutes a real challenge to the traditional power of capital-management. Each side nurses grudges against the other based upon past experience.

Both groups are probably made up of an appreciable number of well-meaning and morally sensitive people, and likewise each group contains persons of whom the opposite could be said. Meanwhile, it becomes increasingly difficult for either group, as a group, to see the problem from the point of view of the other in any real and vital sense. It is not difficult for members of either group to feel that the other has dealt unfairly and unkindly. Each group vies with the other to maintain officials in the government who will be favorable to its cause. The settlement of labor issues tends to be made on the basis of a struggle for dominance, rather than on the basis of understanding.

It is doubtful whether one may reasonably expect much change in the foregoing conditions in the near future. A noted economist has set forth a few of the reasons for this viewpoint: [3]

> Nor are the next twenty years likely to be years of industrial peace. On the contrary, all signs point to labor ferment: the rapid rise of total population without an accompanying rise of working population; the major technological shifts which will change large numbers of jobs from unskilled work to highly skilled; the resulting need for radical change in concepts of seniority and training; and the rapid growth of industry in sparsely unionized areas. Unrest may not arise merely between management and labor but fully as much, perhaps even more, between labor and the public, and within labor itself.

The extent to which labor organizations can meet these new demands and adjust to these changing conditions, then, will in part affect the level of its present political and economic strength.

An older population. The increase in the number and proportion of persons 65 years of age and older represents one of the more dramatic and significant changes that has taken place in our "dynamic society." At the mid-point of the century, it would have just about taken the cities of Chicago, Los Angeles, Philadelphia, Detroit, Washington, D. C., Cleveland, Baltimore, and Boston, at their 1950 population levels, to house all of the old people in the United States; the aged of 1900 could have been housed in *one* of the present-day cities, Chicago.

---

[3] Reprinted from Drucker, *op. cit.*, pp. 55-56, by permission.

While the sheer number of old people is important, it is likewise necessary to realize that the older segment of our population has been growing more than twice as fast as the population in general. Today (1955) the almost 14 million older people constitute 8.6 percent of the total population—double the proportion in 1900 and almost four times the proportion of aged in 1850. The best estimate for the year 2000 places the proportion of the aged between 13 and 15 percent of the national population.

Our society has barely begun to address itself to the imposing catalog of problems related to its aged. We need the productive efforts of our capable older citizens, yet, increasingly, we are fostering the policy of compulsive retirement at age 65. Housing, health, and recreation are three additional areas which will have to receive a decidedly different emphasis if we are to meet the needs of this rapidly increasing segment of the population. At present, it seems unlikely that the immediate future will see much relief in these problem areas, and it is probable that some of the problems of the aged will become intensified before, as a society, we can make the necessary adjustments in our thinking and our policies.

The immediate future in "our dynamic society." In the preceding pages we have reveiwed some of the recent changes in American society. In most cases, too, we have at least commented on whether this or that trend would continue, be reversed, or be accentuated in the immediate future. But it must not be imagined that most future changes, or even the most important future changes, will take place in the various foregoing areas. A well-known economist, Peter F. Drucker, has isolated eleven issues which he considers will be of political importance roughly twenty years hence. These issues have one point in common: in most cases, so few realize or understand the underlying conditions that there can scarcely be said to be a "public opinion" or, for that matter, a political policy concerning them. Let us look at these "eleven coming issues." [4]

---

[4] The following has been adapted and summarized from Drucker, *op. cit.*, pp. 52-59.

Water conservation. Population growth but chiefly industrial growth will increase our demand for water tremendously. At the same time, we are already depleting our water resources. Water conservation laws and policies are therefore expected to be important issues.

Power. Power needs are expected to increase even faster than water needs, and the use of atomic power will raise touchy political issues. The issues are expected to center around government regulation of atomic power facilities and government "partnership" in the production of atomic power.

Transportation. Most people are aware of the outmoded state of our highways. But future population and industrial growth will increase the demands on all types of transportation. Perhaps the most controversial issue will be the role of the federal government in building and maintaining an adequate and unified transportation system.

Housing. Within the next twenty years houses constructed some thirty years ago will have to be replaced. Modern housing will not fare much better, for even that which is relatively expensive is not necessarily well-built. Reasonably sound homes at a moderate price will be in great demand, and policies to provide them will be in the fore of local and national political controversies.

Schools. Population trends alone indicate an increased need for school facilities and personnel from kindergarten through college. Yet building programs do not even keep up with present demand and fewer teachers are presently being trained. The financing of higher education will be of particular concern.

Medical care. There will be increased demand for some method of providing adequate medical and hospital care for everyone, and even for the so-called "catastrophic illnesses." Proposals for the provision of such care for those who presently cannot afford it will be politically tense issues.

Labor unions. The four big issues with regard to trade unions are expected to center around the use of the strike, the conflict between union security and "the right to work," union restrictions of access to a craft, and the unionization of various categories of "white-collar" workers.

Economic equality of the Negro. Continued industrialization and emigration of the Negro from the South will combine to make the "race problem" an industrial one. The issue will shift from equal opportunity for employment to equal opportunity for advancement. While this would amount to complete economic equality, it may well encounter resistance.

The older worker. Legislation to prevent discrimination against the older worker is expected to be in demand. The increasing number of aged plus industrial change will necessitate new policies with regard to the hiring and retirement of the older worker.

Government spending and the tax program. Always a controversial issue, government spending will continue to be so but will receive a different emphasis. Major tax changes may be necessary to provide for government revenue, the need for which is expected to remain high whether or not expenditures for armament are needed.

Inflation. Inflation rather than unemployment will constitute the big economic threat of the future. Government action to safeguard monetary stability will be required but may not be acceptable or even felt necessary by an "unemployment-depression"-minded public.

Even a cursory glance at Drucker's "eleven issues" would illustrate that the next couple of decades are expected to be marked by much and by dramatic change in heretofore unanticipated areas. And these expected developments are no mere idle guess but constitute in Drucker's terms, "the future that has already happened." By that it is meant that the foundation for these problems has already taken place, that present and past economic, population, industrial, and other trends are almost certain to lead in the postulated direction. There can scarcely remain any illusions concerning the dynamic nature of American society.

▶ SUMMARY

In this chapter we have attempted to investigate the nature and extent of change in recent American society and to provide some interpretation of its meaning. Technological inventions have occurred at a tremendous rate and have had far-reaching effects, but various "social inventions" likewise have had their impact, although their importance is sometimes not recognized.

Within the last 150 years this nation has evolved from a nation composed almost entirely of rural people to one in which two thirds of the people live in cities. There are over three times the number of people living in cities than there were just fifty years ago; the proportion of the population living on farms has dropped to about 15 percent.

Coincident with the shift from rural to urban living has occurred a change in America's occupations. A vast decrease in the proportion of farmers and unskilled laborers and an increase in the proportion of professionals, proprietors, sales and clerical personnel, and skilled workers are among the occupational shifts that have taken place. The occupational demand for better trained and educated personnel has been, and will continue to be, reflected in the nation's educational attainment. In about one generation the proportion of college graduates has more than doubled, high school graduates have increased almost fourfold, and the relatively unschooled have shrunk by about 80 percent. Elementary and secondary schools are today grossly overtaxed, and it is probable the situation will become worse in the immediate future. An acute college situation is also foreseen inasmuch as enrollments are expected to increase three- or even fourfold.

The impersonality of relationships constitutes one of the major changes in the economic area. The great mass of Americans work at tasks which are highly specialized, thus reducing the satisfaction from a job well done, and are for the most part far removed from the consumer of goods they produce. A separation also exists between management and the worker which, while probably not deliberately fostered, constitutes a stubborn problem in the solution of economic problems.

The labor union movement has recently risen to a position of strength and political power. Organized labor will have to meet such challenges as the larger requirement for skilled workers and resulting changes in the concepts of seniority and training, the growth of industry in sparsely unionized areas, and the rapid rise of total population without an accompanying rise of workers, in order successfully to maintain its present level of political and economic strength.

The increase in the number and proportion of the aged represents the final change in our society which we investigated. In 1955 the almost 14 million older people constituted 8.6 percent of the total population, double their proportion in 1900. The best estimates for the year 2000 place the proportion of the aged between 13 and 15 percent of the national population.

Future change in our dynamic society will not be restricted to the foregoing areas. It has been suggested that within the next twenty years we will be witness to eleven issues which, for the most part, are scarcely recognized as problematical today. These issues fall in the areas of water conservation, atomic and other power regulation, transportation, housing, schools, medical care for the masses, labor unions, economic equality of the Negro, the older worker, government spending and tax programs, and control of inflation.

SUGGESTED READINGS

Dewhurst, J. Frederic, and associates, *America's Needs and Resources*, New York, The Twentieth Century Fund, 1955. A massive compilation of factual data and interpretations of the demands, needs, resources, and capacities of the American economy. A thorough treatment of pre- and postwar trends and a projection into the immediate future.

Drucker, Peter F., "America's Next Twenty Years," *Harper's Magazine*, Vol. 210 (March-June 1955). In a series of four articles, a well-known economist plots the direction and nature of industrial, economic, educational, and other changes in the near future. These are no mere speculations but careful forecasts based on analysis of available trend data. A fascinating glimpse of the next decades in our dynamic society.

Lee, Alfred M., and Elizabeth B. Lee, *Social Problems in America: A Source Book*, rev. ed., New York, Henry Holt and Co., 1955. Chapter 3, entitled, "Societal Change," contains several well-selected readings paralleling our treatment in this chapter. Excellent materials.

Ogburn, William F., *Social Change*, New York, Viking Press, 1950. This is a revision of a pioneer work in the field which has been very influential because of its emphasis upon the "cultural lag" theory of social change. The theory is not without its critics, but few would deny that Ogburn's interpretation calls attention to an important truth about the dynamic nature of modern society.

———, and Meyer F. Nimkoff, *Technology and the Changing Family*, Boston, Houghton Mifflin Co., 1955. Changes in one institution, the family, are viewed in the light of influences of many different inventions, discoveries, and ideological forces. An interesting method of analysis and a vivid portrayal of the complexity of social change.

STUDY QUESTIONS

1. Cite one technological invention and briefly describe the areas of life in which its effect can be felt.

2. What is meant by "social inventions"? List what you consider the five most important social inventions that have occurred within the last fifty years.

3. How do you account for the great rural-urban population shift? For how much longer would you estimate this trend could continue?

4. What occupational group increased the most between 1910 and 1953? Which one decreased the most?

5. Comment upon the changes that have occurred with regard to the proportion of the population with grade school, high school, and college education.

6. What is the relationship between the changing occupational structure of our society and its educational changes? Show how changes in one of the areas affects the other.

7. What is meant by the impersonality of economic and other relationships? What problems are associated with this type of relationship?

8. Briefly review the change that has taken place with regard to the number and proportion of people 65 years of age and older. What "new" problems are likely to be associated with this change?

9. List Drucker's "eleven coming issues" in the order of what you consider their importance for society as a whole. Then arrange them in the order of which you believe will be the most controversial.

10. Of which of the "eleven coming issues" were you most aware? Of which the least? How do you account for this?

· 3 ·

The Nature of
Social Problems

A few years ago one of the authors had the opportunity to discuss current American and Japanese social problems with students at a Tokyo university. It was amazing to discover how accurately the Japanese were able to isolate the "trouble spots" in contemporary American society. But they, like many Americans, were at something of a loss to explain why some conditions, in both of our societies, are viewed as social problems and others, perhaps objectively as serious and as "problematical," are not. It is the purpose of this chapter, then, to shed some light on this enigma and to investigate in what way conditions labeled "problems" occur.

▶ UNDESIRABLE CONDITIONS AS SOCIAL PROBLEMS

Social problems are often regarded simply as undesirable social conditions. But *undesirable* (*a*) to whom, and (*b*) by whose values? As one tries to answer these secondary questions, he faces difficult and complicated considerations.

To whom is a condition undesirable? To probe one of these questions—undesirable to whom?—let us consider the position of the Anti-Nicotine League of America. This group holds that the use of tobacco in any form is highly undesirable, harmful— in fact, immoral. Does this make tobacco smoking and chewing a social problem? Apparently not to the majority of American citizens who are smokers nor to many others who are nonsmokers. *It is a problem, then, to persons who evaluate human behavior*

28

in the way in which the Anti-Nicotine League does. [Until or unless a sizable or influential group becomes convinced that some social condition is "really" undesirable, then that condition cannot be considered a social problem.] In our foregoing example, a large majority of people, including those recognized as medical "experts," seem to be unconvinced that the use of tobacco is a seriously harmful condition in American society. It therefore cannot, for the present at least, be accurately referred to as an "American social problem."

What values determine undesirability? Let us examine another aspect of our question—namely, what values are to be used to determine the "desirability" or "undesirability" of a social condition. Is the Negro's inferior status in American society, for example, "undesirable" and a social problem? Many Negroes, social scientists, and a growing number of civic groups consider it one of the most serious social problems in American society today. According to many other persons and groups, especially in the South, the inferior status accorded the Negro is desirable, is "his proper place."

Role of experts in defining social problems. What criteria, then, can be used in deciding whether or not a given condition is a social problem? Ultimately there are two answers: (1) expert opinion, and (2) public opinion. In many "problem" aspects of everyday life, we follow the dictates of expert rather than public opinion. If, for example, the construction engineer states that serious "problems" prevent the location of a dam at a particular point in a stream, we accept his evaluation of the "problem situation." We do not ask for a popular vote on the question of the exact location of the dam. If the physician diagnoses the patient's "problem" as diabetes, the patient accepts this "expert opinion" without insisting on a public-opinion poll in regard to the matter.

Such "expert opinions," however, are used as criteria in "problem" situations only where the public has accepted the "experts" as such or where value agreement is so complete that no other course of action is open. In the trouble areas of our society generally labeled "social problems," we have no such popularly approved experts. For problems relating to race relations, unemployment, international conflict, old age and health security, crime and juvenile delinquency, who are to be regarded as "experts" with public recognition comparable to the acceptance that is accorded physicians, engineers, physicists, chemists, and others in their special fields? "Expert opinion" as the basis for decision regarding the presence or absence of a problem situation rests ultimately upon public acceptance of the "expert." Since society fails fully and consistently to accept "experts" on societal phenomena, our only source for the objective determination of social problems is public opinion on the matter.

We have just noted that the authority of "expert opinion" rests upon public opinion because the people of the society must recognize and accept experts as experts before their opinions have dominating weight. The absence of such general approval of the "experts," however, does not mean that their voices are totally ineffectual. "Public opinion" in regard to a social condition derives from the exchange of opinions by individuals composing the society. Social scientists, as only partially recognized experts on social problems, are among these individuals. As writers, teachers, consultants, and speakers, social scientists can and do influence public opinion about the desirability and undesirability of various social conditions. Put briefly, public opinion determines the presence or absence of social problems; social scientists have *a* voice, but not *the* voice, in this public opinion.

In so far as public recognition of authority in relation to social problems goes, a better case can be made for the acceptance of politicians as "experts" than for the acceptance of social scientists as such. Apparent public resentment of "harebrained professors," or the "brain trust," in government is an indication that social scientists are considered by at least some people to be less competent to deal with various social problems than the average-run politician. Appointments to many of our most important federal, state, and local boards and commissions are obviously often made from the ranks of politicians rather than from those of social scientists; and yet it is these very governmental bodies that have been designed to deal with problem aspects of our society. Although gradually more social scientists are entering governmental fields (generally, still, not in chief policy-making positions), major public recognition of competency to treat "social problems" continues to be accorded politicians.

▶ VALUE CONFLICTS AS THE SOURCE OF SOCIAL PROBLEMS

Public opinion, as any kind of opinion, is based on values. Values have often changed, and sometimes radically so, in the course of man's cultural history. According to earlier values held in our own society, such conditions as war, mental and physical illness, slavery, racial discrimination, poverty, child labor, and dangerous and unhealthful working conditions were not social problems: they were inevitable and acceptable patterns of human living. That we no longer treat all of such conditions as inevitable and acceptable is evidence that public opinion has acquired values which are contrary to such conditions and has forced the attack upon those problems.

Democratic values and the planning ideology. Two of the most significant values that modern American society espouses are what have been called the "democratic ideology" and the "planning ideology." An increasing number of our citizens have learned that they need not accept the inevitability of any specific social system or any part of it. There is a growing consciousness of power on the part of many disprivileged persons and groups to remove or to better those conditions which seem not conducive to their welfare. Witness, for example, the rise of various pressure groups to improve the living conditions of the aged in our society; the increasing number of labor organizations demanding health and welfare funds, higher wages, better working conditions, and even (the formerly unthinkable!) a voice in management; the increasing insistence upon fully adequate medical care for everyone regardless of income; the demand for desirable housing conditions for all the people. Social planning is the vehicle of such "changes of the inevitable"— that is, the democratic ideology makes possible the expression of dissatisfaction with an undesirable condition by a disprivileged element of society, and the planning ideology contains the means believed to lead to the change of this condition. In brief, modern Americans are becoming increasingly aware of social problems and increasingly convinced that they can "do something" about them.

Not all members of our society adhere to the democratic and planning ideologies, but there are enough who do to make a concerted and consistent impact of effort in the direction of rational modification of many parts of the social structure. And it is the efforts of these groups and the counterefforts of their opponents which make certain areas of modern life problem areas. Probably no condition, however intolerable one might think it, is a self-evident social problem: the problem aspect inheres in the fact of value conflict, not in the deplorable condition *per se*.

Three levels of social problems. Richard C. Fuller, in "The Problem of Teaching Social Problems," [1] which we have already referred to, summarizes the three levels of social problems thus:

1. There are those conditions which all individuals and groups define as bad, but value-judgments do not cause the condition itself and there is very little if any conflict in social policy over what "ought to be done." This is true of certain physical ailments and natural catastrophes the causation and cure of which are essentially "technical" [and] not a social problem, e.g., the malfunctioning of the endocrine glands, medical care of the organic insanities, drought and flood control. Medical or engineering experts may disagree on causes and solutions, but since the problem is primarily physical rather than social it is narrowly confined to the bailwick of these specialists. In fact, although these situations constitute serious problems, we may query whether they are "social" problems at all.

2. There are conditions upon which there is general agreement that they are undesirable, but where value-judgments not only help to create the condition but frustrate its solution. Hence, though criminal acts such as murder and robbery are clearly a violation of our mores, other mores such as our pecuniary values and our individualistic philosophies serve to cause criminal be-

---

[1] Reprinted from Richard C. Fuller, "The Problem of Teaching Social Problems," *American Journal of Sociology* (The University of Chicago Press, publishers), Vol. 44 (1939), pp. 419-21, by permission.

havior in one instance and on the other hand stop us from agreeing on programs of prevention and control. Likewise, though illness and disease among the poor may be looked upon with concern by all social classes, it is a "social problem" partly because our unequal income distribution serves the double function of being the formal cause of much illness among the low-wage groups and the essential obstacle to their purchasing proper medical treatment.

3. There are those conditions upon which there is considerable but no general agreement that they are undesirable, and since these conditions grow out of a conflict in values, there is no accord as to solutions. Here fall such problems as child labor, low wages and long hours, the status of unorganized labor, the status of the unemployed, divorce, and race discrimination.

What light does this tentative classification throw upon the utility of the social disorganization approach, which views the social problem as a function of the breakdown of traditional behavior patterns as social controls over individual conduct?

Where the problem is simply technical, as on the first level, there is a unilinear relation between causes and solutions. This is because the general public is not torn apart by decisions over policy. There is no question of social disorganization involved.

At the second level there is general agreement on the harmfulness of the condition, and social disorganization theories are applicable in the sense that they assume that all "right-thinking" people regard a given condition such as crime as a departure from a socially desirable norm. The danger here, however, is that we are also likely to assume that, since there is unanimous accord in defining the condition as undesirable, solutions must follow as a matter of course. This is true only in those rare instances where solutions may be worked out without necessitating any revisions of the value-scheme. In such cases the problem is merely one of reconstruction, i.e., readjusting the individuals or conditions which are out of line with the value-structure of our culture. Thus, a juvenile delinquency clinic which seeks to analyze and treat problem children antagonizes very little in the *status quo*. More deepgoing solutions for delinquency, however, do stir antagonism precisely because they do disturb the value-scheme. Thus, the suggestion that a community spend less money on the salaries of officials and more on libraries and playgrounds will evoke considerable dissention. Similarly, subsidizing medical care for the poor in private hospitals is acceptable, whereas public health insurance has innumerable enemies. Social disorganization theories will not suffice for problems at this level until they realistically consider the value-judgments which are a part of the causality pattern of the problem and include within their analysis the conflict of social interests which arises, when a program of reform seeks to revise these values.

On the third level neither is there general agreement that the given condition is a problem nor can those who define it as a problem agree on solutions. Consequently, treating these conditions, as do many contemporary texts, as if they were objective states of social disorganization gets us nowhere. We have social problems of this type precisely because some individuals and groups define a given state of affairs as disorganization and have diversified ideas of what ought to be done about it, whereas other individuals and groups do not define the condition as disorganization and consequently do not think that anything should be done about it. This is as true with regard to unemployment, which certain economists and employers view as the inevitable mechanics of competition in the labor market, as to divorce which many regard as a logical release from unhappy marriages. The same logic applies to child labor, the condition of unorganized wage earners, war, and many other major social problems.

Two main phases of value conflict. It seems apparent, then, that *value conflict tends to center around two main phases of a social problem.* First, the clash of values often relates to the issue of *whether or not a problem really exists.* A given condition is a "problem" only when it has come to be regarded as a problem. Before it is so regarded, the "inevitable or acceptable" philosophy holds sway. For example, many authorities on human behavior are currently concerned with what they call a "mental hygiene problem" in the United States. It has been evidenced by such conditions as the high Selective Service rejections of young men with various kinds of mental-emotional personality deviations and the large number of army discharges for the same reasons. As will be aptly demonstrated later in our discussion of mental health, the amount of human unhappiness and inefficiency due to mental-emotional disturbances is appalling. Yet, it appears doubtful whether one may say that this condition is "a problem" in the minds of the rank and file of American people in the same sense that housing, the automobile accident rate, or the infantile paralysis rate is a problem to them. On the basis of the evidence now available, the actual danger of harmful effects to the average person may be greater from the mental hygiene problem than from many conditions more generally recognized as problems. But the mental hygiene problem, as is the case with most problems before they are widely recognized as such, must go through this stage of value conflict as to its existence as a major problem before there can be broad consideration of what ought to be done about the condition.

Second, once considerable agreement has been reached that a certain condition is undesirable, the value clash shifts to *what society can and should do*. Several possible courses of action usually emerge in this stage of the conflict of values. One course invariably recommended is to do nothing at all. This argument is often phrased in some such way as these: (1) granting the undesirability of the conditions, proposed actions would make for "worse conditions than those existing," or (2) the problem is "too large and complex" to handle, or (3) the existing undesirability is "just human nature" and the proposed treatment is contrary to human nature. While the sincerity of the "do-nothing" advocates is sometimes indisputable, there is evidence that some interests taking this stand are not loathe to misrepresent difficulties involved in proposed "solutions." Owners of real estate in slum areas, for example, have been known to exaggerate the difficulties of constructing better housing because some of them, at least, have considered it to their financial interest to keep the slums. In other words, if the argument could be shifted from discussion of the seriousness of the problem to the magnification of the difficulties of solving the problem, the same end would be attained—namely, inaction. Thus the opponent of change would remain, in the eyes of some people at least, a person who is not insensitive to the plight of the slum dweller.

But even among those who sincerely wish the problem attacked and solved, there is likely to be disagreement as to course of action for reaching the desired end. Values are often involved here, too. Many persons, for example, feel that a large portion of our population receives inadequate medical attention. Numerous surveys give indisputable factual substantiation for this feeling, and few deny the "undesirability" of conditions thus exposed. It is at the point of what to do about inadequate medical treatment that conflict arises. The means to the desired end of improved medical care differ widely and reveal sharp conflicts of values. Some advocate the government's taking over medical facilities; others recommend compulsory health insurance with practice still in the hands of private physicians; still others propose voluntary insurance; and some defend a continuation of present conditions as better than the socialism, which, according to them, would inevitably follow upon "tampering with private medical practice." Better medical care for more of our people, yes, we agree; but on the methods, bearers of conflicting cherished values, we fight. On this social problem, as with almost any other you choose to consider, disagreements as to methods are numerous; much discussion and much compromise must generally precede action in relation to the condition.

▶ OBSCURITY AND COMPLEXITY OF "CAUSES" AND "EFFECTS"

The clash of values as to methods to be used in order to treat a condition that is deemed a social problem often stems from failure clearly to recognize the source of the problem. This failure need not arise from superficiality of investigation nor from willful neglect upon the part of those seeking a solution to a problem. Our cultural patterns are so complexly interrelated that it is often impossible to discern either the cause of an "undesirable" condition or all the effects of a designated "cause." Then, too, the designated "cause" of one social problem is often itself an "effect" of other not readily distinguishable causal factors. What, for example, "causes" crime in a community and what can be done to prevent people from behaving criminally? Everyone agrees that crime, like sin, is undesirable, but the methods proposed for ridding society of crime vary from removal of slums, drinking places, and poolrooms to required courses on marriage and the family and to the cottage system of prisons. Proposed methods for removing or reducing crime as a social problem are, in short, as numerous as the alleged "causes" of crime; yet such alleged "causes" as slums, broken homes, psycho-pathic personality conditions, frustrated desires, and parental neglect are themselves complicated social conditions with multi-ple and not clearly delineated "causes." Even where the connec-tion of one social condition with another is clearly demonstrable (and such is very rarely the case), the other effects of the same cause may be highly prized by some members of the society. Drinking of alcoholic beverages produces the "problem" of chronic alcoholism. Whatever the more subtle psychological "causes," one cannot be a chronic alcoholic unless alcohol is available. Yet, judging from our repeal of the "noble experi-ment" of prohibition, most people felt that some other effects of alcoholic drinking than chronic alcoholism were not unde-sirable. Alcohol causes alcoholism, but the simple expedient of dispensing with alcohol failed to "solve" that problem and "caused" others.

Conflicts over what means to use in "solving" a social problem may arise on another score than difference of opinion as to the causes of the condition. Disagreement of values also occurs in regard to the complete removal or partial improvement of a condition. Involuntary unemployment, almost everyone agrees, is a social problem. Should we, however, remove unemployment from our society? Some think we should and proceed logically to demonstrate that it is possible to do so only by considerably altering certain attributes of our economic system. Here the advocates of removal crash head-on into values highly esteemed by many members of our society. Among the latter are advocates of amelioration; they will support insurance programs and other means of easing the difficulties of the unemployed, but oppose the radical social surgery apparently necessary for the *removal* of the social problem of unemployment.

Differential effects of social problems. At the beginning of our chapter, while considering the "undesirability" of a condi-tion labeled a social problem, we raised the question: Undesirable to whom? There we referred the "whom" to the persons eval-uating the undesirability, and used the example of the Anti-Nicotine League of America holding an opinion apparently not shared by the majority of Americans that the use of tobacco constitutes a social problem. We may raise the question of "to whom is a condition undesirable" in another way. If—continuing the nicotine example—tobacco is undesirable, it is presumably less undesirable for the nonuser than for the user. That is to say, the "harmful" effects of a social problem do not often affect all of the people in a society in the same way. For whom is child labor undesirable? More undesirable, obviously, for the children employed than for children not employed or for adults. From the standpoint of the employer of children, who thus has cheaper labor than if he employed adults, child labor is not perceived as an undesirable "social problem." Unemployment is more a problem for the working class than for employers; "Jim Crowism" is more a problem for Negroes than for whites; and so on with many other examples of social problems. It has sometimes been pointed out that such social problems as unemployment or discrimination against minority groups ultimately affect the welfare of those who, on superficial analysis, seem not to be concerned, but the effects are felt by some persons less acutely and less immediately.

Since social problems affect people differentially, pressure groups which arise to advocate methods of change meet with strong resistance from opposing pressure groups representing the interests of those who are less affected or differently affected by the "undesirable" condition. Thus, it is often contended that the *real* social problem is the pressure group who advocates the change. Franklin D. Roosevelt, for example, is held by some interests to have "created the problem of class consciousness" in our society by his support of organized labor and "the forgotten man" and "the ill-clad, ill-housed, and ill-fed," and by his attack on various business groups and political interests as "economic royalists." Roosevelt's defenders maintain, on the other hand, that he merely pointed out the existence of social problems on which action was long overdue. Here again, then, we see values in conflict.

"Solutions" sometimes create new problems. When clashes of values are resolved or compromised and when action on a problem is agreed upon and taken, new "problems" are very often created. Various legal reforms, for example, leading to the emancipation of women were achieved only after bitter battles with many men and some women in the latter part of the nineteenth and early part of the twentieth centuries. Today most persons of both sexes would grant that the emergence of women as persons whose freedom is comparable to that of men has constituted a desirable social change. Women are now free to acquire an education, provide for their own livelihood, follow careers of their own choosing, and participate in many recreational practices formerly denied to them. But along with these "desirabilities" have come apparent "undesirabilities." Many women who are now educated to assume career roles outside the home find themselves torn by conflicts between the traditional duties of housewives and mothers and the unsatisfied desires and interests of outside careers. Some try to carry both domestic and out-of-home responsibilities, and not a few of these find the load too great. In like manner, many men have learned to enjoy the equality companionship of women, but find persistence of attitudes of male dominance incongruous with the new equality. Much of the instability and conflict currently evident in marriage is attributed to confusion as to the role of women in modern society divorce as a "problem" seems to have been greatly intensified by the emancipation of women. Children in our society have likewise reaped some undesirable consequences from woman's changed role. When children were their mother's chief responsibility and interest, conflicts of interest were less likely to center in offspring. Today many women find their children to be the major block to fulfillment of desires arising from their emancipated education. In many instances children are neglected, in whole or in part, by mothers who pursue outside interests or are either emotionally rejected, on the one hand, or smothered with affection, on the other, by mothers who have been frustrated in their desires for out-of-home roles. Such neglect, rejection, or overprotection leads to the development of inadequate personality in the child, according to many psychiatrists and psychologists, and contributes to the increase of neurotic or delinquent behavior disorders. These in themselves are becoming serious contemporary "problems." A "desirable" social change, then, such as the emancipation of women, can produce unforeseen "undesirabilities."

▶ SUMMARY

The question of what constitutes a major social problem is not so easily answered as first consideration might indicate. The mere "undesirability" of a condition does not automatically place it in the category of a social problem. The condition must be recognized as "harmful" and "changeable" by a large section of the public before it becomes a significant "problem" in that society. Such recognition depends always upon value judgments; public opinion must hold that a certain condition is contrary to desired values before the condition becomes a social problem.

Clashes of values tend to center around two main questions: first, does a problem really exist, and, secondly, what can and should a society do about this undesirable condition. The complexity of "causes" and "effects" of a specific problem contributes significantly to confusion over methods to be used to remove or alleviate an undesirable condition. Disagreement among values also occurs at the point of preferability for alleviation or for removal of a problem. The cost in loss of other values is often considered too high in the case of problem removal.

It was pointed out, further, that social problems often have differential effects on a population, and resistance to improvement of an undesirable condition often derives from groups who are less immediately and less acutely affected by the "undesirability." Even when "desirable" action is taken by a society, some of the consequences may be "undesirable," so that problem amelioration in one area may create new or intensified "problems" in other areas of our social living.

SUGGESTED READINGS

Frank, Laurence K., *Society as the Patient*, New Brunswick, N. J., Rutgers University Press, 1948, Chap. 2. In this essay Professor Frank examines the relationship between social problems in general and the particular social conditions from which they arise. The remaining essays in this book treat various societal conflicts and difficulties of individuals as different expressions of the same forces.

Fuller, Richard C., "The Problem of Teaching Social Problems," *American Journal of Sociology*, Vol. 44 (1939), pp. 415-35. This article contains the original complete development of the "clash of value-judgments" theory of social problems. Evaluation of the theory by other sociologists follows the main article.

———, "Social Problems," Part I, in R. E. Park (ed.), *An Outline of the Principles of Sociology*, New York, Barnes and Noble, 1939. This is an excellent brief treatment and classification of social problems for the beginning student by the author of the "value-conflict" theory.

Furfey, Paul H., "The Social Philosophy of Social Pathologists," *Social Problems*, Vol. 2 (October 1954), pp. 71-75. An examination of all articles in the first five issues of *Social Problems* with the purpose of determining whether the authors inclined to a particular social philosophy and, if so, whether this could constitute a threat to their objectivity. Summarizes the values espoused by the various authors.

Social Problems. This is the official quarterly publication of the Society for the Study of Social Problems. It began publication in 1953. Each issue contains reports of recent research and study on contemporary social problems.

STUDY QUESTIONS

1. What difficulties are likely to occur when we attempt to define social problems as undesirable conditions? Illustrate.

2. To what extent are the "expert opinions" of social scientists used as criteria of social problems? How do you account for this situation?

3. What criterion other than "expert opinions" can be used to decide whether a given condition is or is not a social problem?

What are the advantages and disadvantages of the use of this criterion?

4. What are two significant values of American society that affect its awareness of social problems and its action with regard to them? In what sense do these two values "create" social problems?

5. Explain what is meant by the "three levels of social problems." Give an example of a social problem that is at each of the three levels.

6. Give an example other than that used in the text of value conflict with regard to the course of action necessary to attack a social problem.

7. What are some of the difficulties involved in isolating the "cause" of a social problem? Present an example other than that used in the text of how a "cause" of a social problem may have other desirable "effects" for some members of society.

8. Explain what is meant by the "differential effects" of social problems.

9. How can the "solution" to one social problem create new problems? Illustrate.

10. Evaluate: "If no one had pointed out that the poorest segment of our society is unable to receive adequate medical attention, there would be no social problem in this area."

· 4 · The Treatment of
Social Problems

The concept of *treatment* of social problems is one abounding with difficulties and with differences in value opinions. A casual eavesdropping among the so-called idealists may reveal much noisy concern and virtual clamoring that "something" be done immediately, once and for all, to "remove" that which is viewed as a problem; a similar observation of the cynic leaves one with the impression that really it is of no use to tackle social issues, for the few that have been "solved" seem to have been supplanted by even more serious problems. Intermingled with these ideological opposites are found the ostrichlike ignorer, the militant reformer, the esoteric concerned only with his astral charades, and the embittered iconoclast. But probably the most important value distinction which needs to be made regarding the treatment of social problems is between the philosophy of *laissez faire* and that of directed social change. These two value positions are basic to so much social problems thinking that they require careful examination.

▶ "LAISSEZ FAIRE"

The *laissez-faire* philosophy originated in Europe as a protest against excessive government regulation of society, especially of business, during the eighteenth century. It means, literally, let [people] do, or make, [what they choose], hence noninterference. The implication is that social problems are "inherent in the scheme of things" and cannot, therefore, be successfully

43

treated by collective, especially by governmental, action. The historic quotation, "That government governs best which governs least," has become a *laissez-faire* slogan with which almost everyone is familiar. The *laissez-faire* concept is also found in The Holy Bible where the somewhat cynical statement "ye have the poor with you always" is embedded in a body of otherwise largely idealistic writing. The modern person who opposes almost every attempt to attack poverty, immorality or squalor finds little difficulty in pointing out that we not only have the poor always with us but so also the weak, the blind and the lame, the criminal and the prostitute, the racketeer and the exploiter, and that, in spite of all collective efforts to stamp out vice and misery, it seems to recur in one form or another with heart-rending vitality.

Consistency in "laissez-faire" advocacy. It should be emphasized, however, that some of our loudest advocates of *laissez faire* in modern times have been anything but consistent in their advocacy of this policy. Certain business groups in recent years have protested loudly against subsidies for the agricultural industry, pointing out that subsidies create "artificial prices" and "encourage inefficient production," while at the same time they advocate protective tariffs, which almost in identical ways create artificially high prices and encourage inefficient industry. Similarly, many industrialists oppose governmental measures which fix prices or in other ways tend to restrict the "free operation of the competitive system," and yet these same industries have shown a tendency for the last seventy-five years to form trusts, mergers, chains, and other devices designed precisely to eliminate competitors and prevent the operation of a free competitive system. Likewise, labor groups at times cry out in protest against any government support of the monopolistic tendencies of big business, while building for themselves the best monopoly they can and doing their utmost to prevent government from interfering with that monopoly by some of the same tactics as those used by big business to protect its monopoly. The situation is such that it is easy to conclude somewhat cynically that everyone is an advocate of *laissez faire*, so long as it is to his advantage to be free, but comes quickly whining for governmental or other protection whenever the existence of a *laissez-faire* policy is in the leastwise hurtful. Although there is lip service paid to the *laissez-faire* philosophy by many groups in American society at any one time, a more careful examination of the same groups' past and present actions almost always reveals that either now or recently they have pressed for governmental or other collective action when it is to their advantage.

Over-all "laissez faire" v. piecemeal control. Thus far we have spoken, of course, of *laissez faire* in rather specific terms, that is, in regard to such matters as tariff, labor legislation, farm subsidies, and the like. But *laissez faire* as an "over-all philosophy" may seem, to the beginner at least, to be something quite different.

It is sometimes argued that *laissez faire* should apply to the "over-all plan of the society" and that there is nothing inconsistent with *laissez faire* if some group tries to secure for itself through government or other collective action some specific privilege or benefit. Careful examination readily shows, however, the spuriousness of this distinction. Specific regulations by government or other power groups quickly add up to the existence of an over-all negation of *laissez faire*. For example, if big industry wins its present fight to end the legality of the closed shop, it might seem on superficial observation that we are back to *laissez faire* in labor matters because the monopoly of organized labor has been broken and the individual worker is free to make the terms of his wage contract directly with his employer without the union as a necessary go-between. What is frequently overlooked, however, is that, while one aspect of monopoly is broken, the other is still retained by industry, to a considerable extent everywhere, but especially in the one-industry town. In other words, whether so intended or not, virtually every decision which is made by the government vitally affects the over-all make-up of the society and is a denial of the *laissez-faire* idea. The only issue is the matter of sides: whose side—farmer, employer, teacher, miner, consumer, etc.—has been favored or would be favored by the change? Each group cries out for "freedom" when it thinks that it would be better off by the removal of some restriction; and each group cries out against "regimentation" when the regulation imposed upon it seems not to be advantageous.

Thus the *laissez-faire* philosophy, though easy to phrase in academic language, is in practice a "glittering generality," if not a deliberately misleading "red herring." Many propagandists, sensing the Americans' long-standing adherence to the concept of freedom, have used the *laissez-faire* generality as a propaganda device to win friends to some cause, either unknowingly or unscrupulously using it in such a way as to mislead. *Laissez faire* no longer exists in fact, if it ever did. As laws and other kinds of collective control come into being and pass out, there is no returning to or departing from *laissez faire*. *Laissez faire* is gone— the only remaining question is not *whether* there shall be influence by organized groups, but *what kind* of influence and *which groups* shall have it.

▶ PURPOSIVE SOCIAL CHANGE OR PURPOSIVE SHAPING OF SOCIETY

The idea that a society can and should direct its own development is an old one. Whether it is older or younger than *laissez faire* or fatalistic philosophy is impossible to determine. As with *laissez faire*, one must distinguish between the general proposition and the specific application of it. Speaking in general terms, it is easy to demonstrate that there is wide acceptance of the idea that a society can shape its destiny and also the acceptance of the position that the society should do so. The very concept of limited democracy as outlined in the Constitution of the United States illustrates this. There is, for example, provision for a Congress, the major purpose of which is to pass laws. To what possible purpose could the Congress pass laws other than in some way or other to modify the existing scheme of things—that is, to limit the operation of *laissez faire* in some way or other?

The people's choice!   We have pointed out that, in the name of *laissez faire*, programs inconsistent with that philosophy have been sold to society. In similar ways the philosophy of purposive social change has been distorted by the advocates of this or that specific proposal, objective, or plan. Perhaps the chief misrepresentation lies in the assumption which every advocate makes—namely, that his proposal represents "the people," "*all* the people," or "the *real* people." Such statements usually come very close to being sheer nonsense.

"The people" is a catch phrase of very many meanings. As we have seen in previous chapters, there are many diverse interest groups in a society and frequently some one of these groups is best served, or thinks it is, by a form or action of government which another group finds not to its interest or liking. Thus opposing factions all claim to represent "the people," meanwhile incidentally, using all the forms of influence and propaganda available with a view to convincing as many people as possible that what that group wants is really in the interest of all. Thus the "Divine Right" king in medieval Europe represented not only "the people," but also the "Will of God." Hitler claimed to represent the people. In short, the prevailing government and the challenging group may often both claim with logic to represent the people. But in reality both only represent *some* people.[1]

Uncritical claims. Another naïveté which all too frequently is passed off uncritically by purposive change advocates is the glib assumption that by collective action a society can accomplish anything. Of course, no one actually says this quite so bluntly, but the implication is clear that many reformers act and think *as if* such were the case. Present experience to date, while it gives reason to believe that much can be accomplished by collective attack upon social problems, does not permit us to be entirely confident that all social problems are amenable to control, even under reasonably ideal circumstances. The current high death rate from automobile accidents is a case in point. More people in the United States are killed each year by automobile accidents than were killed during the first two years of American participation in World War II. Generally speaking, there is no one who stands to gain anything by a high automobile accident rate, and

[1] Reprinted from John F. Cuber, *Sociology: A Synopsis of Principles*, New York, Appleton-Century-Crofts, 1951, p. 486, by permission.

thus everybody agrees that it ought not to occur. Our best collective efforts to date, although they have probably reduced materially the number of deaths due to automobile accidents, have not prevented the rate from rising steadily throughout the peacetime years.

Then there is probably the most fundamental question of all —what to do about war. War is the number one social problem of the world. Few persons profit by war, either individually or as groups, yet in spite of all of our efforts, we are by no means sure that we have eliminated, or even materially reduced, the prospects of another world war.

Achievements of the control idea. The advocates of purposive social change, however, can and do present an impressive array of accomplishments of collective societal action upon which there would be substantial if not unanimous agreement. By collective social action in America, during the last one hundred years or so, we have abolished slavery, established a free public school system, given to women many of the same rights as men, radically reduced and sometimes eliminated many epidemics, and built a network of highways such that almost any point within a thousand miles is accessible by automobile within two days. These and many other accomplishments serve to give us what faith we have in the ability of men to work collectively for the solution of problems and for the achievement of purposes upon which they can agree.

Summary. Although much more could be said about the two basic value positions on social problems—*laissez faire* and directed change—we have perhaps indicated enough of the implications to achieve our purpose—namely, to show (*a*) that both philosophies are simpler to state in the abstract than to apply concretely to the specific situations in hand; (*b*) that both philosophies have at one time or another been both innocently and maliciously distorted by persons with "axes to grind"; and (*c*) that there are some very real difficulties in practical situations. It is now necessary to analyze further the directed social-control philosophy into some of its various emphases.

▶ IDEOLOGIES FOR THE TREATMENT OF SOCIAL PROBLEMS

The use of the term "ideologies" in the above caption may be somewhat misleading. As popularly used in America, the term has a narrow connotation making it largely synonymous with the philosophy of communism, fascism, or some other radical social system which in the United States we do not presumably have or want. But "ideology"—literally the science of ideas—refers to any more or less integrated system of ideas and values. Capitalism is an ideology, so is Catholicism, democracy, and pacifism. In the following paragraphs, however, we shall not discuss the socialist or the Methodist or the democratic ideologies as such. In other words, we shall not treat the idea-value systems of any organized group. Instead, we shall treat the systems of ideas which one finds implicit or explicit in the writings and comments of a cross section of the American people, irrespective of their group affiliations. Thus we shall discuss "ameliorative" over against "curative" treatment of social problems, "coercive" approach over against control of "educative-persuasive" procedures, "evolutionary" as compared with "revolutionary" attack upon social problems, and "piecemeal attack" as compared with "total attack." This approach seems to us more useful because it helps the student to free himself from impediments to objective thinking which he may have as a result of his membership in, or opposition to, such group ideologies as Protestantism, communism, or pacifism. It seems much sounder to explain, analyze, and evaluate ideas as such, before becoming involved in the unnecessary and confusing practice of name-calling which so easily degenerates into a discussion of empty slogans instead of meaningful analyses.

Amelioration v. curative treatment. Many social problems are of such a nature that they can be handled either by a direct attack upon the basic source of the trouble or by leaving the source untouched and providing palliative assistance to the victims of the condition. Let us take a simple illustration from the field of public health to sharpen the distinction. Suppose there is a lake in the vicinity of a city. The water in the lake serves as a breeding ground for mosquitoes which carry malaria. The malaria menace can be attacked in two basic ways: the city can build hospitals to help malaria victims recover from the malady and inoculations may be offered or required of the population to reduce the vulnerability to malaria. Or, the malaria problem can be attacked at source and cured more or less permanently. The stagnant lake can be drained or the water can be treated with some chemical which would destroy the mosquito larvae.

Now suppose we take an illustration of a social problem of another scope—for example, the baffling problem of caring for the children of divorced parents. The ameliorative method would suggest the use of skilled child guidance and placement experts to assist the court in the best possible placement of the children. Moreover, the children of divorced indigent parents might need to be supported by the state in whole or in part. The curative approach, on the other hand, would get at the root cause—namely, the divorce. Every husband-wife estrangement which can be prevented means one less case of children who will need ameliorative treatment.

In using divorce as the illustration in the above paragraph we have deliberately chosen one of the knottiest problems for illustration. This was done in order to show that curative treatment of social problems can be very difficult, if not an almost impossible task. But it would be an error to end our discussion at this point because not all social problems are as complex as the divorce problem. As we shall see in subsequent chapters, we now have conclusive evidence to show that many problems can be efficiently and successfully attacked by direct curative means.

Amelioration is usually justified as a "less costly" approach. But it is not always such. If the full facts were known, we might easily come to realize that it is much cheaper, especially in the long run, to cure a social problem outright rather than merely to give the victims some "first aid," so to speak, which will tide them over until the next attack to which they will be more vulnerable because of the first one.

In the analysis of specific social problems throughout the rest of this book, the student will do well to direct his thinking to the crucial question of curative over against ameliorative treatment. Caution should be observed, however, not to regard amelioration and curative treatment as mutually exclusive categories. A society may and possibly should attack its problems by *both* procedures. Usually it will be necessary to use ameliorative measures until curative measures have been perfected. Sometimes the final curative program is not discovered until after various ameliorative measures have been tried. Some ameliorative work will probably always be necessary no matter how perfect a social system may be, for there are always unusual circumstances or unusual persons who need assistance under almost any conceivable curative program.

Coercion v. persuasion. It has been said that the American's first reaction to an undesirable condition is to assert that "we ought to pass a law against it." This is an altogether common, initial attitude. If someone is doing something which is inimical to the general good, then he ought to be prevented from continuing the practice. Thus, we prohibit people from driving at excessive speeds, printing counterfeit money, and selling their children.

It is obvious, of course, that the legislative-coercive approach has serious limitations. Sometimes, even though there is rather general agreement that some persons are doing things which are contrary to the public good, it is difficult, if not impossible, to enforce the law which prohibits the unlawful act. The Prohibition experiment of 1919-33 constitutes an excellent illustration. So also did the price control and rationing experiment of World War II.

Another difficulty with legislative coercion is that the remedy may be worse than the disease. The cost of enforcing the law may be burdensome, if not impossible, to bear. The infringement upon personal freedom might be so great that the people would rebel. The change in basic patterns of living might be so radical that, despite the harmfulness of the social condition, many people would rather contend with it than with the substitute. Many Southerners, for example, feel that way about their present system of race relations; many people throughout the country felt this way about price control and rationing after war. Finally, there are many social problems concerning which we lack sufficient knowledge to treat by coercive methods because, frankly, we do not now know whom to coerce into doing what. The great problem of war is a case in point.

Educative or persuasive approaches to social problems are sometimes offered as a substitute for coercive ones. Thus many persons argue that while Prohibition failed, a long, slow process of education concerning the effects of alcohol would dissuade people from using it—at least to excess. Similarly, during the war it was frequently argued that price control and rationing were not necessary, that, if the government simply appealed to the people's patriotism and was honest in presenting the facts and the need, a "self-discipline" would be observed by the people and the problem would be solved. Most unbiased observers would probably disagree with both of the foregoing. A knowledge of the effects of alcohol is now widely diffused in American society and seems not to deter many persons from alcoholic consumption —even to excess. Likewise, the existence of the "black market" both during and after the war demonstrated that, despite persuasion, many persons would not discipline their wants, even to win a war in which their sons were fighting.

It would seem, then, that there are definite limitations both to coercive treatment and persuasive treatment of social problems. Certainly both approaches have their place. No one would seriously argue that capital and labor could at present work out their difficulties without any legislation whatsoever, so that both sides would be free to do whatever they wanted and required to do nothing. On the other hand, particularly where enforcement of coercive measures is impossible, too costly, or too inconvenient, education may remain the only solution. Finally, coercive and persuasive methods may be used simultaneously on the same problem, each buttressing the other. The toll of automobile deaths can be reduced in part by forcing people to drive more slowly, but also by educating them to drive better.

Evolutionary v. revolutionary procedures. Frequently the people of a society have a choice with respect to the relative speed and relative completeness with which to attack a given problem. Almost invariably in such cases, some voices will counsel that "we should proceed slowly, not rush into a radical, untried program," while others will advise that if we do not proceed with haste, "we shall be caught fiddling while Rome burns." Obviously, you can rationalize either position, and even though you try to be objective and unprejudiced in your judgment, you may find it extremely difficult to determine, all things considered, which is the better approach.

Generally speaking, one of the chief impediments to revolutionary change by democratic procedure is the apathy of the great mass of the people, their unwillingness or inability to function outside of traditional grooves. Under conditions of dictatorship, of course, the consent of subordinates need not be secured in support of a revolutionary change, but the inertia of subordinates may create so many resistances and other nuisance inconveniences that the person in position to make the decision often decides against radical change in favor of the path of less resistance.

While in general the above can be demonstrated to be true, there are exceptions, and conspicuous ones at that. The Bolshevik revolution in Russia at the end of World War I, the *coup d'état* of the fascist regime in Italy and Germany are well-known examples of a radical remaking of a social system by revolution. In the crisis of 1933 the Roosevelt New Deal regime, through democratic means, enacted sweeping legislative changes by the so-called 100-Day Congress which altered the structure of American social and economic life at numerous crucial points.

It is always difficult, however, to interpret these seemingly revolutionary changes. It is quite possible, as some contend, that they only represent a sort of "catching up" by a people on reforms which have long been in demand but were held back by the overly conservative government in power. Thus what seems to be a revolution is really only the accumulated impact of accumulated evolutionary plans for change. Others interpret revolutions essentially as plots contrived by a small group of clever men who, regardless of their motives, succeed in foisting a radical program upon a powerless people. In interpreting a revolutionary change, it is very difficult to maintain one's objectivity. Prejudices based upon vested interests (see p. 58) and other factors reach extreme intensity in part because of the magnitude of the change.

Frequently, of course, the only difference between evolution and revolution is the interpretation of the change. As one reads the history of American law, he is entertained by the manner in which people in the past viewed what we now regard as very minor, evolutionary changes. Many, for example, thought that a revolution had occurred when Andrew Jackson became president; many others thought so when Abraham Lincoln signed the Emancipation Proclamation. Perhaps they were right, but as we look today at the history of the United States in the past one hundred years, we see certain long-run trends, which some historians call "the emergence of the common man," and the administrations of Andrew Jackson, Abraham Lincoln, Woodrow Wilson, and Franklin D. Roosevelt seem simply to be a series of not-too-radical steps in the one-hundred-year-old evolution.

Piecemeal attack v. total attack.   Another ideological variation in attacks on social problems pertains to the inclusiveness of the proposed program. Many observers feel that one of the major weaknesses (and wastes) of the "typical American" approach to social problems is the tendency to tackle only one aspect or only one problem at a time, when there really are several aspects of one problem or several problems which can most advantageously be handled together. For example, in one Midwestern state there are currently six separate divisions of the state government which are concerned with the problems of conservation of the state's natural resources—the divisions of game and fish, water, parks, forests, soil, and minerals. These various agencies were created at different times and with different purposes. Better, it is argued, that the whole problem of conservation of natural resources be attacked at once, thus avoiding the waste, duplication, and other interagency inefficiency which is now said to exist. The conservation of forests, soil, and water, certainly, are intimately interrelated, and a sound program which achieves one purpose automatically achieves the others at the same time.

The clearance of slums over against the separate treatment of juvenile delinquency, health conservation, family disorganization, and immorality is another illustration of the distinction between piecemeal and total attack. We now have abundant and conclusive evidence to show that there is an intimate and causative relation between these several problem areas of modern urban life. The root problem is housing; the root solution is the elimination of slum dwellings. And yet for many years we have had numerous agencies, programs, and movements each designed to treat one separate problem at a time as if that one were largely distinct from the others. We in America are notably deficient in the ability and willingness to see social problems in their real relationships with one another. Our professional leadership (social workers, sociologists, and others) has long known and advocated the more total approach, but their appeals have fallen largely upon deaf ears so far as legislators and the general public are concerned. Both continue to think largely in terms of the nonexistent separateness of these social problem areas. The cost of such ignorance—especially in the long run—would be tremendous and staggering if fully known. In the long run—and not necessarily very long—the cost of a concerted, organized attack on groups of related social problems such as those mentioned above and others might be less than the cost of separate, piecemeal attacks. Or, to put it otherwise, per dollar spent the nation would, it is argued with considerable logic, get much more for its money by a total approach than by a piecemeal one.

▶ THE PERSONAL ELEMENT IN THE TREATMENT OF SOCIAL PROBLEMS

Diversity of viewpoint. Even the least informed person must recognize that there exist widespread differences of opinion with respect to the existence of social problems and especially as to their most appropriate treatment. We sometimes write and speak, for purposes of simplicity, in such terms as "the labor view," "the employer's position," "the farmer's outlook," or "the conservative reaction." While such phrases may be useful and necessary before we can proceed in our discussions without undue confusion, it must be emphasized that all such phrases are oversimplifications if not downright misrepresentations. In the first place, what, for example, is *the* farmers' view on farm subsidies? A writer has a large acquaintance with farmers in a Midwest farming community. After extensive inquiry, he is forced to conclude that there is no such thing as *the* farmers' viewpoint on farm subsidies in this area. Some farmers praise farm subsidies, and some oppose it. Some farmers favor subsidy on one commodity, and some on another. Some farmers favor one type of subsidy, while other farmers favor another kind. Meanwhile newspaper editorials, magazine writers, and radio commentators continue to speak and write glibly about *the* farmers' position on farm subsidies. The same is true of labor's position, employers' viewpoint, and so on.

Such phrases as those above might, of course, mean something like "the position of the majority of farmers on farm subsidies," or "the official position taken by organized farm groups with respect to farm subsidies." Interpreted thus, the catch phrase comes nearer to the truth, but is still a stumbling block to clear thinking about farmers in relation to farm subsidies. In the first place, how about the minority; it might constitute 49 percent of the farmers. Furthermore, what percentage of the farmers are members of farm organizations, and for what percentage, therefore, of the farmers of the nation does the farm organization really speak? Finally, when the farm organization takes a position on a crop subsidy law, how is its position arrived at—by vote of all the members, by guesses as to how the farmers would vote if they had a chance, or by the leaders' judgment as to how farmers ought to vote if they were wise? And so we might go on and on to demonstrate that there is far greater diversity of opinion on social problems than the oversimplifications which some leaders like to use in order to win their points in argument.

Why diversity of viewpoint? This great variety of viewpoint is difficult to explain. We do not know why there is so great an ideological diversity with respect to social problems on the part of American people, but each of the following factors, at least to some extent, may help to explain it.

1. *Ignorance.* Few people have first-hand contact with all social problem conditions. Actually many social problems are primarily problems of certain classes or of certain regions. Persons in the unaffected social classes or regions really know little about "how the other half lives." It is unfortunate that we are as ignorant of the facts as we are, but we must face the fact that we are.

Not only are we ignorant of many of the problem conditions, but there is also great ignorance as to the effectiveness, or even the availability, of various approaches. For example, a prominent citizen of a Midwest city entered a lecture hall where the speaker was discussing the court handling of juvenile delinquency, a well-known social problem with which the speaker had had considerable practical experience. The civic leader who had come in late and heard only the last half of the lecture, commended the speaker for "a fine theoretical statement, but you know it can never work in practice." He was much surprised to find out that what he thought could not work "in practice" had been working admirably for fifteen years in his own city.

2. *Purposive misinformation.* It is not surprising that so many people are misinformed concerning the nature and treatment of social problems, in view of the fact that there is so much cleverly concealed and widely disseminated propaganda designed precisely to mislead him. As soon as there is a strike or threat of a strike it is now the vogue for both union and management to put large advertisements in the newspapers, each justifying its own side. Thus, to a disinterested observer, both sides are made to seem to be so completely right, so ethical, so noble in their purpose, that it is hard to understand how such altruistic people could possibly get into an argument. On less dramatic problems than strikes, it is often more difficult to secure reliable information, even if one searches diligently for it. There is always some-

one with an ax to grind who confuses the discussion with a concoction of truth, half truth, and utter falsity, so that the bewildered citizen knows not whom to believe. The greatest tragedy, however, is that the citizen is too often completely sure that his source of information is infallible, that he is possessed of the truth, the whole truth, and nothing but the truth.

3. *Vested interests.* Each person has at one given time some specific relationship to each particular social problem. He is an employer or an employee, a buyer or a seller, a farmer or a nonfarmer, a parent or nonparent. Each of these positions constitutes for a person a vested interest. The outcomes one wants are largely determined by his vested interests. Some persons, because of idealism or breadth of experience, are less narrow in pursuing their vested interests than others, but few persons are able to rise far above their selfish "best interest."

4. *Personality and personal background.* People differ in temperament, in intelligence, in parental and formal education, and in the kind of religious and political indoctrination which they have experienced. People bring to their thinking on social problems, therefore, patterns of prejudice based upon these personal and background factors. This is fairly easy to see when a representative of the National Association of Manufacturers and an officer of the CIO discuss fair wage rates or when an equalitarian and a supporter of the caste system attempt to "discuss" race relations. It may be less conspicuous to the layman, but it is obvious to the behavior scientist that a similar situation exists when a somewhat paranoid neurotic proclaims that there is a communist plot to overthrow the government tomorrow, or when a person whose knowledge of human behavior is fifty years behind the model of his automobile dismisses all social reform with a glib "You can't change human nature," "Negroes are simply like that," "Children just ought to be brought up like I was."

How, then, does each person line up with respect to the value issues in which social problems have their existence? Obviously his position on social problems is a result of the interaction of his vested interests, his information and his ignorance, the ways he has been misinformed, his background, his temperament, and other factors. In this interaction of influence and counterinfluence, many persons experience indecision and conflict as to where they stand on this or that problem. Other persons are markedly stable in the positions which they take. Some try to "reason it out" by the cumbersome process of collecting and evaluating information. Others take their value positions impulsively on the basis of whatever facet of their personality is ascendant at the moment or is dominant in their total personality make-up. This makes the intellectual diversity of viewpoint on social problems which is so patently American. This is the ideological climate in which American social problems live, breathe, and have their being.

SUGGESTED READINGS

Dunham, H. Warren, and Nathan D. Grundstein, "The Impact of a Confusion of Social Objectives on Public Housing: A Preliminary Analysis," *Marriage and Family Living*, Vol. 17 (May 1955), pp. 103-12. City planners, social reformers, organized realtors, tenants, and others sometimes sharply disagree concerning basic objectives of public housing. An interesting specific illustration of "clash of values" at the treatment level of social problems.

Elmer, M. C., "Social Change and Social Reforms," *Social Science*, Vol. 26 (January 1951), pp. 33-35. This article suggests seven standards by which to evaluate the constructiveness and potential efficacy of social reform programs. When judged according to these standards, it is not difficult to understand the failure of many popular proposals for the treatment of social problems.

Fink, Arthur E., *The Field of Social Work*, 3d ed., New York, Henry Holt and Co., 1955. A good survey of the social-work approach to treating social problems.

Lee, Alfred M., and Elizabeth B. Lee, *Social Problems in America: A Source Book*, rev. ed., New York, Henry Holt and Co., 1955, Chap. 24. The readings in this chapter consist of classical and contemporary approaches to social action. An interesting cross section of viewpoints on what can and should be done to remedy societal problems.

Roucek, Joseph S., "Ideologies," *Social Control*, New York, D. Van Nostrand Co., 1947, Chap. 12. A clear treatment of the ideological forces affecting thinking about social problems.

STUDY QUESTIONS

1. What is the literal meaning of *laissez faire?* What is the implication of this philosophy when it is applied to the treatment of social problems?

2. Evaluate: "Everyone is *laissez faire* when it is to his advantage; he is otherwise when *laissez faire* becomes uncomfortable."

3. What is meant by "purposive social change"? Illustrate.

4. Why is the phrase "the people's choice" an empty slogan? In what way is it dishonest?

5. What do you consider some of the major achievements our society has made through purposive social change? What do you consider the most important problems that remain despite societal action to remove them?

6. Distinguish between amelioration and cure of social problems. Are social problems most frequently ameliorated or cured? Why?

7. What are the chief limitations of the coercive approach to the treatment of social problems? What are its advantages? Illustrate.

8. Differentiate between evolutionary and revolutionary procedures for attacking social problems. Illustrate why it is difficult to make this distinction with regard to specific changes that have occurred.

9. Illustrate how a total attack on social problems could be less costly than a piecemeal attack. Why is the piecemeal attack so frequently employed?

10. What four factors help explain the ideological diversity with respect to social problems on the part of the American people? Explain.

Major Social Problems in America

Part 2

Major Social Problems
in America

· 5 ·

Income and Its
Distribution

Any record of man's activities is replete with descriptions of the activities in which he has engaged in order to sustain life. The cave drawings of primitive man, The Holy Bible, and Booth's *Life and Labour of the People of London*, while indicating that he has indeed changed his methods of labor, attest that man's search for an adequate return from his labor has long been fraught with difficulties and frustrations. With the establishment of the practice of exchanging labor for money and the money in turn for goods and services, the problem of income has become somewhat more involved. Another complication has arisen as a result of the intricate division of labor which is so conspicuously a part of modern society. The money system and the division of labor have in many ways aggravated, if not actually caused, many of the modern problems of income and its distribution among the persons and families of the society.

Our task in this section is threefold: (1) to examine the various factors and forces which operate in determining the amount of income a person receives; (2) to investigate the distribution of income in the United States; and (3) to consider the value differences regarding the present distribution of income.

▶ THE INDIVIDUAL WORKER AND HIS INCOME

Differential wage rates. It is one thing to divide up the labor of a society and quite another to reward the various specialties and occupations in ways which are just and practical. If all kinds of work required equal skill, if all occupations had the same degree of pleasantness-unpleasantness associated with them, if all persons had the same preference as to which occupation they would follow, and if all occupations carried the same prestige for the persons engaged in them, the problem of remuneration would be relatively easy—everyone would be paid approximately equally, wages varying only to account for differences in personal skill and industriousness. But as everyone realizes, none of the above assumptions is consistent with the facts. Occupations differ radically in the amount of skill, kind of skill, and the length and type of training necessary, and range from the various jobs done by unskilled labor to the precise specialty of the brain surgeon, the atomic physicist, and the concert musician.

It has sometimes been carelessly said that the positions which require the greater skill and the longer training pay their incumbents higher incomes. That generalization is simply untrue. Teachers, clergymen, and musicians, for example—three of the most highly trained professions in American society—characteristically receive remuneration which is relatively low in comparison even to that of semiskilled workmen whose period of training and whose minimum skills are relatively low. Nor is this a new condition: it has existed for at least seventy-five years.

The reasons for the low pay of these highly skilled occupational groups are, of course, not hard to find. Prestige plays a part. Many people accept the notion that these occupations constitute a kind of "calling," as if the worker in these roles were a peculiar kind of human being, fashioned by God or destiny for this special work and should not, therefore, be compensated on the same basis as are other workers. Another factor may be the relative pleasantness of these professional tasks, "freedom from rigid routine" being an example. Whatever the reason, however, there is little relationship between that income derived from an occupation and the cost and length of training or the degree of required skill.

This is, then, what we mean by the statement that, *between occupations, our system of wages is a "nonrational" one;* wage rates between occupations are more or less arbitrary, and are largely determined by the factor of custom. Nor can it be otherwise, since society has no objective basis (even if it should by some miracle become so inclined) for measuring the comparative worth of the services of a carpenter, a policeman, a television comedian, and a football coach. Certainly no one can say that winning some football game is equivalent to so many arrests, or that hanging a door is worth so many jokes!

Humanitarian ideology. There is at least another factor which affects the income received by individuals. Although difficult to phrase precisely, it seems to be a sentimental belief rather than a matter of economics: that there is some sort of minimum below which no person's reward for service should fall. This belief has taken tangible form during the past eighteen years in laws setting minimum wages of employment. The old justification that a man was not "worth" any more, or that another man could be hired for less, than a living wage has to some extent given way to the humane argument that any worker, as a citizen of a wealthy society, has the right to a "decent" minimum living wage. Any industry or employer who cannot pay such a living wage is thus regarded as uneconomic and incompatible with the general welfare. We do not know whether this view is yet shared by the great majority of Americans, but it is shared by a large enough number so that minimum wage laws have been passed and pressure continues for additional laws along the same line.

A somewhat related logic is incorporated in the concept that there should be a maximum as well as a minimum to the size of personal income. As recent as the 1940's there were recurrent proposals to limit annual personal incomes to $25,000 after payment of federal income taxes. This proposal had the endorsement of the late President Roosevelt in a message to the Congress in April 1943. At about this same time, furthermore, a Public Opinion Poll discovered that almost two thirds of the population thought that such a proposal was "a good idea." [1]

[1] Findings with regard to this opinion poll originally were relased in 1942. See Hadley Cantril, *Public Opinion 1935-1946*, Princeton, Princeton University Press, 1951, p. 313.

Of a similar nature is the higher income tax rate imposed upon people with higher incomes. For example, an individual earning $3,000 in 1955 would pay about 14 percent of his gross income in federal income taxes, while the tax for a person earning $10,000 would be about 21 percent of his income. There are, of course, other reasons than equalization of incomes which are involved in these graduated tax rates, but a reduction of the more extreme differences in income is at least one of them. There are persons who believe that greater equalization should be effected through further tax legislation; others believe that we have already gone far enough.

Total national income. Another factor affecting individual income is the national income or the total worth of the goods and services which can be distributed among the people. The society cannot in the long run consume more than the society produces. The coming and going of periods of boom and depression emphatically bring this fact home periodically to Americans as well as to other peoples of the world. We must be careful not to assume, however, that rising and falling prosperity affects all wage earners equally, or even proportionally, for such is by no means the case. Some of the same factors which affect the amount of income received in normal times also affect the amount or proportion of change associated with rises and falls in the national income.

Real v. money income. Almost all thinking about wages and income is unfortunately confused by the necessity for clearly distinguishing the number of dollars received and the amount of goods and services which the income received will buy. The number of dollars a person receives as cash income is important only for what goods and services the cash can purchase for its owner. If a man earns $100 per week and pays $25 rental for his apartment, for example, he would be no better off should his wages be increased to $125 and his rental to $50. In both instances he would have $75 left for other purposes. The same holds true, of course, for expenditures for goods, clothing, taxes, or any other item. Wages are important only as they relate to prices of goods purchased with them. Doubling wage rates is of no value

Table 3. National Income in the United States, 1929-55 *

(In millions of dollars)

Year	Income
1929	87,814
1930	75,729
1931	59,708
1932	42,547
1933	40,159
1934	48,959
1935	57,057
1936	64,911
1937	73,618
1938	67,581
1939	72,753
1940	81,634
1941	104,710
1942	137,694
1943	170,310
1944	182,639
1945	181,248
1946	179,577
1947	197,168
1948	221,641
1949	216,193
1950	239,956
1951	277,041
1952	289,537
1953	303,648
1954	299,673
1955	311,400

* Statistics taken from *Survey of Current Business*, Office of Business Economics, U. S. Department of Commerce (July 1955).

to the worker if the prices of the goods and the services he buys are also doubled. Thus, wage rates may be going up, but the persons who receive the increases may be getting poorer because prices have risen more rapidly than have the wage rates. The reverse trend may also, of course, be true: wages may be going down but prices may be dropping even faster. It becomes very difficult, therefore, to discover the significance of constantly changing wages and prices upon the level of living of the worker and his family. And yet unless and until one relates these two interdependent items, he cannot accurately determine the true status of the income recipient or the actual trends in the standard of living which are taking place.

A glance at Table 4 will illustrate the point. From 1929 to 1950 money income per family increased 92 percent. But let us adjust

Table 4. How Much Have Incomes Changed? *

Year	Average family income	
	Current dollars	1950 dollars
1929	2,322	3,267
1935-36	1,631	2,937
1941	2,209	3,664
1946	3,940	4,592
1950	4,461	4,461

* Adapted from Goldsmith and others, "Size Distribution of Income Since the Mid-Thirties," *Review of Economics and Statistics*, Vol. 36 (February 1954), p. 3.

the figures to take into account the price changes since 1929. This can be done by converting dollar figures for all years into dollars of 1950 purchasing power. It is now evident that "real" income increased but 37 percent. In a similar manner, although the average money income was less in 1941 than in 1929, purchasing power actually was somewhat greater.

Money v. other "income."   Income must not only be related to the price of goods, or purchasing power, but also to any change in the necessity for purchasing some goods or services at all in order to maintain a given standard of living. Industrial, white-collar, and professional workers, for example, increasingly are receiving at no cost or at greatly reduced rates sickness and accident insurance, life insurance, retirement benefits, and the like, all of which are not considered part of their dollar income. Nevertheless, these "benefits" have a dollar value, and the worker who receives a company "health insurance" policy does not have to spend his income for such a policy or for hospital bills. Then there is the federal Social Security program. In addition to the fact that as a nation our purchasing power has increased, millions of Americans now find that they have one less item to purchase— a minimum retirement income. Since each employee makes a small contribution to this program, it would perhaps be more accurate to say that workers are purchasing retirement insurance at extremely low rates. But should not, then, the difference between the cost to the worker of Social Security and that of a comparable insurance policy through a commercial concern be counted as part of his "income"? Other-than-dollar income has become increasingly important in the last several decades and further complicates the determination of actual trends in living standards.

Summary. These, then, seem to be the major factors, aside from differences in ability, which at present are known to influence the amount of income which the various persons in America receive: (1) the customary and nonrational differentials between occupations; (2) humanitarian considerations designed to limit, to some extent at least, minimum and maximum income limits; (3) the total national income to be distributed; (4) the interplay of rising and falling prices which determine the real income which a money income can provide; and (5) the receipt of other-than-money income.

▶ HOW WELL OFF FINANCIALLY ARE THE AMERICAN PEOPLE?

Upon first thought it might seem that the facts about the distribution of incomes could be secured easily. The truth, however, is otherwise. To secure even an approximately accurate compilation of income figures is a gigantic undertaking and one fraught with knotty theoretical and technical problems.

Current income is, of course, not the only index to the economic welfare of a people. "Liquid" savings, that is, money or other possessions readily convertible into currency, are also of significance for at least two reasons. (1) The amount of savings is a measure of the adequacy of income. If a people can save substantial portions of their current incomes, it is reasonable to conclude that their incomes are more than adequate for their needs. (2) Liquid savings constitute a cushion, so to speak, to help the person or family over financial crises due to illness, accident, unemployment, or other contingency.

We shall now turn to an examination of the available facts relative to the distribution of incomes among American wage earners and families and to the volume of their savings.

Savings: fact and myth. Ever since World War II there has been widespread supposition that the great bulk of Americans have fairly extensive savings. It is often said that the working classes in particular, as a result of their wartime wage rate and the tendency of their wages to keep pace with postwar inflation, have amassed a considerable amount of savings. The facts, however, do not support this conclusion.

In 1954 half of the families in the United States had less than $350 savings. And this is *gross* savings; outstanding debts, sometimes amounting to more than the savings, have not been subtracted. Only one third of the families had what could be called a "good-sized" savings account, that is, one with $1,000 or more.

Looking at it a bit differently, we can discover *who* has the savings. The top 20 percent of income recipients have a little over half of all the national savings. The bottom 60 percent, or "most of us," do not quite have one third of all the savings. Apparently, then, it is mostly myth that there is a great "stockpile of unspent savings" in the purses of American families of moderate means.

It should be remembered, of course, that the type of savings we have been discussing is "liquid assets" which include money in bank accounts, government bonds, and the like, but do not include, for example, the equity one may have in his home. There are more homeowners in the nation than ever before; over half of the families, excluding farmers, are buying their homes and of these over half own their property outright. Added to this, as we have noted previously, is the fact that Social Security, unemployment compensation, and other types of insurance have

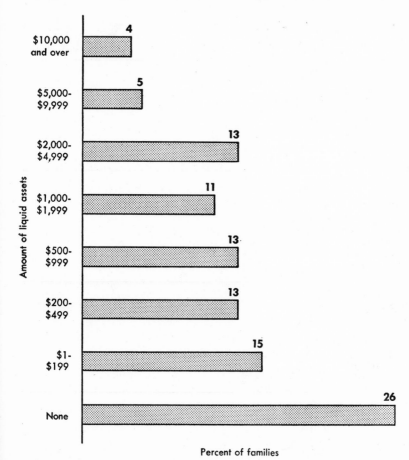

Fig. 2. How large are families' savings? (Data from *Federal Reserve Bulletin*, July 1954, p. 3.)

removed at least some of the previous "risks" of life. Indeed, in times of full employment, with a high rate of homeownership, and with a growing proportion of the nation insured against some of the uncertainties of life, it is appropriate to question whether savings are at all necessary or even desirable. To be sure,

Fig. 3. Who has the nation's savings? (Data from *Federal Reserve Bulletin*, July 1954, p. 11.)

every American would probably like "a little money in the bank," and no one is seeking to deny him the "security" this apparently provides nor the acquisitive pleasure of reaping the fruits of compound interest. And it is still true that many Americans have very little "money in the bank." The point is at least tenable, however, that in our present economy the need for savings is not so great as once it was and that liquid savings, therefore, do not constitute an adequate measure of the financial and other well-being of the population.

Personal income: fact and myth. As with popular misimpressions concerning the extent of savings among the rank and file of the people, there is also much misconception relative to the size of family incomes during so-called "prosperity periods." The average family income, about $4,500 per year, is often used to illustrate the belief that *most* American families are "well off." But averages can be misleading. Such a figure does not take into account the number of persons in the family nor the number of wage earners in the family necessary to produce the family income. Many persons will probably be surprised to learn the facts concerning the distribution of family income in the United States.

During the year 1953, generally labeled as a "prosperous" year,

Table 5. Family Income in the United States in 1953 *

Total yearly income of all family members	Percent of families	Actual distribution
Under $1,000	9	30% of American
$1,000-$1,999	10	*families* live on
$2,000-$2,999	11	less than $58 per
$3,000-$3,999	15	week
$4,000-$4,999	16	31% of all families
$5,000-$7,499	23	earn between $58
$7,500-$9,999	8	and $96 per week
Over $10,000	8	

* *Federal Reserve Bulletin* (July 1954), p. 13.

nearly one third of the families of the nation received incomes of less than $58 per week to be allocated among the needs of the several family members. Not even one family out of five was in the so-called "higher brackets" receiving $7,500 a year or more. And these figures are for total money income received by all members of the family before payment of income taxes; about 40 percent of all families apparently find it necessary to have more than one wage earner.

▶ THE TREND IN INCOME DISTRIBUTION

It is generally recognized that "people are getting more money" today than they did years ago. Even when allowance is made for price increases, it is evident that the purchasing power of American families, considered as an aggregate, has increased. But has this affected families at all income levels?

Are incomes becoming more equal?   Over the period of eighteen years covered by the chart of Figure 4, income distribution has remained *approximately* the same. To be sure, the top 20 percent now receive about 46 percent of the total income instead of about 52 percent, but the over-all trend can scarcely lead to the conclusion that anything approaching a great "leveling off" of incomes has taken place. More detailed analysis, incidentally, shows that the decline in the relative share of the income obtained by the top 20 percent was largely borne by the top 1 percent of consumer units.[2]

The effect of income taxes.   Lest there be some confusion, it should be pointed out that data used to study the trend in income distribution are for total money income before taxes. Income taxes have a tendency to "equalize" incomes, but do so to no great extent. For example, in 1951 the 10 percent of the popula-

[2] In analyzing the decline in the share of income obtained by the top 20 percent between the years 1935-36 and 1950 Goldsmith concluded that the decline was heaviest for the top 1 percent; the next 4 percent were affected much less; the next 5 percent maintained their relative position; and the remaining 10 percent in the top quintile actually showed a small gain. See Selma Goldsmith and others, "Size Distribution of Income Since the Mid-Thirties," *Review of Economics and Statistics,* Vol. 36 (February 1954), p. 13.

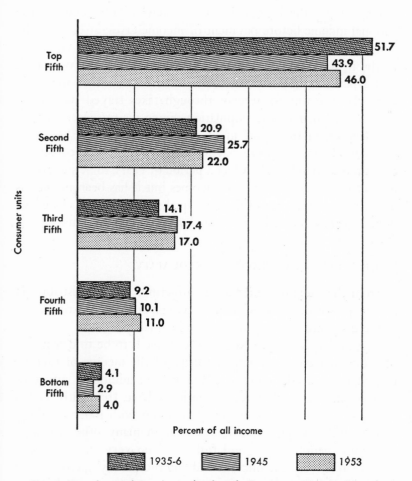

Fig. 4. How the total income is distributed. Consumer units receiving the lowest 20 percent of the national income obtained about the same share in 1953 as they did in 1935-1936. Some quintiles received a larger share in 1953, while the top received a smaller share. Generally, the distribution has remained the same through the years. (Data from Selma Goldsmith and others, "Size Distribution of Income Since the Mid-Thirties," *Review of Economics and Statistics*, Vol. 36, February 1954, p. 3; and *Federal Reserve Bulletin*, July 1954, p. 698.)

tion receiving the highest incomes received 31 percent of the national income before payment of income taxes; after taxes the comparable figure was 28 percent.[3] In the same year the share of the national income obtained by the lowest-paid 20 percent was 4 percent, both before and after taxes. Most of the share "lost" by the top 10 percent through taxes stayed within the highest-paid half of the population. Since we are interested, in this section, in the *trend* in income distribution, it should be understood that taxes are having virtually no more equalizing effect today than in 1935. Over a period of years, to be sure, there has been *some* equalization of incomes but it has been neither as little as the proponents of greater equality would have us believe nor as great as those who abhor such an idea seem to think.

▶ THE MEANING OF INCOME INEQUALITY

From the facts of, and factors affecting, income distribution among persons and families in American society, we turn now to the daily-life *meaning* of income inequality.

A pecuniary society. No American needs to be told that one of life's chief concerns is the security of the income of each of us and the consideration of planning and additional effort to achieve increased income. Romanticists have frequently called attention to the American's preoccupation with money-making and money-seeking, pointing out that in many other parts of the world people live "good full lives" on very small incomes and are relatively unconcerned about the money factor in the standard of living. We have used the word "romantic" in the above sentence advisedly to call attention to the unrealistic nature of the implication. Because people in *other* societies are not concerned with financial matters is largely irrelevant in respect to people in *this* society who, generally speaking, cannot escape from having such a concern. The romanticism springs from the failure to recognize the fact that America is a pecuniary society—the predominant system of values operates in terms of pecuniary

[3] U. S. Bureau of the Census, *Statistical Abstracts of the United States: 1953,* Washington, D. C., U. S. Government Printing Office, 1953, p. 286.

considerations. This is sometimes construed as revealing selfishness, ignorance, and poor judgment, as if the "good" person somehow rises above or beyond pecuniary valuation. With rare exceptions, one cannot escape the fact of the ascendancy of pecuniary values in the American's *modus operandi*. Let us now turn our attention to the reasons underlying pecuniary valuation.

"Life chances" and income.   In American society one's life chances are in large measure determined by his financial status. The goods and services necessary to maintain life must be bought and paid for out of the accumulated wealth or current earnings of the person or his family. Broadly speaking, quality varies with cost. The principle is the same whether the person is buying potatoes, securing music lessons for his child, or purchasing medical care. The better potatoes cost more, so do the music lessons taught by more competent teachers, and so do the services of medical specialists run higher, particularly when one considers such added costs as X-ray, various laboratory tests and other aids to more precise diagnosis and treatment by the specialist.

Life itself can frequently be preserved only at considerable expense. We have long known, for example, that a larger percentage of the babies born to parents in the higher income groups survive the first year of life than among persons of lower income. Not only is infant mortality affected by income, so also is the incidence of various illnesses. (See charts pp. 100 and 101.) Accident statistics also show that life is safer for persons of higher income. It is small wonder, then, with the characteristics of the good life so much a matter of dollars and cents, that people are preoccupied with money-making.

Social status and income.   Social status, too, is largely, though not entirely, a product of the amount of money which one has to spend for status-giving goods and services. Given sufficient income one can live in a better house, in a better part of town where his children may attend better schools and be less likely to associate in play groups with children who show delinquent patterns of behavior. Everything from automobiles to membership in exclusive clubs is largely available on the basis of whether or not the person has the wherewithal to qualify. This is not intended to deny that there are other factors than income which affect one's social status. The point is that income is a large factor and directly and indirectly affects other factors which seem at first not to be matters of income at all.[4] Frequently what are designated as "traits of a good personality" are not inherent in the person but rather are the accumulated results of association with certain people, the results of education, and the effects of clothes, possessions and other attributes for which someone had in some way to pay. These indirect effects of income, and the lack of it, are frequently overlooked by the person who glibly asserts that "after all it is personality, not money, that counts." The error lies in failing to recognize the many connections between money, or the lack of it, and the desirable traits of the personality.

Thus we see that ours is the type of society in which wealth and income are very important, not only because wealth can purchase the so-called luxuries, but, more importantly, because social status and life chances for attaining the goals which society holds as good are in so great a measure the result of ability to buy the goods and services which typify the good life in America.

▶ CONTEMPORARY VALUE ISSUES REGARDING WEALTH
   AND INCOME

Income and its distribution in the United States are social problems primarily because of the "clash of values" regarding existing conditions. Is the present state of affairs "right," "the best," or, should "something be done about it"? Value judgments interpret the problems of income and its distribution with two prevailing antithetical emphases: (1) ideologies which rationalize the *status quo* in some way or other and (2) ideologies rationalizing modification of the *status quo*. We shall treat each of these only briefly since practically every person who has attained early adulthood

---

[4] The relationship between social status and wealth has been repeatedly demonstrated by sociological studies. See John F. Cuber and William F. Kenkel, *Social Stratification in the United States,* New York, Appleton-Century-Crofts, 1954, and references cited therein.

has already encountered a number of them, either in his own thinking or in the stated opinions of other people he has known.

Rationalizations of the "status quo." One frequently encounters a justification of the present distribution of wealth and income on the ground that inequality is "inherent in the nature of things" and that unequal income is merely a reflection of differences in ability. To be sure, there are individual differences in almost every known ability, but it does not follow from this fact, as we have seen in previous paragraphs, (*a*) that the differences in ability are equal to the differences in income or (*b*) that there are no other systems of compensating differences in ability than the one which happens to be current in our society at the present time.

Another familiar rationalization holds that differences in income are necessary in order to "spur" people to greater exertion and self-denial, in order that they may appreciate later the somewhat higher level of living which the eventually larger income may open up. The American folklore is replete with tales containing an admixture of truth and fiction, explaining how many of our colorful national figures such as John Jacob Astor, Cornelius Vanderbilt, and Henry Ford had humble financial beginnings, persevered amid deprivations, and eventually were rewarded with social position and a somewhat belated but abundant financial reward. The possibility that some lowly born child may some day be President of the United States or Chairman of the Board of United States Steel Corporation has satisfied many persons that our present distribution of income is morally right and has beneficial results.

A related defense of the *status quo* in income distribution is simply that "it works." It is pointed out, for example, that at present our warehouses are bulging with consumer goods, our farmers produce more food than we can eat, and, in time of war, we prove that our production capability allows us to defeat aggressors. In short, the motives and incentives furnished by the present income distribution seem to result in a workable system and a high national standard of living. It scarcely needs to be mentioned that such a view ignores the host of other factors, population density, and natural resources, to name but two, that affect our production rate. Then too, such a view seems tacitly to imply that a workable system cannot be improved.

One frequently encounters the rationalization that a grossly unequal distribution of wealth is a desirable condition, because of the good moral effect of poverty. "Character" is alleged to be best developed under conditions of deprivation and deteriorates under conditions of opulence. Tales of the "moral decadence of the rich" are cited as proof and undoubtedly are so accepted, at least by some people. There are others, of course, who will be inclined to doubt whether their inability to afford an electric refrigerator is likely to insure either their own morals or the characters of their children. Other justifications will undoubtedly occur to almost anyone reading this account. It is not our purpose to provide an exhaustive treatment. In the interest of conserving time and space, we have contented ourselves with only this brief synopsis.

The argument for smaller income differentials. In clear opposition to the foregoing arguments, some economists have pointed out that gross inequality of incomes is detrimental to full employment and to the national standard of living. The crux of the argument is that great income inequalities can result in underconsumption of goods, and thus, in less need to produce goods and less need for workers.

The workers of the nation produce various goods and services which collectively are known as the "national product." As long as this national product is consumed, there will be need for workers to produce more of the same. If as today, however, the poorer 80 percent of the nation receives but about half of the national income it means that this portion can buy only about half of all goods produced and, consequently, the other half is available to the remaining 20 percent of the population. Since it is unlikely that the top fifth of the nation's earners can consume half the national product, it means that soon there will be a surplus of goods and, following this, a decreasing need for workers to produce goods. And as unemployment increases, there will be even less ability to buy goods.[5] This is an admittedly simplified version of the economic theory, but the point is merely that there are extremely practical reasons for suggesting that the present inequality in incomes be reduced.

Attempts at income modification. As in the foregoing paragraphs, we shall again not attempt an exhaustive treatment of all the currents of value judgment which attempt to rationalize one or another of the stream of proposals for changing the income distribution system. A few examples must suffice. Others appear in almost every chapter in this book, because since America is a pecuniary society, almost every problem is related in some way or other to income and every proposed treatment of social problems reflects pecuniary values in one way or another.

It is obvious to almost any moderately informed citizen that various groups in a society from time to time attempt by force to increase the proportion of income which they receive. Strikes and lockouts are perhaps our best illustration. In strikes over wage rates, workers refuse to work unless their demands for higher wages are met or approximated, relying upon this threat to bring for themselves the increase in income which they desire. The lockout proceeds from the same kind of logic. Thus employer and employee struggle with one another for the purpose of effecting change, in however slight or great a degree, in the distribution of the joint product of labor and management which the industry produces. Consumers' "strikes," although much less prevalent and effective, have been attempted in recent years for a similar reason—namely, to force prices down under threat of refusing to purchase at all.

The creation of artificial scarcities, which we have noted earlier in this chapter, is another device which is both advocated and practiced in our society. For example, one of the factors

[5] For sake of simplification, we have ignored the matters of exports and of war. Exports obviously would have to exceed imports if they were effectively to relieve a surplus of goods and, although war is a great consumer of goods, it is rarely proposed as a means of maintaining a stable economy. For a lucid treatment of the relationship between consumption, purchasing power, and full employment, see H. Gordon Hayes, *Spending, Saving and Employment*, New York, Alfred A. Knopf, 1945.

which is said to have influenced the abolition of price controls at the end of World War II was the practice by some merchants and producers of holding back goods or cutting down production in order to create scarcities which would cause a pressure toward higher prices and black markets. It should be noted that this kind of scarcity is not a natural scarcity, but rather a scarcity *created* deliberately for the purpose of someone securing a greater share in the distribution of income than he would if the scarcity had not been induced. Other examples have been cited previously.

In recent years there have been a number of proposals for the collective ownership, or at least collective control, of some of the important want-satisfying industries in the society. Some communities own and operate their own electric light plants, street railways, and other public utilities on a nonprofit basis, thus indirectly affecting wealth distribution by eliminating profits or giving service to the people of the community at reduced cost. In more recent years we have had some experience in this country with collective ownership of housing. Other pending proposals vary from collective ownership and control of medical facilities to similar control of the mining industry. In the past we have limited our collective ownership to such things as the public school system, the post office, bridges and highways, and a few other parts of the economic system. Somehow, the idea never took root that such organizations and services as these should be operated for private profit. In more recent years the collective ownership ideology has been extended to cover such additional services as public recreation facilities and a few of the so-called public utilities.

There are some indications that this point of view is growing not only in the United States but more patently in other parts of the world, notably in England. It is true that in the last few years the experiences in both countries would seem to negate this. England has attempted to "de-socialize" some industries and in the United States, to cite but one example, the "government monopoly" in the field of atomic energy has been broken. The *long-run* trend, however, has been toward more, and not less, collective ownership. Whether the present experiences represent a temporary slowdown in the trend or a true reversal cannot at this time fully be determined.

Earlier in this chapter we have alluded to minimum and maximum limits upon personal incomes. These practices represent values which imply that the *laissez-faire* concept should not be accepted without at least some minimum and maximum qualifications. The limiting of maximum profits, attempted during the war and at other times, is another current idea which has at least some adherents.

Another point of view designed to work in the direction of reducing income inequalities is known as the "principle of progressive taxation." The word "progressive" is not used in the sense of being modern or forward looking; it means rather that the proportion of income taken by the government for taxes should increase as the amount of income increases. For example, if we taxed each person 10 percent of his total income, we would not be taxing progressively, but if we taxed persons with higher incomes at higher percentages, then the tax rate would be progressive. To some extent the present federal income tax structure is based on the principle of progressive taxation. Many persons believe that the tax rates should be more progressive than they now are; others allege that we have already "stifled the initiative" of many enterprising people in the higher income brackets by taking as much of their personal income for taxes as we now do.

The concept of "social security" is an older attempt to handle some of the more extreme inequalities of personal and family income. Under present laws both employer and employee, with some exceptions, are required to make contributions to the federal government for the purpose of building up a fund out of which small incomes for aged people can later be paid. Recent laws, enacted under both Democratic and Republican administrations, have extended the coverage of Social Security to more segments of the population and have increased the benefit payments. Some states have laws under which they, in conjunction with the federal government, also pay unemployment benefits to persons who are out of work and thus without income from wages. It is felt by many that a national system of health and accident insurance, operated more or less like old age and unemployment compensation, is a desirable next step. (See Chapter 6.)

It should be stressed that all of the proposals for modifying income distribution which we have discussed, constitute rather minor modifications of our traditional *laissez-faire* capitalistic system. They amount, in the main, to (*a*) setting income maximums and minimums for certain categories of people, (*b*) securing somewhat better incomes for one group at the expense of another, and (*c*) supplementing money income by providing some collective governmental service in which all persons regardless of wealth or income may participate equally. Over against these proposals we should mention, of course, such propositions as those which maintain that all incomes should be approximately equal, irrespective of differences in ability or the social need for the occupation in question. Such ideas are, of course, more truly "communistic," and the prevailing value position of our society seems to be adamantly set against them. For the time being, at least, issues centering around income redistribution seem likely to continue to be those of strikes, collective bargaining, attempts to "corner the market" by creating artificial scarcities, movements to "socialize" some one or more of the organizations now running for private profit, struggles over taxation, laws instituting minimum and possibly maximum incomes and attempts to modify the prevailing system of social security. These are the devices through which various groups for some time now have been attempting to alter their destinies so far as their personal share of our collective income is concerned. It seems likely that these struggles will continue and that they will take new forms which are not now wholly apparent.

There are those people who believe that the over-all trend in our society is toward a more equalitarian or communal-like system of income distribution. Such a view of the matter represents either a hope or a fear, depending upon one's personal values, but hardly a fact which one could demonstrate on the basis of figures on income and its distribution in the United States.

▶ SUMMARY

The intricate division of labor and the money system have aggravated many problems of income and its distribution in modern society. Following an investigation of the major factors, aside from differences in ability, which at present are known to influence the amount of income which the various persons in America receive, we turned to an investigation of the financial well-being of the American people.

The distribution of savings was analyzed, and it was discovered that some common beliefs in this area cannot be supported by facts. In 1954 half of the families in the United States had less than $350 savings; only one third had savings of $1,000 or more. The point was made that in our present economy the need for savings is not so great as once it was and that savings, therefore, may not constitute an adequate measure of the financial well-being of the population.

Analysis of income distribution revealed much inequality. Even in the "prosperous" year 1953, 30 percent of American *families* received incomes of less than $58 per week to provide for the needs of the several family members. For the past eighteen years income distribution has remained approximately the same, with the top 20 percent of income recipients receiving roughly half of the income. Income taxes have had some but no very great equalizing effect.

From the facts of income distribution we turned to the daily-life *meaning* of income inequality in America. The relationship between "life chances" and income and social status and income were viewed against the backdrop of the pecuniary nature of American society.

Value judgments regarding income and its distribution center about two prevailing antithetical emphases: (1) those which rationalize the *status quo* and (2) those which rationalize modification of the *status quo*. Among the more frequent justifications of the present distribution of wealth and income are found the notions that the present system is "inherent in the nature of things," is necessary to encourage work, or simply that it "works" reasonably well. Still others emphasize the alleged development of "character" under conditions of deprivation. The argument for smaller income differentials selected for comment was that which holds there are extremely practical reasons for suggesting that the present inequality in incomes be reduced. Finally, several examples were given of recent attempts at income modification

SUGGESTED READINGS

Achinstein, Asher, *Introduction to Business Cycles*, New York, Thomas Y. Crowell Co., 1950. A comprehensive treatment of the subject. Critically evaluates "classical" and other economists and summarizes the mass of empirical work on business cycles.

Blum, W. J., and Harry Kalnen, Jr., *The Uneasy Case for Progressive Taxation*, Chicago, The University of Chicago Press, 1953. A scholarly essay that grapples with the economic, ethical, and legal arguments for and against progressive taxation.

Bowen, Howard, *Social Responsibilities of the Business Man*, New York, Harper & Bros., 1953. Part of a series on Christian Ethics and Economic Life sponsored by the National Council of Churches. Searches for the proper relationship between private control of enterprise and the general welfare and the responsibilities of "big business" to society in general.

Dewhurst, J. Frederic, *America's Needs and Resources*, New York, The Twentieth Century Fund, 1955. A massive compilation of factual data and interpretations of the demands, needs, resources, and capacities of the American economy. A thorough treatment of past trends and a projection into the immediate future.

The Editors of *Fortune*, *The Changing American Market*, Garden City, N. Y., Hanover House, 1955. An enthusiastically written account of recent changes in income and consumption habits of Americans. Presents a detailed analysis of each of the major markets for goods (food, housing, etc.). See especially the changes in income and consumption estimated for the future in Chapter 12, "The Consumer Markets: 1954-1959."

Hayes, H. Gordon, *Spending, Saving, and Employment*, New York, Alfred A. Knopf, 1945. A challenging answer to the problem of chronic unemployment. Income inequality, savings, and investment are considered in relationship to full employment and a high standard of living.

STUDY QUESTIONS

1. Criticize the position that the differential wage rates among occupations are a reflection of the different amounts of skill and training required to fill the occupation. Cite as much factual evidence as possible.

2. How do you account for the fact that society manages to fill its occupations requiring considerable skill and training although it does not always attach much financial reward to such occupations?

3. What is the "logic" of a minimum wage for any type of employment? Of a maximum wage? What are your own positions on these two issues?

4. What is meant by the statement that many workers receive "income" from their jobs other than the wages or salary received? How is this other income related to purchasing power and standard of living?

5. Defend the position that today Americans in general do not need to have cash savings to the extent that they did several decades ago.

6. Is it true that the income distribution in the United States has been becoming more equalitarian? Cite the evidence.

7. What is meant when it is said that in our society one's life chances are in large measure determined by his financial status? To what extent does this contribute to the fact that income distribution is a social problem?

8. Defend the position that the present distribution of wealth and income in the United States requires no modification.

9. Defend the position that there are practical reasons why the present distribution of wealth and income in the United States requires some modification.

10. How much did the dollar income of families in the United States change between 1929 and 1950? What was the change in "real" income?

·6· Physical Health

It is probable that matters of health would appear on many a layman's list of "problems." Man has for a long time concerned himself with alleviating his ills, remedying his bodily complaints, and prolonging his life. He has improved his methods throughout the years, but the charms and potions of the past and the medicine and surgery of today are alike in intent, if not in kind. Traditionally, it seems, we have given more attention to the sick body than we have to the sick mind. But the distinction between mental and physical health is artificial. Medical and psychological research increasingly demonstrates that the individual functions as a mind-body whole in illness and in health. Since health problems are so numerous and so complex, however, some kind of division must be used in discussing them. We herein employ the artificial and traditional distinction between mental and physical health problems both because this distinction is firmly fixed in the literature and because value judgments and value conflicts differ regarding the two phases of health. Hence, in this chapter we treat health problems which are traditionally regarded as "physical," and in Chapter 7 those generally considered "mental."

Poor health is now almost unanimously recognized as undesirable. At least in the area of physical health, most of the conflict of values centers around disagreements as to the best methods of meeting the problems rather than questioning their existence. Such was not always the case. Until very recently in our cultural history, illness was considered the concern and misfortune of the diseased individual and his family and not of the general society. The whole concept of public health and sanitation measures is a relatively new one. While today we take for granted that technological medical improvements will be passed on to the patient and that our public health agencies will prevent and control epidemics, every step of the way to this point of view was fraught with conflict. A brief historical review will help us to understand present health problems and differences of opinion as to methods for solving them.

▶ MEDICAL STRUGGLES OF THE PAST

Theoretical and technical conflicts. Advocates of dissection, Harvey's theory of the circulation of the blood, the theory of percussion, asepsis, antisepsis, vaccination, etc., met with violent opposition from practicing physicians and the public of their day. Yet today these theories and practices are part of the very heart of medicine. The chief reason for such opposition was that preconceived values were encroached upon by the new theories and techniques. Resistance to technical and theoretical medical progress was as strong a century or so ago as resistance to social medical progress (change in the methods of distributing medical services) is today. Harvey, Pasteur, Lister, Ehrlich, and other proponents of new technical theories and methods were even more denounced by defenders of what was then the *status quo* than are proponents of group medical practice or of compulsory health insurance at the present time.

It is not to be inferred, however, that difference of opinion no longer exists in regard to medical theories and techniques. The important change in social attitude is that the physician proposing a new theory or method today is much more apt to be given a fair hearing. His "radical" views are much more likely to be tested clinically and, if proved true, soon incorporated into the body of medicine.

Another unjustified inference from the foregoing account is that every new medical idea is a sound one. Simply because it is "new" does not mean that a specific plan is basically sound. It is not, on the other hand, necessarily "crackpot" or "dangerous." A lesson that we should learn from the history of theoretical and technical medicine to apply to contemporary social medicine is this: *Test the new idea to see whether or not it is sound.*

Opposition to public health policies. Even more violent battles have raged in the field of public health than over medical techniques and theories. If a smallpox epidemic were to break out in one of our communities today, we would not only insist upon public control, but expect public enforcement of preventive methods through the use of vaccines and by other measures. But for many decades such procedures were forcibly resisted on professional, religious, economic, and political grounds. Physicians felt then that they were the only ones capable of dealing with disease and resented attempted enforcement of reports, quarantines, etc. Many religious groups defied isolation and quarantine as interfering with the Divine plan, and commercial interests opposed them on the basis of interference with trade and closing of markets. Added to these professional, religious, and economic objections was the political philosophy of individual rights. If a man wanted to have smallpox in his home or place of business, it was his concern, and he did not want any snooping public health officials interfering with his God-granted individual rights.

All resistance to the improvement of public health facilities has not disappeared. Such blocks as remain, however, stem largely from ignorance and from inability or unwillingness to finance public health programs properly. Many parts of the nation fail to meet the most minimal public health standards. It is estimated, for example, that almost a million American homes have no toilet facilities at all while about 10 million more are lacking adequate flush toilets. During a recent twenty-five year period an estimated quarter of a million persons were affected by intestinal disturbances due to impure water supplies.

All too frequently communities exhibit a "do-nothing" attitude even after facts as startling as the following are disclosed: [1] (1) 6,000 persons in a small city were taken ill in one week due

[1] Reported in Rolf Eliassen, "Environmental Health Responsibilities for the Next Century," *American Journal of Public Health*, Vol. 43, Part II (June 1953), pp. 26-27.

to air pollution, and this was the city's second "smog attack" in four years; (2) 100 cases of encephalitis (sleeping sickness) were uncovered in California and traced directly to inadequate mosquito control; and (3) 8,000 entire communities lack adequate refuse disposal facilities. These are but a few isolated illustrations of the inadequacies in public health that still exist and which *could* be remedied.

In spite of continuing problems, however, considerable progress has been made over epidemic diseases. In the years from 1900 to 1950, for example, the mortality rates of diphtheria, typhoid fever, whooping cough, and measles were reduced between 94 and 99 percent, and of tuberculosis by over 85 percent. As late as 1920 there were over 100,000 cases of smallpox in the United States; in 1950 there were 39. Even for "polio," which has of late reached epidemic stages in some localities, the results are encouraging; *before* the use of the famous Salk vaccine, the mortality rate had been reduced by over 50 percent, despite the occurrence or discovery of more actual cases. Epidemic diseases already have disappeared from the lists of major causes of death and industrial absenteeism; medical research and public health advancements share the credit.

▶ THE PRESENT STATE OF THE NATION'S HEALTH

It is frequently stated that Americans have the best medical care and are the healthiest persons in the world. Even if we grant the truth of the statement, a glance at some of the facts about the nation's health and medical treatment will assure us that the best in the world is, in the light of modern medical knowledge, very poor indeed.

Amount of physical illness. It is difficult to determine the extent of illness in a large group at any specific time. Much ill health not only escapes enumeration in mass studies but goes unrecognized (while taking its toll in efficiency and happiness) by the persons having the diseases. Under present medical procedures, often only the gross maladies and defects become known. During the last twenty-five years, however, there have been several intensive studies of large samplings of the population which have provided a basis of estimation more accurate than guess-work.

One of the first large-scale "health surveys" was that conducted by the "Committee on the Costs of Medical Care" between 1928 and 1932.[2] This committee, privately sponsored and supported, was composed of 48 outstanding physicians, dentists, and laymen. Under their auspices a survey was made of 9,000 families living in 130 communities in 18 states, a sample carefully chosen to be representative of the nation as a whole. The study discovered that on the average there were 3.8 illnesses per family per year and 0.84 illnesses per individual per year. Variations, ranging from 14 percent less than the average to 45 percent more, occurred when income and size of community were taken into account. All in all, the study disclosed that there was a great amount of illness among the "healthiest people in the world."

In 1935-36 the United States Public Health Service sponsored a survey of illness known as the National Health Survey.[3] The sample consisted of more than 2.5 million people living in 83 cities. Twenty-three rural counties were included in order to study the rural health problem. A striking amount of illness was uncovered. On the very day of the interview, for example, almost one out of twenty persons interviewed was disabled. A chronic disease or impairment was reported by 17.7 percent of the sample. In addition, 171 out of every 1,000 persons were disabled for a week or longer during the year preceding the interview. The study also disclosed that there was a strong correlation between low income and high incidence, duration, and severity of illness. It may be surprising to some to realize that the sickness and mortality rates for the poor in our large cities were discovered to be as high in 1936 as they had been for the country as a whole *fifty years previous.*

The Selective Service examinations during and after World

[2] Committee on the Costs of Medical Care, *Medical Care for the American People*, Chicago, The University of Chicago Press, 1932.

[3] U. S. National Institute of Health, *National Health Survey: 1935-1936*, Washington, D. C., U. S. Public Health Service, 1938.

War II probably offer the best nation-wide data we have on the physical status of the male population. Government reports indicate that despite the repeated lowering of Selective Service physical standards, near the end of the war, of the 16,000,000 youth examined, fully half were unfit for military service. These consisted of 5 million rejectees, 1.5 million men with rejectable defects who were inducted into the armed forces and rehabilitated, and an additional 1.5 million men who were inducted but who had to be discharged for mental and physical defects not acquired in the service.

Government figures further indicate that some type of illness or physical defect was present in eight out of every ten persons examined under Selective Service. A half to two thirds of the physical conditions among the rejectees could probably have been prevented or rehabilitated with timely care. Highest rejection rates were in rural areas and in the Southeastern states.

A study of the draftees for the Korean war showed that, between 1950 and 1951, 15 percent of those examined were totally rejected for medical reasons only. The rate is lower than World War II's, it is held, not because the health of the nation has improved but *because the physical standards for military service have been lowered.*[4]

The most recent large-scale study of America's health needs was conducted in 1952 by "The President's Commission on the Health Needs of the Nation," appointed by President Truman in December 1951. This fifteen-man commission was made up of representatives of the medical, dentistry, and nursing professions as well as outstanding citizens with nonmedical interests. The five-volume report covering the medical needs of the nation, resources and finances available for meeting them, and committee recommendations, was presented to the President under the title *Building America's Health.*

Basically, the President's Commission utilized many existing studies made in various parts of the nation, drew them together,

[4] President's Commission on the Health Needs of the Nation, *Building America's Health*, Washington, D. C., U. S. Government Printing Office, 1952, Vol. I, p. 10.

reached conclusions, and made recommendations on the basis of a vast amount of evidence. A study in Baltimore, for one example, found that almost 12 percent of the men and 17 percent of the women interviewed had a major chronic disease. A study on the opposite coast, in San Francisco, found that 63 percent of some 4,000 longshoremen had a positive reaction (medically unfavorable) to one or more of a series of medical tests.

The Commission discovered that "many countries of Western Europe have much lower death rates for certain population groups, especially adult males, than does the corresponding white population of the United States." [5] It concluded that all evidence points to a higher incidence and longer duration of illness among people in low-income families than those with a higher income. Specific rates of illness varied in the different studies investigated by the Commission, but in general, they were consistent with those of the National Health Survey, the Committee on Cost of Medical Care, and others referred to earlier.

Probably no one knows accurately just how much illness exists in the United States. But survey after survey, year after year, point to the conclusion that physical illness is all too prevalent. How much of this illness is "disabling" is another worth-while area of investigation.

Extent of disabling illnesses. A disabling illness is one that keeps a person from his work, school, or other routine. The latest nation-wide investigation of the extent of disabling illness was conducted through the joint efforts of four governmental agencies, the Social Security Administration, the Office of Vocational Rehabilitation, the Public Health Service, and the Bureau of the Census.[6] A house-to-house survey of 25,000 households was made in February 1949, and a "repeat study," using 25,000 different households, was made in September 1950. The sampling techniques were such that estimates of disabling illness based on these samples are reliable, within small margins, for the United States as a whole. The studies were limited, however, to the civilian

[5] President's Commission, *op. cit.*, Vol. II, p. 11.
[6] Theodore D. Woolsey, "Estimates of Disabling Illness in the United States," *Public Health Monograph*, No. 4 (August 1952), p. 11.

noninstitutional population between 14 and 64 years of age. Not included would be those members of the armed forces who are on the sick list and all disabled persons in prisons, homes for the aged, mental hospitals, tuberculosis sanitariums, and the like. Those over sixty-four and those under fourteen are also excluded.

On an average day about 4 million Americans between the ages of fourteen and sixty-four are absent from their work or usual pursuit because of illness. Another 750,000 disabled persons are in resident institutions. Others are in military hospitals. The total would probably exceed 6 million if we also included persons under fourteen and over sixty-four. And *over half* of the disabled have been too ill to follow their usual pursuit for three months or more. Each year the 100 million civilians between fourteen and sixty-four lose over 4 million man-years. The productive working time lost due to disabling illness is tremendous, to say nothing of the toll in human happiness that is exacted. It has been estimated that in 1950 approximately $5 billion in income was lost as a result of nonoccupational illness.[7]

Not all disabling diseases are preventable or curable, but many are. There is no major disabling illness that could not be markedly reduced in amount and intensity by currently known preventive and therapeutic measures.

Changing nature of health problems and health objectives. While the contagious and epidemic diseases linger on as important aspects of illness in general and disabling illness in particular, health problems and goals are gradually shifting their center of attention from the conquering of gross physical maladies to methods of extending life and promoting efficiency for the total population. Stated differently, the principal goals of modern medicine are (1) shifting from treatment of the acutely ill to treatment of the chronically ailing, and (2) raising the health standards of the relatively unailing. It is on these new goals that the greater amount of value conflict over medical practices and health measures focuses today.

This alteration in goals is bringing into being a whole new

[7] Oscar Serbein, Jr., *Paying for Medical Care in the United States*, New York, Columbia University Press, 1953, p. 55.

philosophy of the nature of illness and of society's responsibility in attacking the health problem. The focus of medical research and practice is shifting from illness as such to ill or ailing persons. Recognition of the importance of personality factors in the source and continuance of disease is increasing markedly in medical circles. The new emphasis on the personality of the ill or ailing person constitutes the *psychosomatic* approach in medicine.[8] As the term implies, this approach is based on the realization that the mind and body of a person are different aspects of the same entity, that mental and physical health are indivisible. Functional disorders (mental in source) are frequently the early phases of organic diseases. Distinctions between mental and physical illnesses are, according to the psychosomatic approach, largely ones of *time* rather than of *kind*.

The psychosomatic emphasis has not only centered attention on the psychological and social factors involved in chronic illnesses, but has brought greater awareness of the health problems of persons, most of whom seldom are seen by a physician under our present organization of medical services. Our society seems to be producing an increasing number of persons who have physical complaints neither sufficiently acute nor specific to be recognized as "illnesses," but whose vague and shifting "ailments" greatly reduce their efficiency in work and pleasure. These people (to some extent most, if not all, of us) constitute an important part of modern society's health problem.

▶ ARE MEDICAL SERVICES MEETING HEALTH NEEDS?

"Are medical services meeting health needs?" Little time for pondering is needed to answer this question in the negative. A glance at the foregoing facts about the nation's most easily observable conditions of illness is sufficient to dispel any notion that

---

[8] "New," that is, for modern medicine and as substantiated by scientific research. The basic conception of mind-body medicine was held by some ancient and medieval practitioners. See, for example, Edward A. Strecker, "The Leaven of Psychosomatic Medicine," *Annals of Internal Medicine*, Vol. 18 (O.S., Vol. XXIII), No. 5 (May 1943), pp. 736-40, for illustrations of time-honored psychosomatic views.

fully adequate medical care is being provided the American people. It is our purpose in this section, however, to arrive at a clearer understanding of the degree of inadequacy and of some of the reasons for it.

Degree of fulfillment. The President's Commission on the Health Needs of the Nation, earlier referred to, has made a careful study of America's health resources (physicians, hospitals, clinics, dentists, and the like) on the one hand and of the country's health needs on the other. The results are available for all to inspect. It was discovered, for example, that the nation has about half as many mental hospital beds as it now needs. We have but 15 percent of the beds needed for the care of the chronically ill. Despite the reduction in the incidence of tuberculosis, hospitals for the treatment of persons now afflicted with the disease are only 60 percent adequate. It has been estimated that less than 30 percent of the population receive an adequate level of dental care; to attain an adequate dentist-patient ratio we need fully twice as many dentists as we now have.

There is general agreement that we need more physicians; there is little agreement concerning *how many* we need. Confusion arises partially because of the failure to distinguish the *demand* for medical care from the *need* for such care. In a given area, for example, there may well be enough doctors to care for the people who seek their attention. But many others may *need* medical care in the sense that they have conditions or symptoms which, according to medical authorities, require medical attention. Because of confusions such as this, estimates concerning our need for physicians range all the way from the position that we have about as many physicians as we need to the position that we need about 30,000 more.

Other general studies and special surveys bear out the facts concerning the adequacy of our national health resources. It is obvious that the health needs of the nation are a long way from being met. Our next question, then, is why this is true.

Economics of medical practice. The nation's total medical bill for 1953 was in excess of $10 billion; it has been estimated to be as high as $15 billion. Almost three fourths of the money was paid to physicians, hospitals, and dentists; the remainder was spent on medicines, medical appliances, laboratory and nursing services, the service of paramedical personnel, such as chiropractors, naturopaths, chiropodists, and the like.

Over-all national estimates for the cost of medical care tell only part of the story. Let us think, instead, in terms of the "average family." If the total cost of health services were divided among all families, the typical family would find it was spending

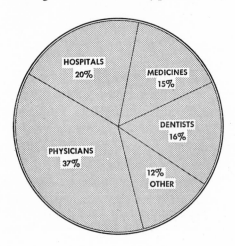

Fig. 5. How America spends its medical dollar. (Data from Odin W. Anderson, *National Family Survey of Medical Costs and Voluntary Health Insurance,* New York, Health Information Foundation, 1954, p. 32.)

$42 per year for hospital charges, $75 for physicians, $31 for medicines, $33 for dentists, and $26 for other medical services and goods, a total of $207 per year.[9] It would seem from these figures, and the national total, that as a nation we are spending enough money to buy adequate medical care. But it must be remembered we have been talking about "averages"; the actual distribution of medical costs is a different matter.

Great differences are noticed in the cost of medical care for different income groups. The cost for families earning less than $2,000 was $54 per year; families earning $7,500 spent about $238 for health services. It has been argued that these figures simply indicate that "the rich" are charged a high fee for

[9] Odin W. Anderson, *National Family Survey of Medical Costs and Voluntary Health Insurance,* New York, Health Information Foundation, 1954, p. 27.

basically the same medical care that the rest of the population receives at a more modest cost. It is a prevalent belief that any family, regardless of income level, can and does obtain adequate medical care for its members. But let us examine the facts.

In 1948 a state-wide study of the extent of the unmet need

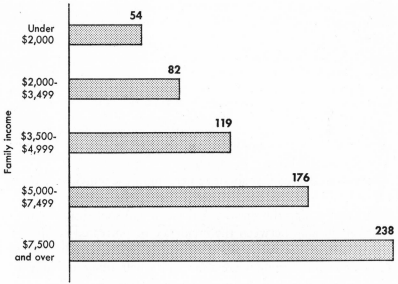

Fig. 6. Variations in the cost of medical care by income. The cost of health insurance, if any, has not been included nor has an attempt been made to attach a value to any free medical care received. (Adapted from Odin W. Anderson, *National Family Survey of Medical Costs and Voluntary Health Insurance*, New York Health Information Foundation, 1954, p. 35.)

for medical attention was conducted in Michigan using the "symptoms approach." [10] Individuals in a carefully selected sample were presented with a list of 27 important "symptoms" or "conditions" which, in the opinion of medical experts, would indicate that the attention of a physician was required. Unmet need for medical attention was thus defined as the presence of

[10] Charles R. Hoffer and others, *Health Needs and Health Care in Michigan*, Special Bulletin 365, East Lansing, Michigan State College Agricultural Experiment Station, 1950.

Table 6. Family Income and Medical Charges *

Family income	Percent with no charges	Percent with charges of $1-$94	Percent with charges over $95
Under $2,000	16	49	36
$2,000-$3,499	11	46	42
$3,500-$4,999	6	39	54
$5,000-$7,499	5	33	61
$7,500 and over	3	25	71

* Adapted from Odin W. Anderson, *National Family Survey of Medical Costs and Voluntary Health Insurance*, New York, Health Information Foundation, 1954, p. 37.

one or more such symptoms for which the persons had not sought medical help.

It was discovered that about 22 percent of the individuals interviewed had one or more untreated symptoms during the six months preceding the survey. A decided and statistically significant relationship between the incidence of untreated symptoms and family income was also discovered. Individuals in the "under $1,000" income group were four and a half times as likely to have untreated symptoms or conditions as those in families earning over $5,000 per year. And this general relationship is consistent with the findings of various earlier studies that have approached the problem somewhat differently. The following are among the discovered relationships between income and health needs or health care: (1) relief clients had three times as many days of chronic disability per person annually as persons in upper income groups; (2) the proportion of families receiving no physician's care was four times as great among the lowest-income group (under $1,000) as among families with incomes of $3,000 or more; (3) relief clients were twice as likely to have a disabling illness lasting one week or more and not treated by a physician as persons earning over $3,000; (4) the most prevalent stated reason for not consulting a physician, when positive symptoms indicated the need for attention, was the expense of the treatment; and (5) persons in families with an income of $5,000 or more were almost three times as likely to consult a dentist once a year as those with an income of $1,000 or less. The list could be continued. The "recurring theme" in the various studies is

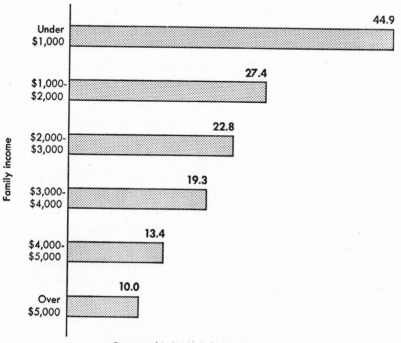

Percent of individuals having one or more untreated
medical symptoms

Fig. 7. The relation between income and untreated medical symptoms. (From Charles R. Hoffer and others, *Health Needs and Health Care in Michigan,* East Lansing, Michigan State College, 1950, p. 78. Used by permission.)

simply that those with the lowest income are *least* likely to receive medical care and *most* likely to need such care.

It should not be construed from the foregoing that the economic problems of medical care are just the "concern of a few unfortunates." Over half of all families have annual medical bills of over $110. More than 10 percent, or about 5.5 million families, incur charges in excess of $395 per year. One family out of five either has outstanding medical debts or has borrowed money to pay for its medical expenses. The economic facts of medical care may be unpleasant, but they cannot be ignored.

Maldistribution of medical personnel and facilities. Both physicians and facilities are very inequitably located in relation to the population. Health resources at the present time tend to be distributed, not on a basis of need, but on a basis of "effective demand." This demand derives from the two main sources of (1) ability to pay for the services and (2) health consciousness. Both of these factors are more abundant in the urban sections of the nation and of the states, and the predominantly rural states and the rural areas of even the most urbanized states are inadequately supplied with medical care.

It is difficult to determine just what is a "satisfactory" ratio of physicians to population. A careful early study, computing among other things the amount of physicians' service necessary for the treatment of various diseases and the rates of these diseases, concluded that there should be one doctor to over 742 persons for the adequate prevention, diagnosis, and treatment of medical ills.[11] During World War II the War Manpower Commission determined that 1,500 persons per effective physician was an absolute *minimum*; beyond this, civilian health would be endangered. Thus the doctor-population ratio considered "adequate" depends on whether we want full medical attention, including *prevention* of disease, or whether, as in time of war, we must be satisfied with a ratio that will not endanger civilian health. Under ordinary circumstances, then, it can be estimated that 1 doctor per 800 persons would be an *optimum*, rather than a *minimum* ratio.

These difficulties with determining a desired doctor-population ratio not withstanding, it is clear that there are gross differences in the ratio among and within the states. In over two thirds of the states, as shown in Figure 8, p. 103, the doctor-population ratio does not come up to the suggested standard; in fourteen

[11] Roger I. Lee and Lewis W. Jones, *The Fundamentals of Good Medical Care*, Chicago, The University of Chicago Press, 1933, p. 108.

states the ratio meets or surpasses the standard.[12] In the District of Columbia there is 1 physician for every 375 persons; in New York State the ratio is 1 to 510. In Mississippi, by way of contrast, there is but 1 doctor for over 1,500 persons. In Alabama, South Carolina, New Mexico, and South Dakota the situation is

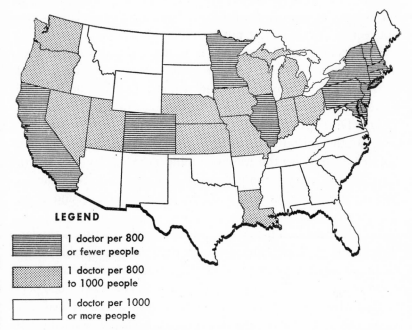

LEGEND

1 doctor per 800 or fewer people

1 doctor per 800 to 1000 people

1 doctor per 1000 or more people

Fig. 8. Distribution of nonfederal physicians. (Based on data from George W. Bachman and Associates, *Health Resources in the United States*, Washington, D. C., The Brookings Institution, 1952, p. 300.)

not much different, 1 doctor for every 1,400 persons. Of course, the ratio in a section of a given state may be higher or lower than for the entire state. While the over-all ratio in Missouri is 1 doctor per 779 persons, the ratio in a twenty-county rural area is 1 doctor for 1,812 population. In Minnesota, 84 percent of all physicians are in places with a population of 2,500 or more.

[12] The various statistics in this and following sections on distribution of medical personnel and facilities, unless otherwise documented, have been taken from George W. Bachman and associates, *Health Resources in the United States*, Washington, D. C., The Brookings Institution, 1952.

There were more than twice as many incorporated places in Minnesota with no doctor in 1949 as there were in 1912. Minnesota as a state has a satisfactory doctor-population ratio; it is a matter of distribution.

In the United States there is 1 dentist to about every 1,800 persons. The military services try to keep the ratio at a dentist for every 500 servicemen. Probably the civilian population does not require the same ratio, but even if we set the standard at 1 per 1,000, it is obvious that we have a shortage of dentists. To make matters more difficult, dentists are not equally distributed throughout the various states and regions. The Middle Atlantic states have 1 dentist for about 1,300 persons. In New York State and the District of Columbia the ratio is close to 1 per 1,100. The East South Central states have 1 dentist per 3,800 population. South Carolina has the least favorable ratio of any state, with 1 dentist for every 5,200 persons; this is more than ten times as many people per dentist as sought by the military and more than five times the suggested standard.

For other medical personnel and services the picture is similar. The Middle Atlantic states, for example, have 8 acceptable hospital beds per 1,000 population; the East South Central states have 5. New York State has twice as many hospital beds per 1,000 persons as Mississippi or West Virginia. Alabama has 3.5 beds for every 1,000 persons; the District of Columbia 8.3. The Pacific and New England states have about 90 pharmacists per 100,000 population, the South Atlantic and East South Central states about 40. The distribution of nurses and optometrists is anything but even.

Further illustrations of the unequal distribution of medical personnel and facilities could certainly be supplied. It is not too much to assume that the medical requirements of people in the United States vary not nearly so much as do the services to meet these requirements. But need, recognition of need, and ability to pay are not the same.

Current efficacy of private medical practice. Some of the noblest words in our language have been written and spoken in defense of the private system of medical practice. While we shall take occasion to examine critically some of the alleged values of private practice under modern social conditions, the student should not overlook the fact that tremendous advances in medical knowledge have been made under this system. We in no way detract from past achievements by raising questions concerning the fulfillment of present needs.

Since we have already observed that many health needs are not being met under the contemporary system of predominantly private practice, questions regarding the efficacy of this system are, to a considerable extent, already answered. Opponents of change in the current procedures for health care, however, maintain that there are certain highly important values inherent in the private, individualized form of medical practice that we cannot afford to lose as a society.

Removal of the physician's incentive to do competent work, deprivation of the patient's right of free choice in consulting a doctor, and destruction of the personal relation between physician and patient are often cited as desirabilities that would be lost by proposed changes. Riesman, a nationally known physician, questions the validity of these value claims. In speaking of the personal relation between physician and patient, he states:

> That relation had certain admirable qualities, but it applied mainly to curative medicine and had little bearing on preventive medicine. But even in the former it is fast disappearing in many fields. The patient is referred to a surgeon previously unknown to him; or to specialists; to experts in certain technical branches—electrocardiography, X ray, basal metabolism, allergy. No close relationship is established between the patient and these various doctors.[13]

Concerning the loss of values of the patient's free choice of his physician and of the physician's incentive to do competent work, Riesman continues:

> A further objection has been made on the ground that a more socialized type of medicine deprives the patient of his free choice in consulting a doctor. This is closely related to the previous ob-

[13] Reprinted from David Riesman, *Medicine in Modern Society*, Princeton, Princeton University Press, 1938, p. 202, by permission.

jection. At first sight that seems a weighty argument. Most of us are accustomed to choose our own doctor, dentist or lawyer. Yet the man who goes to a hospital or to a dispensary has no choice. He sees the doctor on duty; he may not see him on his next visit. . . . While it is desirable to retain the freedom of choice in as large a degree as possible, it is not so vital an element in the doctor-patient relation that a wise social plan should be sacrificed to it.

It has been claimed that socialized medicine will remove the stimulus to self-improvement inherent in the competitive system of practice. I believe that fear is not warranted. First, the main stimulus for self-advancement in knowledge always comes from within, and I have reason to believe that it is stronger in the American doctor than in any other. Secondly, there will always be, in any form of medical practice, strong external pressure, none stronger than the approbation of colleagues, expressed in respect, confidence, and in positions in medical societies. Furthermore, the medical journals by their process of selection of articles, exert a definite stimulus. Finally, there are the abundant post-graduate courses given throughout the land, which make the acquisition of new knowledge easy, besides providing good fellowship and relaxation.[14]

Again Binger appears to have adequately summarized, by analogy, the relation of private medical practice to our complex, industrialized society.

Just as modern industry has grown from individual craftsmen through guilds to labor unions and eventually to highly organized units for mass production, so medicine seems to be developing. The doctor with his little black bag was once the sole dispenser of the healing art, like the cobbler who sat patiently and even lovingly over his last. Certainly shoes would be too costly today if they were made in the old way, and there would not be nearly enough to go around. Though the individual doctor is still the essential unit in good medical care, there is a tendency for him to join with others not only for the purpose of pooling knowledge and mutual education but also in order that his services may reach more people.[15]

[14] Reprinted from Riesman, *op. cit.*, pp. 203-4, by permission.
[15] Reprinted from Carl Binger, *The Doctor's Job*, New York, W. W. Norton & Co., 1945, p. 217, by permission.

▶ CHANGING METHODS OF MEETING HEALTH NEEDS

Almost everyone is willing "to go on record" as being opposed to sickness, disease, and other marks of poor health. When new health measures are suggested, however, we frequently find anything but unanimity of opinion. Sometimes the clash of values is manifested by the failure of the public to support, financially and otherwise, new methods of treating and preventing disease or new plans for financing the cost of medical care. Other times the clash is more obvious, as when a spokesman for organized medicine labels the report of the President's Commission on the Health Needs of the Nation as "creeping socialism." In any case, when it comes to new health measures, it is clear that "some of us" are not always in agreement with what "others of us" are doing, are failing to do, or are merely suggesting. Let us look, then, at some of these changing practices and the reactions to them.

Extended public health services. The idea of public health is now well-rooted in American society. The President's Commission on the Health Needs of the Nation sums up the history of public health as follows:

> Traditionally, health departments have sought to minimize the most important day-to-day threats to health. Fifty to 100 years ago these major threats arose from gross defects in the environment. . . . Hence, health departments first developed environmental health services to improve water supplies and assure the sanitary disposal of sewage. . . .
>
> Recently, public health officers have been seeking methods for attacking accidents and chronic disease—heart disease, cancer, diabetes, and others—which now represent the major causes of death in America. Health education, epidemiologic investigation, early detection—these and many other techniques which have proved so successful in combating the communicable diseases are likewise useful for the chronic diseases. Efforts in these new fields have been greatly aided by Federal categorical grants for cancer and heart disease control.
>
> Public health services, like all other health resources, reflect changes in the character of health needs. New problems require

new techniques, and different modes of organization. It is as unrealistic to tackle today's health problems with a type of service
developed for the problems of 50 years ago, as it would be to base
modern traffic regulations on the pre-automobile era.[16]

Granted that the scope of public health is greatly increased,
just what would be needed to develop *adequate* public health
services commensurate with today's needs? We would need more
money, a great deal more money, than we now appropriate for
such purposes. Is this money readily available? Certainly not
in many of our small, poor, rural counties where current public
health services are most inadequate. Should states provide the
funds to poor counties? Here we step on some political "value
toes." When the states provide funds to counties for any purpose,
they demand that certain standards be met in the use of those
funds. State-dictated standards are not always identical with the
standards of county politicians, and even where there is no sharp
disagreement as to standards, the "dictation" process itself is often
resented and brings about conflict. Furthermore, many states
indicate that they cannot or will not markedly increase expenditures for public health. In these states there could be no other
alternative than supplementation of state financing by federal
funds, with resultant conflict even greater than at the county
level.

Whether funds were derived from city, county, state, or federal sources, there would be a necessary increase in taxation.
Here the taxpayer who is "all for improved public health services" would find his ardor for the program cooling, would find
his public health values in conflict with other values contingent
on lighter taxation. Even with money forthcoming, many a
politician at our various governmental levels would find it difficult not to attempt to divert some of the funds into channels
that would seem of greater immediate political worth than an
"adequate public health program."

Organized medicine would not find itself free of all conflict
in regard to really *adequate* public health services. Many physicians would have to choose between a radical altering of their

[16] President's Commission, *op. cit.*, Vol. II, p. 215.

type of private practice or a joining of the public health staffs. Young graduates of medical colleges (most of whom indicate a preference for private practice in large urban centers) would also find their values disturbed, for a large number would be needed in small communities and rural areas where public health services are now least adequate. The very organization of our medical colleges would probably need to be radically revised, for it is extremely doubtful that present medical school facilities could be stretched to meet the demands for an *adequate* public health service staff for the whole nation.

Governmental finances would be required for subsidizing the education of young men and women who would serve as public health physicians, dentists, nurses, and social workers. Many of the capable persons who would be needed as personnel in an adequate public health program would be unable privately to finance the necessary education. Such governmentally provided education is contrary to the principles of many of our legislators and their constituents, although the GI Bill has changed some minds.

Many a value of certain business interests would be crushed by adequate public health services, for not a few of our industrial structures and processes and our business-operated dwellings are not conducive to optimum public health.

Values such as "my home is my castle" would have to tumble for a large number of our "average citizens." Obviously an adequate public health program could not succeed with every person's continuing with the sort of life, however unsanitary and unhealthful, he pleased within "his own four walls."

Huge appropriations would be necessary for alteration of the physical equipment, facilities, and instruction provided the nation's school children; similarly large funds would be needed for improving the quality and quantity of public recreational facilities. The evidence is indisputable that public health is closely related to what the public learns and what the public does with its leisure. And so, almost infinitely, with major changes necessary in our society in order to provide *adequate* public health services. Everyone agrees the goal is a desirable one, but the methods necessary for achieving the goal bring numerous values into conflict.

Group practice. The term "group practice" covers a wide variety of medical programs. Basically, a medical group consists of a number of physicians practicing in a common, formal association. Medical groups vary, however, in size (number of physicians), comprehensiveness of services offered, ownership of the group facilities, and the methods by which the patients meet the costs of treatment.

Perhaps the most familiar type of medical group is the privately owned clinic (Mayo Clinic in Rochester, Minnesota; Lahey Clinic in Boston; Caylor-Nickel Clinic in Bluffton, Indiana; Crile Clinic in Cleveland). In the Mayo Clinic, for example, patients are billed, on a straight fee-for-service basis, but by the business office rather than an individual doctor. Physicians receive a straight yearly salary not dependent on the number of patients they treat. Any surplus earnings of the clinic are used for medical research and education.

Despite the generally good reputation of some private clinics, based on their volume of significant research and their successful therapy, they are said to have several inadequacies as far as the total health problem is concerned. They have failed (1) to provide much leadership in the development of preventive medicine (they are "swamped" with the sick), (2) to offer a solution to the problem of costs of medical treatment for the large groups of Americans falling somewhere between the well-to-do and the indigent, and (3) to provide health services for any large segment of the population.

In some cases, a medical group may use some type of "prepayment" method of compensation for its services. Such is the case with the Ross-Loos Clinic in Los Angeles. Some 40,000 subscribers pay a flat monthly fee which entitles them to the services of salaried physicians at the clinic, in their own homes, or at a hospital. Prevention of disease and early diagnosis are emphasized, and it is suggested that these aims can best be met when the patient is not charged on a fee-for-service basis. But organized medicine generally opposes payment plans that operate on other than a fee-for-service basis.[17] The Los Angeles County Medical Society voted to expel Drs. Ross and Loos from their membership. Although the founders of the clinic were subsequently reinstated, perhaps this illustrates the opposition to innovations in medical practice.

Another form of group practice that has not developed very extensively is the industrial group-practice plan. The most notable example of this type is the Permanente Foundation medical service for employees of the Henry Kaiser shipyards. On the basis of payroll deductions, the employees and their dependents receive a comprehensive medical service at home and in the hospitals and clinics built for them by the Kaiser Company. All fees and costs are covered, and, since they are prepaid, the patient is encouraged to report for examination and treatment before serious stages of ill health have been reached. It has been suggested that only under this general type of group practice can preventive health measures be very effective.

It is reported that the county medical societies have resisted the Permanente Foundation in various ways. Dr. Garfield, its founder, has been accused of unethical behavior by the disciplinary boards of the societies. On all but one charge he was acquitted; he was judged guilty of unduly promoting the health plan and was reprimanded.

The Group Health Association of Washington, D. C., is the outstanding example of the consumers' cooperative group-practice plan. The services are similar to those provided under the Kaiser plan, but the plan differs from Kaiser's in that the consumers have a vote in how the plan will be managed and in that there is a standard membership fee rather than payroll deduction.

Organized medicine, in the form of the District of Columbia Medical Society, attacked the Group Health Association almost from its inception in 1937. It was charged that the practices would lead to compulsory health insurance in this country.

[17] For a brief account of the difficulties encountered by the Ross-Loos Clinic, the Permanente Foundation, and the Group Health Association, consult James Howard Means, M.D., *Doctors, People, and Government*, Boston, Little, Brown and Co., 1953, pp. 130-32 and 172-75.

Group Health contended that its purposes were beneficial to the public and countercharged that the American Medical Association and the District of Columbia Medical Society were intimidating the group's doctors, threatening to have them excluded from the use of hospitals, and the like. The American Medical Association and three affiliated societies were indicted by a federal grand jury. After years of complicated litigation the American Medical Association and the Medical Society of the District of Columbia were found guilty and were fined $2,500 and $1,500 respectively. The case finally reached the United States Supreme Court where the verdict of the lower court was upheld.

The four-year dispute between organized medicine and the Group Health Association represents more than a "family squabble" among members of the medical profession. It shows the intensity of opposition which sometimes meets any departure from the traditional means of dispensing medical goods and services and of collecting medical fees.

Still another type of group plan is typified by the community-sponsored prepayment plan of New York City. The Health Insurance Plan (HIP) of Greater New York provides for physician's care at home, in a hospital, or in the doctor's office, for a fixed annual premium. Included are periodic health examinations and immunizations, and not merely treatment for existing conditions. The yearly premium is based on the size of the family and the family income. HIP requires its subscribers to join some hospitalization insurance plan so that the combined plans give fairly complete coverage for medical and hospital care.

HIP has organized its participating doctors in some 30 teams or groups, each composed of general practitioners and various specialists. The 400,000 HIP subscribers have the choice of (1) any of the 30 groups, and (2) any of the general practitioners within the group. In addition, they are free to change groups or to go to a different doctor within a group.

The history of HIP apparently has been marked with medical success, but not by the absence of attacks. A past president of the Medical Society of the County of New York, writing in

1952, sees HIP as ". . . a major step in the road to the socialization of medicine." [18] "When HIP was being planned," he charges further, "its founders envisioned, among other possibilities, that it would be a forerunner of a system of compulsory health insurance by the federal government. . . ." [19] Refutations and countercharges, of course, were quickly forthcoming. It is but another example of the controversy that frequently arises when new medical practices are initiated.

The President's Commission on the Health Needs of the Nation, after evaluating the needs of the people and the efficacy of the resources for meeting these needs, came up with literally hundreds of recommendations. Relating directly to group medical practice, it was recommended that:

(1) Group practice be further developed as a means of concentrating and coördinating the skills of specialists for the needs of patients.

(2) General physicians in rural areas establish group practice arrangements, if necessary with specialists in nearby urban areas, in order to bring the benefit of all medical skills more readily to rural people.

(3) Federal loans be made to local organizations desiring to institute prepayment plans associated with group practice, for the purpose of encouraging the establishment of group practice facilities.[20]

The reaction of organized medicine to such proposals needs little comment. Apparently anticipating the response, the President's Commission found it necessary further to recommend that "Organized medical bodies review their attitudes toward group practice in a spirit of tolerance." Despite the benefits of group practice claimed by its adherents and despite the recommendations of the President's Commission, it seems that there is plenty of ammunition on the other side. The group versus private practice controversy is likely to continue. And frequently in the middle is the patient.

[18] Arthur M. Master, "Impact of Medical Care Plans on the Medical Profession," *Journal of the American Medical Association*, Vol. 150 (October 25, 1952), p. 767.

[19] *Ibid.*

[20] President's Commission, *op. cit.*, Vol. I, p. 38 and p. 70.

Voluntary health insurance. There are over 100 voluntary prepayment hospitalization plans offered by commercial insurance companies in the United States. In addition, in 1952 there were 81 Blue Cross hospitalization plans, operating on a nonprofit basis throughout the nation. The many commercial and Blue Cross plans differ, sometimes substantially, with regard to the rates they charge and the benefits they offer.

A fairly typical plan would provide for $5 to $10 per day for a maximum of 60 to 90 days room and board in a hospital. About two thirds of the plans do not provide nursing care. Diagnostic treatment in a hospital is almost universally excluded, and most plans do not pay for the treatment of chronic or other conditions that existed before the contract was purchased. Most nonprofit hospitalization contracts cost a famliy between $25 and $60 per year.

In addition to hospitalization plans, there have arisen many prepayment plans to cover the cost of surgery and general medical attention while in the hospital. Frequently these plans have a schedule of fees for specific types of surgery. For example, the insurance company may pay $75 for an appendectomy or $35 for a tonsillectomy. In 1952 the costs of such contracts, for nonprofit companies, ranged between $30 and $48 per year per family. Thus, hospitalization and surgical insurance combined frequently ranges between $50 and $100 per year.

Apparently many Americans are convinced of the value of health insurance. In 1953, 57 percent of the population had some kind of hospital insurance.[21] About 48 percent had surgical or medical insurance, but only a small group, estimated at 3 percent, had insurance that covered substantially complete physician's service.

It is significant to note that twice as many families earning over $5,000 have some voluntary insurance as families earning under $3,000. Urban families are more likely to have insurance than farm families, and the general category of white-collar workers are more likely to carry insurance than blue-collar workers.

[21] These and the following data on hospital and surgical insurance from Anderson, *op. cit.*, p. 11 ff.

Despite the fact that many Americans have some kind of voluntary health insurance, several criticisms are consistently levied against the various plans. It has been pointed out that (1) too much must be paid for too little coverage; (2) individuals in the low-income categories, "those who need it most," cannot afford insurance; (3) persons with chronic illnesses, who badly need care, are frequently excluded; (4) only serious illness, rather than preventive treatment, tends to be included in the plans; and (5) there is a great duplication and waste in operating hundreds of small voluntary plans. That such plans do not provide the final answer for financing the medical costs for the masses should be obvious. In addition to the limitations mentioned earlier, it should be recognized that most of the insurance plans make no attempt to cover the cost of extended treatment in mental hospitals, tuberculosis sanitariums, and the like. A quite recent development, however, is the so-called "catastrophe insurance" offered by a few companies to cover the cost of prolonged sickness. The fact that half of the population hold some type of voluntary health insurance tells one side of the story; that half cannot or do not purchase such insurance, coupled with the criticisms of existing plans, presents the other side.

Compulsory health insurance. Efforts toward procuring legislation for compulsory health insurance date back to the passage of workmen's compensation laws in many states prior to World War I. With the prosperity period of the 1920's, the campaign for such legislation died, only to be reborn in the depression of the 1930's. Legislation for providing compulsory medical insurance has repeatedly failed to gain the approval of Congress. The Roosevelt administration, the Truman administration, and organized labor have strongly advocated this legislation, but organized medicine and other powerful business and professional groups have bitterly attacked it. Even the more limited request of President Eisenhower for federal aid for providing private health insurance for the indigent has been denied by Congress, reportedly because it would be an "inroad" to compulsory health insurance.

Dr. Morris Fishbein, outstanding American Medical Association opponent of compulsory medical insurance, has written that proposed legislation "would abolish the volunteer control and inspiration that have brought medical education, hospital management, drug purity, research, and medical service to their present eminence." [22] Proponents of compulsory medical insurance deny that "volunteer control and inspiration" would be abolished. Robert F. Wagner, retired Senator from New York and one of the authors of the original bill which proposed compulsory medical insurance, has stated: "The bill rests upon free initiative and private medical practice as it has been developing in the United States. Rejecting any plan of socialized state medicine, the bill simply brings doctor and patient closer together because the bills are paid by the insurance fund." [23]

As in any area of sharp value conflict, epithets are hurled at those advocating compulsory medical insurance. The most effective "bad name" attached to compulsory medical insurance has been that of "socialized medicine." Since many Americans are automatically opposed to anything socialistic, this technique has been successful thus far in arousing much opposition to the proposed legislation. What has been proposed is an insurance system by which medical and hospital services are provided out of a fund derived from the wages of employed persons in much the same fashion as unemployment compensation operates today. The "compulsory" aspect of the insurance is based on the calculation that only in that way could a sufficiently large fund be accumulated at sufficiently low cost per worker to be practicable for the low-income groups in our population.

Proponents of compulsory medical insurance have likewise not been consistently above name calling and imputation of undesirable motives on the part of their opponents. Some of them have said that certain physicians not only lack genuine interest in the health of the American people, but that as "unscrupulous businessmen" rather than true "servants of the

[22] Morris Fishbein, "Does the United States Need a Medical Revolution?", *Journal of the American Medical Association*, Vol. 123 (Oct. 16, 1943), p. 418.
[23] Quoted by Oliver E. Byrd (compiler), *Health Instruction Yearbook, 1944*, Stanford, Stanford University Press, 1944, p. 317.

people," they fear a system that would prevent them from charging fees out of proportion to services rendered.

Socialized medicine. The adverb "fully" must be used in this connection, for we now have a partially socialized medicine. As the term socialized, as opposed to private, is used in connection with medicine, it means control and planning of medicine by society (specifically, government) rather than by individuals or groups not officially representing society. In short, socialized medicine means governmentally controlled medicine. Federal, state, and local governments now engage in numerous medical operations and controls, such as operation of hospitals, planning and management of public health and sanitation programs, gathering of vital statistics. *The issue, then, is not whether or not we should socialize medicine, but how much further we should socialize it.*

Some say that the government's role in medicine is already large enough; the President's Commission reports otherwise. Many, but certainly not all, of the Commission's recommendations advocate increased federal expenditures for such items as (1) the expansion and modernization of schools of medicine, dentistry, and nursing; (2) the general operation of such schools; (3) scholarships for students who could not otherwise afford to attend a school for education in the health professions; (4) development of chronic disease control; (5) medical research in general; and (6) other more specific health measures. The reaction to such proposals was swift and strong. In an article in the *Journal of the American Medical Association* the report of the President's Commission was labeled "socialistic." The Commission was said to be ascribing to the "poor, dumb peasant theory" which holds ". . . that the American people are such poor, dumb peasants that they do not know how to spend their money wisely and that it must be taken away from them in taxes by an all-wise government that know best. . . ." [24] After reviewing many recommendations in the five volumes point by point, it

[24] This and the following quotation from Frank G. Dickinson, "Building Health by Commission," *Journal of the American Medical Association*, Vol. 151 (March 21, 1953), pp. 1032-39.

was suggested that, "Taken as a whole, this report should be filed away in the archives marked, 'Creeping Socialism.' "

President Eisenhower admitted the inadequacy of private insurance and asked for some type of federal aid to cover the health insurance of those unable to provide it for themselves. Undoubtedly this suggestion is "too socialistic" for some while others feel it is not going "far enough." And so the controversy continues. What *is* the government's role in medicine? And who is to decide?

▶ SUMMARY

Poor health is now almost unanimously recognized as a matter of social concern. Like most social problems, however, it passed through stages of value conflict in becoming so regarded. This conflict over new medical theories and techniques and over the development of public health was comparable to value clashes centering today around recommended alterations of medical services. A lesson to be derived from the earlier conflicts and applied to the present ones would seem to be the appropriateness of testing new ideas as to their soundness, rather than emotionally rejecting them without fair trial.

Opposition to at least the aspects of public health services relating to epidemic prevention and control has largely disappeared, and the inadequacies that remain derive chiefly from public ignorance, inadequate personnel, and insufficiency of funds appropriated for these activities. Striking successes have been achieved in this phase of the health problem.

Although the health and medical services of our society are often praised, the present amount of illness in general, and of disabling illness in particular, is still tremendous. Health goals, however, are gradually shifting from the sheer conquering of gross physical maladies to methods of extending life and promoting efficiency for the total population. There is a new emphasis on psychological and social factors involved in ill health, the personality of not only the ill but the ailing person, and methods of increasing the good health of the unailing. The term "psychosomatic medicine" has come to apply to this emphasis.

An examination of data provided by general surveys and special studies reveals that the medical services are not adequately meeting the health needs of the nation at the present time. The nation spent over $10 billion for health measures in the year 1953, but apparently this is not enough, or the amount was not spent wisely, or was not spent by the right people. Surveys repeatedly indicate that large percentages of Americans are in need of medical care. On a typical day 6 million people are prevented from pursuing their usual activities because of illness and half of these have been disabled for three months or more. The cost of medical care is high. Half of the nation's families spend over $110 per year on health services, but the lowest income groups, in whose ranks are found the most disabled, sick, and otherwise unhealthy persons, spend far less than average. Since health resources tend to be distributed on a basis of health consciousness and ability to pay, rather than on a basis of health needs, large sections of the nation are inadequately provided with medical personnel and facilities.

The private system of medical practice has brought great advancements in knowledge and techniques, but appears not to be fully efficacious in relation to contemporary health needs. Alleged values of the current system that would be lost by alteration of medical practices have been challenged by members of the medical profession itself.

We have witnessed in our time some major departures from the private, individualistic form of medical practice. Some of the changes, or suggested changes, have been accepted by the public and have received the support of organized medicine. But still there is much dissension. Extended public health service is accepted in theory but is not always supported in practice. Group medical practice is generally accepted by the public and by a growing number of physicians, but frequently organized medicine does not approve of the way in which the medical groups are paid for their services. Voluntary health insurance is purchased by over half of the people in the country but we find much discontent in the kind of policies offered and the premiums that are charged. Then too, lowest paid workers, with the greatest medical needs and the least ability to pay for them, are the least likely to buy voluntary health insurance. Perhaps the greatest conflict rages with regard to the proper role of the government in providing health services for the people. To some, the government has gone far enough or perhaps, too far; others would like to see the government take an even more active role in the prevention and treatment of disease and in medical research. Compulsory health insurance is favored by some and abhorred by others. Federal aid for health insurance for the aged and indigent is labeled both "too socialistic" and "the only humane thing to do." There is little indication that the many conflicts over health and medical services will be resolved in the near future.

Many obstacles block the path to the removal or major amelioration of the health problem. If a large-scale program for bringing good health to the whole people is undertaken, major alterations in many other social values would appear to be necessary. A need is manifest for the American people to decide whether or not they prize optimum health more highly than other values with which it is in conflict.

SUGGESTED READINGS

Anderson, Odin W., *National Family Survey of Medical Costs and Voluntary Health Insurance*, New York, Health Information Foundation, 1954. This recent nation-wide study is an excellent source for data on extent of voluntary health insurance, family expenditures and debt for health services, and utilization of health services. Breakdowns by age, rural-urban, and income present a compact and provocative picture.

Bachman, George W., and Lewis Meriam, *The Issue of Compulsory Health Insurance*, Washington, D. C., The Brookings Institution, 1948. Recommendations regarding compulsory health insurance based on analysis of health status and needs of Americans and consideration of cost of a government system of medical care. A thorough and well-documented study.

Davis, Michael M., *Medical Care For Tomorrow*, New York, Harper & Bros., 1955. A thorough analysis of economic, social, scientific, and medical forces which have altered medical practice and which are thought to bring further changes in the future. Defines a course of action to benefit both consumer and producer of medical services.

Means, James Howard, *Doctors, People, and Government*, Boston, Little, Brown and Co., 1953. A physician's forthright evaluation of medical resources and needs. Health planning, the government's role in medicine, and current medical practices are courageously discussed in nontechnical language with no attempt to "whitewash" his profession.

President's Commission on the Health Needs of the Nation, *Building America's Health*, Washington, D. C., U. S. Government Printing Office, 1952. (In five volumes.) The most complete documentation of the health status of Americans and the nation's health needs and resources. A wealth of factual data drawn from numerous studies furnishes the background for specific recommendations concerning the need for medical personnel and facilities, medical research, and the financing of health services.

Serbein, Oscar, Jr., *Paying for Medical Care in the United States*, New York, Columbia University Press, 1953. A comprehensive study of the cost of medical care and methods used to meet it. Contains much factual data on prevalence of illness, medical prepayment plans, and government health programs.

STUDY QUESTIONS

1. In what ways is physical health an old problem? In what ways is it a new one?

2. Cite some existing inadequacies in public health that could be remedied. Why do you think they have not been remedied?

3. To what extent does the use of data based on Selective Service examinations underestimate the extent of physical illness and disability in the population? Could it also result in an overestimation?

4. Evaluate the "symptoms approach" as a method of determining the extent of illness and disability in a society. To what extent do you feel it gives an accurate picture?

5. It is sometimes said that there are about enough physicians in the United States. In what sense may this be true? In what sense is it not wholly accurate?

6. How do you account for the fact that there is an unequal distribution of medical personnel and facilities in the United States?

7. What is the general relationship between income and cost of medical care? Between income and condition of health?

8. What are the major value clashes between the supporters and opponents of group medical practice?

9. What segments of the population and what types of medical care are presently not covered by voluntary health insurance? In view of this, do you think voluntary health insurance can become a feasible method of meeting all major medical costs of the population as a whole?

10. What is meant by the statement that we now have a partially socialized medicine in the United States? Explain why you believe medicine will be more fully socialized or less socialized in the future.

· 7 ·   Mental Health

In our last chapter we pointed out that poor physical health is almost unanimously regarded as a matter of social concern and that the value conflict centers around the means of ameliorating this problem. With regard to problems of mental health, however, the clash of values is largely on the level of whether or not a problem actually exists. Professional judgment seems unanimous that the state of the nation's mental health is a matter of concern, and an ever-growing body of laymen are aware of the undesirability of existing conditions. For some segments of the population the value conflict has actually shifted to the level of disagreement on what to do about an admittedly serious social problem. But by and large there is still much apathy and indifference. Almost anyone realizes that it is far easier to obtain public support to "fight" a much publicized physical disorder like poliomyelitis than it would be to obtain like support for research and treatment in the field of mental illness.

It seems that much of the indifference with regard to mental health stems from ignorance—ignorance of the extent of this problem, ignorance of the nature and causes of mental disorders, and ignorance of the curative and preventive treatments that are already possible. In this chapter, therefore, we shall present evidence that should clear up many of the misconceptions in these areas.

▶ SYMPTOMS OF PERSONAL AND INTERPERSONAL TENSIONS

Although the clashes of values continue to be largely in the area of gaining general social recognition of the existence of a major social problem of mental health, it is not at all difficult for even an untrained observer to find evidence, if he will admit of it, that many Americans are mentally and emotionally unwell. If one were asked to choose a single word for characterizing many Americans both individually and in their relationships with one another, considerable justification could be made for the selection of the term "maladjusted." Many persons in our society seem tense, anxious, unhappy, dissatisfied, fearful, skeptical, cynical, pessimistic, and depressed. Not very many Americans indicate that they have found entirely comfortable roles in life and are satisfied with them. The observer finds it difficult to discover more than a few people who are not complaining about one or another aspect, or the totality, of their estate in life. Anxiety seems to pervade the personalities of many members of our society, and tension seems to characterize their interrelationships.

We do not, however, need to rely on such a subjective impression to have evidence of mental health difficulties in American society. More objective symptoms of maladjustment, tension, and distress are available, and it is to an examination of some of these that we now turn.

Divorce.   It is in the marriage institution that we have the most highly publicized evidence of personal and interpersonal unhappiness. Numerous studies have established the fact that a large percentage of husbands and wives are unhappy in their marriages, and, although the divorce rate has declined somewhat from its postwar peak, the long-term divorce trend continues upward. While there is no scientific evidence on which to base an assertion that Americans in the earlier periods of lower divorce rates were correspondingly happier in their marriages, it is clear that many present-day Americans *are* unhappy in their marriages.

Whatever the alleged causes of divorce or the moral implications of a rising divorce rate, they need not here concern us. Regardless of the particular factors contributing to increased divorces in the United States, the generalization that a growing number of Americans are openly dissatisfied with the marital phase of their lives would appear inescapable. Whatever else it does or does not represent, the rising divorce rate may be taken as symptomatic of widespread tension in one important area of modern social living.

Juvenile delinquency. Other statistical symptoms of tension and maladjustment in American society are the misbehavior and legal transgressions of youth that are customarily lumped together under the heading of juvenile delinquency. While crime- and delinquency-rate comparisons in time and place may not be considered highly reliable (see Chapter 8), the consensus is that juvenile delinquency is on the increase. Just as in the case of divorce, we need infer nothing about the specific causes of delinquency to regard it as symptomatic of personal adjustment. Since, by definition, the delinquent is a person who behaves contrary to established rules, delinquency may be considered as another evidence of tension between the individual and his society. Although the individual delinquent, like the individual divorcé, is not necessarily a victim of serious mental illness, a rising rate of delinquency demonstrates growing dissatisfaction among young people with traditionally approved ways of life.

Psychosomatic disorders. Still another significant evidence of the extent of mental health problems is found in the growing research in the field of psychosomatic medicine. As Dr. Jack R. Ewalt, along with many other physicians and psychiatrists, has pointed out: "It becomes increasingly evident that emotional factors play some role in all the illnesses of man, and these forces must be evaluated in any study of the cause and treatment of human sickness." [1] There are four general types of illness, however, where psychological expressions using bodily systems have been most frequently observed by internists: cardiovascular (the heart and its system); gastrointestinal (stomach, intestines, and related organs); the whole group of cephalalgias, arthralgias, and myalgias (aches and pains in the head, joints, muscles, eyes, etc.); and the allergies.

Much more research is needed in the field of psychosomatic medicine before any completely indisputable statistics may be

[1] Jack R. Ewalt, "Psychosomatic Problems," *Journal of the American Medical Association*, Vol. 126, No. 3 (Sept. 16, 1944), p. 153.

presented on the extent to which various bodily pathologies are influenced by and stem from mental and emotional maladjustments. The foregoing material, however, is illustrative of information that has already accumulated in sufficient amount and reliability to indicate that personality difficulties of various types play a tremendously important role in contributing to health problems traditionally considered in strictly "physical" terms.

Occupational maladjustment. Occupational unrest is another symptom of tensions in personal mental hygiene and in interpersonal relationships. Turnover and absenteeism are two major problems in many of the vocations in modern American life. While other factors contribute to these conditions, mental hygiene difficulties are significant causal agents. Failure to get along with his fellow workers or "bosses," home worries, general life dissatisfactions or unhappiness, specific distaste for the type of work, alcoholism, illness, and related reasons frequently appear on reports as reasons for absence or separation from employment, and all of these factors contain, in full or in part, evidence of personality difficulties that fall into the general category of mental health problems.

Even many workers who are seldom or never included in statistics on absenteeism or turnover indicate in numerous ways their varying degrees of occupational maladjustment. The extent to which major industrial and commercial establishments are turning to psychiatrists, psychologists, and sociologists for assistance in constructing "worker surveys" and "worker guidance programs" is in itself testimony to the growing seriousness of morale problems in many occupations. And many of the surveys instituted by management, labor unions, and various agencies of the government add still further weight to the generalization that a high percentage of Americans are unhappy in their work.

Escapist roles. The tensions and maladjustments of many members of our society manifest themselves recreationally as well as occupationally. Much of commercial recreation (which holds a dominant position in the leisure-time pursuits of Americans) is of the escape variety.

The most obvious evidence of "flight from reality" is presented by the increasing use of narcotics. The most consumed drug is, of course, alcohol. All recent studies indicate that not only are more men and women using alcoholic beverages but that the number of "heavy, escape drinkers" and chronic alcoholics is growing. Although exact statistics on the extent of alcoholism in previous generations are not avaialable, the proportion of alcoholics, especially among women, probably exceeds that of any previous period in our history. In like manner, an increasing number of persons apparently need some sort of sedative all or part of the time in order to sleep. Because the sale, purchase, or use of most other types of narcotics (such as opium, morphine, marihuana) is illegal, any accurate estimate of the number of users is impossible to determine, but such indication as may be inferred from police reports shows an upward trend.

Less dramatic evidence of the need for escape from reality may be found in the popularity of various types of fantasy literature (comics, pulp magazines, romantic novels, etc.) and similarly "unreal" moving pictures and radio and television programs. The authors do not contend that every "Superman" radio story or comic or every literary "flight into fantasy" is undesirable, but merely that the extremely widespread use of these recreational forms may be taken as indicative of a large number of people's dissatisfaction with and maladjustment to the world of reality. Put differently, when people turn enthusiastically to escapist activities, there is some attitudinal condition within them escape from which is appealing.

Severe mental illness and deficiency rates. Most obvious evidence of all that the mental health of the American people is a matter of grave concern is the number of persons who become so acutely ill that they require attention at a mental hospital. On the basis of 1952 rates of admission, it has been estimated that one person in twenty will, in the course of his lifetime, require hospitalization for mental illness.[2] On a given day 800,000 people,

---

[2] Data on mental illness and deficiency rates taken from President's Commission on the Health Needs of the Nation, *Building America's Health*, Washington, D. C., U. S. Government Printing Office, 1953, Vol. V, pp. 466-72 ff.

about one out of every two hundred Americans, are in hospitals for mental disease, epilepsy, and mental deficiency. Mentally ill patients alone occupy slightly more than half of the nation's hospital beds. Each year 250,000 new patients are admitted to mental hospitals, and 100,000 former patients are readmitted. Another 200,000 people are treated at psychiatric out-patient clinics.

It has been further estimated that from 1 to 3 percent of the general population is mentally deficient, that is, they lack in varying degrees a normal intelligence. This means that there are between 1.6 and almost 5 million people in the United States with incomplete development of mental ability. It means, too, that there were at least 40,000 mentally deficient babies born in 1954. Probably few parents realize that the possibility of their child being crippled by polio is about 1.4 in 1,000 while it is about 10 in 1,000 that he will have a permanently crippled mind.

These are some of the basic facts about the prevalence of *severe* mental disorders and deficiencies. When we add the somewhat less emphatic, but equally tangible, indications brought out in the foregoing paragraphs, further apologia of the subject seems superfluous.

▶ A CLASSIFICATION OF PERSONALITY DISORDERS

Most laymen have little conception of the nature of mental disorders and are even less likely to be able to distinguish the various types. For this reason, let us turn our attention briefly to a classification of personality disorders. We have yet to see such a classification about which no valid objections could be raised. This generalization certainly applies to the classification presented in this section of the chapter. At least two major reasons account for the inadequacy of existing categorizations of personality disorders: (1) Psychiatry has not developed the exactness of other branches of medicine. This lack of exactness has been due considerably to the centering of the highest quality and quantity of medical research on physical illnesses. Part of the inexactitude, however, is probably inherent in the very nature of psychiatric subject matter, which brings us to our second point. (2) Mental illnesses present less stable, tangible, definable symptoms than most physical illnesses. Personality disorders consist, by definition, of aberrations from socially determined norms of mental, emotional, and moral behavior. Relatively speaking, the symptoms of a person suffering from pulmonary tuberculosis are definite and fixed and readily discernible by a skilled clinician. These tubercular symptoms are (again, relatively speaking) quite distinguishable from the symptoms of a person suffering from some other organic pulmonary condition, such as pneumonia. Two competent physicians are not likely to disagree as to whether the patient is suffering from tuberculosis or pneumonia. Even "normal" variations of mental, emotional, and moral expressions, on the other hand, are so variable and dynamic and intangible that much confusion may appear in the precise diagnosis of a personality disorder. The patient at the time of one examination, for example, may be in a mood where he manifests little anxiety; at the time of another examination the patient may appear so filled with irrational fears that he is obviously suffering from an anxiety neurosis.

Partly because of the foregoing difficulties and partly because of a realization of the relative unimportance of precise classification, psychiatrists have come to concentrate more on the source and symptoms of, and most effective therapy for, the individual patient's difficulties and to be less concerned about placing this patient in a "textbook" category. It is useful, however, in order to have an understanding of the immense range of personality disorders, to attempt some classification. The student, then, should realize that the following classification is offered as a rough guide to the varieties of mental illness and not as a precise classificatory device for the diagnostician. Four main categories of personality disorders will be discussed under the headings of (1) psychosis, (2) psychoneurosis, (3) psychopathic personalities, and (4) amentia.

Psychosis. The most severe and readily discernible form of mental illness is psychosis, which is roughly synonymous with what in lay and legal terminology is referred to as "insanity" or "*non compos mentis.*" Psychoses are usually roughly classified into two main subdivisions: organic and functional. A person suffering from a psychotic condition is generally quite noticeably out of touch with reality. He often manifests what psychiatrists term hallucinations, delusions, and illusions; he indicates by his words or his actions that his ideas, emotions, sense perceptions, or memory differ considerably from what his society designates as "normal."

Organic psychosis. An organic psychosis is one in which the principal source of the condition is a structural pathology of the brain or central nervous system. The most frequently occurring organic psychosis is paresis, which is caused by spirochetes (syphilis germs) lodging in brain tissue. Meningitis (inflammation of the meninges or membranes covering the brain) and encephalitis (inflammation of the brain, popularly known as sleeping sickness) are two other examples of brain infection that may produce psychotic conditions. Some of the many other types of organic psychoses may result from brain trauma (injury); disturbances of the circulatory system (most familiar of which is cerebral arteriosclerosis, or hardening of the brain arteries); prolonged, severe, and frequent epileptic seizures; brain tumors; and toxic conditions (external, such as alcohol, morphine, or an industrial poison; internal, such as diabetes, uremia, and pellagra).

Functional psychosis. Functional psychosis is a severe mental disorder for which no structural basis has been discovered. No brain lesions or biochemical irregularities can be found that are demonstrably causal factors for the psychotic condition; or, said more simply, there seems to be no organic source of the mental illness.

The leading functional psychosis is schizophrenia. Approximately 20 percent of all first admissions and one half of the patients resident in mental institutions are diagnosed as having this type of psychosis. Schizophrenia, meaning "split mind," is an appropriate term in two respects: (1) the patient has divorced himself from effective contact with the physical and social environment, has "withdrawn into a world of his own"; and (2) the patient manifests a "split" between his thoughts and his feelings, has emotional behavior that is incongruous with his ideational processes (may laugh uproariously, for example, when stating that his mother has died).

Schizophrenics can and do recover from their illness. Although there is little consensus on the exact recovery rate, there is good agreement that many patients originally diagnosed as suffering from schizophrenia have returned to useful lives in their communities.

The cause or causes of schizophrenia are largely unknown. Studies of identical twins and investigations of family histories seem to indicate that for *some* patients inherited characteristics cannot be ruled out. Many other schizophrenics are "recruited" from the mass of apparently normal families. For this reason, attention is more frequently turned to the stresses and strains of life and other environmental factors that seem to suggest to some that it is better to forsake the complicated world of reality for one of their own creation.

The second most common of the extreme functional disorders is manic-depressive psychosis. Patients with this disorder constitute about 10 percent of first admissions to mental hospitals and about 12 percent of the resident hospital population. Characteristically the patient demonstrates extreme shifts of mood from extreme elation, excitement, and activity (manic stage) to extreme despondency, melancholia, and stuporous depression (depressive stage). Some patients do not go through the mania-to-depression (or vice versa) cycle, but exhibit the symptoms of only one phase.

Manic-depressive psychosis has a higher recovery rate than schizophrenia. Two thirds or more of all patients recover, and in more than half of the cases there is no recurrence of the disease. In some cases, a recovered patient has another attack, just as some heart patients apparently recover completely while others suffer repeated attacks. Hereditary factors are stressed a bit more for this disorder than for some others, but the results are far from conclusive. One authority, reporting on many studies, found that the parents of manic-depressive patients were more likely to have had the disease than the general population, but brothers and sisters of the patients contracted the illness in only 7 percent of the cases.[3] Despite repeated investigations of patient's bodily chemistry, glandular functions, and the like, little really is known about the causes of this illness.

Psychoneurosis. The psychoneurotic individual, unlike the psychotic, maintains considerable contact with reality. He is often able to adjust for long periods of times to many aspects of his environment, and his mental illness may become apparent to the untrained observer only in what, for the patient, constitutes a crisis situation. Numerous categories of neuroses have been proposed; the four most frequently found in the more recent literature are (1) anxiety states, (2) conversion hysteria, (3) neurasthenia, and (4) obsessive-compulsive reactions.

Anxiety states. It is probable that anxiety lies at the root of all psychoneurotic conditions. Some neurotic patients, however, have a chronic sense of apprehension as their outstanding symptom, and it is this group of patients who are placed in the present category.

Anxiety differs from "normal fear" in at least two fundamental respects. Anxiety, first of all, unlike fear, appears either with no observable stimulus or to a degree that is out of proportion with the stimulus.[4] If, for example, one's life is being threatened by an armed gangster, to turn pale, perspire, experience palpitations of the heart, feel gastronomic disturbances, and develop a tremor would be "normal" fear reactions. To experience comparable responses daily upon boarding a streetcar, however, would constitute an "abnormal" anxiety state. In the first example, the psychosomatic reactions were in harmony with the external danger stimulus; in the second illustration, the same kind of reactions were disproportionate to the

[3] Carney Landis and M. Marjorie Bolles, *Textbook of Abnormal Psychology,* New York, The Macmillan Co., 1947, p. 60.

[4] For a clarification of the nature of anxiety, the authors are principally indebted to the writings of Karen Horney. See, especially, her discussion of the subject in *The Neurotic Personality of Our Time,* New York, W. W. Norton & Co., 1937.

stimulus. Fear is predominantly rational, and anxiety is pre-dominantly irrational in respect to the stimulus.

A second way that "normal" fear differs from "abnormal" anxiety is that the source of anxiety tends to be largely un-known to the person experiencing the fear. The source of the anxiety is "hidden in his unconscious mind." In the foregoing example of the person experiencing extreme psychosomatic reactions upon boarding a streetcar, he cannot give an adequate explanation of why he feels as he does. The real source of his anxiety stems from conditions "buried" in his past experiences. The person experiencing fear can consciously account for his reactions on the basis of the immediate stimuli in his environ-ment.

It should be noted at this juncture that so-called "normal" people are not free from unreasonable fears or anxieties. The panic reactions into which not a few persons are thrown by the presence of mice, by the need for handling worms or garter snakes, by a walk through a cemetery at night, etc., are of the same species as the anxieties of a psychoneurotic. The difference between a "normal" person's anxieties and those of a neurotic is largely a matter of intensity of reactions, frequency and per-sistence of responses, and the degree of social maladjustment re-sulting from the specific nature of the anxieties.

Conversion hysteria. It was pointed out that a person suf-fering from an anxiety neurosis is generally unaware of the real source of his "fears." He is, however, acutely aware of the anxiety reactions themselves. In hysteria, on the other hand, the source of the neurotic condition has been repressed so deeply into the unconscious mind that the individual denies the very existence of anxiety or of any type of mental or emo-tional conflict. The hysteria type of neurosis does not express itself in consciously recognizable anxiety reactions, but takes the subtler forms of symptoms of bodily disease or physical disabil-ity. The mental conflict is "converted" into a physical complaint; thus, the patient is no longer aware of conflict or anxiety, but merely aware of his apparent disease or disability.

The simplest explanation of conversion hysteria is that the

psychoneurotic unconsciously seizes upon a physical disease or disability as a means of escaping his anxieties and conflicts. By developing physical illness he not only excuses himself from the necessity of solving his difficulties, but he accomplishes this result by a method for which he is apparently not responsible. He has escaped his conflicts (at the conscious level), and, at the same time, developed a condition for which he is likely to receive sympathy and special conveniences from his associates.

The student must remember, however, that this process just described (in overly simple terms to make it understandable) takes place *below the level of consciousness* of the person developing a conversion hysteria. He does not consciously decide to become ill or disabled; it happens to him, is beyond his conscious control. In like manner, he cannot will to get well. A patient who is suffering from hysterical blindness, for example, is just as unable to see by consciously wanting to do so as he would be were both his eyes removed. Only psychiatric treatment, on the one hand, or some particular type of crisis situation, on the other, can restore his ability to see. The hysteria patient is an *ill* person, not a malingerer.

Neurasthenia. Neurasthenia more nearly resembles the anxiety neurosis than hysteria in the respect that the anxieties and conflicts of the patient are nearer the conscious level. Unlike the anxiety conditions, however, the neurasthenic manifests his illness more in chronic fatigue than in fear reactions. The term "neurasthenia" means "nervous exhaustion"; the exhaustion, however, is not the fatigue of physical tiring but derives from the conflict of emotions. The patient is characteristically struggling to solve problems he does not clearly comprehend and the sources of which are unknown to him. The complete neurasthenic state (popularly, the "nervous breakdown") appears at the climax of frustration where the patient unconsciously "gives up" the battle with these ghostlike emotional adversaries.

A frequent accompaniment of neurasthenia (and one which links neurasthenia more closely with the anxiety neurosis) is hypochondria, which is defined as a "morbid anxiety about one's health." The neurasthenic, baffled by his constant fatigue, is apt to begin imagining he has all kinds of physical illnesses. He hears or reads of the prevalence of tuberculosis, anxiously reads up on the disease, and decides that he has it. His anxiety about his health readily shifts focus. Today he is worried about tuberculosis, tomorrow cancer, the next day brain tumor, and still another day heart disease. The hypochondriac is one of the chief "headaches" of the physician and one of the main sources of income for the quack and nostrum peddler.

Obsessive-compulsive reactions. In the final category of psychoneurosis that we shall briefly discuss are the obsessions and the compulsions. An "obsession" is an idea over which the person has lost control; a "compulsion" is an overt action over which the person has lost control. Many laymen have heard of compulsions such as kleptomania, the compulsion to steal, and pyromania, the compulsion to start fires, but almost any type of behavior can be compulsive for someone. In some cases, a person exhibits both obsessive and compulsive reactions, as in the case of the patient who was obsessed with the idea that she was infecting herself and others by the germs on her hands, and felt compelled, therefore, to wash her hands almost continually and to avoid touching doors and other objects that people before her had touched.

Most normal people have some obsessions and compulsions. Observe, for instance, the number of persons who become uncomfortable if prevented from lifting back the lid of a mailbox after having deposited a letter; they feel *compelled* to do so. Other examples are frequent checkings that doors are locked, pictures are straight, gas fires are extinguished, hands are washed, etc. Obsessions appear in similar fashion. We all have ideas to which we *must* cling, regardless of the proved illogic or inconvenience of holding to them.

It is when the number and intensity of, or social maladjustment associated with, these obsessions and compulsions become patent in the life of the individual that he may be diagnosed as having an obsessive-compulsive neurosis. It is, in short, when his obsessions and compulsions "take over" his thoughts and actions to a sufficient degree to render him obviously inefficient or "abnormal" in various social situations that he is clearly neurotic.

Psychopathic personalities.   Our third principal division of personality disorders is most frequently referred to as the psychopathic personalities. Rottersman, one of the leading investigators of this type of personality disorder, writes of a growing tendency to discard the term and to refer to this category of patients as "neurotic characters." [5] Because of its greater familiarity, however, and because of confusion that is apt to result between the newer term and the psychoneuroses in the minds of elementary students, we have adhered to "psychopathic personalities."

Professional difference of opinion is greater in regard to the nature and origin of psychopathic personalities than in relation to the major psychoses and psychoneuroses. Some psychiatrists feel that many persons described as psychopaths are actually psychotic; others lay great stress on the *constitutional* nature of the illness—meaning that the environment can make the psychopath neither better nor worse.

Amid these and many other differences of opinion, however, a fairly clear clinical picture emerges. The psychopathic personality is characterized more by a moral than a mental defect. His is a character illness. Although psychopaths demonstrate *intellectual* understanding of right and wrong, they indicate incapacity for *feeling* the moral implications of their acts.

> . . . they exhibit a seeming pathological inability to be mindful of routine obligations and sensitive to the rights of others. It is as if they lacked the capacity to appreciate the ethical implications of conduct problems. The word *appreciate* is used advisedly in this context; for with them it is not a question of not *knowing* the "difference between right and wrong," but of not being able to evaluate such a difference emotionally. In a purely cognitive manner they "know" that it is "wrong" to stab a child, to pour acid on a puppy, or to steal money from a blind newspaper vendor. However, they fail to experience the emotional re-

[5] Willim Rottersman, "The Guardhouse Inmate, with a Brief Discussion of the 'Psychopathic Personality,'" *War Medicine*, Vol. 5, No. 5 (May 1944), p. 278.

vulsion which crimes of this character arouse in the average man. Such affective responsiveness is probably more necessary in determining ethical choices than abstract knowledge of legal codes. This was rendered quite evident during the prohibition era when vast numbers of "respectable" citizens violated the law because they "didn't *feel* it wrong to take a drink." [6]

Another outstanding characteristic of the psychopathic personality is his apparent inability to learn from experience. His moral defect is as rigid as the mental defect of a feebleminded person. Pleading, psychiatric treatment, kindness, punishment, and so on, all fail to touch him. At the first opportunity, he reverts to his lying, cheating, stealing, debauching, or whatever other channels in which his psychopathic behavior customarily expresses itself.

Amentia.   Amentia is the technical term for feeblemindedness. In many classifications it is not included among personality disorders, for the amented individual is not a normal one who has become ill, but one who, as a result of genetic or early environmental factors, never developed a normal mental capacity. Since the same objection may be leveled at the inclusion of psychopathic personalities with their moral deficiencies in a categorization of disorders, and since we are openly striving for understanding rather than technically perfect classification, we feel justified, however, in our inclusion of amentia in this section.

Mental deficiency is now generally thought to be approximately 50 percent hereditary. The genetic source of feeblemindedness is not a simple one; various combinations of genes may produce varying types and degrees of deficiency. Since the factors producing hereditary amentia are recessive, normal persons may carry the genes and have feebleminded offspring. For this and other reasons, any program for the sterilization of feebleminded persons as a means for significantly reducing the incidence of amentia is not generally considered practicable.

Half of the cases of feeblemindedness are believed to be nonhereditary. Some of the ways that mental deficiency may be

[6] David B. Klein, *Mental Hygiene*, rev. ed., New York, Henry Holt and Co., 1956, p. 132.

produced by environmental factors follow: (1) endocrine deficiency, especially hypoactivity of the thyroid gland (cretinism); (2) brain trauma (injury to the brain of the child during the process of or shortly following birth); (3) congenital syphilis (where the spirochetes attack the brain of the child in embryo or early childhood); (4) encephalitis, meningitis, and other "brain inflammatory" diseases, when contracted prior to full mental development; (5) epilepsy (occurring in an early and severe enough form to prevent full mental development); (6) severe forms of many of the common childhood diseases; and (7) extreme malnutrition prior to or following birth.

It is in the environmental sources of amentia that the greatest hope lies for reduction of the feebleminded persons in the population. Most of the foregoing conditions are preventable.

Four subclassifications of feeblemindedness are: (1) the idiots, with mental ages extending from approximately zero up to 3 years; (2) imbeciles, mental ages 3 to 7; (3) morons, mental ages 7 to 12; and (4) borderline cases, 12 to 13 mental years.

▶ EXPLANATIONS OF THE MENTAL HEALTH PROBLEM

It has been previously noted that social problems are much more easily described than "explained" or "cured." The mental health problem is certainly no exception to this generalization. Psychiatrists who have worked intensively for many years with the mentally ill admit that their knowledge of etiology and therapy is short of complete or final. The authors, none of whom is a specialist in these matters, merely attempt in this section to acquaint the elementary student with some of the factors frequently associated with the mental health problem and to point out some of the strengths and weaknesses of various hypotheses about the "causes" of mental illness. Many of our remarks will be addressed to explanations for the functional psychoses, the neuroses, and other symptoms of tension that apparently have a social rather than an organic basis. The causes of disorders such as paresis and certain types of feeblemindedness are better understood, but it does not follow, of course, that their complete elimination is immediately possible.

Societal complexity theory.   Most students of human behavior believe that the increasing complexity of society contributes to the growing mental health problem. This would seem to be true in two important respects. First, the number and variety of demands for adjustment placed on the members of our complex society greatly exceed those patterns of behavior exacted from members of simpler societies. The life of modern man is a mass of intertwined institutional exactings; he is obliged to relate himself to many other human beings, most of whom are absolute or relative strangers, in complicated economic, governmental, educational, recreational, and religious settings. His predominantly agricultural forefathers, on the other hand, had most of their relationships confined to the less demanding and far simpler environments of their own families and of neighbors known for a lifetime.

The physical environment of members of simpler societies is characteristically the same plot of land on which they were born (or a very similar one), the old and familiar home and barn, and the livestock; their lives consist, to a great extent, of relating themselves simply to land, home, barn, and livestock. Modern man's physical environment is a gigantic mechanism whose operation is dependent upon complicated cooperation with impersonal laws. He is forced to adjust to many powers and gadgets from income taxes to automatically operated elevators, from traffic signals to juke boxes, from fire departments to subways.

Relative to modern man premodern man was little challenged to modify his behavior. If he once "made the grade" of his society, he could be very secure in his remaining years with the adjustment achieved. Social change was, relative to modern "progress," so slow that it was scarcely perceptible in the longest of lifetimes; there were very few "new things under the sun" in an individual life span. The increasing tempo of change in modern society is too patent to merit illustration. Suffice it to say, by way of further warning of the urgency of mental health problems, that all indications point to increasingly rapid and radical alterations of our behavior patterns that will probably make the period between the beginning of the industrial revolution and the onset of this "atomic age" seem, by contrast, a stable one.

Another way that the increasing complexity of society appears pertinent to an understanding of the rising prominence of mental health problems is through its revealing of maladjustments which would have gone unobserved in a simpler society. The rising incidence of mental illness may be more apparent than real. Rather than *producing* new tension states, in many instances, modern societal situations may merely *expose* tension states that would have passed unnoticed, or at least unreported, in a simpler environment. All sorts of eccentricities that would be considered a "man's own business" in a rural setting, for example, could become highly inconvenient or even dangerous in a complex urban environment. Add to this that one of the increases in societal complexity is advanced skill in recognizing and diagnosing mental and emotional difficulties, and you have the essentials of the "exposure" aspect of the societal complexity theory.

In so far as this second point is true, of course, it reduces the validity of the societal complexity theory as an explanation of the "cause" of increased mental illness, for it calls into question the whole proposition that mental illness is *actually* greater in a complex than in a simple society. The exact amount of truth in either the causal or exposure propositions cannot be demonstrated beyond question. If a man "breaks down" in a complex societal situation, who can state definitely what he would or would not have done had conditions been different at that exact moment in his life? Most observers hold that the truth lies somewhere between "cause" and "exposure," with the weight perhaps more on the latter.

"Schizoid culture" theory.   Another hypothesis in relation to the "cause" of increased mental illness also places the "blame" on modern society, but emphasizes the inconsistency rather than the sheer complexity of contemporary behavior patterns.

The "schizoid culture" theory postulates that modern man is confused not by the number and variety of the demands made upon him, but by the unresolvable conflicts that occur between some of these demands. He becomes unhappy, filled with anxiety, neurotic, psychopathic, psychotic, and so on, not, for example, because both the economic and religious institutions require many things of him, but because some of the things required by his religion cannot be harmonized with some of the adjustments necessitated by his economic system. Such conflicts need not be interinstitutional but may occur within the same institution. In government, by way of illustration, full subscription to the principles of democracy exists side by side with machine politics, graft, manipulation of votes, exclusion of Negroes from participation, etc.[7]

As in the case of the societal complexity theory, conclusive proof or disproof of the "schizoid culture" theory cannot be mustered. That our culture is inconsistent or "split" cannot be denied; that these conflicts between various aspects of our culture "cause" individual mental and emotional maladjustments does not, however, necessarily follow. It could be just as plausibly argued that mentally ill individuals have produced or "caused" this "schizoid culture." Trite though it be, again it is probably correct that "the truth lies somewhere in between." The sociological principle that individuals are molded by their culture and, in turn, mold that culture probably applies as fully to abnormal as to normal behavioral manifestations.

Secularization theory. Still another hypothesis on mental illness singles out one specific social trend and emphasizes its importance in producing anxiety, tension, and maladjustment. Religion has traditionally provided men with a profound, underlying meaning for life, but a growing number of persons in modern society have apparently lost religious convictions. With "real meaning" departed from their lives, these same individuals,

[7] For a graphic development of the "schizoid culture" theory, see Read Bain, "Our Schizoid Culture," *Sociology and Social Research*, Vol. 19 (January 1935), pp. 266-76. For further illustrations and the relation of institutional conflicts to mental health, consult Horney, *op. cit.*

it is contended, lose their mental and emotional stability and develop some type of personality disorder.

Some substantiation for this secularization theory can be found in the results of clinical observations of various psychologists and psychiatrists. The Jungian school of psychoanalysis has particularly stressed the absence of strong religious convictions in many of the patients treated for various types of psychoneurosis.

Once again, however, we must point out that this hypothesis, like its forerunners in our discussion, has been neither proved nor disproved. No statistically significant study has been made, so far as the authors are aware, of the relative prevalence of mental and emotional difficulties among persons of strong religious convictions as compared with persons of weak or no religious convictions. Even if a positive correlation were established between absence of religion and mental illness, no better case could be made for secularization "causing" mental illness than vice versa. Further, it could well be that mental illness and secularization were, independently of one another, related to some unknown other factor or factors. The most we can say, then, is that the secularization theory *may* contain an element of truth.

Overcompetition theory. Other seekers after a "cause" for the increased incidence of mental illness have seized upon another characteristic of American culture—namely, the great emphasis on competition. Mental and emotional breakdown stems, according to the proponents of the overcompetition hypothesis, from the pressures placed upon individuals to equal or exceed the achievements of fellow members of society. From the cradle onward, it is contended, the individual is *forced* to make efforts along lines and to degrees toward which he has no inclination because of the emphasis placed on competitive achievements by society. Strains are thus placed upon members of society in two major respects: (1) Some individuals are frequently forced to make efforts beyond their tension capacity in some situations (and, with sufficient repetition of these situations, mental, emotional, or moral collapse will occur), and (2) conflicts are set up in many individuals between internal desires and the external demands of the highly competitive social environment [these conflicts may lead directly to anxiety states or may indirectly lower the tension capacity of the individual and produce results (1) above]. The overcompetition theory is likewise one of plausibility rather than (thus far, at least) verified fact. It would be difficult to construct a controlled experiment over a sufficiently long period of time to test adequately the hypothesis.

"**Theory of dysgenic population trends.**" Another hypothesis, with both genetic and environmental facets, has been proposed to account for the apparently rising incidence of mental and emotional maladjustment. In its hereditary aspect, the theory holds that the parts of the population with the least favorable genetic characteristics have been consistently reproducing at a more rapid rate than other elements in our society. We are gradually "reaping the rewards" of this dysgenic population trend in getting a larger and larger percentage of the members of society who are hereditarily predisposed toward mental illness.

This "dysgenic theory" is frankly based on the assumption that the lower economic groups in the population are bio-psychologically inferior to the middle and upper classes. Not only is this general assumption unsubstantiated, but the further inference that the alleged genetic inferiority applies specifically to predisposition toward personality disorders is likewise unverified and, in fact, quite dubious.

The case is particularly clear for mental deficiency regarding which we have already noted that half of the cases have no hereditary basis at all. It has been further discovered that: (1) mental defectives have been born of highly intelligent parents from the "best families"; (2) the lowest grade mental defectives are most frequently physically incapable of reproduction; (3) many mental defectives do not even live to physical maturity.

It has been definitely established that heredity plays no part in the causes of some types of psychoses. The clearest cases are those of psychoses due to tumors or injuries to the brain. Although some disorders, such as schizophrenia and manic-depressive psychosis, are somewhat more likely to occur in families with a history of the disease, so many more patients have no such history that the "dysgenic theory" does not seem to hold up. Furthermore, there is no evidence that such patients are more likely to reproduce than the general population.

Other theorists, however, have given the "dysgenic hypothesis" an environmental twist. While it is true, they agree, that the genetic inferiority of the lower economic classes is not established, these groups are not as able to provide their relatively large number of children with *environments* conducive to the development of sound mental health. Hence, a growing number of probably genetically fit persons are being *reared* in conditions predisposing them toward the development of personality disorders.

Increasing realization of the close relationship (really inseparable character) of physical and mental health lends some weight to this aspect of the hypothesis. There is no doubt that families of poorer circumstances are less able to provide the nutrition, physical living conditions, clothes, educational and recreational opportunities conducive to fully healthful living.

It must be pointed out, however, that the economic, educational, and social advantages of a child born in the middle and upper classes may be counterbalanced by certain moral and emotional disadvantages that not infrequently appear in our "better homes." As Dr. Edward A. Strecker [8] and others have pointed out, children from the "better-class families" sometimes fail to mature emotionally, remain overly dependent upon their mothers who have overprotected them from the exigencies of life. Such social products may be even less adequately prepared to meet the moral and emotional demands of adult life in our complex society than persons reared in the homes providing fewer economic, educational, and social advantages. Reports from various psychiatric sources of the high proportion of psychoneurotics and persons with psychosomatic complaints (such as peptic ulcers) who have middle- and upper-class family backgrounds further stress the caution with which we must view even the environmental facet of the "dysgenic theory" of mental illness. Finally,

[8] Edward A. Strecker, *Their Mothers' Sons*, J. B. Lippincott Co., Philadelphia, 1946; "Pops and Popism," *Parents Magazine*, Vol. 22 (May 1947), pp. 20-21 ff.

divorce and "alcoholic escapism" are two indices of mental and emotional maladjustment that show little respect for persons of economically affluent family origins.

▶ TREATMENT OF MENTAL ILLNESS AND VALUE CONFLICTS

Efforts for ameliorating our mental health problem can be broken down into two types: (1) those directed at treating and returning to useful lives as many of the mentally ill as possible; and (2) those aimed at preventing others from joining the ranks of the mentally ill. Conflicts in values are much in evidence regarding both types of programs. The apparent views and feelings of the many make it extremely difficult for the few to carry on their necessary and demonstrably sound preventive and curative work.

Institutional treatment of psychotics.   Most psychotics are unable to cope with the complex problems of life and must, therefore, be removed from their usual social environment. Placed in an adequate mental hospital, chances for recovery are good. Personnel and equipment are available for his treatment, the routine of institutional life eliminates the need for much difficult decision-making, and the patient is assured adequate diet and rest. For the occasional psychotic, removal from society is further necessary to assure that he will not harm himself or others. Thus, the adequacy of treatment of the severely mentally ill largely depends on the adequacy of our mental hospitals.

It is easily demonstrated that our mental hospitals are far from adequate. Overcrowding is quite common, the doctor-patient ratio is too low to allow optimum psychiatric treatment, and physical conditions and facilities are poor. All too frequently this means that the patient can receive little more than custodial care while supposedly undergoing treatment for his illness. The indictment against the people would not be so severe if, as a nation, we did not "know any better." But psychiatric knowledge has advanced rapidly in the last decades and recommendations repeatedly are made concerning the treatment of hospitalized psychotics necessary to insure their recovery or improvement.

There are several reasons for the considerable lag between psychiatric knowledge and institutional practices.

Finances. The most important cause of this lag is an economic one. Today, in order to meet accepted standards, we need 300,-000 additional mental hospital beds.[9] Older hospitals have to be improved and new ones should be built. To operate a scientifically modern mental hospital takes a great deal of money—much more money than the people and the legislatures of most states have indicated that they are willing to spend for this purpose. Modern buildings and equipment are expensive, and so are the best qualified personnel to staff the institution. To lure psychiatrists and psychiatric social workers and nurses into arduous institutional work, salaries must be paid that are somewhat commensurate to those obtained with private agencies and in private practice. Likewise wages providing a comfortable standard of living rather than current "starvation wages" must be paid to secure high quality personnel in the psychologically important roles of attendants. Until the necessary amount of finances are provided for adequate buildings, equipment, and personnel, all the "horror stories" and "public exposures" are not likely to alter significantly the facts about which they are written.

Time. In the second place, if ample finances, by some miracle, were immediately available for modernizing our mental institutions, radical changes would not take place overnight. It takes time to erect modern buildings and to secure the best available equipment, and it takes even more time to translate scientific findings into effective practice.

Personnel. Thirdly, there is a tremendous shortage of properly trained psychiatric personnel. According to standards established by the American Psychiatric Association, there is an overall shortage of about 65 percent of psychiatric personnel. It has been estimated that there is a shortage of about 15,000 psychiatrists.[10] Not all of them are needed in mental hospitals, but as long as the shortage exists, hospitals, with their generally lower

[9] President's Commission, *op. cit.,* Vol. I, p. 59.

[10] Data on need for psychiatric personnel from President's Commission, *op. cit.,* Vol. II, p. 53.

bargaining power, will be hard pressed to fill their needs. Only five states have 80 percent or better of their needed psychiatrists. New needs are growing much more rapidly than the new supply of psychiatrists. Even if a sufficient number of properly qualified persons can be persuaded to undertake psychiatric training, it will be at least a decade before the need will be met, for a minimum of five years' training following the receipt of an M.D. degree is necessary to produce a fully qualified psychiatrist. No state has more than half of the psychiatric social workers necessary to meet the standards and nineteen states have less than 10 percent. Thirty-five states do not reach 20 percent of the standard for psychiatric nurses. The country as a whole needs an additional 14,500 such nurses.

The foregoing comments are not made to decry current journalistic demand that "something be done" about our mental hospitals, but merely to point out some of the obstacles in the way of immediate achievement of this desired goal. Only by even greater arousal of public protest against contemporary conditions will the finances, altered practices, and increased quantity and quality of personnel be obtained.

Lack of early treatment. Finally, psychiatric practices do not keep pace with knowledge because many patients simply do not reach a mental hospital in an early enough stage of their illness for most effective treatment. Public misunderstandings and misconceptions are greatly to blame for this. As this is being written, there is still one state (Texas) where a mentally ill person must be adjudged "insane" at a jury "trial" before he can be admitted to a state mental hospital. Under this system, quite prevalent just a decade or two ago, the patient is brought into court and witnesses, frequently relatives, must describe his behavior and testify that in their opinion he should be "committed" to the state institution. The jury then weighs the evidence and decides whether the patient is sufficiently ill to require treatment. Such a practice indicates a basic and gross misunderstanding of the nature of mental illness, and it is no wonder that only the most advanced cases, with the least favorable prognosis, reach hospitals.

Public misunderstanding still operates to prevent early treatment for many of the mentally ill. Because of the "shame" and "disgrace" still attached to such illness, the afflicted person and his family are not prone to admit that he is sick and requires professional care. It is paradoxical that if a wife urges her husband to "see a doctor" because of a physical complaint she is considered solicitous, while if she tells him that he "better see a psychiatrist," she is insulting!

Treatment of mental defectives. The most serious cases of amentia are usually institutionalized and "treatment" consists almost exclusively of helping the patients to be as happy and useful as possible in the permanent institutional situation. This is quite difficult under present conditions of overcrowding, poor physical facilities, and lack of personnel. Even quite deficient patients can be taught simple skills as dressing and feeding themselves, but this takes time and personnel and money; less defective patients can be taught to perform various "housekeeping" tasks.

It may be surprising to some to learn that in many of our institutions for the feebleminded are people who, with proper education and special placement programs, could become partially or fully self-supporting. As a result of a recent "drive" in Iowa, for example, over 250 patients were successfully placed on jobs outside the institution.[11] The savings to the state, less the cost of administering the placement program, amounted to over $150,000, and the patients earned in wages almost $240,000 in several years. Thus, there is a practical as well as humanitarian reason for "reclaiming" the best of the mental deficients who now reside in public-supported institutions.

▶ SOME METHODS OF PREVENTION AND VALUE CONFLICTS

A mere naming of all the possibilities for preventing mental illness would require more space than is available in the remainder of this chapter. Fundamental preventive attack on prob-

---

[11] Albert J. Shafter and Charles S. Chandler, "The Economics of a Hospital Social Service Department," *American Journal of Mental Deficiency*, Vol. 59 (July 1954), pp. 107-09.

lems of mental health would indisputably require radical alteration of our whole social structure. It would mean the removal of
the related problems of misconceived parenthood, poor physical
health, malnutrition, inadequate housing, unemployment, crime,
ineffective religion and education and recreation, malpractices in
government, occupational misplacement, etc. All of which is to
say that mental health problems are closely interdependent with
the other social problems of our society and will not be solved
apart from amelioration in all societal areas.

Within our present social structure, however, there are several immediately available points of attack. The National Mental
Health Act of 1947 makes it possible for state and private agencies and individuals to obtain federal funds for research in mental
health, for the provision of community mental health programs,
and even for the initiation and expansion of diagnostic mental
health clinics. Various agencies and persons throughout the country, most notably the National Association for Mental Health
(which represents a recent merger of several previously existing
national associations), and the state and local mental hygiene
societies, are making some progress in all of the areas suggested
below.

**Encouragement of competent persons to enter psychiatric
services.** The gross inadequacy of the number of persons trained
as psychiatrists, psychiatric social workers, psychiatric nurses,
and attendants has already been discussed in another context.
The three main methods by which the future quantity and quality of psychiatric workers of all types may be increased to a
point that will meet the needs for their services are (1) educating
young men and women to the needs and opportunities of the
various types of psychiatric work, (2) subsidizing the necessary
education for competent persons who cannot themselves afford
to undertake psychiatric training, and (3) increasing from governmental funds the financial remunerations for the various psychiatric services.

Increasing funds available for psychiatric research. We have
already pointed out that about one half of all hospital patients
are mentally ill. It might be supposed, then, that funds for mental

health research would approach that of all other medical research combined. But during a recent five-year period grants for mental health research accounted for only *4 percent* of all medical research grants. Roughly $24 million a year is being spent on research for one physical disorder—cancer—while about $6 million a year is spent on research for *all* types of mental disorders.[12] Commenting on the federal research funds available, the President's Commission on the Health Needs of the Nation reports that "expenditure for research into mental diseases is less per year than *a single bomber* of the newer type will cost."[13] While money spent is not the sole criterion, modern research in any field cannot proceed adequately without considerable funds being made available. Whether increase in financial assistance for psychiatric research stems chiefly from governmental or private sources is not so important as that it be quickly provided to meet the growing crisis in mental health.

Provision of mental hygiene clinics in local communities. It is ridiculous to talk about preventing mental illness so long as most communities do not at the present time have competent psychiatric services available even for the minority of the population who can afford to pay private fees. Even in the relatively well-staffed metropolitan areas, most psychiatrists are able to handle only the cases most severely in need of assistance. And the great mass of the people cannot pay the fees demanded by private psychiatric practitioners.

The only practical answer to the problem of meeting the needs of the majority of persons in the local communities is the mental hygiene clinic or guidance center. Again we run into difficulties of finances and insufficient personnel. The latter must come by the means already indicated, and the former must be derived from a combination of governmental and philanthropic sources. But, until the "normal" person has a reliable place to take his worries and fears and maladjustments, talk of preventing "abnormalities" is rather meaningless.

[12] President's Commission, *op. cit.*, Vol. I, p. 41.
[13] President's Commission, *op. cit.*, Vol. II, p. 236.

Provision of competent counseling services in the schools. While it is rather fantastic at the present time to think of providing actual psychiatric service in most public schools, it is quite feasible to inaugurate more and better educational programs for training counselors. These persons would be able to treat minor personality difficulties among school children and to recognize more serious difficulties for referral to the community mental hygiene clinic. This would be a most significant aspect of prevention, for it would catch most mental illnesses in their initial stages when psychotherapy would be most effective and efficient.

Modernization of mental institutions. We have already discussed the obstacles to the achievement of this objective. It is relevant to our present consideration of preventive measures chiefly in relation to research and to the training of psychiatrists for noninstitutional service. Since most of the research in mental illness and most of the training in psychiatric methods must proceed in mental hospitals, the need for the most modern facilities and most competent personnel is quite evident.

Extension of on-the-job counseling services. A number of the more progressive industrial and commercial establishments now provide counselors for their workers. It is a service that should be made available in all establishments hiring more than a few workers and could be linked to the mental hygiene clinics of the community in much the same fashion as suggested for counseling in the schools. Many workers have personal problems with which competent counselors could assist; some of these problems, without counseling help being available (as it generally is not at present), grow into serious mental health difficulties. Even when personal problems remain relatively small ones, they greatly reduce the efficiency and happiness of workers. From a strictly business point of view, management has found that a counseling service more than "pays for itself." Furthermore, potentially serious personality maladjustments in some workers may early be detected and referred to the mental hygiene clinic for effective psychiatric treatment.

Prevention of mental deficiency. Earlier it was mentioned that any program for the sterilization of feebleminded persons as a means for significantly reducing the incidence of mental deficiency is not generally considered practicable. This does not mean that nothing can be done to prevent the yearly addition of tens of thousands of mental defectives to our population. Basically, the problem is one of understanding the causes of arrested development. One type of amentia has been tentatively linked with prenatal oxygen deficiency. Why do some fetuses fail to receive their proper supply? Could this be discovered during pregnancy and corrected? The mother's body chemistry, her age, and a host of other factors have also been investigated for their possible link with amentia, but the results are generally inconclusive. The simple fact is that our knowledge is all too limited. This suggests, obviously, that the first step in a preventive program would be to increase our knowledge. Again, the lack of funds looms large in the picture. In a report of the President's Commission on the Health Needs of the Nation it was pointed out that during a given year an average of $2 per new victim was spent on research into mental deficiency.[14] Roughly $70 was spent for research per each new case of crippling polio. Could this be a partial explanation of why less than sixteen years after the polio foundation was established a preventive is in use? How much nearer would we be to sound knowledge of preventive treatment for mental deficiency if we had been spending thirty-five times more on research?

The lack of support for mental deficiency research has its roots in the misconceptions and indifferences of the nation. Too many believe that "nothing can be done" and too few realize the prevalence of this problem. There is evidence that an increasing number of people are aware that *a problem does exist.* Over fifty groups, largely parents of the afflicted, have been formed throughout the states and there is a National Society for Retarded Children. Nevertheless, the clash of values is still between the many who believe there is no "real" problem and the few who have learned otherwise. Until the few can become many, the hopes for sound preventive measures are not strong.

[14] President's Commission, *op. cit.*, Vol. V, p. 466.

▶ SUMMARY

Mental health as a social problem is still considerably in the phase of value conflict centering around recognition of its existence as a major problem area. The general public seems quite unaware of the nature of mental illness and the widespread extent of this problem. Data continue to accumulate, however, to demonstrate the presence of serious and widespread tensions and maladjustments in the mental and emotional life of the American people.

Numerous theories have been advanced to explain the apparently increasing incidence of mental illness. Societal complexity, the "schizoid" nature of our culture, secularization, over-competitive processes, and dysgenic population trends are among the more prominent hypotheses. It is probable, with certain reservations and modifications, all of these theories contain some element of truth.

A convenient classification of personality disorders for discussional purposes is the four categories of psychosis, neurosis, psychopathic personality, and amentia or mental deficiency. Psychoses are further subdivided into functional and organic, and the four main types of psychoneurosis are referred to as anxiety states, hysteria, neurasthenia, and obsessive-compulsive reactions. The psychopathic personality is a moral defective analogous to the mental defective.

Psychotics can be treated most efficiently and effectively in institutions designed specifically for such purposes. Thus, the adequacy of the treatment of the severely mentally ill depends on the adequacy of our mental hospitals. There are several obstacles to the program of bringing institutional practices more fully in line with psychiatric knowledge, but an increasing number of people are being aroused to the inadequacies of current practices.

A full program of prevention of mental illness would require the radical alteration of our social structure, but a more limited preventive therapy is possible under existing conditions. Some of the measures for prevention are encouragement of persons to enter psychiatric services, the increasing of funds available for psychiatric research, provision of mental hygiene clinics in local communities, provision of counseling services in the schools, the modernization of mental institutions, and extension of on-the-job counseling services. A beginning step in preventing some types of mental deficiency is the allocation of far more funds for research into the nature and causes of amentia.

SUGGESTED READINGS

American Academy of Political and Social Science, *Annals*, Vol. 286 (March 1953). This issue is entitled "Mental Health in the United States." A compact survey of extent of mental disorders, mental health resources, and community goals for mental health.

Beers, Clifford W., *A Mind That Found Itself*, Garden City, N. Y., Doubleday & Co., 1948. First published in 1908, this is an autobiographical account of the pre-institutional and institutional experiences of the man who gave impetus to the establishment of the Mental Hygiene Movement. Vivid and insightful portrayal of treatment and care of the mentally ill at the turn of the century.

Buck, Pearl S., *The Child Who Never Grew*, New York, John Day Publishing Co., 1950. A novelist's account of experiences with her mentally defective daughter. A sympathetic story that should provide many insights into this problem.

Burling, Temple, "Psychiatry in Industry," *Industrial and Labor Relations Review*, Vol. 8 (October 1954), pp. 30-37. The industrial psychiatrist is shown to have a position analogous to the safety engineer, locating hazards to mental health within the plant and suggesting remedies. Illustrative of the all-encompassing nature of mental health and a relatively new industrial practice.

The Council of State Governments, *The Mental Health Programs of the Forty-Eight States*, Chicago, 1950. Presents nation-wide resources in personnel, physical plant, and facilities for care and treatment of the mentally ill. For quick overview of adequacy of resources and recommendations to bring them up to standards see "Summary and Recommendations," pp. 4-13.

English, Oliver S., and Gerald H. J. Pearson, *Emotional Problems of Living*, New York, W. W. Norton & Co., 1945. A good cross-section view of difficulties of individual and group adjustment to the complexities and conflicts of modern social living.

Horney, Karen, *Neurosis and Human Growth*, New York, W. W. Norton & Co., 1950. A brief, clear, and recent summarization of the point of view of the "Horney school" of psychoanalysis. Chiefly because of its greater emphasis on cultural factors, this point of view has had wide acceptance in social psychological and sociological circles and should be familiar to the student of mental health problems.

Maholick, Leonard T., and Mitchell H. Wetherhorn, "A Proposal for Community-Wide Mental Health," *American Journal of Public Health*, Vol. 44 (October 1954), pp. 1345-48. Outlines the functions of a community guidance center and suggests the necessary programs, staff, and facilities. Emphasis is on preventive measures and early treatment to limit the spread of emotional disorders. Specific recommendations should be useful to the health-minded community.

Menninger, William C., and Munro Leaf, *You and Psychiatry*, New York, Charles Scribner's Sons, 1948. The psychoanalytic theory of personality structure and growth written in informal language for the layman. Should clear up misconceptions on psychoanalytic psychiatry and the process of psychoanalysis.

Weinberg, S. Kirson, *Society and Personality Disorders*, New York, Prentice-Hall, 1952. Deals with the kinds of social relations which lead to disordered behavior. Major psychoses and neuroses are related to experiences in the family, school, and occupational and other groups. Social aspects of treating and rehabilitating mental patients receive attention.

STUDY QUESTIONS

1. Why do you think it is more difficult to obtain public support and interest for research into mental illness than for physical illness research?

2. Why or why not do the number and proportion of people in mental hospitals constitute a good indication of the general level of mental health of the society?

3. What is a psychosomatic disorder? Why would it be difficult to determine whether the prevalence of such disorders has increased or decreased?

4. How would you explain to the average layman the difference between a psychosis and mental deficiency?

5. Why does our actual treatment of the mentally ill generally lag behind psychiatric knowledge concerning optimum treatment?

6. In what sense does the lack of public recognition of mental illness as a problem contribute to its becoming an even greater problem?

7. Why or why not would a program for sterilizing mental deficients result in a substantial reduction of mental deficiency? What would be the principal value clashes concerning such a program?

8. Do you see any relationship between what are called "escapist roles" and the psychosis schizophrenia?

9. Cite several measures for preventing mental illness. Why have these measures not been fully put into effect?

10. Show how each of three theories of mental illness could account for the increase of poor mental health in American society.

· 8 ·　Crime and the Criminal

During an average day in 1954, 39 homicides, 48 rapes, and 252 felonious assaults were committed in the United States. There occurred 197 robberies and 1,454 burglaries, in addition to 3,683 larcenies and 608 auto thefts.[1] Americans do not have to be told that there is a *crime* problem. But much ambiguity, ignorance, confusion, and out-and-out contradiction are apparent when even a roomful of lay people attempt to discuss the nature of crime, the "causes" of crime, and methods for "solving" the crime problem. Criminologists and other professional persons can contribute much factual information in each of these areas. Broadly conceived, whether in a preliterate society with unwritten mores or in a complex society with a written criminal code, crime may be defined as any *intentional violation of the rules considered essential for the welfare of society.* The criminal codes of modern societies, like the mores of simpler societies, designate certain values as important to the general welfare and therefore not to be violated. Crime, then, is any action *officially* considered to be contrary to the important values held by a society. For example, kidnaping, in the American legal code, has been officially defined as a crime. Once it has been proved in court that a person "carried off another person by unlawful force or by fraud," the crime of kidnaping has been officially committed and the perpetrator is a criminal.

[1] Federal Bureau of Investigation, *Uniform Crime Reports*, Vol. 24, Washington, D. C., U. S. Government Printing Office, 1954, p. 3.

Only those are criminals who have been adjudicated as such by the courts. Crime is an intentional act in violation of the criminal law (statutory and case law), committed without defense or excuse, and penalized by the state as a felony or misdemeanor. In studying the offender there can be no presumption that arrested, arraigned, indicted, or prosecuted persons are criminals unless they also be held guilty beyond a reasonable doubt of a particular offense. Even less than the unconvicted suspect can those individuals be considered criminal who have violated no law. Only those are criminals who have been selected by a clear substantive and careful objective law, such as obtains in our courts. The unconvicted offenders of whom the criminologist may wish to take cognizance are an important but unselected group; it has no specific membership presently ascertainable.[2]

▶ CHANGING CONCEPTIONS OF CRIME AND THE CRIMINAL

When we define crime as "a breach of the legal norm" and the criminal as "the individual who has committed such acts of breach," we have set up no categories of "universal" or "natural" or "unchanging" crimes. Just as there is wide variance in other social values, there is likewise much difference from time to time and place to place as to what constitutes criminality. The criminal code of our society not only differs in some respects from that of any other society, but is in a constant process of redefinition to meet our own changing social conditions and values.

The laws at any particular point in American history include two sources of norms of right and wrong conduct: the "age-old" mores and the more recent rationally formulated ideas. Thus, a "modern" criminal may have violated one or more of the legal norms long established in our social heritage, such as those pertaining to murder, rape, or theft (but it is to be noted that the legal definition of even these crimes varies from state to state and from time to time within the same state), or he may have

---

[2] Paul W. Tappan, "Who Is the Criminal?", *American Sociological Review*, Vol. 12 (February 1947), p. 100. For a view of a type of "crime" not included in Tappan's definition (to which we adhere in this chapter), see Edwin H. Sutherland, "White-Collar Criminality," *ibid.*, Vol. 5 (February 1940), pp. 1-12, and Edwin H. Sutherland, *White Collar Crime*, New York, Dryden Press, 1949.

committed a breach of recently defined legal norms relating to the manufacture, sale, or use of foods and drugs, to gambling, or to traffic regulations.

Crime as a career. A considerable, but not precisely known, amount of crime in American society is committed by careerists. The term "recidivist" is used to refer to those criminals found guilty of second, third, fourth, or more offenses, and criminals are sometimes classified on a scale ranging from "one-time offenders" through "occasional offenders" through "habitual criminals" and "racketeers" to "professional criminals." Such categories obviously are not clear-cut and are subject to many errors arising from inefficiencies of arrest, conviction, incarceration, and reporting by police, courts, and prisons. A person classified as a one-time offender may, for example, be a professional criminal fortunate and clever enough to have been caught, convicted, and imprisoned only once!

Sufficient study has been made, however, of recidivists in crime so that the modern criminologist now knows some of the characteristics of a criminal career. The process whereby a person becomes a careerist in crime apparently does not differ fundamentally from the process whereby a person becomes a careerist in law, plumbing, medicine, business, carpentry, or baseball. The novitiate to crime passes through an apprenticeship in which he learns, through association with "experts," the skills, attitudes, terminology, and philosophy of the racketeer or of the professional criminal.[3] As with other types of careers, the individual becomes a professional criminal or a racketeer through association, training, and experience. Furthermore, in-group associations of criminals appear comparable to the unions and professional societies of other occupational groups. The novitiate must be "taken under the wing" of one of the criminal groups and pass

---

[3] The stereotyped distinction between the "racketeer" and the "professional criminal" seems to have considerable validity. The former typically is a member of an organization operating in such activities as bootlegging, gambling, sponsoring of prostitution, and various "shakedown" activities; the latter, by contrast, tends to be a "smooth," quiet operator of confidence games, counterfeiting, forgery, and the like. The socialization of these two types of criminals differs in content and in personalities "selected" but seems to be similar in process.

through a probationary period of "learning the ropes" before he can achieve the status of a professional.

"Schools for crime."   The major recruiting stations for careerists in crime appear to be the reform schools, jails, prisons, and reformatories. There the first-time or occasional offender may make the "proper contacts" with professional criminals and racketeers for developing a criminal career. He not only establishes friendships with and learns skills and attitudes from professional criminals who are his fellow inmates, but he receives informal credentials to the "right people" in the criminal world outside the institution. For a criminal a short "stay in the stir" is almost a prerequisite to getting ahead in his chosen profession. Through the gradual acquisition of skills, attitudes, and contacts, the perpetrator of petty, unskilled offenses moves upward in the criminal profession to the status of one sufficiently skilled and sophisticated to commit a major, complicated crime.

Choice of career.   What causes some persons to choose a criminal career? Despite many claims made as to positive knowledge of causes by various individuals and agencies in our society, specific answers to this question have not been validated. Increasing consensus among criminologists, however, is to the effect that the *causes of persons choosing criminal careers are as varied and as difficult to determine and classify as the causes of some persons becoming politicians, others dentists, and still others high school teachers.*

Relation of crime to changing social norms.   As we have seen, crime is most clearly defined as an intentional act in violation of the criminal code. The provisions of the criminal code depend, obviously, upon what values the *controlling element* of a society decide should not, without punishment, be violated. Such values change in time and place and this change is reflected both in what is considered a crime and society's reaction to transgressors.

Social values and definition of crime.   A well-known criminologist reports that some years ago it was discovered that about three fourths of all inmates of state and federal prisons were there for committing acts that had not been crimes fifteen years earlier.[4] The many relatively new laws concerning business and occupational practices, employment of children, and conservation of natural resources, provide further evidence of the changes that have taken place with regard to what is and what is not allowable under the law. It has been estimated that since 1900 over 500,000 new state laws have been enacted.

The changing definitions of crime also operate to remove some acts from the category of criminal behavior. Prior to the repeal of the Prohibition Amendment, any person selling liquor anywhere in the United States under any circumstances and for any purpose other than medicinal was upon arrest, conviction, and imposition of a penalty, a criminal. Today this is still true in a few states and in some counties of some other states, but in most places in the country is no longer true. Other laws in regard to the sale of liquor render other acts crimes, however. In Ohio, for example, to sell on Sunday any alcoholic beverage other than a certain percentage beer is a criminal offense. If this law is repealed, it will no longer be categorically criminal to sell stronger alcoholic beverages on Sunday.

Social values and reporting of crimes. Social values affect the crime in a community in many other ways than through definition of an offense in the criminal code. Since the criminal in modern society, for all practical purposes, is the individual who is reported to the police, arrested, tried, found guilty, and sentenced, many *social values can intervene at any point in this sequence to render an act officially criminal or noncriminal.* In the matter of reporting the crime to the police, for example, there may be many blocks; *until the crime is so reported, it does not officially exist.* In America, such crimes as homicide, theft, and rape are rather consistently reported, but other crimes such as blackmail, embezzlement, fraud, and abortion are not consistently reported. Social values of persons against whom the offense is committed, of friends and relatives of the offender, and of observers of the offense obviously will differentially affect the reporting of crime. If my house is burglarized, I am very likely

[4] Harry Elmer Barnes and Negley K. Teeters, *New Horizons in Criminology,* 2d ed., New York, Prentice-Hall, 1951, p. 77.

to report it to the police; if I am being blackmailed, I am much less likely to do so. If my neighbor is a thief, I shall hasten to report the fact; if my neighbor confides that he has been "cheating" on his income tax, I may feel that it is "his business."

Social values not only affect the reporting of crimes differentially, but such values change as to what should be and should not be reported. Abortion, for example, is designated as criminal by our legal norms in essentially the same way that it was several generations ago, but, judging from such evidence as is available concerning its increase, it is considered more lightly by a growing number of members of our society. Kinsey has pointed out that many, many American males and females, according to laws now on the books, could be placed in prison for various sex offenses. Many of these offenses are probably known to others who could report them to the police if they felt they "should" do so.

Social values and arrests. Social values also affect arrests. Not all crimes reported to the police end in arrest of the offender even when he is apprehended. Aside from corruption of police by bribes (which is an appreciable factor in stopping the official process of justice at least at some times and in some communities), there are many reasons why the police may feel that arrest of the offender is not advisable and, hence, no crime gets on the books. As practically everyone realizes, prostitution is widely practiced in all large American communities and in most smaller ones. When a reform drive is in progress, many arrests of prostitutes are made; when "the heat is off," the prostitutes, not unknown always, at least, to the police, return to the community and resume their activities. The attitude of many Americans on the subject of prostitution seems to be that it is criminal and, when forced upon their attention, should be prosecuted, but that, unofficially, it is not undesirable and may be tolerated.

Other influences of social values on crime. Trial, finding of guilt, and sentence or suspension of sentence are likewise influenced by social values, changing public sentiments. Public opinion, with no apparent rationality, varies from indignation to apathy in regard to various types of offenses officially defined as crimes, and the crime rate varies with it. Frequently a crime wave is undoubtedly nothing more than a change in social values, usually quite temporary, which influences reporting to police, arrests, trials, convictions, and sentences in such a way as to increase the number of "crimes."

Fallacy of statistical analysis of crime. The student has probably realized from the foregoing section that statistics based on crimes reported to the police, arrests, indictments, and convictions are so influenced by social values currently existent that they do not afford highly reliable bases for comparing crime rates. Suppose, for example, that we wish to know whether a certain crime—say counterfeiting—has increased during the past decade in a specified community and how the rate in that community compares with the rate in another community. We immediately encounter numerous problems, of which the following would be typical. Is the enforcement of the law against counterfeiting more or less effective today than ten years ago? In Community A as compared with Community B? What are and were the strength of community sentiments against counterfeiting (and, hence, consistency of reporting to police) today and ten years ago in the two communities? If differences are thought to exist, how much allowance can we make for them in adjusting our statistics and how can we scientifically justify the degree of adjustment? What are current sentiments and policies in regard to arrest, trial, sentence, and imprisonment of known counterfeiters as compared with ten years ago, in Community A as compared with Community B? How do the activities of the federal government against counterfeiting compare in the two time periods and in the two communities? How do we interpret our statistics on these matters and how do we justify our interpretations?

Social class and criminal statistics. Another differential affecting statistics of crime not yet touched upon is that of social class. The boy from a lower-class family who steals an automobile will almost invariably be reported to the police, arrested, tried, convicted, and sentenced. The boy from a family of means *may* go through the same procedure, but he is less likely to do so. The report of his "crime" is apt to get no further than his father, who is trusted by the person whose car has been stolen to deal properly with the matter. If the theft is reported to the police, they may deem it wise, because of the respectable reputation of the family, not to "book" the boy, but merely to warn him and his father. If the arrest takes place, the judge may dismiss charges upon assurances from the boy and his father that "it will never happen again." If the boy of means is tried and found guilty, sentence may be suspended. And so on with other differentials based on class privilege, including various legal loopholes available to the better-class boy through the employment of high paid and competent legal talent. Hence, crime statistics in the *same city* at the *same point in time* are not necessarily reliable indices of offenses committed.

Limited use for criminal statistics. Crime statistics are not totally useless in this connection. If used cautiously within narrow limits for a few crimes known to have wide public cooperation in reporting (of a very public nature and considered highly injurious to the public welfare, such as murder, rape, or robbery), statistics may give rough indices of volume of crime. But so far as being reliable and valid indications of general crime as a social problem, particularly in time and place, crime statistics are very nearly worthless.

Fallacy of causation. Proposed "causes" of crime are probably more numerous than the suggested "causes" of any other societal phenomenon. Theories of causation have been so numerous that a mere listing of them would cover many pages; they fall into several main categories: geographical, hereditary, constitutional, psychological, and social.

What is a cause? Rather than go into a detailed examination of the proposed causes of crime, it is advisable, first of all, for us to understand what we mean by a cause. Its popular usage is quite loose and unscientific. You may say that sitting in the draft or getting your feet wet or staying up too late was the "cause" of your catching cold. While such things may or may not be predisposing factors—that is, increase your likelihood of catching cold providing the causal agent is present—none of them "causes" the common cold. A cause of anything, in the scientific usage of the term, is the "sufficient and essential forerunner" of the specified result. Not only, to return to our example, do people sit in drafts, get wet feet, and sit up too late without necessarily catching cold, but people sometimes catch cold without undergoing any of these conditions. None of these things, therefore, can be considered the "cause" of your catching cold.

Difficulties of isolating causes of crime. When we turn to the proposed causes of crime, we find ourselves in a position very comparable to our foregoing example. Feeblemindedness, endocrine disturbances, psychopathic personality, insanity, social disorganization, slums, bad companions, broken homes, movies, alcoholism, economic depressions, etc., have been suggested, both casually and by the process of laborious research, to be the "causes" of crime. And yet we not only find persons exposed to or falling into any one or any combination of these categories who do not become criminals, but we find criminals who fail to meet these causal requirements. There are, for example, criminals who come from broken homes, but noncriminals also come from broken homes, and all criminals do *not* come from broken homes. Broken homes, therefore, are not the "cause" of crime, for they are not the sufficient and essential forerunner of criminality. The same goes for any other suggested cause or combination of causal factors.

Since social conditions will probably never be sufficiently controllable to isolate causal factors in such complex behavior as criminality, the search for causes in crime will undoubtedly remain a fruitless one. As we shall observe later in this chapter, professional criminologists are increasingly turning their attention to more productive research. It is sufficient to observe here that knowledge of actual "causes" of crime is by no means necessary for progress to be made through empirical research regarding predictive, preventive, and control factors in crime. Scientifically based changes which effect crime reduction may be made in society without concern about whether or not ultimate causes of criminal conditions have been isolated.

▶ POPULAR PROPOSALS FOR REDUCING CRIME

The search for causes of crime, however, appears as strict rationality and rigid science compared with proposals for "curing" the criminal and reducing or "wiping out" crime. It has become fashionable to claim that almost any public or private agency's request for funds will, if granted, bring about the reduction of crime and juvenile delinquency in the community and help "straighten out" young men and women who have already committed crimes. The recreational program of, for example, the YMCA or the local settlement house is not to be defended on its own merits alone; the subscriber is assured that his contribution will prevent crime and lead to the reform of criminals. Sex education is not to be thought of as desirable in itself; such education will prevent delinquency. With all respect for the sincerity of motives of such claimants, it is obvious that their hopes tend to influence their judgments, for they offer nothing approximating scientific evidence for their claims.

Stricter penalties and better law enforcement. More rigid enforcement of our criminal laws and more severe punishment of offenders are two of the most frequently recommended methods for reducing the amount of crime in our society. Better law enforcement in itself, it is interesting to note, would actually increase the crime rate, for, as we have observed, the only totally practical definition of the criminal in our society is that of an offender who is arrested and proved guilty of the alleged offense. Hence, the more offenders caught, arrested, tried, and proved guilty, the higher the official crime rate. Obviously, then, the argument for more rigid law enforcement as a means of reducing crime depends upon what we do as a society with those who are officially proved to have committed crimes. Let us, therefore, examine the proposition of stricter penalities as a method of reducing crime.

Strict punishment as a deterrent. The strictest penalty possible for a crime is, of course, death for the offender. Until about three centuries ago almost all crimes were punishable by hanging.

Social justification for hanging was simply that the crime had injured society and that society not only deserved vengeance through the payment by the criminal with his life, but needed to show potential criminals that "they couldn't get away with that sort of thing." The evidence is fairly clear that the existence of the death penalty does not serve to deter people from committing crime. In eighteenth-century England, for example, public hangings of pickpockets had to be discontinued because too many people had their pockets picked while witnessing the hanging of pickpockets. A current study in the United States shows that the seven states without the death penalty all have "murder and nonnegligent manslaughter" rates lower than the national average. It has even been suggested that the death penalty actually may serve to increase the crimes for which it is stipulated. An early case in point is that of the English bankers in 1830 who petitioned for the abolishment of the death penalty for forgery since, because of the severity of the penalty, too few convictions could be secured.[5] More recently, a noted criminologist has pointed out that the Lindbergh Act, which makes kidnaping a capital offense when the victim is carried over a state line, may encourage a kidnaper to kill his victim rather than release him and risk the chance of exposure.[6] It is not to be construed from the foregoing illustrations that there is an inverse relationship between crime and the severity of the punishment. Rather, they indicate that criminals are apparently not deterred by the realization that severe punishment awaits them if they are caught.

For most crimes in modern society the only forms of penalty that have public approval are imprisonment and fines or a combination of the two. Stricter penalties through a system of fines would have practicability for only a relatively small percentage of offenders, those in a financial position for paying heavy fines. Since a large percentage of at least the habitual offenders come from the lower economic classes in our society, stricter penalties through heavier fines would not seem to offer very fruitful crime-reducing possibilities. Even in those cases where the

---

[5] Barnes and Teeters, *op. cit.*, p. 77.
[6] *Ibid.*, pp. 74-75.

penalty for the crime is a fine, the alternative to payment (an alternative that many offenders are forced to take) is incarceration. In addition, there are many crimes for which the only penalty offered is imprisonment.

The argument for stricter penalties for crime seems to reduce itself, then, to longer prison sentences. The popular supposition that this would reduce crime finds no support among professional workers in the fields of criminology and penology. The "threat" of a long prison term does not seem to deter criminals and a long sentence in a conventional prison does not seem to "reform" them. Even prison officials themselves, those whose livelihood depends upon the continuance of the prison system, have little to say in its support.

Limitations of punishment. After a thorough analysis of justifications for punishment and the data available in regard to the efficacy of current punitive usages, Reckless, one of the nation's outstanding criminologists and penologists, arrives at the following conclusions:

> It is already apparent that there are definite limitations to punishment, in spite of the generally accepted justifications for it. On the positive side, *i.e.*, from the standpoint of what it actually does to the offender, (1) it may make him cautious about concealing his activities; (2) it may stigmatize him and isolate him from the society to which he should be adjusted; (3) it may martyrize or heroize the culprit; (4) it may develop in him an antisocial grudge and a strong resentment of authority, not conducive to law-abiding existence. On the negative side, *i.e.*, from the standpoint of what it does not do, (5) it does not prevent crime in others or relapse into crime; (6) it does not repair damage to society; and (7) it does not reconstruct the personality of the offender.[7]

In speaking of the ineffectiveness of imprisonment as a method of reforming the criminal (and, hence, reducing crime), Sam A. Lewisohn, then president of the American Prison Association, stated:

> Too many of our citizens believe in the "cash register system of justice." When a man commits a crime, they feel a judge should

7 By permission from *Criminal Behavior*, by Walter C. Reckless. Copyright, 1940, p. 276, New York, McGraw-Hill Book Company, Inc.

press his finger on a key marked "burglary" or "robbery" or "larceny" or "felony," and presto! Out comes a piece of paper saying, "You owe society a debt of so many and so many years." And off the offender goes to prison to be punished.

But soon after that offender is given a number he hears the strange word "rehabilitation." He wonders—and so do I—if he can be punished and rehabilitated at the same time. And he is also confronted with a maze of inconsistencies.

Suppose he is rehabilitated long before the expiration of his term. He must still remain behind bars at a cost to the state of $500 a year. Suppose he does learn a trade. When he is released from prison, state laws prevent him from engaging in that trade. And too often he cannot even obtain a job because of his past indiscretions. Is it any wonder then, that so many offenders return to prison? [8]

With such evaluations of the effectiveness of our present punitive practices by experts it would hardly seem sound logic for us to subscribe to the hypothesis that more of the same, only worse, is a solution to the crime problem. There would seem to be no evidence that stricter penalties would reduce the amount of crime.

Education and religion.   Two of the most general of the popular proposals for reducing crime are increase in the effectiveness of education and religion. So long as the proposals are kept at the general level of discussion, there is hardly room for dispute, but, likewise, there is nothing to be done to implement them. That is to say, one can scarcely deny that in some way through the institutions of education and religion noncriminal rather than criminal behavior patterns should be inculcated in the members of our society. It is when we come to examine the specific methods of changing the programs of the church and the school in order to prevent the development of criminal behavior patterns that we encounter difficulty. To say that the home and the church should prevent crime is one thing; to know how this is to be accomplished is quite a different matter.

[8] Sam A. Lewisohn, "Presidential Address" given at the 76th Annual Congress of Correction, sponsored by the American Prison Association, Detroit, Mich., Oct. 4, 1946.

Role of the church in reducing crime. The role of the church in crime reduction is usually conceived in terms of increasing the church's effectiveness as an agent in equipping the individual with a system of morals that will lead him to resist and reject criminal behavior patterns. That is precisely what the church has been attempting to accomplish for centuries, and, although scientific proof is not available, to some extent probably has accomplished. Yet the church today fails to reach roughly half of the noncriminal population and seems at a loss as to methods of increasing its appeal. That criminals and potential criminals can be readily convinced of the desirability of their becoming active church participants (and, hence, be subject to whatever reformation program the church undertakes in their behalf) seems highly doubtful. Put differently, the church probably does not, for the most part, effectively reach the criminal and potentially criminal elements in our population and does not, to date, give indications of knowing how to reach them. Even granting that contemporary religious programs would divert persons from criminal patterns (which, in itself, is not an established fact), we seem at present ignorant as to means to induce criminals and potential criminals to participate in these programs.

Public school v. crime. With compulsory school attendance, the problem for education differs from that for religion. The school reaches, for a time at least, those who adopt criminal as well as noncriminal careers. But apparently many school programs are ineffective both for discovering the predelinquent and dealing with the already delinquent child. A recent study of 500 delinquents discovered that almost one third were less than eight years old when they first exhibited serious maladaptation in school.[9] Almost all had a history of truancy; two thirds "skipped school" regularly; and half began their truancy before they were ten years old. Most did not like school, their teachers, or their playmates. Their scholastic achievement was considerably lower than a group of nondelinquents with whom they were "matched" on such factors as age and intelligence. Looking at it from an-

[9] Sheldon Glueck and Eleanor Glueck, *Delinquents in the Making*, New York, Harper & Bros., 1952, pp. 69 ff.

other direction, a prison official examined the records of 634 consecutive prison commitments.[10] Seventy-eight percent of the recidivists and 61 percent of the first offenders had "truancy from school" as the first entry in their crime ledger. Many more prisoners had been truant from school but it was not officially recorded.

Many school authorities recognize the school's ineffectiveness in dealing with predelinquency and delinquency and various remedial programs have been suggested. Most of the proposals involve some form of provision of clinical and social services. Child guidance clinics, mental hygiene clinics, and child welfare agencies have been suggested as additional services needed to make it possible to recognize, understand, and treat various categories of children requiring special help. Although such services would seem educationally desirable and very worthy of trial, there is still too little scientific evidence for substantiating the claims that crime and delinquency would thereby be reduced.

Even if we were to accept on faith the efficacy of recommended clinical and social services in the school, the economic wherewithal for the implementation of such programs on a wide scale would not seem to be readily forthcoming. As this is being written, communities throughout the nation are having difficulty meeting the economic needs of regular personnel without undertaking to provide what (to be effective, at least) would have to be a costly clinical and social program. Added to this is the current scarcity of personnel qualified to operate such a program. For the time being, therefore, these proposals would seem to lack widespread practicality.

Platitudes on crime reduction. Description of popular programs for reducing crime would not be complete without mentioning some of the many platitudes uttered on the subject.

Blame on the home. One of the most frequently heard of the weak, empty remarks is that "the home is at fault." How this is believed to have meaning as a solution is difficult to under-

[10] Arthur C. Johnson, Jr., "Our Schools Make Criminals," in Clyde B. Vedder (ed.), *The Juvenile Offender*, Garden City, N. Y., Doubleday & Co., 1954, pp. 88-92.

stand, and yet many persons who believe that they are speaking quite seriously on the subject of crime utter similar sayings. That most of the basic aspects of personality are formed in the home environment, few psychologists would deny, but application of such a general truth to the likely inception of criminal behavior patterns provides us with no specific program for the reduction of crime. Just what about some homes predispose some of the children in those homes to adopt criminal ways? And, then, knowing that, what specific programs of home change would be feasible? Facts resulting from specific research, rather than the pointing of a platitudinous finger at the home, may bring us a starting point in crime prevention at one of its likely general sources.

Mental illness. Another frequently encountered platitude in crime prevention is one to the effect that criminals "ain't right." Mental illness as a "cause" of criminality would seem to be implied in this statement. While the earlier criminological literature often gave a good deal of weight to mental disorders of various types, recent studies fail to back up these claims. Since a very small proportion of criminals have been adjudged feebleminded or insane, and since a very small proportion of the feebleminded and insane manifest criminal tendencies, neither mental condition may be considered a significant source of crime, much less a helpful lead to crime solution.

The individual himself. Another empty saying that is found among proposed solutions to crime as a social problem is that "it depends on the individual." As it stands, of course, the statement has no meaning. The vague notion, however, that often seems to underlie the platitude is a partially digested conception of modern education's emphasis on individual differences. Another implication sometimes apparently included is that the individual who has fallen into criminal patterns must by his own efforts extricate himself; little or nothing is said about how the criminally inclined individual is to be instilled with the motivation to effect his behavioral changes. Neither the implication that individuals differ nor that reform must come from within the individual helps us to formulate a program of crime prevention or control.

"Born criminals." One of the most futile of the platitudes is that "criminals are born that way." Even if we were to assume hereditary sources of criminal behavior (and none of the many contentions made in this regard has been validated), no eugenical program for reducing the number of criminals in our population is considered practicable.

Our analysis of platitudes could go on for many more pages. It is hoped that the examples have been sufficient to caution the student to avoid the all too frequent tendency to seize a catchphrase, without analysis, and to present it as a solution to a complicated social problem.

▶ PROFESSIONAL CONCLUSIONS ON SOURCES OF CRIMINALITY

As has been previously indicated, the "causes" of crime and the criminal are currently unknown and, to a considerable extent, probably unknowable. This does not mean, however, that criminologists have made no progress in the understanding and control of crime. In the remaining sections of this chapter we shall consider, first, professional conclusions regarding the sources of criminal behavior patterns and, secondly, professional recommendations for the reduction of crime as a social problem.

Differential contagion and risk factors. Although studies of the sources of crime have produced no conclusive results concerning causation, they have pointed to various factors in both the individual and the environment that are correlated with the appearance of criminal patterns. These studies have further indicated that most criminal behavior is directly acquired from persons in the individual's association who already manifest the behavior. Such information has led to the use of such terms as "risk factors" and "differential contagion" to refer to the conditions conducive to the adoption of criminal behavior patterns. As the terms imply, the criminologist is placed in a position analogous to that of the physician dealing with a disease such as poliomyelitis (infantile paralysis). The causes of crime, like the causes of poliomyelitis, are not completely known, yet a number of helpful facts are known about both "diseases." Crime, like polio, is contagious, that is, caught from those who already carry the germs. In addition, contagion follows certain selective patterns, not all aspects of which are known, rather than indiscriminately affecting all persons exposed to the disease. Just as physicians have found various factors such as age, time of year, lowering of resistance, and exposure in certain public places (such as swimming pools) increase the risk of the individual's contracting poliomyelitis, the criminologist has found such factors as age, sex, class, and exposure to certain residential areas increase the risk of the individual's "contracting" patterns of criminality.

Place of residence. It is generally true that the incidence of crime is higher in large cities than in small towns and rural areas. As indicated in Table 7, this is more true of the most prevalent crimes—theft, burglary, and auto theft—than it is of the less frequently occurring "crimes against the person." Large cities, of course, offer greater opportunities for gainful crime, for disposal of goods, and for secrecy. Certain types of criminals whose operations depend on large numbers of people, as the "bookie" and the "number writer," obviously work where large numbers of people are found. Furthermore, since more criminals are found in cities than rural areas, an urban child has more opportunities for first-hand experience with crime and criminals.

Many studies have been made to determine the relationship between crime and place of residence *within* the city. While some cities do not fall neatly into geographical patterns, it has been found, in general, that most forms of crime decrease progressively as we move from the center to the periphery of a city. Stated differently, these studies show that place of residence is one important risk factor in criminality, that criminal contagion is highest in the central core of the city and diminishes in amount in proportion to distance away from this center. Since these centers are characterized by much transiency and lack of community stability, they make possible easier rebellion against established law and order by the individual and also make more likely

Table 7. Crime Rates by Population Groups, 1954 *

Type of community	Rate per 100,000 inhabitants				
	Murder and manslaughter	Rape	Robbery	Burglary and theft	Auto theft
All Cities	3.9	5.9	37.1	735.3	93.6
Over 250,000	5.2	9.0	64.8	806.1	125.9
100,000-250,000	4.3	4.9	28.5	843.7	102.6
50,000-100,000	3.2	3.7	16.3	717.3	76.7
25,000-50,000	3.1	3.0	12.9	703.4	63.7
10,000-25,000	1.9	2.9	10.6	631.8	52.3
2,500-10,000	1.9	2.9	8.2	464.2	42.3
Rural Areas	5.0	6.0	10.0	270.1	29.7

* Federal Bureau of Investigation, *Uniform Crime Reports*, Vol. 24, No. 1, Washington, D. C., U. S. Government Printing Office, 1954, pp. 6-8.

his "contagious contact" with criminals who thrive in the anonymity of these areas.

Social status. Since there is a tendency for people living in the same section of the city to be of somewhat similar status, this factor is related to the foregoing one. Studies have repeatedly discovered, nevertheless, that the lower status person is more likely to "run afoul" of the law than the higher status person. In a seven-year study of arrests in a New England town, Warner discovered that the lower 58 percent of the population contributed 90 percent of the arrests.[11] Sixty-five percent of all arrested criminals were "lower-lower class," which class constituted but 25 percent of the community. As we have already indicated, this relationship is at least partially explained by differential crime reporting and differential treatment of persons suspected of committing crimes. From the point of view of "risks," however, it is nevertheless true that the odds favor the lower status person having his name recorded on a police blotter.

[11] W. Lloyd Warner, *Social Life of a Modern Community*, New Haven, Yale University Press, 1941, p. 376.

Other risk factors.   There are still other differences in crime rates of various population categories. The statistics on these, as on those previously cited, are by no means conclusive. The following summarizes some of the remaining risk factors.

> Examination of the age curve of the criminal population shows that persons in the young adult, postadolescent ages are disproportionately the most criminal in modern societies. The statistical chances of individuals' becoming violators appear to be less and less with advancing age. The age factor in criminality reflects a differential opportunity or risk of persons, by virtue of their age position in society, for getting into difficulties.
>
> Males are disproportionately more criminal than females because of the differential workings of social institutions on the two sexes and because of physical disabilities of females as compared with males. The differences in types of offenses by sex reveal the fact that certain offenses are much more characteristically male or female offenses. Such variations likewise indicate the differential workings of sociological and biological factors on the activity and participation of the two sexes.
>
> Race and nationality variations in crime tend to suggest that these factors operate pretty much as class factors. Individuals of racial and national groups occupying a minority status are exposed to many of the same risks for getting involved and caught in crime to which individuals in the lower class ranks are exposed. Furthermore, individuals as a result of their membership in specific racial and national minorities are disadvantaged in reference to making adequate adjustments to the social order and codes of the dominant people, unless their groups are able to maintain strong counteracting systems of regulation over behavior.[12]

A "medieval penology."   It has long been realized that one of the most important sources of crime is the very penology presumably designed to prevent and "cure" criminality. The very concept of penology is rooted in the idea of punishment for the criminal; the notion of reforming the criminal is a relatively recent one in our cultural history and has been superimposed upon the idea of punishment. Although reform of the criminal is the most frequently expressed purpose of our police, court, and prison practices, these practices have remained more nearly

[12] By permission from *Criminal Behavior,* by Walter C. Reckless. Copyright, 1940, p. 120. McGraw-Hill Book Company, Inc.

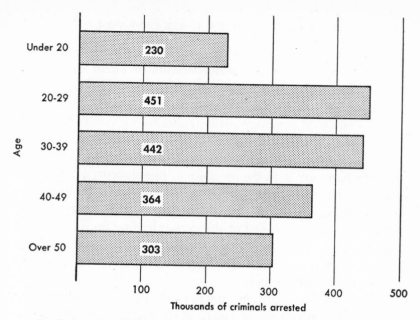

Fig. 9. Age as a risk factor in crime, 1953. (Based on Federal Bureau of Investigation, *Uniform Crime Reports,* Vol. 24, No. 2, Washington, D. C., U. S. Government Printing Office, 1954, p. 110.)

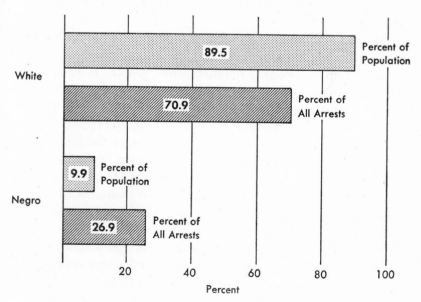

Fig. 10. Race as a risk factor in crime, 1954. (Based on Federal Bureau of Investigation, *Uniform Crime Reports,* Vol. 24, No. 2, Washington, D. C., U. S. Government Printing Office, 1954, p. 114.)

aligned with the punitive ideology of an earlier period than with modern theoretical pronouncements of intent to reform. There is increasing evidence that criminal punishment and criminal reform are irreconcilable social goals.

The "medieval penology" as it applies to our courts takes the form of punitive justice dispensed to individuals who fall into specified categories of violation of the criminal code. Legal justice is in harmony with the ideology of punishment: crime committed, price to society paid. It is not, however, in harmony with the ideology of reform, which must take into account the individualized background of the person leading up to the committing of the crime and the individualized needs present which must be met in order to help the person to divert his behavior into noncriminal channels.

In like manner, current practices of penal institutions are geared to the dispensing of justice in the form of punishment to the individual for having gone contrary to the criminal code, but are not designed to provide individualized treatment to the offender to help him achieve noncriminal methods of social functioning.

The revealed experiences of persons who have been subjected to the justice of our courts and the "reforming" of our reformatories add up to a weighty testimony that "justice" is much more likely to engender contempt for the law and desire for revenge than to stimulate motivation for reform and that penal institutions increase motivation, knowledge, and skill in criminal, rather than noncriminal, behavior patterns and render the inmate less acceptable for noncriminal roles upon his return to outer society.

It is not herein suggested that no sincere efforts have been made to improve court handling and penal treatment of criminals. Progress in the direction of individualized treatment has been made with the increasing use of probation and parole, the indeterminate sentence, lessening severity of punishment, development of dormitory-type, minimum-security institutions, attempted separation of first offenders from recidivists, etc. But most of these attempts at individualized treatment of the offender have been piecemeal rather than thorough and consistent reformulations of court and penal practices. The basic tenets of punishment have remained, and relatively superficial tenets of reform have been added. Our courts still, for the most part, send violators of criminal codes to penal institutions to be punished, and, while there, many of these violators (both out of reaction to the court "justice" dispensed and the penal treatment received and out of contacts with more experienced criminals in the institutions) are processed into more thoroughgoing criminals than they were when they entered. It appears to some observers that the superimposed notions of reform have done little other than render the ideology of punishment less efficient. Be that as it may, it would seem undeniable that the persistence of a "medieval penology" must be reckoned with by modern society as one source of persisting criminality.

Inherent problems of institutionalization. Institutionalization of any type for the criminal constitutes a problem in his reform and must, in itself, continue to be a source of further criminality. To institutionalize a criminal is to remove him to a special social world where his chief contacts will be with other violators of the criminal code. It is to remove the criminal from the society to which you hope to stimulate his noncriminal adjustment, to accustom him to a process of special-world adjustments, and to return him, regardless of the special-world treatment, to an outer society in which he carries the label of "ex-convict." He is apt to find that this label lacks censure in only one section of outer society, namely, the criminal group. That there is relapse to criminality following the most "progressive" type of institutionalization should cause us small occasion for wonder.

The proper classifications and segregation of inmates who are exposed to an enriched institutional program, based on the offenders' needs and interests in work, education, and recreation, can likewise reduce some of the schooling in crime that takes place under the surface of life in penal institutions. But such a program cannot eliminate further corruption and maturation of inmates. Interaction between inmates and the effects of inmate contacts will continue in any system; they continued *sub rosa* even under the most rigid silence rules and under the system of single cells. Parole supervision and prisoners' aid societies have attempted to assist the convict in his postinstitutional adjustments but they have not remade a world that is suspicious of and distant to ex-convicts.[13]

While improved institutional practices are not only justifiable upon humane bases in themselves, but are likely to reduce the amount of crime-breeding and crime-entrenching within these institutions, any institutional program will probably continue to be a source of criminality.

▶ PROFESSIONAL RECOMMENDATIONS FOR AMELIORATION OF THE CRIME PROBLEM

It is certainly apparent to the student by now that crime is a deeply entrenched social problem concerning which causes and full-blown solutions are unknown. To date our scientific knowledge of criminal behavior must be stated largely in negative terms, i.e., that claims of such-and-such individuals and groups regarding causes and solutions to crime are unwarranted or unverified. The general summary of criminological investigation is that no panacea to eliminate crime either exists or is likely to be forthcoming. While in themselves programs of greater economic security, more and better education, better use of leisure time, better health, slum clearance, and the like, are certainly worthy social goals, their relation to crime prevention or reduction has not been demonstrated. Four specific proposals for crime reduction stemming from professional criminologists would seem to merit further consideration and experimentation.

Reducing crime by revising the criminal code.   One obvious way to reduce crime in a society is to reduce the number of offenses which are defined as criminal. This proposal is not so evasive and insipid as first thought might indicate. It would mean the discarding by society of many petty rules, the elimination of small penal sanctions, of which the greatest proportion of modern social offenses consist. It would permit society to concentrate its criminal code on those values deemed most thoroughly related to the general welfare and to free its police, its courts, its reform-

[13] Reckless, *op. cit.*, p. 362, by permission.

ing institutions, its probation and parole officers, etc., for full attention to these major violators and their reformation. Our juvenile courts and our juvenile and adult probation have already set precedent for the "excusing" of certain types of offenses under certain circumstances. But this has, again, been the superimposing of new rules designed for reformation upon old rules designed for punitive justice. Complete renovation of our criminal code to render it a relatively simple instrument defining crime as violations of major social values, rather than continued additions to the present mass of criminal laws, constitutes this proposal.

This implies, of course, that society is able to "make up its mind" on which are its major values. Gambling is a much publicized case in point. In some states it is now legal to bet on the outcome of a horserace provided the bet is placed at the track's parimutuel window. To make the same kind of bet through a "bookie" is illegal. Some contend that "people will always gamble" and suggest that much illegal behavior could be reduced if the public were provided with a legal, readily available outlet for their gambling urges. The gambling syndicates that stand to lose considerable revenue and those that feel gambling is categorically "wrong" obviously oppose "legalized gambling." The pros and cons of this particular issue are too numerous to present here, but it illustrates how value conflicts can and do interfere with the job of much needed renovation of our criminal code.

Guidance of the "natural leader." Regardless of their specific sources, most criminal behavior has its inception in childhood and adolescent delinquency. This has long been recognized, and many youth agencies have claimed to have programs that "prevent and reduce juvenile delinquency." Since, until very recently, no controlled experiments have been conducted as part of the procedures of these agencies, there has been no verification of their claims and, on the contrary, some evidence for doubting them.

Probably the first approach to producing a program which, on the basis of control groups, could be shown to reduce delinquency in high delinquency rate areas was the Chicago Area

Project. It was set up in such a way as to use natural instead of artificial groups and local instead of imported leaders. Further characteristics of the project follow: the program is determined locally rather than by following standardized procedures imposed from the outside; already existing neighborhood facilities and institutions are employed; trained personnel are kept in the background, but are constantly available for assistance to the "natural" leaders in improving operational effectiveness; data and records are accumulated whereby results may be frequently evaluated.

Comparison of the reduced number of arrests of persons in the experimental area with those in a carefully matched contiguous area (where no comparable program was in progress) has at least tentatively demonstrated the effectiveness of the "natural leadership" techniques employed in the Chicago Area Project. While further and more extensive experimentation is needed, the superiority of this type of guidance program for youth, rather than the standardized program superimposed on the community by out-group leadership, would seem to be indicated.

Improved social-work programs. A more general attack on crime, primarily through work with delinquents and predelinquents, consists of improving the services offered by casework and group-work agencies. A concerted effort to raise the standards and practices of social-work programs related to young people and their homes was begun by the National Conference on Prevention and Control of Juvenile Delinquency. Space does not permit even a complete summary of recommendations made by the Conference, but a few of the many important proposals follow: [14]

1. Development by casework and group-work agencies of a program designed to inform their communities about the services they are prepared to give and the resources, both material and staff, they need to provide adequate services.

[14] Material taken from various publications of the Conference, especially Attorney General's Office, the National Conference on Prevention and Control of Juvenile Delinquency, *Summaries of Recommendations for Action*, Washington, D. C., 1947.

2. Strengthening and extending of existing social services and creating of new ones to meet such needs as more and better casework services in the schools; special training for truant officers in casework techniques; development of more cooperative planning of leisure-time activities of schools and group-work agencies *with*, rather than *for*, youth; child guidance centers with psychiatric services; employment of additional qualified probation officers by juvenile courts; employment of social workers to do interviewing and referral by police departments or their juvenile aid bureaus; setting up of research programs for discovering new and additional needs in the field of juvenile delinquency and of more adequate educational programs for keeping the public informed of these needs and progress made in meeting them.

3. More effective co-ordination and integration of private and public social services.

4. Assuming of greater responsibility on the part of community leaders for establishing the structure and on the part of the staff for making continuous evaluations of both the quantity and quality of the social services in light of current needs of children and adults of the community.

5. More effective efforts to attract competent college students to the field of social work.

6. Further encouragement of and impetus to research in the field of juvenile delinquency and its prevention, and in ways of developing more effective social work techniques for meeting needs in the field.

Development of predictive devices. In our discussion of the sources of criminality we mentioned the study of risk factors related to the development of criminal behavior and the contemporary inadequacy of the results of this study. It seems very probable, however, that considerable hope for improvement of social controls over crime and the criminal will stem from the accumulation of more accurate data in regard to criminal risk or liability. Out of studies providing us with more accurate statistical information concerning various risk factors associated with criminal behavior various predictive scales will be developed. Some progress in the development of predictive devices in the field of crime has already been made, but, since they are based on inadequate knowledge of risk factors, they may be regarded only as crude beginnings.

The development of accurate predictive instruments regarding those likely to adopt delinquent or criminal patterns of behavior and of those likely to revert to such patterns following treatment would provide society with means to curtail futile expenditures of time, money, and energy in misdirected preventive and treatment programs and to concentrate full efforts where they would bring the desired results. Devices already developed, while crude according to the best scientific standards, are great improvements as bases, for example, for predicting success or failure on parole compared with the combinations of guesswork, "insight," and sentiment currently employed by most of our parole boards.

In conclusion, the student is cautioned to remember that, while an overwhelming bulk of literature going under the name of "criminology" has accumulated for centuries, only recently have criminologists in large numbers begun to attack scientifically the very important social problem of crime. For those seeking swift cures for the problem, the present status of our knowledge is indeed discouraging; for those recognizing the complicated nature of social behavior generally, and of criminal behavior specifically, that we have come so far in so little time in the development of scientific methods for dealing with crime and the criminal should be amazing.

▶ SUMMARY

Although various other definitions of crime have been suggested, the only fully workable one appears to be that which makes crime "a breach of the legal norm" and the criminal "the individual who has committed acts of breach." The legal norms, or criminal code, of contemporary American society combine "age-old" mores, gradually redefined, together with enactments of recent laws.

A considerable, but not specifically determined, amount of crime in American society is committed by careerists. The process whereby a person adopts a criminal career does not apparently differ fundamentally from the process whereby a person adopts a career in any other field. The novitiate to crime passes through an apprenticeship in which he learns the skills, attitudes, and philosophy of the professional criminal or racketeer. The reasons causing individuals to adopt criminal careers would seem to be as varied as the reasons leading to the adoption of any other specific life activities.

Social values affect crime in a community in several ways. First of all, because of their changing nature, social values produce a continuous redefinition of what constitutes criminality. Since the criminal code does not stay in perfect alignment with the social values of a community, changes in values affect the official crime rate through such practical manifestations as reporting of crimes to the police, policies of arrest, court attitudes, etc. The wide variation in crimes reported, arrests, indictments, and convictions renders rather unreliable the use of crime statistics for comparing crime rates from community to community and from time to time in the same community. Social class differentials also probably reduce the reliability of such statistics.

Although a vast amount of literature has been produced on the subject of causes of crime, no proposed cause has been verified as such. In fact, the whole search for causes of crime is probably a futile one.

Of the many popular proposals for crime reduction and prevention, stricter penalties and more effective law enforcement are among the most frequent. More effective law enforcement would, by definition, increase the amount of crime, and the ineffectiveness of our penal system would make very doubtful reduction or prevention of crime by introduction of stricter penalties.

More effective educational and religious activities have also frequently been offered as methods for reducing and preventing crime. Most of these proposals have been too general to be considered seriously as methods, and the more specific programs are not only unverified, but, for the present at least, impracticable as large-scale efforts.

Samples of platitudinous pronouncements for crime reduction were shown to be, upon examination, largely carriers of nonsense.

The failure of the search for causes of crime does not mean that nothing is known of the source of criminality. Although research has not yet progressed to a fully satisfactory point, correlation of criminal behavior with various risk factors has been demonstrated, and the general belief that crime is contracted through a process of differential contagion would seem to have some substantiation. An important source of persisting criminality is what has been referred to as our continuing "medieval penology." It was pointed out, however, that the very nature of an institution is such that correctional institutionalization will remain a source of criminal behavior under probably the most progressive practices.

While no panacea for the social problem of crime is likely to be forthcoming, several methods which are developing show promise of reducing crime. Four general methods were discussed under the headings of criminal code revision, "natural leader" guidance, social work improvement, and the development of predictive devices.

SUGGESTED READINGS

Barron, Milton S., *The Juvenile in Delinquent Society*, New York, Alfred A. Knopf, 1954. A good text on the young offender. Contends that juvenile delinquency can be understood and reduced by understanding his society.

Glueck, Sheldon, and Eleanor Glueck, *Delinquents in the Making*, New York, Harper & Bros., 1952. A monumental study of 500 delinquents paired with an equal number of nondelinquents by well-known criminological researchers. Accent is on understanding and preventing delinquency rather than describing it.

Hassler, Alfred, *Diary of a Self-Made Convict*, Chicago, Henry Regnery Co., 1954. A straightforward account of the prison experiences of a conscientious objector. Good insight into prison administration and its effect on possible rehabilitation of prisoners.

Kefauver, Estes, *Crime in America*, Garden City, N. Y., Doubleday & Co., 1951. A popular account of "big crime" (the Mafia, gambling syndicates, etc.) in the United States based on testimony received by Senate Crime Investigating Committee.

Reckless, Walter C., *The Crime Problem*, New York, Appleton-Century-Crofts, 1955. A broad, practical textbook. The mature student should consult, especially, the sections on "affiliated problems" and "categorical risks."

Scudder, Kenyon J., *Prisoners Are People*, Garden City, N. Y., Doubleday & Co., 1952. Describes the fascinating experiment with a new type prison. Easily read and extremely stimulating.

Sutherland, Edwin H., *White Collar Crime*, New York, The Dryden Press, 1949. This is a well-documented analysis of a type of "crime" not treated in this chapter.

U. S. Department of Health, Education, and Welfare, *Helping Delinquent Children*, Washington, D. C., U. S. Government Printing Office, 1953. Describes the kind of services that ideally should be rendered by police, detention home, juvenile court, and other agencies in order successfully to combat delinquency. Discusses ways of preventing juvenile delinquency. A guidepost for every American community.

Wilson, Donald P., and Harry Elmer Barnes, "A Riot Is an Unnecessary Evil," *Life*, Vol. 33 (Nov. 24, 1952), pp. 139-50. Two outstanding prison specialists survey the current status of state penitentiaries. Reasonable and practical suggestions, not involving huge outlays of funds, are made to combat such problems as idleness, overcrowding, and brutality.

STUDY QUESTIONS

1. Indicate the similarities between crime as a career and some noncriminal occupational career.

2. How do the values of a society affect its definition of crime? Illustrate.

3. It was pointed out in the text that many Americans have committed sex offenses for which they were never arrested. In what sense are such individuals criminals? In what sense are they not criminals?

4. In view of present knowledge concerning the criminal career, would you suggest sending amateur criminals and recidivists to the

same penal institution? What difficulties would you expect if a relatively expensive program to do otherwise were suggested?

5. Cite as many difficulties as you can with regard to the use of crime statistics. Of what use are such statistics?

6. Describe how the social status of a youthful delinquent could affect "the wheels of justice" from his apprehension to the passing of sentence.

7. Why, in your opinion, is the layman more willing to discuss and list "the causes" of crime than the trained criminologist?

8. Evaluate: "Stricter penalties are needed to deter potential criminals from committing crimes."

8a. Illustrate how increasing the severity of the punishment for a given crime could result in an increase in that particular crime.

9. Describe the age, sex, place of residence, social status, and race of the person most likely to be a criminal. In a similar manner, who would be least likely to be a criminal?

10. Cite as many ways as you can in which the professional recommendations for amelioration of the crime problem differ from popular proposals.

·9· Social and Psychological Deviations

The social problems treated in this chapter directly affect a smaller percentage of the population than any we have separately treated. But most Americans *are* involved in the clashes of values regarding their solutions. The problems to be considered are those of alcoholism, drug addiction, sex perversions, and prostitution. Even a simple enumeration of the conditions may call forth deep-rooted aversions, strong prejudices, stereotyped descriptions of the offenders, and rigid theories for the amelioration of the specific problems. Indeed, it is strong public opinion that renders each of these conditions· a distinct social problem.

The treatment of these problems together in a single chapter is not to suggest some subtle interrelationships; the procedure is justified chiefly by its convenience. Logical analysis might justifiably classify the first two (alcoholism and drug addiction) as special symptoms of mental and physical illness, and the last two might be considered specific demonstrations of the inadequacies of our marriage and family institutions. But, because of the intense conflicts of values inherent in them and surrounding them, we direct particular attention to these four problems in the present chapter.

▶ ALCOHOLISM

Alcohol itself carries clashes of values in its effects. Alcohol can facilitate interpersonal associations and can contribute to their disintegration. It can offer an escape valve for frustrated individuals and can impair potentially valuable social contributions. Alcohol can reduce tension, guilt, and anxiety; but it can reduce operational efficiency and thus, perhaps, increase tension, guilt, and anxiety. Alcohol can be both the elixir and the wrecker of life.

It is necessary to distinguish at the outset the difference between the drinking of alcohol and alcoholism. High rates of consumption of alcohol do not necessarily mean that the individual consumer of large quantities is an alcoholic nor that a society has a correspondingly high rate of alcoholism. Although many different definitions are available, the key point of difference between a drinker of alcohol and an alcoholic seems to be the matter of *compulsive* drinking.

Problems within the lives of individuals or families may result, of course, from noncompulsive drinking. A man who gets drunk only on rare festive occasions may break the furniture, his leg, his good relations with his wife or boss, or do an almost endless series of socially damaging acts. According to the value judgments of a majority of Americans, however, his drinking becomes a serious part of the problem of alcoholism only when it becomes a chronic and compulsive condition. It is then that he is directly on the road to bringing grave difficulties into his own life and into the lives of his family and associates.

We do not know how many Americans drink alcoholic beverages and are even less sure of the number of alcoholics. The best estimate is that some 65 million people use alcohol and that about 1 percent of these are true alcoholics.[1] Some place the proportion of chronic, compulsive drinkers at about 6 percent of those who drink at all. In numbers, then, it has been estimated that there are between three quarters of a million and 4 million alcoholics. There is still too little known about the alcoholic, but enough is known to dispel some possible misconceptions. One authority estimates that no more than 20

[1] Alton L. Blakeslee, "Alcoholism—A Sickness That Can Be Beaten," Public Affairs Pamphlet No. 118, New York, Public Affairs Committee, 1952, p. 4.

percent of alcoholics are the "skid row" or "bowery bum" type of derelicts. In the ranks of alcoholics are men and women, single and married, parents and nonparents, the successful and the unsuccessful. They are drawn from all occupations, all levels of society, and are of all degrees of intelligence. In one sense, then, the alcoholic may be "anyone," the doctor, the factory worker, the suburban housewife, or the clerk. Studies have shown, however, that male alcoholics outnumber females six to one and that over three fourths of the males are between the ages of thirty-five and fifty-five.[2]

Value conflicts as the source of alcoholism. Urbanized America becomes increasingly a society of nonintimate, impersonal, secondary group associations. Aggressive and competitive relationships dominate the lives of individuals, who are encouraged to be self-contained and independent, and who are increasingly removed from each other's interests and activities. Values to be derived from personal, intimate, unsuspicious, pleasant, and unstrained relationships are often largely unsatisfied.

When the individual turns to recreational groups designed to satisfy his needs for primary group fellowship, he is often frustrated by feelings of strangeness, tension, suspicion, ignorance, and indifference in himself and in other group members. Something is needed to bring relaxation to these individuals who, conditioned by secondary group interactions, are seeking primary group values. Alcohol becomes the most readily available and effective relaxing agent. Thus, the "social drinker" is born.

Most social drinkers remain such, sometimes drinking to excess, but usually knowing "when they have had enough." Others, perhaps because of unusual feelings of inadequacy in themselves and because of particular interpersonal tensions in their family or occupational lives, find in alcohol an increasingly welcome "escape from it all." Such persons come to find the world of alcohol the only tolerable world; they become the compulsive, chronic drinkers, the alcoholics.

[2] *Ibid.*

Alcoholics are not without value conflicts. They become aware of the deteriorating effect of alcohol on their physiological, psychological, and social functioning. But the anxieties for which alcohol originally offered "escape value" become less rather than more bearable during sober periods. And whatever counteranxieties existed for the individual before he became a compulsive drinker lose strength as the alcoholic habit becomes more fixed and the will to resist drinking deteriorates.

Value conflicts in the control of alcoholism. The most obvious way for society to deal with the problem of alcoholism is to remove the possibility of individuals' obtaining alcohol. The simple logic of no alcohol, no alcoholism, was tried on a national scale with the Eighteenth Amendment and still operates at the county and state levels with prohibition laws. This method ignores the conflict of values regarding alcohol for large numbers of citizens who are not compulsive drinkers. Prohibition does not remove alcohol; it merely places various obstacles in the path of its procurement. Hence, to the other values of alcohol, prohibition adds the values of prestige of obtaining it and "smartness" of drinking it. Prohibition fails, then, not so much because its values conflict with values held by alcoholics (who are, after all, a small and noninfluential segment of the population), but because its values conflict with values held by nonalcoholics.

Another strong set of values is held, of course, by the manufacturers and distributors of alcoholic beverages and others whose occupations are directly and indirectly related to them. These are in direct conflict with the values of other strong pressure groups representing prohibitionists. The public is propagandized from both sides by the efforts of "wets" and "drys" to convert a majority to their particular sets of values.

With the demonstrated failures of prohibition to achieve its main goals, together with the apparent increase in other social evils during the operation of the Eighteenth Amendment, the conclusion is reached that the reduction of the problem of alcoholism must come through other channels. Educational programs directed toward moderation in drinking may have some effect in preventing some individuals from becoming alcoholics. Curative treatment of those who have already become compulsive drinkers must be based on a knowledge of anxieties and counteranxieties in the individual. The success in some instances of Alcoholics Anonymous would seem to be based on the feelings of prestige and satisfaction created in the individual by his personal and intimate association with other alcoholics who care for and are interested in him and the later satisfactions and prestige derived by providing comparable service himself to other alcoholics.

A society which wishes to solve the problem of alcoholism cannot expect to do so by a negative program of admonition about the evils of alcohol nor by prohibiting its sale or consumption. It must examine the conflicts of values inherent in its present interpersonal relationships and proceed with positive programs for resolving these conflicts by other methods than that of prohibiting alcoholic consumption. Such a program will not succeed if it is based on the values held by reformers. It must be based on a knowledge of the unsatisfied and conflicting values held by a large proportion of the members of our complex, urbanized society.

▶ DRUG ADDICTION

In recent years there has been much public concern with the problem of drug addiction. Particular attention seems to have been directed toward the adolescent addict. Various well-intentioned but often ill-informed groups of citizens have initiated campaigns to combat the "teenage dope menace"; recordings by former addicts have blared forth from our radios as a "warning" to other youths; and newspapers and magazines seem unwittingly to have glamorized the addict in their dramatic attempts to present "the truth about dope addiction."

It is difficult to obtain accurate information on the illegal use of narcotics, but what evidence we have seems to indicate that the recent "dope menace" has been overemphasized. Reliable sources place the number of addicts in the United States at about 60,000.[3] About one sixth of these are adolescents. It is thought that traffic in narcotics has increased since World War II, but even so, there are about half as many addicts now as there were before World War I. Some check-ups indicate that adolescents form a smaller proportion of all addicts than they did a couple of decades ago; others estimate that the proportion was about the same then as now.

The recent public concern with drug addiction provides us with a current illustration of a social problem passing through different phases of value conflicts. What apparently has happened is that a real, but less than imagined, increase in the use of narcotics has led to an awareness of the problem by many who previously did not admit that a problem existed. The clash of values regarding the amelioration of the problem is a matter of public record. Despite the attention the phenomenon has received, however, there appears still to be need for unglamorized information on the sources of drug addiction and realistic views toward lessening the number of addicts.

The sources of drug addiction are very similar to those of alcoholism. In fact, alcoholic beverages may be viewed as readily available forms of a narcotic. By many specialists, however, the term "drug addiction" is applied only to the habitual use of opium and its derivatives, codeine, morphine, laudanum, and heroin. Use of any of the opium drugs, by smoking, eating, hypodermic injection, or snuffing, has a more rapid and disintegrating effect on the user than alcohol or other drugs such as cocaine, marihuana, or hashish.

The problem of drug addiction is further complicated by the fact that both users and distributors become criminals by their violations of both federal and state statutes. Like the chronic alcoholic, the drug addict becomes moody, disorderly, and neglectful of personal and social obligations. Added to this is his criminality, and he pays not only the price of the alcoholic, but the additional costs occasioned by the difficulty

[3] Albert Deutsch, "What We Can Do About the Drug Menace," Public Affairs Pamphlet No. 186, New York, Public Affairs Committee, 1952, p. 5.

of procuring his drug, complete social disgrace, and imprisonment.

Drug distribution is a highly risky but very profitable occupation. Although federal law enforcement has been successful in reducing the traffic in drugs, there seems to be little hope of completely cutting it off. Making a criminal out of the drug addict himself is of doubtful value in controlling the problem. Just as in the case of the alcoholic problem, social attention needs to be increasingly directed toward the conflict of values inherent in and surrounding drug addiction before the problem can be brought under really effective control. Medical rather than penological treatment is needed for the person already addicted. Educational programs which stress the much more devastating undesirabilities of drug addiction (as compared with alcoholism) might prevent some addictions from developing, for many young people seem totally ignorant of the subject. The most effective measures, however, as in the case of the alcoholic problem, must be directed toward constructive satisfaction of the interpersonal needs from which drug addiction derives.

▶ SEX PERVERSIONS

During the past year or so, newspaper headlines have been extensively devoted to sex crimes of various sorts. The uncritical perusal of most of the nation's newspapers would lead the reader to believe that sexual perversions of all types were rapidly increasing. Although there is no evidence that this is true,[4] the great public concern regarding rape and molesting of children has led to a panicky passage of laws in many states and the tightening of police prosecution of all types of sex deviants, including homosexuals, in many American communities.

Psychologists, psychiatrists, sociologists, and other authorities on sex perversions agree that they stem, almost uniformly,

---

[4] According to Dr. Alfred C. Kinsey in an unpublished report to the American Association of Marriage Counselors at their December 27, 1949, meeting in New York City.

from social malconditioning and frustration of those sexual outlets which our society designates as normal. Sometimes sex offenders are out-and-out psychotics or severe neurotics; at other times the individual who is considered in every other way "perfectly normal" will be caught in deviant sex behavior.

Types and sources of perversion. The types of sex perversion which are most often referred to in clinical diagnoses are the following methods of obtaining sexual gratification: (1) by the seduction of children (technically termed *pedophilia*), (2) by practicing intimacies with a member of the same sex (*homosexuality*), (3) by inflicting pain on others (*sadism*), (4) by having pain inflicted upon oneself (*masochism*), (5) by loving things (such as women's hair or underclothes) instead of people (*fetishism*), (6) by looking at other people (*voyeurism*), (7) by exposing oneself to the view of others (*exhibitionism*), and (8) by practicing intimacies with animals (*bestiality*).[5]

Although an occasional instance of homosexuality may be induced by hormone deficiencies, almost all cases of homosexuality and the other forms of perversion seem to be the result of social malconditioning. Many of the forms of perversion, such as exhibitionism, voyeurism, fetishism, and homosexual impulses, are normal enough experiences in the early life of the individual. It is probable that many sexual perverts are emotionally immature persons who have been "stunted" at some point in their growth toward psychological adulthood. Afraid to undertake, or meeting with frustrations in attempts to undertake, adult heterosexual outlets, the maladjusted individual turns to one of the perversions.

As for the other perversions, bestiality would seem to be due most often to the unavailability of human sex objects and the availability of animals, and pedophilia probably arises out of similar circumstances. The greater availability of children and animals may be relative, not absolute; that is, children and animals are less capable of resisting the advances of a pervert than an adult would be.

---

[5] O. S. English, and G. H. J. Pearson, *Emotional Problems of Living*, New York, W. W. Norton & Co., 1945, pp. 375-76.

Masochism and sadism are found to some degree in the normal human being. Neurotic conditions stemming from any number of life frustrations and anxieties could find their easiest channel of expression in a particular individual through masochism or sadism as the chief forms of sexual gratification.

Although the foregoing discussion of sexual-perversion types and sources may seem extremely general, greater specificity is possible only as a result of clinical diagnosis of the particular pervert. Stated differently, specific sources and forms of perversion may be understood only in terms of the life history of the patient under consideration.

Values in conflict. The problem of perversion operates at two levels: (1) the psychological, that is, in the individual pervert, and (2) the societal, that is, the relationship of society to its perverts. The two levels are interrelated. Our society, because of its very strong condemnation of perversion, makes the psychological difficulties of its sex deviants much greater than they were, for example, in ancient Greece. Since we are in no position, however, to offer suggestions for generalized therapy to suffering sex deviants, we shall confine our discussion to the societal level of value conflicts.

Most members of society are extremely disturbed by sexual perversion. Contact with or even a discussion of a homosexual is likely to make the average American shocked, angry, or repelled. Why such reactions to one who, at worst, is an emotionally ill person? Why do many people suggest jailing or shooting the pervert rather than referring him to a psychiatrist or leaving him alone?

One obvious answer is that an occasional sex deviant is dangerous, and there is a tendency to generalize from these few to a fear and hatred of all sexually "queer" people.

A second reason may be found in our long Puritanical social conditioning. To a still considerable percentage of the American population, any kind of sexual activity is a shameful thing. If even marital sexual intercourse is fearsome and horrible, then obviously sexual activity which departs from this channel is to be regarded as disgustingly criminal. This sort of attitude is instilled early in the minds of many American citizens and generally goes unchallenged for the rest of their lives.

It is only recently that even a few courageous professional writers and speakers have dared question the traditional American attitude toward and treatment of sexual perverts. Their efforts have by no means yet begun to stem the tide of public prejudice, panic, and inhumanity regarding its sexual deviants. The resolution of this conflict over what to do about the problem of perversion may, therefore, be considered in its infancy. Gradually, however, psychiatrists, psychologists, and other sexologists are stating that "we can never bring about the reduction of perverse sexual behavior through condemnation, through punishment of the sexually perverse individual, by excluding him from our lives or from society, by bringing him into court and putting him in jail." [6] It is only by understanding, preventing, and changing the conditions that have produced the frustrations lying behind sexual perversion in the individual that we can reduce the number of perverts. Meantime, a more humane and understanding treatment of the sexual perverts which society has already produced will go a long way toward removing perversion from the list of social problems.

The need for research. Throughout this book we have repeatedly indicated that the amelioration of various social problems rests in some part on the objective study of the conditions. In few areas is the lack of factual knowledge more manifest than in that of sexual perversions. Many seem quite content to accept their own interpretation of the situation and hold rigidly to their own beliefs regarding the treatment of offenders. Perhaps to let the psychiatrist, the sociologist, and others study the problem objectively would result in the discovery of too many facts that some would be unwilling to accept or too many implications that they would find uncomfortable. Witness the public reaction to Kinsey's studies. Some completely discounted the facts; others said the facts, even if reasonably accurate, should never have been reported; and some even questioned the morals

[6] English and Pearson, *op. cit.*, pp. 376-77.

of the researchers themselves. But we need to know more about the "normal" individual and we need even more to know about the sexual deviant.

Pedophilia is probably considered the most heinous of sex perversions. One such reported case and the community becomes quite alarmed at the thought that a "vicious sex fiend" is loose in their midst. The results of a recent study in California, however, may serve to make many question their conception of the adult involved if not their recommendations for "stamping out" this type of activity.[7] The psychiatrists and others on the California project found it necessary to distinguish between two types of female child victims, the "accidental victim" and the "participant victim." In only one third of the cases studied was the child classified as an "accidental victim," in which case the act was likely to have occurred with a stranger and to have occurred only once. Such a child usually reported the incident to her mother soon after it occurred. In two thirds of the cases the child was classified as a "participant victim" and here the pattern was quite different. In most cases the adult involved was not a stranger, but a relative, friend, or neighbor of the family of the victim. Sex experiences frequently occurred over a period of time; the child was likely to accept some reward (candy, movies, and the like); and she frequently kept the activity secret for a period ranging from weeks to years.

Almost everyone would agree that children should be protected from sexual seduction by adults. But are not the foregoing facts likely to change some minds on what action should be taken and to whom it should be directed? Studies such as this one may well bring forth some unpleasant facts about already unpleasant situations. But until we are willing to devote more effort to the objective analysis of sexual deviancy and less to the rigid pronouncements on the proper disposition of "sex fiends" our attempts at ameliorating the problem are likely to meet with failure.

[7] State of California Department of Mental Hygiene, *California Sexual Deviation Research*, Monterey, California State Printing Office, Assembly of the State of California, 1953.

▶ PROSTITUTION

Prostitution in the United States has followed an interesting pattern of oscillation between the opposed values of health and morality, on the one hand, and business interests and sexual desires, on the other. Until about the second decade of the twentieth century business and sex dominated societal treatment of prostitution, and it was permitted to exist relatively undisturbed in the segregated districts of most American cities. The antivice campaign that preceded World War I, however, forced public officials to cease open toleration of prostitution. This brought about the concealing, not the permanent closing, of houses of prostitution.

During World War II the federal government was empowered to proceed against prostitution in military and defense-factory centers. This forced local authorities to curb much more efficiently and consistently than they had previously the business of prostitution. Hence, as an open practice, prostitution almost disappeared during World War II. Although the wartime federal powers of enforcement on local authorities have been continued, the effectiveness is apparently gradually falling below the wartime level.[8]

Changing types of prostitution. Today it may be difficult (but by no means impossible) to go down to the "red-light" district of a major American city and point out the houses of prostitution. We rarely read of unsuspecting and naïve girls being lured from home and forced into a great prostitution ring by "white slavers." Even the somewhat overweight and overrouged "street walker" is less seldom seen. There is some evidence that the form of prostitution may have changed; this does not necessarily mean that the extent has been reduced.

Where once the prostitute more or less openly plied her trade individually or was connected with a "house," now she may be quietly and anonymously living in her own apartment where she

[8] Walter C. Reckless, *The Crime Problem,* New York, Appleton-Century-Crofts, 1950, pp. 222-23.

is informed where and when to meet a customer. A number of "call girls" may be loosely organized by some central figure who makes "appointments" for them, or the individual prostitute may make her own arrangements for securing contacts with potential customers. It is always difficult to obtain accurate information on the extent of prostitution and the activities of prostitutes. And this is particularly true of the clandestine activities of the "call girl." It is well to remember that lack of obvious signs of prostitution does not necessarily mean that the activity does not exist.

Sources of prostitution.   One of the chief sources of prostitution would seem to be the desire on the part of a considerable number of males for an easily achieved, nonbinding sexual outlet and their willingness to pay for such an outlet. Without this demand, the supply of prostitutes would quickly disappear.

This desire of some males for such sexual experiences as prostitutes may provide is aided by various business interests not directly involved in prostitution itself. Hotel employees, taxicab operators, restaurant proprietors and waiters, bartenders, and various other types of commercial persons know that there is "money in it for them," directly or indirectly, if they can provide their customers with or refer them to prostitutes.

A third factor is the belief on the part of girls themselves that prostitution is an easier way to make a living than other pursuits open to them. However correct or mistaken the particular girl may be in this judgment, the belief undoubtedly lures many into the occupation.

With demand set up in the form of males ready to pay, with channels of communication improved by greedy merchants, and with the lure of "easy money," the girl herself still has to be vulnerable to such attractions. The girls from whom prostitutes are recruited seem to be, to a large extent, those who come from poor social backgrounds, who have mental or emotional inadequacies (low intelligence, high degree of emotional immaturity, psychopathic tendencies, etc.), who have had previous sexual experience (mostly unfortunate), and who have had contact with persons in or on the fringe of prostitution.[9]

Effects of prostitution. Whatever the beginning of the road to prostitution for the woman, the chances of demoralization, the ultimate of which is the state of the derelict, are great. A few prostitutes probably permanently improve their economic and social status. Others get out in time to escape the occupational hazards. But it would appear that most meet with one or more of the following undesirable consequences: "arrests and institutional sentences, venereal infection, sickness, gynecological complications, marginal living, alcoholism, drug addiction, and so forth." [10]

The effects of prostitution on the rest of society are less easily discerned. According to the official morality of the ages, prostitution is an unmitigated vice. And yet, side by side with this morality, sometimes openly and sometimes partially hidden, prostitution has continued to exist. What the effect is of this perpetual clash of values, and the hypocrisy behind which many members of society hide in an attempt to deny the clash, on the strength and health of society, it is difficult to ascertain. That the effect is undesirable to some degree can scarcely be disputed.

Suppression and prevention. As with any social problem, the reduction or elimination of prostitution postulates a strong public opinion in favor of the laborious study and effective action necessary. Such public opinion has never been consistently present in American society (or, for that matter, in any other large urban society). Any program of complete suppression or prevention would seem to be out of the question.

Some methods for reducing the number of active prostitutes are: (1) insistence on federal surveillance of local officials with the same diligence as was accomplished during World War II (this is legally possibly through the permanent extension in 1946 of the May Act); (2) re-establishment of social-protection assistance to the states of the type used during the war;

[9] Reckless, *op. cit.*, pp. 228-30.
[10] *Ibid.*, p. 234.

(3) more adequate readjustment programs for sex-delinquent girls in juvenile courts and training schools; (4) better assistance to the unattached or stranded woman in finding employment, lodging, and approved recreations; (5) surveillance and protection of female workers and patrons in taverns, restaurants, bars, and other places of moral hazard; (6) creation and application of a more effective sex-education program in the public schools; and (7) provision of far-reaching marriage, vocational, and educational counseling programs.[11]

Such activities as the foregoing would take more time, money, and effort than the American people are now ready to expend. So long as anything less than these things are done, however, any long-term reduction of prostitution seems unlikely.

▶ SUMMARY

Four of the areas of social and psychological deviation about which value conflicts center in our society are alcoholism, drug addiction, sex perversions, and prostitution.

Because of the effects it produces in the individual, alcohol itself may be considered the source of value conflicts. It becomes a social problem largely, however, when it is *compulsively* consumed by certain members of society. These individuals are the true alcoholics, and they are recruited from the social drinkers. The popularity of drinking as a recreational pursuit is apparently enhanced in a complex, urban society where the opportunity for personal, intimate associations of the primary-group variety are at a minimum.

Society faces value conflicts in its attempts to control alcoholism. Prohibition failed because of the conflict in values regarding alcohol on the part of the large percentage of the population which is noncompulsive in its drinking. Added to the values created by the unavailability of alcohol are the values emphasized by the manufacturers and distributors of alcoholic beverages. Educational and therapeutic programs would seem

[11] *Ibid.*, pp. 234-36.

to be the only practicable methods for the reduction of alcoholism, but such programs have not been especially successful to date.

Drug addiction affects a smaller percentage of the population than alcoholism, is more adequately controlled, and more fully penalized legally, but otherwise is quite similar as a social problem to that produced by alcoholism. Judging from the attention this problem has received in recent years, it would seem to have increased tremendously. Actually it has increased some since World War II, but there are nevertheless fewer addicts today than in other periods of the recent history of the United States.

Although sex perversion as a fact is not the serious threat which it has become in public opinion, there are various discernible types of sexual deviation. All of these types seem to be associated predominantly with the emotionally immature individual who is frustrated in his normal heterosexual relations. Current punitive programs will not reduce perversion; such reduction must be based on an understanding and sympathetic treatment of the individual and a removal of the types of environmental conditions which produce retardation of personality development.

Prostitution varies in the openness with which it is practiced in the United States, but attempts at complete suppression have been unsuccessful. The chief sources of prostitution seem to be: male demand for easily accessible sex outlets, monetary interests of commercial enterprises, belief of some girls that prostitution is a better way to make a living than other occupations open to them, their poor social background and personality organization, and previous sexual experience and contacts with others associated with prostitution on the part of the girls.

The effects of prostitution on the practitioner are often of a very demoralizing sort. While the effects on society are less readily discernible or measurable, they are undoubtedly of a disintegrative nature.

While a program for the complete elimination of prostitution is unrealistic, methods for reducing the problem have been recommended. It is unlikely that any such program will be effectively carried out.

SUGGESTED READINGS

Blakeslee, Alton L., "Alcoholism—A Sickness That Can Be Beaten," Public Affairs Pamphlet No. 118, New York, Public Affairs Committee, 1952. In the succinct and readable fashion of the Public Affairs synopses, the reader is given an accurate picture of some of the important aspects of the problem of alcoholism.

Cory, Donald W. (pseud.), *The Homosexual in America*, New York, Greenberg-Publisher, 1951. An autobiographical account of homosexuality. Addressed to the lay reader, it describes the life and problems of a homosexual and makes a plea for more humane treatment of this type of deviant. An interesting and courageous book, although it is not meant to be a scientific explanation of homosexuality.

Deutsch, Albert, "What We Can Do About the Drug Menace," Public Affairs Pamphlet No. 186, New York, Public Affairs Committee, 1952. Recent facts about drug addiction are objectively presented and discussed in this brief treatment.

Journal of Social Hygiene. Almost every volume contains reports and articles on prostitution, particularly as it affects control of venereal disease. A good source for recent information.

Plascowe, Morris, *Sex and the Law*, New York, Prentice-Hall, 1951. Chapters 5 to 10 deal with criminal laws purporting to control various sex crimes. An excellent portrayal of the confused and frequently outmoded state of sex laws.

Podolsky, Edward, *Management of Addictions*, New York, Philosophical Library, 1955. Leading authorities discuss addiction to alcohol and various drugs. Although written largely for the physician, Chapter 35, "The Problem of Narcotic Drug Addiction" is an excellent summary on the nature and effects of narcotics and treatment and prevention of addiction.

Quarterly Journal of Studies on Alcohol, New Haven, Yale University. Recommended to students who wish to keep up with the latest scientific research in problems of alcoholism, methods recommended for its control, and treatment of alcoholics.

Reckless, Walter C., *The Crime Problem*, New York, Appleton-Century-Crofts, 1950. Chapters 10 ("Prostitution"), 11 ("Alcoholism"), and 12 ("Drug Addiction") are all good, short coverages of their topics.

Reckless, Walter C., "Prostitution in the United States," in Morris Fishbein and Ernest W. Burgess, *Successful Marriage*, Garden City, N. Y., Doubleday & Co., 1947, pp. 433-47. An excellent summary of the history, status, and methods of attempted control of American prostitution.

State of California Department of Mental Hygiene, *California Sexual Deviation Research*, Sacramento, California State Printing Office, 1953. A compact study concentrating on sex crimes against children. Offenders and victims are described statistically, psychologically, and sociologically and scientific literature on sexual deviation is reviewed.

STUDY QUESTIONS

1. Approximately how many American adults use alcohol? What proportion of these are alcoholics? What is the relationship between these two facts and the conflict of values over alcohol?

2. Give as many reasons as you can for the failure of prohibition, and for each state the value conflict that was involved.

3. Is it possible that our recent concern with youthful drug addiction could have accentuated this phenomenon? Explain.

4. Criticize: "There must be more drug addiction today because we hear so much more about it."

5. For how many of the different forms of sex perversion can you describe a "normal" pattern of behavior which would seem to be a less extreme manifestation of the same tendency?

6. Why do you think many people find it hard to believe that a sex pervert is emotionally ill?

7. How would the values of American society interfere with a program for enlightening the masses concerning the nature and types of sex perversions? With a program for treatment of known perverts?

8. Distinguish between an "accidental" and "participant" child sexual victim. Of what utility is this distinction?

9. What are the principal sources of prostitution? Which of these do you believe would be the most difficult to change in order to reduce prostitution?

10. Rearrange the seven proposals given in the text for the reduction of prostitution in the order of their immediate effectiveness. Rearrange them in order of their more lasting effects.

· 10 ·　　　　　Adolescence

Judging from the attention the adolescent receives, there can be little doubt that many Americans believe that there is "something wrong" with present-day youth. Parents of teenagers exchange knowing glances, shake their heads in despair, and try to convince one another that sooner or later their offspring will pass through this "stage." Some are not really convinced and seriously question whether the youth of today will ever become responsible and mature members of society. Whatever their specific reaction, many adults are aware that adolescence is a period of strain, for themselves as well as for their children.

Probably the chief value clash which gives rise to what is called "the adolescent problem" is between the vested interests of adults and the vested interests of adolescents. From the point of view of the adolescent, he is an adult. In a gadget-infested culture his adultness is clearly manifest to him, since he can do such things as drive an auto, even "soup it up" into "a hot rod" with frequently more success than can his father. Sexually he is grown up too, with a whole new world of adult-forbidden fulfillments before him. The adolescent wants to prove his "adulthood" by any and all devices available to him. It does not seem unreasonable to him to want to do so, and he champs at the bit when older adults admonish him to "grow up first," to "be a little more patient," to "get some more experience," and "not to be impulsive." The adolescent is in a real sense the sociological version of being "all dressed up with no place to go."

The older adult, on the other hand, sees the adolescent as an irresponsible, not yet *really* mature human being who shows great promise, if he will only stay childlike for a little longer,.

that is, if he will not do adult things or think in adult ways. It is entirely possible, moreover, that some of the superior skills of adolescents may threaten the superiority of older adults, more even than it is easy to admit. If adolescents can only be kept "acting their age" a little longer, there may be more comfort for the status-threatened adult.

Thus the basic viewpoint from which we shall attempt to see the problem of the adolescent is one of neutrality—of stepping aside and trying to understand what, characteristically, the adolescent wants and needs in terms of *his* personality, over against what the older adult wants and needs in terms of *his* personality and social position. Not very many people are capable of this kind of detached objectivity because they have become so ego-involved in *being* an adolescent or an older adult and therefore in *seeing* the social world largely, if not solely, from one age-status position. It is not so much that either adolescents or older adults do not *wish* to see the problems from the point of view of the other group, but rather that they find it almost impossible to free themselves sufficiently from themselves, and from their age-group concepts of the world, to permit more than an occasional glimpse into how the other conceives of reality. In this chapter we shall attempt, nevertheless, to do precisely that—to assay the value perspectives of adolescents and adults with a view better to understand what each group wants and needs and to evaluate the proposals for accomplishing a better liaison between the two.

▶ SOME PRELIMINARY CONSIDERATIONS

Biological v. sociological maturity. The term "adolescent" is frequently used in such a way as to make it appear to be synonymous with the biological term "puberty." A sharper distinction should be consistently held to. *Puberty* is a biological term and refers simply to that stage in the development of a person after which he *seems* to have become an adult in the sense that his sexual characteristics appear mature. Most humans, however, are sterile during the first two years or so of puberty. The organism, moreover, is not mature at puberty in that growth is not yet complete and physical vigor has not reached its apex. *Adolescence*, on the other hand, is a social status in which the human being finds himself just prior to being admitted into the society as a full-fledged adult member with all of the responsibilities and privileges which adults normally have. *Adolescence and puberty may coincide in time, or either may follow the other, depending upon the culture in which the person is reared.* In a given culture, moreover, little allowance is usually made for the fact that different persons attain puberty at different times, and adults tend to treat all of the young alike, as if they became pubertal at the same age. This means that prepubertal children may be treated as adolescents and postpubertal children as preadolescents. Needless to say, this may seriously aggravate for many children the problems of growing up.

An intercultural view of adolescence. In different societies adolescence (*a*) comes at markedly different times, (*b*) has markedly different duration, varying from an almost insignificant period to eight or ten years, and (*c*) is accompanied by unequal amounts of trauma or shock or difficulty.

In many primitive societies, for example, a person simply becomes an adult with the onset of puberty, although usually puberty is marked as a distinct period and is often accompanied by rites and ceremonies which publicly proclaim the fact that the boy or girl has become a man or a woman. Sometimes this period of transition comes immediately at the time of puberty and sometimes somewhat later. Being a sociological rather than a biological state, of course, considerable leeway is allowed, depending largely on the values of the culture in question.

In some societies adolescence is a very brief status. It may consist merely of a short, public ceremony. At the other extreme, adolescence stretches out over a period of eight or ten years. In our own society the average child becomes pubertal at between ten and thirteen years but is not considered an adult, for many purposes, until during the early twenties.

Most importantly of all, a cross-cultural view of adolescence reveals clearly that both the kinds and the amounts of shock or social disturbance which are supposed to accompany adolescence are highly variant. *In some societies adolescent trauma is practically nonexistent.* When children become adults they simply take on adult responsibilities, without fuss and turmoil and all of the many manifestations which adolescence so often has in American society.

We are forced, then, to the conclusion that adolescence becomes a problem in American society because we make it a problem. This does not mean, of course, that we contrive with diabolical sadism to invoke the scourge of adolescence upon our children. Rather, we have built the kind of society, with the kind of values, material culture, and moral concepts which make adolescent trauma a by-product of modern living. *If*, for example, we did not have automobiles, and *if* we characteristically allowed children to go to work at full employment at any age at which they wished, and *if* we allowed "teen-agers" to marry whenever they thought they had found the correct mate, *then* we would be without many of the characteristic problems which bring adolescent turmoil to plague both the adolescents and their elders. It is not meant to imply that we ought to make such changes in our present culture; we are simply stressing the fact that, *given* our particular value system and material culture, it is more or less inevitable that we have the problems between youth and age which we usually do.

Conditions conducive to adolescent trauma.   It is not necessary to restrict ourselves to vague generalizations concerning the conditions in our culture which contribute to making adolescence a period of "storm and strife." In any scientific treatment of the values of American society the cultural sore spots, as far as adolescent difficulty is concerned, are readily apparent. Some of these, as a matter of fact, were isolated some twenty-five years ago by the anthropologist Margaret Mead following her studies of adolescence in various societies.[1] The following are among the more significant features of our culture largely responsible for adolescence constituting the kind of problem it does.

The extent of cultural alternatives. In small, relatively homogeneous societies the "choices" available to a person embarking on adulthood are relatively limited. The paths that can be traversed are few, and the signposts are clearly marked. In our own and other "mass societies," by contrast, the adolescent finds himself confronted with a bewildering array of alternatives. The sheer volume of educational, occupational, economic, moral, and other choices is staggering. The present-day *Occupational Dictionary*, for example, lists over 20,000 job titles. Realistically, these do not represent true choices for every youth, but certainly the task of choosing and preparing for one's life's work is more complicated than it was less than a hundred years ago when it was estimated that there were but several hundred different occupations. And so it is for choices in other areas. Caught up in the swollen stream of cultural alternatives, with its frequent crosscurrents, it is not surprising to find numerous adolescents consciously or otherwise "giving up" in their struggle to make decisions.

Lack of rationale for decision-making. It is somewhat paradoxical that a culture replete with alternatives is found wanting in the preparation for choosing among them. We force the child to make moral choices for which he is unprepared. We stress the importance of "right" and "wrong" and yet can provide no really satisfactory rationale for what acts are clearly to be regarded as right and wrong. What is even worse, we teach the child, more perhaps by example than by formal instruction, that certain things are wrong, but yet we, the adults, do those same things, either characteristically or under certain extenuating circumstances. Smoking, drinking, and sexual behavior illustrate this moral category well. Adults who smoke and drink

[1] See, especially, her "Adolescence in Primitive and Modern Society," in *The New Generation*, ed. by V. F. Calverton and S. D. Schmalhausen, New York, Macaulay Co., 1930.

tell adolescents that they should not smoke and drink "because it is not good for you." "Is it good for you?" asks the adolescent. The adult has no satisfactory answer because there is none. Moreover, in the sexual realm the adolescent is overstimulated by a culture which places emphasis on sexual matters, manifesting this sexual preoccupation with such farfetched evidences as advertising soft drinks with pictures of near nudes in highly suggestive poses, meanwhile pouring forth from radios, television and "juke boxes" a plethora of productions with almost exclusively romantic, if not downright sexual, themes. In this panorama of taboo and indulgence, of inconsistent preachment and example, the adolescent is supposed to make moral choices with greater discretion than his parents!

Negative conditioning.   Not only do we require the adolescent to make decisions for which he is not prepared—and for which many adults are not either—we actually *unfit* him for wise choices during the adolescent period. Again, we do not do this consciously, and certainly not with the desire to make life difficult for him. But regardless of our intentions, the consequences are the same. In no area of life is this more true than in the area of sex. Here the characteristic adult mode of handling the "problem" is a combination of withholding pertinent information from the child for as long as possible, and then, when procrastination is no longer expedient, of presenting him with a pattern of fears and phobias which are designed to keep him "pure," but which are more likely to make him neurotic. In this atmosphere of too little information coming too late and distorted by instilled fears, the adolescent is expected by righteous adults to make wise decisions in sexual matters and is condemned brutally when he fails.

Emphasis on "peer competition."   From the time the child enters school, great stress is placed upon competition, and high standing is attached to being successful in competition with those of older age levels. From the time that "mama" takes great pride in the fact that "Junior, only two, wears suits sized 3½!" until the same mother boasts that Junior has "graduated from college, the *youngest* member of his class," he is almost constantly subjected to competition that drives him to be like someone older than he. Then, when Junior wishes to reap the rewards of his successful emulation of older persons, he is promptly told that he is too young for them. Seen in this way, the so-called adolescent rebellion is not difficult to understand.

Impersonal social relationships.   As we have shifted from a predominantly rural to a predominantly urban society, there has been a decline in the personal, face-to-face, type of social relationship. The social control previously exerted by almost daily association with members of a tightly knit primary group is not felt to the same degree in the more fleeting contacts with secondary-group members. Modern urban living readily allows the average adolescent to escape from the watchful eye of parent and sibling, church and neighbor. Where he goes and what he does no one knows—and shortly no one really cares.

The role of material culture.   Our material culture, that is the objects or "things" that we have created, has contributed its share of hazard and confusion to adolescence. As accident statistics indicate, an automobile in the hands of an adolescent is a 200 percent more lethal device than when it is in the hands of an adult over thirty-five. This is not opinion, it is sheer statistical fact. In other less dramatic ways the automobile multiplies adolescent problems. The automobile parked a few blocks or a few miles from home may be used almost as effectively for a boudoir as for a vehicle of transportation. While certainly sex was invented before the automobile, and equally obviously morality did not end with it, it is no less true that the anonymity and intimacy fostered by the modern automobile are contributing factors in the difficulties which many adolescents have in working out a code of sexual conduct which will give them a maximum of long-term life fulfillment.

Adolescent trauma begins early.   It cannot be stressed too forcibly that much of the adolescent's difficulty, hostility toward parents, maladjustment in school, mental-health problems, and the like, does not *originate* with adolescence. These symptoms are merely more *conspicuously* manifest at that time. There is much comment, for example, concerning "adolescent rebellion," which term usually refers to the fact that very often during adolescence children rebel against their parents and other authority and give other evidence of their refusal to act as they are expected to. What is frequently overlooked is that such behavior is the *end product* of all of the child-rearing practices to which the child has been subjected. If parental disciplining is inconsistent, if parents are not honest in answering children's questions about sex, if the parents' own moral conduct is not consistent with their moral preachment, an intelligent adolescent can hardly be expected either to rely on his parents' advice or to feel too kindly toward them when they attempt to force it on him. This is not to be taken as a categorical assertion that adolescents are always blameless or that all adolescent irresponsibility is to be tossed like a dead cat on the doorstep of parents. Obviously, in individual cases other circumstances besides child-rearing practices operate. But taking the society *as a whole*, the evidence is clear that much of the tempest in the adolescent experience is the consequence of the accumulation of little whirlwinds of parental ineptitude.

Nor can it be stressed too forcibly that we are not here speaking of the *individual* parent and his *individual* offspring. This is a *societal* problem, rather than an individual one. Some particular parents, for example, may rear their children with wisdom and empathy, only to find their best efforts defeated because their child has come under the influence of other children who were not so fortunate in their parental influence, but who serve thereafter as a sort of emotional contamination. In other words, this is a *social* problem and cannot be solved solely, even somewhat effectively, by the individual parent working alone, as if he lived in a vacuum. *How other people rear their children can be a decisive factor in the eventual outcome for one's own.* Long ago we learned this lesson with respect to contagious-disease control—the same principle holds for the mental hygiene of adolescence.

▶ INDICES OF ADOLESCENT DIFFICULTY

The purpose of this section is to bring together some of the lines of evidence now available which demonstrate either the nature of typical adolescent difficulty in our society or the extent to which these difficulties exist. It must be admitted at the outset that for many of the most serious adolescent difficulties, notably those in the realm of mental hygiene, there are no clear or convincing statistics of the true extent of difficulties. If a child does not commit a delinquency which results in his getting caught (and very, very few ever get caught), if he avoids failure or major disciplinary action in school or court martial in the army, or if he is not cornered somewhere by an ambitious researcher who pries into his private life,[2] the torments of his adolescence go unrecorded and unknown. Certainly one is no alarmist if he points out that for every school failure that is recorded there must be many near-failures and many who find the going very, very painful. For every child who commits a delinquent act and gets caught there must be many more who suffer considerable indecision, conscience trouble, and other emotional discomfort, caught as they are in the same crosscurrents of cultural inconsistency as is the technical delinquent. Realizing, then, that only the more extreme and more dramatic instances become matters of record, it may be useful to look at the record for more tangible evidence of the difficulty of the adolescent period in American society.

Delinquency. It is very difficult to be objective about delinquency. No one knows what a "normal rate" of delinquency in a city is, and from at least one point of view, even one delinquent act is a tragedy which should have been prevented. Those persons, however, who are responsible professionally for juvenile delinquency are not primarily concerned with official delinquent acts which result in apprehension by the police and jurisdiction by the juvenile court. Numerous as such cases are, and serious as are the consequences, everyone but the very naïve person real-

[2] See Chapter 7 on Mental Health.

izes that such cases are but a negligible proportion of the actual number of adolescents who have made moral choices contrary to the expected code. Moreover, even among the apprehended delinquent, recidivism is very high, even under conditions of expert guidance by probation officers and other juvenile-court personnel. Substantial numbers of juvenile offenders do not regard their criminal acts as wrong, and even when they do, they often find it impossible to avoid repetitions, even soon after the first act.

It is sometimes alleged that there has been a long-time rise in the rate of juvenile delinquency in the United States. This may or may not be true. Statistics are practically meaningless because (1) so many delinquent acts do not result in arrest, (2) rises and falls in delinquency rates reflect more the changes in law-enforcement policy than they do changes in the actual behavior of juveniles. This is not to say that it is not *possible* that there may have been a long-time increase in juvenile behavior contrary to the law, but simply that evidence of such is largely lacking.[3]

School failures.   By "school failures" are meant not merely those persons who fail to maintain minimal standards of academic achievement, but rather the much larger group of adolescents who remain in school, but for whom the school experience is a continuously frustrating one, or one which does not provide for them the degree of satisfaction and growth in experience which it could and should. It is customary for many superficial adults to jump hastily to the conclusion that it is the adolescent's fault if he fails to "get enough out of" his school experience. Just what is meant by that is not always clear, but the implication apparently is that the school is a sort of reservoir of goodness from which a good child drinks long and heartily and the wayward or willful or "problem" child refuses to drink at all. What is overlooked in such a conception of the matter is that not all of the responsibility rests with the adolescent. To return to our

---

[3] For a discussion of the difficulties involved in computing crime rates see Chapter 8.

figure of speech, if the water supply is contaminated, it may be a sign of good judgment rather than poor judgment if one refuses to drink. Many of our more penetrating students of education have come to the conclusion that the phrase "failure *of* the *school*" to interest the adolescent is a more accurate way of putting it than is the more familiar "failure *of* the *adolescent*" to be interested in school. In many schools the curriculum content, the teaching skills of the staff, and the whole concept of child development is so foreign to what we know scientifically about the needs of adolescents that "failure of the school" rather than "failure of the adolescent" seems a more accurate way of stating the case.

Morals. The tendency of adults to decry the morals of youth is older than Methuselah. Each generation seems to torture itself with the "certain" knowledge that its youth is going to the dogs! Careful research on moral conduct is not as abundant as one might expect in a scientifically minded nation. Moreover, "morals" is a slippery concept to manipulate. It means different things to different people, and different things to the same person in various contexts. To many persons "morals" is synonymous with sexual conduct. Just why a breach of conduct in the sexual area should be more serious or important than a breach of conduct in business dealings is not wholly clear. Many students of adolescent behavior feel there has been a far greater revolution in moral precepts in the realm of business ethics than in sexual ones.

Moreover, phrases like "moral degeneracy" are frequently misleading, because they imply a static concept of moral conduct. Many people in our society and in others adhere to a static concept of moral conduct, accepting the idea that a given behavior is right or wrong *per se*, and that it makes no difference *when* the behaving is done. To such persons it is futile to argue that it once was wrong for a woman to smoke or wear shorts in public, but that it is not so today. To them, morals are morals, and they go on forever unchanged and unchangeable. History, however, has it otherwise. It records a continuously changing concept of right and wrong in every society that has a written history, and a great variation in moral conduct among societies at any one time. Thus many of the "immoral" acts of adolescents as seen by older adults may be the "moral" acts of the next generation. This is evidenced most vividly in the recent history of women's conduct, although it could be illustrated in many other ways as well.

Insofar as there have been careful studies of the sexual morality of persons of different ages, notably those of Alfred Kinsey and his staff, the differences alleged between present-day adolescents and their elders do not show up. Kinsey's research fails to show that there is any marked difference in the sexual conduct of American adolescent males, their fathers, and their grandfathers. Much of our so-called moral revolution may lie in the realm of conscience and tolerance rather than in overt action. Adolescents today may talk more freely about sexual matters and judge violators of the expected codes less severely than they used to. Moreover, there appears to be a greater freedom to experiment with erotic satisfactions short of coitus than there was in the past, and a greater casualness with respect to the identity of the partner. Whether such acts and such judgments are immoral or not would seem to depend largely upon the point of view of the evaluator. That is why it is difficult to say whether the freer conduct of adolescents in this area of life constitutes immorality or not.

A sociological sage once wrote, "The imaginations which people have of one another are the solid facts" of human life. In this frame of reference the frequent adult charge that adolescents are immoral is both real and important. It is real in that adults base their judgments of adolescents and their efforts to control adolescents on the supposition of juvenile immorality. Whether that assumption is right or wrong, they act and talk as if it were correct, and for practical purposes, therefore, it might almost as well be. In a second sense, the adolescent-immorality charge may be socially significant, namely, in its effect upon the adolescent. There is an adage that "one may as well have the game, since one has the name." Just how far such a realization may influence present-day adolescents is of course not known, but it would not be surprising if it had some influence, nor if that influence were in the direction of encouraging some adolescents at least to take greater liberties with the traditional code than they otherwise would.

Economic frustration. Theoretically, an adolescent in America may choose, after he has fulfilled the minimum compulsory school attendance, whether he shall go on to college or go to work. Whichever role he chooses, there are many more impediments in his path than are ordinarily recognized. If he chooses "to go on to college and make something of himself," he may encounter any one or more, or possibly even all, of the following serious hurdles: (1) He and his parents may not have the money necessary to enable him to go to college. (2) If he belongs to certain minority groups, he may find himself excluded categorically or by a "quota system" from some or all of the colleges he wishes to attend. (3) He may find, after admission to college, that his skills, abilities, temperament, intelligence, or what not, may not be suited to the requirements of the school or the profession he has chosen. (4) He may find that his desire to get married, or the fact that he is already married, interferes with his attending school. (5) Even after the successful completion of four or more years of study he may find that he is still expected to "start at the bottom" in his chosen career at a salary that suggests still further postponement of marriage. A moment's reflection will indicate that these hazards are by no means to be minimized. The adolescent who wishes to attend noncollegiate training schools faces the same type of problems, but not, perhaps, to so sharp a degree.

If, however, the adolescent chooses not to go to school, he encounters serious difficulties too: (1) Even in times of relatively full employment, he may discover that what he considers a "good job" is hard to find. A common complaint is that most of the better jobs require "experience," and this the fresh-from-high-school youth does not have. (2) The job he finally accepts and its pay may not be too much to his liking. There is almost certain to be disappointment when he realizes that being financially "on his own" means that, for some time at least, he may have a lower standard of living than he had while living with his parents. (3)

He will shortly, probably, wish to get married. Wage rates for unskilled workers of comparative inexperience do not conduce to marriage. Even with husband and wife both working, frustrations are numerous. With or without children the couple's standard of living cannot be very high. Advertisements for "dream homes," new automobiles, and northland vacations leave an understandably bad taste. (4) Not infrequently there is some "unfinished business" with parents, relatives, and friends who may have expected the young man to further his education, there being a widespread American ideal that a young man ought to start out at a somewhat better job than his father had. Parents and friends frequently let it be known, in rather more than subtle ways, that he is something of a disappointment!

Thus, whether he chooses the narrow and somewhat demanding path of higher education or the somewhat less exciting path of early and romantic "independence," the adolescent finds the adult world difficult to "crack." Perhaps that is why he finds it necessary to "zoom" in and out of the lines of traffic with his "hot-rod jalopy," just to show his middle-aged elders in their shiny cars that he can do *something* conspicuously!

▶ PROPOSED SOLUTIONS

Everyone, it seems, has a solution for the adolescent problem. These solutions vary markedly in their approach, their basic assumptions, their feasibility, and certainly in their comprehension of the problem. Loosely classified, they seem to fall into two main categories: (1) repressive measures, and (2) constructive measures. A brief consideration of each type will enable almost anyone to supply further illustrations based upon his own observations of persons and communities with which he is familiar.

Repressive measures. "Now, when I was a boy, parents got tough with kids. When I was seventeen, my father and I made a trip to the woodshed. . . ." Anyone can finish the sentence. So usually begins the "get-tough" orator. The supposition here is that there are adolescent problems because adolescents willfully refuse to follow what adults know to be appropriate courses of action, which, if followed, would solve all of the adolescents' problems. The trouble, as these persons see it, is that adolescents are willfully disobedient or heedless. Consequently, the correct course of action is to get tough with them. A student on a campus of 20,000 is involved in a traffic accident, and immediately the "get-tough" advocates wish to deny all students the right to drive cars! Juvenile delinquency authorities who try to solve personality difficulties by removing the causes are constantly subjected to ridicule for being "too easy" and "soft." The local newspaper plays up some juvenile delinquency, and the town fathers are barraged with petitions to invoke curfews requiring all persons under eighteen to be "off the streets" by 10:00 P.M.! Parents are admonished to make their children work harder, but no one knows how to *find* work enough in a five-room apartment for the mothers, much less for the children. And so on and on. What all of these measures have in common is a rather transparent disregard for (*a*) the need to examine the *causes* of the difficulty, and (*b*) the fact that times have changed and that, therefore, measures presumably appropriate to another era may no longer be appropriate to this one. The chief sociological significance of the "get-tough" policy is its nuisance value to the advocates of careful analysis of the problem and of intelligent effort to solve the problem in accordance with reality.

Constructive measures. Under this caption are subsumed a number of widely variant proposals which have one basic and important attribute in common, namely: they seek to reduce some problem for the adolescent either by removing the cause or by in some way counterbalancing it. Some of these proposals are undoubtedly more effective or more feasible than others, but this attribute of rational attack is the common ingredient.

Improved parent education. As we have seen earlier in this chapter, adolescent problems are largely mental hygiene problems and, as such, go back to the child-rearing practices of the adolescent's parents. It is important, therefore, that parents learn how and why the consequences of their child-rearing techniques do not show up today or tomorrow, but ten or twenty years

from now. For example, it might solve today's disciplinary problem with Billy to compare Billy unfavorably with his older
brother Jack, but if such disciplinary techniques create sibling
rivalry in Billy, we may develop an adolescent who hates both
his brother and his parents and is not too much at peace with
anybody. This is undoubtedly an oversimplified illustration, but
it is accurate as far as it goes, and typifies the point we are discussing. A very important part of this parental education should
consist in teaching parents the necessity of not pushing children
beyond their own real abilities and desires, because to do so is
to aggravate adolescent turmoil.

Educational reform. There is great need for a more realistic
approach in American education. Generally speaking the school
system is an unrealistic system predicated on concepts of adolescence, of how learning takes place, and of ways to teach morality
which are hopelessly out of line with our scientific knowledge
about these things. Generally speaking, professional educators
are aware of this but cannot institute reforms as rapidly as they
would like for fear of incurring community disapproval. Regardless of the reason, however, the fact remains that we can do much
better in implementing sound and realistic educational philosophies than we now do. The result would be a lessening of school
failures, fewer "dropouts" in high school and college, less unhappiness about school work, and surely an improved mental hygiene
in general.

Free education. It has been revealed by almost every relevant study that has been made that numerous persons of talent
are prevented from furthering their education because of inadequate funds. Not very many unskilled workers' families could
afford to send a promising son to college, even if assured of his
exceptional competency. It was recommended to the President
by the Commission on Higher Education that there should be
made available, on a competitive basis, a considerable number of
scholarships at federal expense to insure the education of capable
young men and women in the lower-income groups. The so-
called G.I. educational program demonstrated that there are
many persons of talent who wish to and can successfully attend

college. The argument runs that they should be encouraged to do so, not only in their own interests but for the good of the nation as a whole.

Improved community recreation. Adolescents, like adults, frequently have time on their hands. They have no desire, as a rule, to use it in antisocial or harmful ways, but they may do so because there is often no real alternative. Commercialized recreation does not fully meet the need, partly because of cost, but more importantly because it does not create, as a rule, sufficiently consuming and enduring interests. Accordingly, it is often argued that communities should provide extensive year-round public recreation for adolescents. While the total cost of such a program seems impressive, the per-capita cost to the taxpayer is very low. Parks, playgrounds, athletic leagues, swimming pools, hobby clubs—the list is almost endless. Not only do such activities use up available recreational time and superabundant physical energies, but participation in them creates and cultivates recreational skills which may be useful and pleasurable over the years.

Other kinds of constructive proposals have been made. We have singled out these four as being fundamental, widespread, and typical of the approach.

▶ ADOLESCENT PROBLEMS GENERIC TO THE SOCIETY

In separating the problem of the adolescent from the rest of the social problems of our time, we have of course committed a certain violation of reality. Most, if not all, of the adolescent's problems are present in the larger society and are only *reflected in* the adolescent. Problems of job frustration, bad mental health, and delinquent conduct are certainly not unique with the adolescent. They may even be less prevalent among adolescents than among adults, and may only be brought to a focus in adolescence because of our sharper scrutiny and stricter control of the young. Other problems, like the failure of the school to inspire a larger proportion of adolescents, are really not adolescent problems at all. They represent the failure of the society to do an effective job in rearing its own young. To be sure, the adolescent bears the brunt of adult ineptitude here as elsewhere, but this should not obscure the fact that the root cause is societal, not individual. It has been suggested that what we call "adolescent problems" are merely the outward sign of an unhealthy and inefficient society so far as rearing its young is concerned, that the troubled adolescent is the symptom, not the disease.

▶ SUMMARY

In the problem of the adolescent we find a cardinal expression of the sociological principle that a refusal to be realistic aggravates a social problem. Another way of saying this is that when values are predicated upon inaccurate and unrealistic assumptions, programs based on those values either fail to solve the problem or make it worse.

The foregoing paragraph may seem to oversimplify the adolescent problem. If we left the matter at that, it would, but we hasten to add that there is a second aspect which may be even more important. Numerous observers have pointed out that ours is a society trying to "face both ways," that is, that we face choices which we will not make or cannot make. The alternatives may be dilemmas such as the following. We know the hazards of child labor, so we have abolished it. We now have the hazard of enforced adolescent idleness, especially among the lower-class adolescents. Who can prove which is worse? The dilemma is even more pronounced in the case of sex. We are aware of the hazards of early marriage, but what of the hazards of delayed marriage? Who can say in which course of action, fostering early marriage or delaying marriage, the greater social good lies? And, even if we can decide objectively, can we translate our decision into effective action, and are we prepared for the consequences of our decision? Both appear doubtful.

Dilemmas also appear with respect to philosophies of solution. We have pointed out that the "get-tough" philosophy breeds resentment, hostility, or further alienation from adults and from the values which adults are fostering. But a "get-soft" policy could conceivably be worse. What we have called "constructive" solutions sound good in theory, but may have practical consequences in fact which may render them impractical. Values are in great chaos: adolescents' needs versus archaic adult conceptions, adults of varying philosophy and familiarity with the problem working at cross-purposes. Meanwhile the problem persists.

SUGGESTED READINGS

Barron, Milton L., *The Juvenile in Delinquent Society*, New York, Alfred A. Knopf, 1954. Chapter 12 presents a vivid account of the values and value conflicts faced by adolescents in our society. Emphasis is on the cultural values that motivate delinquents and nondelinquents.

Baruch, Dorothy W., *How to Live with Your Teen-Ager*, New York, McGraw-Hill Book Co., 1953. Although primarily written for parents, this book will nevertheless provide insight into the nature of adolescence and problems of this period of life. Clear, forceful, and objective.

Duvall, Evelyn M., "Community Codes by Common Consent," *National Parent Teacher*, Vol. 49 (December 1954), pp. 8-10. A brief but interesting account of what different communities have done to enable parents and adolescents to "get together" on expected behavior.

Havighurst, Robert J., and others, *A Community Youth Development Program*, Supplementary Educational Monograph No. 75, Chicago, The University of Chicago Press, 1952. A university research group teamed with community agencies initiates a ten-year study to screen all children of a certain age and to treat any cases of personal or social maladjustment. Although results will not be in for some years, this report summarizes the ambitious plan. Useful as an illustration of constructive, preventative youth programs.

Hollingshead, August B., *Elmtown's Youth*, New York, John Wiley and Sons, 1949. A thought-provoking study of the impact of social class on the lives of adolescents. Part III, "The High School Students" and Part IV, "The Out-of-School Adolescent" provide excellent case material on the behavior, problems, and frustrations of adolescents.

Strain, Frances B., *But You Don't Understand*, New York, Appleton-Century-Crofts, 1950. Twelve case histories of adolescents written from the point of view of the youth experiencing the difficulty. A sympathetic and insightful portrayal of the sometimes wide gulf that separates adolescents and their parents.

STUDY QUESTIONS

1. What are the essential differences between puberty and adolescence? In a given culture, why is it that puberty and adolescence do not necessarily coincide in time?

2. Of what value is it to study adolescence in various societies? What are some of the conclusions that have been reached regarding adolescence as a result of such cross-cultural studies?

3. State the six features of present-day American society which are said to be largely responsible for adolescence constituting the kind of problem it does. Can you think of any other characteristics of our society that contribute to making adolescence a period of "storm and strife"?

4. Give an example, other than that used in the text, of how the material culture of American society has contributed to the confusion of adolescence.

5. How do you account for the fact that adolescence is not a period of trauma for all young people in our society?

6. In what sense is the extent of juvenile delinquency a fairly good index of adolescent difficulty? In what sense is it misleading?

7. What is the evidence concerning the alleged lower sexual morals of present-day adolescents? How do the values of our society make it difficult to prove or disprove the assertion?

8. What possible frustrations does the adolescent who does not continue his education face? Show the value conflicts that could arise in the larger society from a program designed to minimize one of these frustrations.

9. What are the chief difficulties with repressive measures for dealing with the "adolescent problem"? Can you think of ways in which such measures could encourage the type of behavior they purport to discourage?

10. Name three constructive measures for combatting adolescent problems and indicate the value conflicts that prevent the full incorporation of such measures in our society.

· *11* · Pressure Groups

To a people who have been called a nation of joiners it is scarcely necessary to point out that their society contains numerous and varied special-interest groups. Many Americans are aware, too, that there are thousands of special-interest groups that have as one of their avowed aims the attempt to impose their policies on the larger society. Organizations so engaged in the competitive struggle for power are called pressure groups. If everyone had the same interests and held them with equal intensity there would scarcely be a need for special groups to exert "pressures" in behalf of these interests. Thus, the existence of pressure groups represents the crystallization of value conflict; to ignore such groups and their activities would be to ignore some of the noisiest, if not the most severe, value clashes in American society. In addition to the value conflict manifested by the divergent interests of pressure groups, there is some evidence of a clash of values concerning the *fact* of pressure groups. That is, regardless of why or what they are "pressuring," some hold that such groups are not only unnecessary but downright "dangerous." Others see pressure groups as completely compatible with democracy and indeed part of the "American way" of getting things done. But it seems that not everyone on either "side" of the issue fully understands the nature and workings of pressure groups. In this chapter, then, we will take a look at the activities and operations of pressure groups and investigate some of the major groups in existence today. We will then be in a position to evaluate the extent to which such activities constitute a "problem."

▶ THE NATURE OF PRESSURE GROUPS

We have said that a pressure group can be defined as an organization engaged in the struggle for the control of power. Pressure groups work to protect or to further the interests and privileges of *certain* people. Frequently the "certain people" are a specific segment of the population with similar economic or occupational interests. But pressure groups also have been formed to protect or further a host of values other than strictly economic ones. Some examples of such groups that immediately come to mind are the Anti-Saloon League, the Anti-Vivisection Society, and the Council on Christian Social Progress.

Scope of pressure group activities.   Pressure groups vary, too, with regard to their scope and power. The "big" groups like the National Association of Manufacturers and the American Medical Association are fairly well known, but the majority of pressure groups are far more limited in scope. The activities of the Clothespin Manufacturers of America or the Committee Against Discrimination on Small Catalog Postage Rates are relatively specific and restricted. Occasionally pressure groups are at least purportedly organized in the interests of the whole citizenry. The American Civil Liberties Union is an example of this type of pressure group, for it "pressures" for the defense and advancement of the civil rights of all citizens.

Growth of pressure groups.   The federal Regulation of Lobbying Act of 1946 requires the registration of all organizations collecting money to be used to influence legislation by Congress.[1] Any individual paid to influence legislation must also register and must state his employer and his purpose. The resulting list of paid lobbyists becomes a matter of public record. Despite this convenient catalog of lobbyists, we still do not know how many pressure groups exist in our society. There are several reasons for this. In the first place, a pressure group could operate without a Washington lobby; it could attempt to promote its interests

[1] For the text of the Lobbying Act see Franklin L. Burdette, *Lobbyists in Action*, Manassas, Va., National Capitol Publishers, 1950, appendix.

solely through other channels, such as by attempting to mold opinion through mass-media advertising. In the second place, the existing law has sufficient "loopholes" to allow an estimated 75 percent of paid lobbyists to remain unregistered without fear of reprisals. Presumably many such lobbyists represent real pressure groups.

Judging from their increasing numbers, there is some justification for the belief that pressure groups are fast becoming the third house of Congress. Today over 500 organizations have registered under the Lobbying Act. This represents an increase of one third over 1941 and is more than double the number of pressure groups thought to be in existence twenty-five years ago.[2]

More important than sheer numbers, however, is the amount and extent of influence exerted by pressure groups. It is interesting that some of the most notorious victories of pressure groups involved an influential and vociferous minority influencing legislation that affected the country as a whole. The famous Yazoo land frauds of the early 1800's cost the taxpayers $8 million, the sum voted by Congress as compensation to a handful of land speculators. No less a personage than the Postmaster General acted as lobbyist for the claimants. Americans will long remember, too, the powerful influence of the Anti-Saloon League. Judging from the initial response to prohibition and its eventual repeal, the wishes of the majority of Americans were ignored or misconstrued on this issue.

Many more famous or infamous examples of influential pressure groups can be gleaned from history. There is some evidence, however, that pressure groups are becoming increasingly more influential. Literally millions of dollars are spent annually by pressure groups in their twofold task of shaping public opinion and directly influencing legislation. If we turn to an examina-

[2] Current data on lobbies taken from House of Representatives, House Select Committee on Lobbying Activities, *Lobby Index*, Washington, D. C., U. S. Government Printing Office, 1950. Data on lobbying activities in previous years cited in Donald C. Blaisdell, "Government Under Pressure," Public Affairs Pamphlet No. 67, New York, Public Affairs Committee, 1946.

tion of the "workings" of pressure groups, we shall gain a better idea of just how influential and important such groups have become.

▶ THE WORKINGS OF PRESSURE GROUPS

In order to impose their policies on the larger society, pressure groups operate in two general ways: (1) by attempting to influence and mold public opinion, and (2) by striving to influence government agencies, particularly the legislative branches. These channels are by no means completely separable. A public conditioned by the activities of a pressure group may itself elect legislators who hold the values it has been taught are "right." Again, a pressure group working to defeat a bill before Congress may attempt both to influence legislators directly and to "educate" the public who, in turn, may let their views be known to their representatives.

Influencing public opinion. Pressure groups cannot ignore public opinion. New laws can be "pressured through" or attempts at legislation can be blocked by frontal attacks upon legislators, but a sufficiently aroused public can undo both. In the long run, a pressure group is better off if it manages to mold public opinion to its liking. If it can sell an idea to the public, or arouse public opinion on an issue, or sometimes just create good will for its interests, the pressure group has a chance of making a stronger and more lasting impression on the American scene.

The specific techniques used to influence public opinion are many. Even a superficial survey of advertisements in magazines and newspapers shows that many are selling ideas rather than, or in addition to, products. An industrial organization may utilize a full newspaper page to explain its version of the "American way." A union may buy newspaper space to present "labor's side" of a current management-labor dispute. Pressure groups prepare pamphlets, books, and periodicals. They buy radio and television time, produce motion picture films, and issue speaker's guides. During one nine-month period, for example, the National

Association of Manufacturers produced over 800,000 copies of 45 pamphlets, booklets, leaflets, and the like.[3] The yearly advertising bill for this organization is reported as $2 million.[4] Labor and other organizations likewise mass produce literature in support of their values.

It is not always easy to recognize the source or sponsor of attempts at opinion molding. A pressure group may be organized as an educational foundation, thereby being exempt from federal taxes, and, in addition, it may publish with a certain anonymity or at least obscurity. Even if the name of the organization appears on the literature, the average citizen may not realize the intent of the organization, or the source of its support. For example, the major function of the Foundation for Economic Education was described by a Congressional committee investigating its activities as "the preparation of pamphlets, booklets, and articles presenting one side of public issues." [5] This foundation, which considers its functions as purely educational, receives the bulk of its support from "big business." It has published under such titles as *So You Believe in Rent Control?*, *The TVA Idea*, and *Illusions of Point Four*. An estimated total of 4 million booklets and pamphlets were distributed by the foundation during its first four years of operation. During this time it received about two thirds of its support from twenty large business organizations and the remainder chiefly from a number of other similar organizations. Although the foundation prints its name on its publications, it is unlikely that many of the message recipients recognize its sponsorship or are aware of the Buchanan Committee's conclusion that it consistently presents but one side of public issues. And this is but one example. It is doubtful that an impartial committee would judge many of the publications of the former CIO Political Action Committee as anything but one-sided. Sometimes the public fares even less well, for the message it reads or hears is apparently unsponsored. Some group is behind it, but which one?

[3] Cited in James MacGregor Burns and Jack Walter Peltsson, *Government By the People,* 2d ed., New York, Prentice-Hall, 1954, p. 282.
[4] *Ibid.*
[5] Reported in Karl Schriftgiesser, *The Lobbyists,* Boston, Little, Brown, and Co., 1951, p. 180.

Somebody has paid for it, but who? The simple fact is that educators, clergy, labor leaders, and millions of private citizens are almost constantly being exposed to the opinion-molding activities of pressure groups. Frequently, the sponsorship of the activities is obscure or unknown.

Political, legislative, and administrative pressures.   Many pressure groups do not restrict themselves to the shaping of public opinion but carry on activities more directly related to the influencing of actual legislation. If its policies are reflected in laws, the pressure group has come a long way in the struggle for power and influence. In their attempts at influencing legislation, pressure groups operate at various levels and employ a host of techniques.

Pressure groups and political parties.   Pressure groups do not usually form political parties with their own total platforms and their own slates of candidates. Rather, working through existing parties, they attempt to influence the party policies and to elect the "right" candidates. No political party can completely ignore the views of large organized pressure groups. Such groups are powerful and may be able to influence a sizable bloc of voters. Such groups also may make sizable financial contributions to the party. Party platform drafters sometimes find diametrically opposed pressure groups clamoring for their attentions. They can either "choose up sides," or, more likely, they can write their party policies with sufficient lack of lucidity to accomplish the well-known feat of fence straddling. But while party platform drafters may keep one ear tuned to the large but somewhat vague "public," it is politically expedient that the other give its attention to the vociferous minority represented by pressure groups.

If the pressure group fails to exert its influence at the platform-drafting stage, there is always the matter of elections. The pressure group does not usually endorse a particular party consistently or even all members of a party in a given election. The best pressure group is nonpartisan, or better, omnipartisan. Its work must continue regardless of the party in power. During a given election, however, a pressure group may well openly support one candidate and oppose another. Its force and skill in propaganda may be aimed at the outcome of an election. The pressure group's financial contribution to individual or party "war chests" can be important at this stage. Thus, by influencing party platforms and by helping to elect legislators and administrators who are friendly toward its interests, legislation unfavorable to pressure group interests can be prevented from ever making its appearance.

Maintenance of a lobby. The expression "lobby" obviously grew out of the name for a public waiting room where persons could meet and attempt to influence public officials. A lobby thus consists of those who attempt to bring pressure on public officials, particularly legislators. Lobbying is as old as legislation, it is legal, and it is big. We have already commented upon some of the influential lobbies of the past. These and their modern counterparts operate within the law, protected by the first amendment to the Constitution which provides that Congress shall make no law abridging the people's right to petition the government for a redress of grievances.

Lobbyists use various techniques in their attempts to assure the passage of legislation. It is well known that many of the bills introduced by members of Congress have been painstakingly prepared by the legal force of a lobby. When a bill reaches the committee stage, the lobbyist can often exert sufficient pressure to bring about a public hearing on the bill. If the hearing is granted, the lobbyists may arrive like a well-tutored and effective sales team. Hours of preparation allow the lobbyist to have on hand minute facts about the bill in question, the testimony of influential citizens, and perhaps the results of public opinion polls conducted at the expense of the lobby. The material is usually artfully presented and witnesses are strategically introduced. Lobbying is a big business; it is also something of an art and a science.

Pressure groups also maintain lobbies in Washington and state capitals to attempt to *prevent* passage of legislation contrary to their aims and purposes. The lobbying techniques may be similar to those employed when acting *for* passage of a bill. The lobby becomes thoroughly acquainted with the proposed measure and its legality and is prepared to exert pressures at various points to assure that the bill never becomes a law. The "tricks of the trade" are legion and many are apparently quite effective. Lobbies have instigated the timely arrival of thousands of messages from the legislator's own constituents demanding the defeat of a bill. What legislator can remain impervious to the opinions of his supporters even though it may have taken a strong pressure group to create or intensify the opinions?

Pressure at other points. If the battle to prevent the passage of inimical legislation, or to render it relatively ineffective by "crippling amendments," is lost, pressure groups by no means withdraw from the fight. Veto of the legislation by the administration can be sought, and, failing that, adequate appropriations for administering the new law can be prevented, and, failing that, pressure may be brought to bear for the appointment of administrators of the law who are friendly to the pressure group. Furthermore, the act may be repealed or rendered ineffective by later legislation. And, as a last resort, interpretations of the law may be made by the courts that reduce or remove its disagreeable characteristics.

▶ MAJOR UNITED STATES PRESSURE GROUPS

As indicated previously there are literally hundreds of pressure groups actively at work in the United States. The pressure groups we have selected for further analysis are important because taken together they frequently involve major value clashes, they collectively include a large number of people, and they are apparently quite powerful. These groups fall into three major divisions: (1) business, led by the National Association of Manufacturers and the Chamber of Commerce of the United States, (2) organized labor, major representatives of which are the combined Congress of Industrial Organizations and the American Federation of Labor, the United Mine Workers, and the railway brotherhoods, and (3) farmers, represented principally by the

National Grange, the American Farm Bureau Federation, and the National Farmers Union.

Business, the "American ruling class." Some four hundred national organizations have permanent representatives in Washington, and a preponderant number of these groups are directly or indirectly attached to general or specific business interests. Business pressure groups are of two types, principal and satellite. The former range from groups lobbying for interests that business enterprises hold in common (Chamber of Commerce and National Association of Manufacturers) down to specific business or industrial interests (Edison Electric Institute's lobby, National Coal Association, American Short Line Railroad Association, etc.). The satellite groups are many of the professional associations, revolving about business and partly dependent upon it for their support (American Bankers Association, American Pharmaceutical Association, American Bar Association, American Newspaper Publishers Association, etc.).

Although there have been and continue to be challenges, the business control of power has been such, at least since the Civil War, that many students believe business may be properly referred to as the "ruling class." Social critics hold that, since power has come to reside largely in the hands of business, most of its activities as a class, especially in its manifestations as a pressure group on government, have been to maintain that power.

Public "good will." Power rests ultimately upon public acceptance of it, and business has come more and more to realize the importance of a public opinion favorably disposed toward it. In a social environment traditionally hostile to monopolies, business has been able to achieve and maintain a tremendous accumulation of power and apparently to concentrate the control of this power into ever fewer hands. It is contended that through various propagandistic channels, both revealed and concealed, the public has been led to believe that general social welfare and business-class welfare are synonymous, that, in other words, the interests of society in general are identical with the interests of the business class.

Some support for this contention can be gained from a recent study of popular attitudes toward big business. The conclusions were based on a national sample of 1,227 adults representing a cross section of the American public.[6] Although everyone did not agree with all of its policies and actions, big business was found to have a good place in the public esteem. Fully three fourths of the people felt that, everything considered, the good effects of big business outweigh any bad effects. There was some discontent, however, with the amount of power and influence that big business has "on how things go in this country." [7] Unfortunately there are no strictly comparable earlier studies with which to compare this recent one; it is difficult to determine whether concern with the relative power of big business is increasing.

Legislative battles.   Any bills proposed for significantly extending the power of any other group, be it farmer, labor, government, the consumer, or the general public, arouse open or covert business opposition. When a group has obtained a position of overwhelming power in a society, its chief function inevitably becomes the protection of that power from either direct reduction or indirect reduction (through extension of more power relatively to other groups in the society).

As seen above, the main pressure of business has apparently been brought to bear against proposed legislation directly or indirectly limiting its power, but it has also sought to extend its power through positive legislation. The chief type of positive legislation successfully advocated has been the protective tariffs, which amount to an indirect subsidy. Some businesses, notably the shipping industry, have obtained direct governmental subsidy.

Advantages of business in the struggle for power.   As principally obstructors of legislation, however, business pressure groups have had a tremendous advantage over other class interests in their propagandistic and lobbying activities. Because of the human tendency to cling to the comforts of the customary, it is almost always easier to convince people of the undesirability,

[6] Burton R. Fisher and Stephen B. Withey, *Big Business as the People See It*, Ann Arbor, The Survey Research Center, University of Michigan, 1951.
[7] *Ibid.*, p. 27 ff.

rather than the desirability, of experimenting with new social patterns. The greater burden of proof tends to fall upon the proponent, not the opponent, of change. It is only when a people is close to desperation (as in the early days of the New Deal) that it is very receptive to tampering with the *status quo*.

Linked to this fundamental advantage of business is the equally important one of great financial resources. Not only is the bulk of the nation's wealth represented by business, but a very considerable percentage of the wealth is concentrated in a relatively few large corporations. Since in our society wealth and power are to a considerable extent inseparable, the amount of pressure that can be brought to bear upon the American people and their government by business in general and large corporations in particular is terrific. By no accident, business lobbies are the most consistently successful lobbies. We are reminded of the adage concerning the relationship between the ability to pay a piper and the privilege of calling tunes.

These two outstanding advantages of the business class can be successfully combated on specific issues only by an intensely and consistently aroused public opinion contrary to the position of business on these issues. It is rarely that such arousal of opinion occurs with sufficient intensity and staying power to combat the powers of business. So consistently, in fact, are the American people given propaganda friendly to business that nothing short of crises of the magnitude of a major economic depression or a war seems to bring about the passing of legislation fundamentally curtailing the control of power by the business class.

It is not here contended that business always uses its control of power in efforts that are contrary to the public welfare or that all legislation inimical to the interests of business is for the public good. Much proposed regulatory legislation is probably unworkable, and much more is undoubtedly suggested and undertaken without sufficient information in regard to the complicated problems and possible consequences involved. We have merely attempted to demonstrate that the *balance of power in pressure politics is heavily weighted in favor of the business class* and that this class pressures for its own interests, whether or not these interests are in harmony with the general welfare.

Business satellites. The pressure groups representing the professions have traditionally had two important roles, the first of which has been to gain control of the making and administering of laws vitally affecting their members and the second of which has been, to a large extent, the support of the interests of the business class in matters of public policy. The two most powerful professional pressure groups are the American Bar Association and the American Medical Association, and the policies of these two organizations have been almost without exception pro-business policies. A growing minority of physicians are indicating their disagreement with the AMA on some issues (such as compulsory health insurance), and a cleavage among lawyers gained official status with the organization of the more liberal National Lawyers Guild in opposition to the very conservative ABA. On the whole, however, physicians and lawyers, and the majority of the membership of the other main professions as well, have been, and apparently continue to be, largely identified with the business class.

Rise of organized labor. The greatest potential challenge to the business ruling class comes from organized labor. It is only very recently in our cultural history that any organization of labor as a class has been sufficiently effective to constitute a real threat to the concentration of control of power in the hands of business. There have been two main reasons for the historical ineffectiveness of labor organization. First, the control of government by business had been so complete and absolute prior to the 1930's that most attempts upon the part of labor to gain more control of power were efficiently smashed. Secondly, and still more important, the nongovernmental controls of business, especially in the use of propaganda, were so effectively wielded that, until very recently, a vast majority of labor has believed that its interests were synonymous with and well represented by the interests of the ruling class. Many working people did, and not a few still do, so identify their interests with those of the business class that they felt that the very organization of labor to bargain with management was "wrong," "un-American," and contrary to their welfare.

During the first century of our national history practically no legislation for the benefit of labor was even attempted by our government. After about a decade of agitation by labor groups, Congress finally, in 1884, created a Bureau of Labor in the Department of Interior. The function of this bureau was solely to gather information. Not until 1913 was a Department of Labor established with a head of Cabinet rank. At this time, to the information-gathering functions were added the directions to attempt to mediate labor disputes. No real power over either business or labor was given to this Conciliation Service.

As interpreted by the Supreme Court the Sherman Anti-Trust Act of 1890 had had, in many respects, a more restrictive effect on labor than on business, for the Court held that the Act applied to such concerted acts of workers as strikes and boycotts when designed to interfere with interstate commerce. An attempt by labor organizations through pressure on Congress to include in the Clayton Act of 1914 several provisions removing labor activities from the Sherman Anti-Trust Law was nullified by the Supreme Court. It was not until the Norris-La Guardia Anti-Injunction Act of 1932 that the federal courts were prohibited from issuing injunctions in labor disputes; contained in this Act was the first general statement by Congress that labor organization and collective bargaining are desirable.

Labor becomes "recognized." Not, then, until 1932 was labor officially recognized as having the right to organize and meet the business class as a theoretical equal in the struggle for control of power. The major economic depression that had begun in 1929 had reached a sufficient state of crisis by 1932 to create a public opinion in support of legislation that organized labor had long desired. In that year a majority of Congress and a President were elected on a platform which promised the enactment of legislation establishing old-age pensions and unemployment insurance and regulating wages and hours. The assumption of duties by this Congress and President Roosevelt in 1933 marked a major turning point in the attitude of government from a weak toleration to a program of positive assistance to organized labor.

The first legislative act of positive assistance to labor in guaranteeing its right to organize and to bargain collectively was Section 7A of the National Industrial Recovery Act of 1933. When NIRA was invalidated by the Supreme Court, the National Labor Relations Act was passed in 1935. This Act guarantees to employees "the right to self-organization, to form, join, or assist labor organizations, to bargain collectively through representatives of their own choosing, and to engage in concerted activities, for the purpose of collective bargaining or other mutual aid or protection." It also prohibits certain specified "unfair practices" on the part of employers which are calculated to prevent or discourage collective bargaining. The National Labor Relations Board was given semijudicial powers to decide when "unfair practices" interfering with collective bargaining were being used by employers and to determine the legitimate bargaining unit in an establishment.

The greater power equality which labor had achieved in its struggle with business under the National Labor Relations Act was somewhat reduced by the Labor-Management Act of 1947 (passed June 23, 1947, this Act is more popularly known as the Taft-Hartley Law). Although there is considerable difference of opinion regarding the amount of curtailment of labor's rights by the Taft-Hartley Law, all of the major unions have bitterly attacked the Act as a severe restriction on the rights of organized labor.

Labor's strengths and weaknesses. Although organized labor is in a position relatively weaker than that of business, it has won a number of victories through collective bargaining with industry. Labor's big continuing pressure battle is to maintain these gains. But it has a more positive program for which it has already begun to fight. Two of the principal aims of this program are guaranteed full employment and a guaranteed annual wage. For labor fully to achieve these aims and for it even to maintain its present position, it will be necessary for it to build further upon its strengths and to control its weaknesses.

Labor has an advantage in the sheer number of people who qualify for membership in its ranks. In addition, more and more workers are becoming "organized." The American Federation of Labor includes 9 million members, the Congress of Industrial Organizations about 6 million. Another million workers belong to the railway brotherhoods. But labor's potential strength is not realized because of the disunity within its ranks. Until recently, there was the major schism between the AF of L craft unions and the CIO industry-type unions. Then there are the thousands of local unions not affiliated with a national organization and there are the millions of workers who do not belong to a union. The remerger of the AF of L and the CIO has been in effect for so short a time that it is not yet possible to evaluate its success.

Even in its present position organized labor has sufficient power and wealth to conduct its own propaganda program and to maintain its own lobbies in Washington. Direct political action has been attempted through the Political Action Committee of the CIO and the Progressive Citizens of America, a national organization of supporters of similar liberal political policies. The various pressure groups within the ranks of labor can and do unite on major issues, but the potential influence of a fully organized and united labor group is so much greater still.

In addition to its lack of unity, there are several other factors which appear to have contributed to labor's failure to gain more control of power. First, there has been a lack of strong and effective pro-labor leadership in the White House. Eisenhower, although receiving some popular support from workers at the polls, certainly cannot be considered a "labor president."

Secondly, prosperous times seem to be poor times for labor to make legislative gains. When jobs are plentiful and money relatively abundant, the public tends to follow the philosophy of "let business have its way." Public opinion not only is indifferent to, but occasionally resentful of, any challenge to the power controls of business in government "when everything is going along smoothly."

A third current weakness of labor in its challenge to the ruling class is that, unlike business, it has never had a strong voice of its own for reaching the people and gaining the support of public opinion. Labor's gains, for the most part, were made not directly through its own channels, but through legislators and a chief executive particularly sensitive to labor's causes. Most of these governmental "friends of labor" have departed from the national scene and have been replaced by men some of whom are cool toward labor's challenge to the power of business and others of whom are actively hostile.

Labor racketeering. Another internal weakness of labor is the occurrence of monopolistic practices and racketeering in union organization. Power is a tempting plaything wherever it occurs—in government, in business, in labor, or in other activities. Some labor leaders have been as ruthless and dictatorial in their policies as have some businessmen and some politicians. Others have accepted bribes and determined union policies for their own benefit rather than for the benefit of the workers. Although the number of monopolistic and racketeer-led unions is very small compared to the bulk of democratically conducted unions, their number has been sufficient to give business interests an excellent discrediting device upon which their propaganda can play. It is important to remember that much of the public's information about unions derives from business sources.

"Featherbedding." Still another internal weakness of organized labor is the occasional (and, when it happens, highly publicized) practice of "featherbedding." Featherbedding is the union practice of creating superfluous jobs, preventing the introduction of modern machinery, and forcing unnecessary work to be done. It is a procedure comparable to that of some employers in buying up patents to prevent the introduction of superior methods of production and of restricting output of needed goods to obtain higher profit. Just as employer featherbedding arises from desire for profit, labor featherbedding arises from desire for employment. Partly, again, because of the effectiveness of business control of propaganda, labor featherbedding has been considered more reprehensible in the eyes of the public than has its employer counterpart.

Farmers. Various pressure groups representing the interests of farmers have at times come in conflict with the interests of business, although at other times they have conceived of their interests as nearly identical with those of business. While the farmer, like the worker, has sometimes sought control of power at the expense of the business class, he has seldom felt his interests to be merged with those of organized labor, has, in fact, often bitterly opposed the rise of organized labor. Politically, and often directly contrary to his rather obvious interests, the farmer has most frequently had his vote counted on the side of the business class. And yet pressure groups representing some of these same farmers have frequently achieved tremendous strength in getting legislation designed to benefit various groups of farmers.

The greatest periods of prosperity for the farming interests in the United States in the past several decades have been during the course of two World Wars. Shortly after World War I, world demand for American agricultural products declined, and the farmer entered a period of economic depression which, despite various relief measures provided during the 1930's, lasted until the beginning of World War II. Most of the current activities of pressure groups representing farmers may be understood in the light of the farmers' attempts to maintain the favorable economic position they achieved during World War II and to prevent a recurrence of the economic disasters following upon World War I. Unlike business, farmers are not in a position to maintain their economic welfare by a *laissez-faire* governmental policy; positive governmental protection is needed. Farmers lack economic security both because of the decline in relative importance of agriculture in our national economy and because of the increasing susceptibility of agriculture to financial maladjustments in our growingly complex and interdependent society.

Just as labor lacks unity, the various pressure groups representing farmers do not have identical interests. The three main groups are the National Grange, American Farm Bureau Federation, and National Farmers Union. While each group tries to cover the nation and "speak for the American farmer," each represents sectional and other specialized interests which influence its policies.

The National Grange.   The oldest and most conservative group is the National Grange, which draws its membership heavily from the traditionally Republican Northeastern states. Its policies reflect the fact that many of its farmer members produce for strictly domestic consumption, reside in traditionally conservative areas, and are advantageously situated in relation to rich domestic markets. The Grange is opposed, for example, to the continuance of the Reciprocal Trade agreements and stands with manufacturing interests in supporting a strong tariff and in demanding curbs on labor groups along the lines followed in the Taft-Hartley Act. The Grange has likewise showed little enthusiasm for various programs for the control of agricultural production, in part, presumably, because Eastern farmers have less to gain by such programs than do farmers in other sections of the country. Although it favors government subsidy for domestically consumed agricultural products, it is against federal subsidies for agricultural exports.

It is difficult to determine just how effective the National Grange is as a pressure group. In its monthly publication to its 750,000 members it boasts that it "almost single-handedly brought the benefits of Old Age & Survivor's Insurance to farm operators." [8] It describes its annual policy-making meeting as a "little Congress" and promises that following this session "The Washington office will then have its marching orders for the next 12 months." [9] Although not as powerful an organization as it once was, the National Grange can still exert considerable influence.

The Farm Bureau.   The American Farm Bureau Federation comes closer to covering the country than does the National Grange, but its principal strength is concentrated in the Midwestern area from Ohio to Kansas to Minnesota. Although it agrees with the Grange on many issues, the Federation's policies have been less conservative, less friendly toward big business,

---

[8] *National Grange Monthly*, (November 1954), p. 20.
[9] *Ibid.*

more friendly toward labor. Since more of the farmers represented by the Farm Bureau are dependent on the world market, it has supported reciprocal trade agreements and compulsory production control. The Farm Bureau actively supported the Agricultural Trade Development Act of 1954 and, indeed, claims to have laid the groundwork for expansion of foreign trade in agricultural products.

The Farm Bureau, with its 1 million members, is the largest and probably the most effective farmers' organization. A recent special issue of its *The Nation's Agriculture* is devoted to the changes in federal laws and policies affecting agriculture that were adopted during the 83rd Congress.[10] The Farm Bureau contends that most of its policies designed to improve the farm program were enacted by this Congress and that frequently it alone supported a proposition. There is no doubt but that pressures exerted by this group can be strong and effective.

The National Farmers' Union. The mildly "radical" element among the American farmers is represented by the National Farmers' Union. Many of the members of the union are farmers on the western margin of tillable lands (Colorado, Oklahoma, Iowa, Kansas, Nebraska, and the Dakotas). Its policies often differ sharply not only from those of the Grange, but also of the Farm Bureau Federation (reputedly composed chiefly of the more prosperous farmers).

From the Farmers' Union comes the strongest support for legislative proposals to bring to the farmer a return guaranteed to be equal to his cost of production. The Union further demands gradual movement of our economy away from private enterprise to cooperative business that is "owned by producers and consumers."

▶ AMELIORATION OF PRESSURE GROUP PROBLEMS

The foregoing descriptions of some of the major pressure groups in the United States should leave no doubt but that these

[10] The special issue was a miniature pre-print of *The Nation's Agriculture*, Vol. 29, November 1954.

groups represent intense value clashes. Although their interests may occasionally overlap, it seems that they are more frequently competitive. Often the interests of business simply cannot be reconciled with those of labor or those of labor are antithetical to those of farmers. Pressure groups represent "values in conflict" in no uncertain terms.

Earlier it was pointed out that there is a certain amount of conflict over the very existence of pressure groups. Some look upon them as an abortion of democracy and claim that our "founding fathers" never intended that all of us should be governed according to the dictates of powerful and influential cliques of some of us. Others see pressure groups as completely compatible with democratic processes but feel that certain controls are necessary to assure that their activities do not "get out of hand." Suggestions for the amelioration of the problem of pressure groups, therefore, are necessarily contingent on whether or not they are defined as a problem, and if so defined, to what extent the problem is thought to exist.

Elimination of pressure groups. Those who argue for the complete elimination of pressure groups will point out that such groups tend to become too powerful. Strength and power and influence are, of course, relative characteristics; what is meant is that some pressure groups exert influence far beyond that which is warranted by the number of people that they represent. A second argument is that pressure groups, regardless of their size, are unrepresentative even of those people they purportedly represent. Thus, the leaders of a labor group may not really speak for all members of the group, let alone all workers; and a farm group, as we have seen, may act only for a certain segment of farmers.

It can scarcely be denied that there is *some* truth in both of the foregoing arguments. Some difficulty lies in assessing just *how much* truth these assertions contain, but the major quarrel is with the recommendation for correcting the situation. It is here contended that complete elimination of pressure groups is an unrealistic proposal. As long as there are numbers of people with similar interests and as long as the first amendment to the Constitution is interpreted as it is today, pressure groups will continue to exist. It would take stringent and unpopular legislation to prohibit groups from attempting directly to influence legislation, and it would require still more encompassing laws to prohibit men from attempting to influence legislation indirectly by propagandizing their fellow men.

Regulation of pressure groups. There are those who feel that in our mass society with its particular type of representative government, pressure groups are not only permissible but necessary. Such individuals contend that some type of functional representation is needed to complement the geographical representation on which our system of government rests. A manufacturer in Iowa, for example, probably shares far more interests with fellow manufacturers throughout the country than he does with many fellow Iowans. In a very real sense our manufacturer may find that he is unrepresented in Congress, particularly if the bulk of people in his district are farmers. Thus, there is said to be need for representation at the legislative level along economic and other lines and that pressure groups fill this need.

Many of those who grant the utility of pressure groups admit that at present a certain amount of "housecleaning" is in order. One serious complaint concerns the anonymity that sometimes surrounds the activities of pressure groups. Some feel that anyone who attempts to influence legislation should be made to tell who he is, what he wants, and who is paying his way. Some feel, too, that there is no place in a democracy for anonymous propaganda or out-and-out attempts to sway public opinion under the guise of publicity or education.

It is no easy matter to secure legislation that will force the activities of pressure groups out into the open. This has been demonstrated by the only partial effectiveness of the federal Regulation of Lobbying Act which has been in existence for over nine years.[11] The act provides for the registration of anyone paid to influence the passage or defeat of a bill. Such a person must state his employer, and must file statements of money collected

---

[11] For an evaluation of the Lobbying Act see Burdette, *op. cit.*, and Schriftgiesser, *op. cit.*

and used for lobbying purposes. The law is so written, however, that many true pressure groups can continue their attempts to influence legislation without registering under the act. In addition, the constitutionality of some aspects of the act has been questioned.

Any attempts to regulate or control the propagandizing efforts of pressure groups are likely to be met with cries about invasion of basic rights and liberties. It is generally agreed that freedom of speech does not give one the right falsely to cry "Fire!" in a crowded theater, but it is not always so easy to set forth just what is covered by this "first freedom." Does one, or should one, have the right anonymously to propagandize his neighbors for whatever cause or interest? Who is to decide what is and what is not propaganda? And what restrictions, such as disclosure of sponsor, should be placed on that which is found to be propaganda? These are all serious questions and the fact that simple answers are not immediately forthcoming should not discourage serious thought. For as long as strong minorities, largely making their own rules as they go along, can directly and indirectly influence the legislation affecting the majority, there is likely to be some discontent within the pressured public.

▶ SUMMARY

American society contains thousands of organizations that have as one of their avowed aims the attempt to impose their policies on the larger society. Such pressure groups represent the crystallization of value conflict. There is some value conflict, too, concerning whether or not pressure groups are compatible with democratic government.

Pressure groups are formed to protect and further a host of values, but many are organized along economic lines. Pressure groups vary, too, with regard to their scope and their power. The number of pressure groups is thought to have increased markedly over the last twenty-five years.

In order to impose their policies on the larger society, pressure groups operate in two general ways: (1) by attempting to influence and mold public opinion, and (2) by striving to influence governmental agencies, particularly the legislative branch. Propaganda aimed at molding public opinion is put forth by many pressure groups, and some groups conduct this phase of their activities anonymously. Pressure groups attempt to influence legislation more directly by having their policies incorporated into political party platforms, by supporting candidates at elections, and by maintaining a lobby in Washington.

The major pressure groups in the United States fall into three broad divisions: (1) business, (2) labor, and (3) farmers. Business pressure groups have the advantage of fighting to maintain the *status quo* and of having the financial resources necessary to pursue their pressure activities on a large scale. The principal challenge to business has been the recent successful rise of organized labor. Labor's potential strength lies in the mass of people who qualify for membership in its ranks. Part of its ineffectiveness derives from advantages held by business and another part stems from weaknesses inherent in the present organization of labor itself. Farmers are represented by three main pressure groups. Although the interests of the three farmers' groups sometimes overlap, there is a certain amount of sectionalism in the policies of each and none can speak for all farmers.

Suggestions for the amelioration of the problem of pressure groups are contingent on the extent to which such groups are thought to constitute a problem. Elimination of pressure groups is sought by those who see them as being too influential and unrepresentative. Despite whatever truth lies in these assertions, the complete elimination of pressure groups is thought to be an unrealistic goal. Even those who grant the usefulness of pressure groups admit to some shortcomings in the present situation. A serious complaint concerns the anonymity with which pressure groups sometimes conduct their activities. It is no easy matter, however, to secure legislation which will bring pressure group activities out into the open without at the same time modifying our historical concepts of freedom of speech and freedom to petition the government for redress of grievances. But as long as strong minorities can directly and indirectly influence the legislation affecting the majority, there is likely to be some discontent felt by the pressured public.

SUGGESTED READINGS

Brady, Robert A., *Business as a System of Power*, New York, Columbia University Press, 1943. The scope, extensiveness, and complexity of the power of big business is thoroughly described and evaluated. An admittedly controversial issue.

Burdette, Franklin L., *Lobbyists in Action*, Manassas, Va., National Capitol Publishers, 1950. A quick overview of lobbying, its techniques, and its regulations. Contains the federal Regulation of Lobbying Act.

House of Representatives, House Select Committee on Lobbying Activities, *Lobby Index*, Washington, D. C., U. S. Government Printing Office, 1950. Published regularly, this report lists the names of all lobbies registered under the Lobbying Act, the organization represented by each, and the amount of money spent for lobbying purposes.

Key, V. O., Jr., *Politics, Parties, and Pressure Groups*, 3d ed., New York, Thomas Y. Crowell Co., 1952. Not only an informative account of governmental activities in our society in general, but specifically useful for gaining an understanding of pressure groups in operation. Treats minor pressure groups as well as larger movements.

Lee, Alfred McClung, *How to Understand Propaganda*, New York, Rinehart and Co., 1952. Chapter 8, "A General View of Propaganda," and Chapter 10, "What Can Individuals Do About Propaganda?" are especially recommended as thought-provoking coverages of their subjects.

Marsh, Benjamin C., *Lobbyist for the People*, Washington, D. C., Public Affairs Press, 1953. A fascinating history of a half century's experiences of the "People's Lobby" written by its founder who was said to be 2,000 years ahead of the progressives in Congress. Good account of specific lobby issues and illustrative of lobbying techniques.

Odegard, Peter, *Pressure Politics, The Story of the Anti-Saloon League*, New York, Columbia University Press, 1928. Few pressure groups have had the vast organization and tenacity of the Anti-Saloon League, and few have left such an imprint on the American scene. An absorbing history of the League replete with reproductions from its pamphlets, speeches, and slogans.

Schriftgiesser, Karl, *The Lobbyists*, Boston, Little, Brown, and Co., 1951. A comprehensive treatment of the Lobbying Act, its historical antecedents, and its intended and actual effects. Any skepticism about the extensiveness of lobbying will be quickly dispelled by a perusal of Chapter 11, "Lobbying by the Billions."

STUDY QUESTIONS

1. What is meant by the statement that pressure groups represent a crystallization of value conflict? What is the evidence that there is a clash of values over the fact of pressure groups?

2. Distinguish fully and show the relationship between a pressure group and a lobby.

3. What are the two general ways in which pressure groups operate to impose their policies on the larger society? Show by specific examples of pressure group activities why these channels are not completely separable.

4. Outline the specific ways in which a pressure group could attempt to influence legislation.

5. What are some of the advantages of "big business" in the struggle for power? Are these partially offset by any disadvantages?

6. How do you explain the fact that labor has failed to gain more control of power than it has? Do you think that labor's share of power will increase in the future? Why?

7. What are the three main farmers' groups in the United States? Is it likely that they will merge in order to form a stronger pressure group? Why or why not?

8. What is meant by the statement that pressure groups are considered by some as the third house of Congress?

9. What is the legal status of pressure groups? Of lobbies? Explain why you feel it would or would not be feasible completely to eliminate pressure groups.

10. What are some of the common criticisms of pressure groups? Which of these do you consider the most serious? Why?

· 12 ·   Race

Race has been called *the* American problem. A witness to
many vigorous discussions of "the race problem" sometimes
encounters more garrulity than knowledge and more emotion
than insight. Added to these difficulties is the fact that the concept of race is a fuzzy one and, scientifically speaking, race itself
is not a social phenomenon. Race, usually defined as "a group-
ing of human beings distinguished by the possession of similar
combinations of anatomical features due to common heredity,"
is in the province of the physical anthropologist, not the sociologist. In so far as race has any scientifically clear meaning at all,
then, it refers to a subdivision of mankind based upon hereditary
anatomical characteristics.

Even when the term "race" is carefully restricted to hereditary physical characteristics, the precision and clarity of the concept are not impressive. Anthropologists have evidenced great
difficulty in agreeing upon criteria acceptable for racial classification. Singly and in combination, many standards have been
used—shape of head, skin pigmentation, shape of the hair in
cross section, stature, color of the eyes and hair, amount of
body hair, shape of nose, and others. The results of using such
bases for the determination of race have consisted of contradic-
tory classifications. For example, the most commonly employed
classification is skin color, but there is no logical or scientific
defense for the employment of this particular criterion. When
skin color is used, a large number of peoples (such as many residents of India) are included in the "black race," who, by the use
of almost any other criterion would fall into the Caucasian (predominantly "white") race. In addition to such "misclassifica-
tions," there are always groups of people who simply cannot be

classified at all as belonging to the Negroid, Caucasoid, or Mongoloid race. Such are the Ainu of northern Japan with their light-to-dusky skins, their "Caucasian nose," and some Mongolian features. The aborigines of Austrialia and other groups present a similar problem. This confusion has led some anthropologists

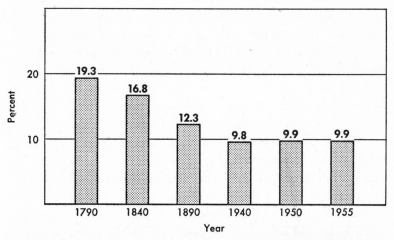

Fig. 11. Approximate percentage of population of the United States which is Negro, 1790 to 1955. (Data assembled from reports of the Bureau of the Census; 1955 data have been estimated.)

and sociologists into taking the position that race, even when used to refer only to strictly hereditary physical similarities of a subdivision of mankind, has become a meaningless concept. The most reasonable conclusion from a strictly scientific point of view seems to be that there is only one human race.

Which is most important? Skin color, hair, the nose, or the skull? Perhaps one can here venture the opinion that the chief trouble is that none of them is important. They are all empty things, and we have the impossible task of arranging them in some order—empty, emptier, and emptiest. And that has never been satisfactorily done.[1]

[1] Brewton Berry, "The Concept of Race in Sociology Textbooks," *Social Forces* (The Williams & Wilkins Co., publishers), Vol. 18, No. 3 (March 1940), p. 416.

▶ THE MYTH OF RACE

Because "race" does not seem to be a scientific reality from a physical anthropological standpoint does not mean that the concept is of no social significance. Mistaken ideas are as real as accurate ones to the person who believes them and, through his actions, to people who do not believe them. "Ghosts" and "witches," for example, are not scientifically demonstrable entities. If a person or group believes in ghosts or witches and these imagined spirits influence his behavior, they become a factor which must be taken into account in understanding the behavior of the "believers" and also of the "nonbelievers" with whom they interact. The delusions and hallucinations of a mentally ill person, by way of another illustration, are "real" to him in his reactions to his environment, even though his physician can demonstrate that "in fact" they lack objective reality. While the delusions and hallucinations are not experienced by the friends and family of the deranged individual directly, these mistaken ideas and sensations become part of the social reality of these persons in their dealings with the ill person. In like manner, the erroneous subjective nature of the concept of "race" does not render it *socially* insignificant. Many people act as if "race" were a scientific reality. Race attitudes, conflicts, discriminations, and inequalities are very real and very significant aspects of our problem society.

Races are fictions—the modern counterparts of witches, ghosts, and goblins—existing only in our minds, although we commonly treat them as though they were real, objective entities. But, you are probably saying, do we not see them with our eyes? Does not everyone know to which race he belongs? Well, so did our ancestors actually see witches and ghosts, and there were many who even confessed that they were witches. The five senses are by no means infallible.

This belief that races are real things is betrayed in the questions one frequently hears. How many races are there? To which race do the Polynesians belong? To which the Hindus? As well to ask, How many slices are there in a pie? Two, four, six; it all depends.

Or this, On which shelf of a bookcase should one put *The Autobiography of Benvenuto Cellini?* The assignment of people to races, like the carving of a pie or the cataloging of books, is an arbitrary affair, depending on the whim of the carver, the criteria chosen, the purpose of the classification.

. . . Except for our prejudices, we should probably agree that such things as intelligence, health, and temperament are important differences, but that it matters not whether the nose is straight or aquiline, whether the hair is curly or wavy. But suppose the hair is kinky? Suppose the nose is broad and flat? Very important indeed, so far as the status of the individual is concerned; more important even than intelligence and temperament. Quite so; but only because we have arbitrarily attached social significance to these biological trivia.[2]

Because so many Americans treat racial myth as if it were racial fact, we are obliged to consider some of the evidence deriving from various scientific sources which establish the mythical nature of beliefs about races.

Biological evidence of the myth of race. As brought out earlier in this chapter, "race" is a concept that is falling into increasing disrepute because of its lack of precision as applied even to strictly physical traits of people. Popular beliefs in regard to "obvious" biological differences between the Negro and white groups are numerous and persistent, however. Some of the biological evidence that points to the mythlike nature of certain of these popular beliefs will be examined in the following paragraphs.

"Apelike" characteristics. One of the arguments in the folklore justifying "white supremacy" in American society is that the Negro is closer to the ancestral anthropoid stock and represents an inferior, more "apelike" species than is the Caucasian stock. Since the customary distinctions between the Caucasian and Negro "races" break down under close scrutiny, such an argument runs into difficulty at the outset. Even if we accept the customary classification, however, the stereotyped Negro

[2] Brewton Berry, "A Southerner Learns About Race," *Common Ground* (Common Council for American Unity, publishers), Vol. II, No. 3 (Spring 1942), p. 89.

resembles the anthropoid less in some respects than do either the Caucasian or the Mongolian stereotypes. The wide flat nose and the long arms of some Negroes, for example, may be more "apelike," but their characteristically thick everted lips and smaller amount of body hair are least "apelike." With respect to thickness of lips, the thin-lipped Mongolians are closest to animals, followed by Caucasians, since apes have very thin or practically no lips. With respect to body hair the Caucasian is clearly the most "apelike." Careful anthropological studies indicate that there is an approximately equal number of anthropoid characteristics in the three traditional races and that none of these characteristics has demonstrable correlation with social or psychological factors.[3] Yet not a few members of our society continue to react to the "reality" of the "apelike nature of the Negro."

"Natural" correlations. Arguments closely related to the foregoing are often based on the "fact" that biological differences between the races "naturally must" be correlated with physiological and psychological differences. For reasons unexplained, it is argued that "superior" characteristics occur only in the "white race." No facts, however, are available to substantiate this belief in the superiority of "white" people. Logically we should expect to find none, for the best biological inference, based on a mass of empirically derived data, is that skin color and other similar gross anatomical characteristics are a product of natural selection acting upon mutations. The probabilities are high that this form of natural selection would have absolutely no social or psychological significance. The burden of proof, in any case, is with those who contend such significance, and proponents of the hypothesis of relationship between such anatomical characteristics as skin color, on the one hand, and such psychological attributes as mental ability, on the other, have yet adequately to shoulder this burden of proof. According to Klineberg, an outstanding investigator of alleged race differences, "there has been no demonstration that psychological differences of any signifi-

[3] See, for example, A. L. Kroeber, *Anthropology*, New York, Harcourt, Brace & Co., 1923, pp. 62-65, and Franz Boas, *Anthropolgy and Modern Life*, New York, W. W. Norton & Co., 1932, pp. 38-39.

cance are associated with the physical features used in race classification." [4]

Cultural evidence. But if there are no significant differences
among the races, why has the white man advanced so much
further than any other race? This question, or some variation of
it, is frequently advanced in the form of "irrefutable" argument
in favor of white supremacy and superiority. Let us examine the
reasoning underlying this argument.

"Superiority" of "white" civilization. First of all, on what
criteria do we base our judgment of the "further advancement"
of the white man? Obviously we take our own particular type
of cultural achievements and judge other civilizations in terms of
these achievements. To evaluate the civilizations of the Chinese
or Indian or African peoples on standards derived from Euro-
American culture is somewhat analogous to judging the com-
petence of lawyers or ministers or engineers on criteria set up
for members of the medical profession. The Western white man's
particular type of cultural achievements focalize in his mechanical ingenuity and skill and in his conquest of physical nature,
but the overwhelming evidence of the "problem nature" of his
society is testimony enough to his failure to date to develop a
generally successful formula for living. An impressive case can
be made for the greater success of other cultures in developing
such a formula. Long ago, for example, the "lowly Eskimo" had
achieved one of the primary goals toward which Western man
is still striving—the absence of warfare, full "peace on earth." If
we take almost any other criterion than sheer bulk of material
"progress," we can find other cultures with more convincing
achievements than that of Western civilization. There is no universal standard which we may employ to rate one culture superior to another.

When superior? In the second place, historical perspective is
needed in any attempted judgment of the superiority of one
culture over another. Even if we were to grant the superiority
of Western culture at this point in history (which, as we have

[4] Otto Klineberg, *Social Psychology*, rev. ed., New York, Henry Holt and
Co., 1954, p. 320.

just seen, is an unwarranted assumption), we may not legitimately argue from a temporary to a permanent superiority, based on biological factors. Western culture at the time of Columbus, for example, did not even compare favorably on materialistic grounds alone with such civilizations as the Chinese and East Indian. Much of the activity of Western nations in the fifteenth and sixteenth centuries was directed toward acquiring some of the "superior" material comforts and conveniences of Eastern societies. Not a little of the material progress of Western culture, in fact, may be traced to the borrowing of ideas and material inventions of non-Western, nonwhite peoples.

"Racial impurity." Thirdly, any close relationship between race and culture may be questioned on the grounds of "impurity" of any racial stock in a specific culture and of variability in the cultural achievements of any specified race. Western culture, for example, is the product of nonwhite as well as white peoples. The most "primitive" tribes of Siberia are of the same racial stock as the most "cultured" Chinese. American Negroes are thought to be "naturally musical," and yet ethnologists report that many tribes in Africa have little or no music. Any alleged "cultural superiority" of a designated "race" breaks down under examination of either the whole culture or the whole race.

Psychological evidence. Another line of attack of the proponents of "white superiority" has been the psychological, especially in reference to the "lower intelligence" of Negroes. The high incidence of illiteracy among Negro groups, the relatively small number of Negroes who have attained educational and scientific distinction, and the poorer average performance of Negroes on a number of "intelligence tests" are all cited as "objective evidence" of their native intellectual inferiority. In regard to "intelligence test" results, the earlier contentions of psychologists that such examinations were a measurement of "native intelligence" have more recently been recanted. Environmental factors have been proved to be of considerable significance in determining test performance, and the consensus among contemporary psychologists seems to be that of Garrett and Schneck that "the examiner must always remember that comparisons are permissible only when environmental differences are absent, or at least negligible." [5] In a white-dominated society, environmental differences are not "absent or negligible" for the American Negro. He is not given the same educational opportunities in many American communities, and even where the school facilities and personnel for the Negro are comparable to those provided the white child, comparisons of the two groups are not thereby made justified. The preschool and out-of-school experiences of a child greatly affect his school performance. Evidence abounds that the social and economic conditions of many Negro homes are not conducive to the development of alert and interested "scholars."

Regardless of whether it is eventually established that Negroes are as intelligent, more intelligent, or less intelligent than whites, it must be remembered that it would be on *a group basis*. In a cross-section sampling of any physical type, wide variations of performance on intelligence tests or any other kind of psychological scale are always found. In *any* of the above three cases, then, it would still be true that many Negroes would be superior to many whites. And, of course, the less intelligent a white person is, the greater would be the number of Negroes who would have an intelligence superior to his. Perhaps it is this thought that prompts some to cling to the presently untenable position that "all Negroes are inferior."

▶ RACE PREJUDICE AND THE AMERICAN SYSTEM

As we have seen, lack of scientific evidence does not prevent the members of society from developing attitudes toward groups with alleged or real physical differences that are based on assumptions of the inferiority of such groups. Race prejudice is rampant in our society, and it is this prejudice that accounts for the development and maintenance of unequal social opportunities. Unequal opportunities to participate in various cultural patterns produce, in turn, personality characteristics (such as greater

[5] Henry E. Garrett and Matthew R. Schneck, *Psychological Tests, Methods and Results*, New York, Harper & Bros., 1933, p. 24.

illiteracy in the Negro group) which are evaluated as "inferior" by the dominant group and give further basis for prejudice. But how does such prejudice originally develop?

Source of race prejudice. Various hypotheses have been advanced to account for the development of race prejudice. None is fully proved or seems to cover all possibilities; some lack plausibility in the light of modern knowledge of attitude formation. Several of the more common attempts to explain the formation of race prejudice are discussed in the following paragraphs.

Is prejudice innate? It has often been contended that each individual is born with some kind of biological mechanism that causes him "instinctively to prefer his own kind" and to recoil from other races. The best indication that "dislike of the unlike" is not innate in human beings is the research revelations that children, especially very young children, do not show race prejudice. Their likes and dislikes for other children are based upon criteria other than physical appearance. As children get older, of course, and learn more of the adult evaluations, they take on the characteristic race prejudices of their groups.

Another evidence against any innate basis for race prejudice is the wide cultural variability of race attitudes. American Negro soldiers, for example, were as generally welcome during World War II in the various activities of the English and French societies as were American white soldiers. Even within our own society we find so many variations in the nature of prejudice that any hereditary basis appears ridiculous. In the South, where race prejudice is regarded as most categorical, many white parents refuse to permit their children to attend the same school as Negro children. Many persons in the North do not object to their children attending the same school with Negro children, but do object to having Negroes living in their neighborhood. But Southern families not only have Negroes in the same neighborhood, but permanently living within their own homes and entrusted with such intimate matters as the preparation of food and care of children. If there were an innate basis for race prejudice, such intimate physical contact could hardly be tolerated.

Finally, there is no evidence whatsoever that an attitude pattern, like race prejudice, can come to a person through the germ plasm. All patterns of evaluation, like other attitudinal phenomena, are learned through the real or vicarious experience of the person.

It is probably seldom a deliberate, formal, teaching and learning situation, but prejudice is nevertheless learned. As it is expressed in a less publicized verse from *South Pacific*, "You've got to be taught to hate and fear . . . You've got to be *carefully taught.*"

What are the true reasons for race prejudice which underlie the rationalizations submitted by the prejudiced? The extreme lengths to which some white members of our society will go, often at great inconvenience to themselves, to "keep the Negro in his place" indicate that *race prejudice must serve some purpose for the prejudiced.*

Economic factors. The primary motive seems to be an economic one. Throughout history we find numerous examples of the exploitation of minority groups for the fruits of their labor. The ancient Romans and Greeks justified their use of other peoples as slaves on the basis of innate superiority over these groups; the medieval lord was, by birth, a superior brand of human being compared to his serfs; the Nazis, as members of a superior Aryan race, were justified in their own minds in appropriating the property of groups they considered inferior; and so with hundreds of other possible examples. In these instances, just as with the American white and Negro, the dominant group found distinct economic advantage in its prejudice against the dominated group. Physical characteristics, such as the skin color of the Negro, serve as very convenient marks of distinctions between the two groups. Dark skin indicates at once in American society an individual who can be economically exploited with impunity. By virtue of its prejudice, the dominant white group in America may appropriate for itself the best jobs, the greatest wealth, and the resulting "better things of life."

Psychological factors. Another reason for the development of race prejudice is the sense of security and self-confidence derived by the least successful members of the dominant group from feeling superior to another group. It has often been observed that the lower economic classes among the whites frequently manifest the most intense prejudice against Negroes. Studies have shown further that individuals who are frustrated in various of their life goals are likely to find in a disfavored minority group a convenient "scapegoat" for their troubles. It does not solve one's problems to see in "the Negroes," "the Jews," or for that matter one's boss or one's wife, the cause of his frustrations, but it reduces the need for self-blame.

Perpetuation of race prejudice.   Although race prejudice serves a purpose for the prejudiced, there may be an unawareness on their parts of such a purpose and an honest belief that their attitudes are merely the reflection of "obvious facts." It requires considerable intellectual effort, together with some knowledge of the results of scientific investigations, to arrive at an understanding of the myths involved in the "facts." It is so much easier to go on believing what one was conditioned to believe early in life. Even when intellectual understanding of the false basis of race prejudice is achieved, very often the emotions, the real "stuff" of prejudice, remain unaltered.

"Vicious circle."   Once a prejudice has become ingrained in a people, then, it is hard to root out. One contributing cause of the persistence of prejudice is that the bias itself deprives the group against whom it is directed of opportunities necessary for them to acquire the type of behavior patterns considered desirable by the dominant group. The operation of prejudice becomes "self-feeding"; since the minority group is kept "unequal" to the dominant group, it is forced to have the "inferior" attributes against which the majority group is prejudiced. It is a "vicious circle" somewhat comparable to a parent's prohibiting a child from attending school and then being "prejudiced" against this same child because he does not know how to read.

Persistence of stereotypes.   Prejudice is not only self-perpetuating in the foregoing sense but, once instilled in the minds of a people, tends to continue, and even to intensify, itself through many channels of socialization. Stereotypes operate through literature, the radio, the movies, jokes, and "art" in insidious ways, which—often unintentionally—create and perpetuate race prejudice. Seldom does a Negro appear in a movie or a television program other than in a stupid, lazy, good-natured, superstitious, ignorant, humorous role. If he is a "good Negro," he properly and good-naturedly "knows his place" as a porter, cook, chauffeur, or some type of unskilled worker. If he is a "bad Negro," he is evilly engaged in some sort of immoral conspiracy against "white rights," which, he is too stupid or mean to realize, are not for the "likes of him." Other channels of communication follow this same general pattern.

In time many an American forgets to question, even if he at one time did, whether the stereotyped portrayals of Negroes are correct or not. If he does have doubts, he is likely (since his few observations of Negroes are generally confined to those with least education in various menial roles around him) to find "evidence" of the stereotype of the "lazy," "stupid," "superstitious" Negro. If he is still not convinced, he is very apt to learn that the questions he raises are not welcomed by his white associates and that his only comfortable role in his own group is one of echoing the stereotypes. Thus even white persons who "know better" often contribute to the perpetuation of race prejudice.

Is there an American caste system? Social scientists use the expression "caste" to refer to a stratification system characterized by definite status, power, and privilege differences which are relatively permanent. Movement between castes is prohibited, and a person who is born into a given caste cannot marry a person from another caste. How well does the term "caste" apply to Negro-white relations in the United States? Mobility is rigidly limited: you cannot be born a Negro or a white and then proceed to pass from one status to the other unless you are an individual bearing physical traits (principally color) characteristic of the other group and unless you move to a community where your family history is completely unknown. Intermarriage is specifically prohibited for Negroes and whites in twenty-nine of the forty-eight states and is severely frowned upon by whites in the nineteen states where legally it is possible. Where children are born, in or out of wedlock, in a Negro-white mating, they are universally relegated to the Negro group, regardless of how "white" they may be according to any anthropometric test. These are some of the reasons why the Negro in the United States is frequently said to constitute a caste. But many of the castelike qualities of Negro-white relations are gradually disappearing. Employment and educational opportunities for the Negro are increasing, and civil rights are slowly becoming equalized. It is permissible to speak of the American Negro group as a caste so long as it is realized that some of the castelike qualities are disappearing or have already been removed. The caste line, that is, the definition of who belongs in which caste, has remained rigid.

Lower caste restrictions. Myrdal has also set forth what he calls "the white man's rank order of discrimination," together with the Negro's inverse "rank order" of resistance to discrimination. The rank order which Myrdal believes is held nearly unanimously by white Americans is the following:

Rank 1. Highest in this order stands the bar against intermarriage and sexual intercourse involving white women.

Rank 2. Next come the several etiquettes and discriminations, which specifically concern behavior in personal relations. (These are the barriers against dancing, bathing, eating, drinking together, and social intercourse generally; peculiar rules as to handshaking, hat lifting, use of titles, house entrance to be used, social forms when meeting on streets and in work, and so forth. These patterns are sometimes referred to as the denial of "social equality" in the narrow meaning of the term.)

Rank 3. Thereafter follow the segregations and discriminations in use of public facilities such as schools, churches, and means of conveyance.

Rank 4. Next comes political disfranchisement.

Rank 5. Thereafter come discriminations in law courts, by the police, and by other public servants.

Rank 6. Finally come the discriminations in securing land, credit, jobs, or other means of earning a living, and discriminations in public relief and other social welfare activities.[6]

[6] This and subsequent quotations reprinted by permission from Gunnar Myrdal, *An American Dilemma*, New York, Harper & Bros., 1944, Vol. I, pp. 60-61.

Negro resistance to restrictions. In accordance with his immediate interests, the Negro resists most the restrictions placed upon him in the lower ranks of the white American's discriminations and resents least the higher ranks of discriminations.

> . . . Negroes are in desperate need of jobs and bread, even more so than of justice in the courts, and the vote. These latter needs are, in their turn, more urgent even than better schools and playgrounds, or, rather, they are primary means of reaching equality in the use of community facilities. Such facilities are, in turn, more important than civil courtesies. The marriage matter, finally, is of rather distant and doubtful interest.
>
> Such reflections are obvious; and most Negroes have them in their minds. It is another matter, however, whether the white man is prepared to stick honestly to the rank order which he is so explicit and emphatic in announcing. The question is whether he is really prepared to give the Negro a good job, or even to vote, rather than to allow him entrance to his front door or to ride beside him in the street car.[7]

What it means to be "lower caste." Being a Negro—a member of the lower caste of American society—means, then, being subject to many disabilities in practically all spheres of life. For a child to be born of Negro parents is to have "the cards stacked against him." Part of the American social world is inaccessible to him entirely, and other parts are made extremely unlikely of attainment. Barriers set up for him as a lower-caste member furthermore reduce his motivation in fields that are at least partially open to him. Since the upper caste may arbitrarily withdraw possible rewards for his efforts, or even punish him for "trying to act like a white person," it is small wonder that some Negroes lose motivation for conscientious study, learning a skilled trade, or observing the "white man's laws." The amazing fact would seem to be, on the contrary, that, despite the restrictions placed upon them as lower-caste members, so many Negroes succeed in so many spheres of our social life.

[7] *Ibid.*, p. 61.

▶ THE AMERICAN RACE PROBLEM

We have discussed thus far in this chapter discrepancies between facts and popular beliefs about "races," the sources and
perpetuation of race prejudices, the existence of an American
caste system, and the restrictions this system places upon lower-
caste members. Such things are important, but do not in themselves make a "race problem." It is necessary background for
understanding the social problem of race in modern society to
know the attitudes of the dominant white group toward the
Negro group[8] and the lack of scientific basis for these attitudes.
Despite the "unscientific nature" of race prejudice and discrimination, however, race would not constitute a social problem
were it not for the fact that the values inherent in race prejudice
and discrimination are in sharp conflict with other values highly
esteemed by American society—namely, those which have been
called "the democratic ideology."

Race discrimination v. the democratic ideology. The race
problem is one of the most complicated, if not the most complicated, of American social problems. This is true not merely
because some aspects of the race problem become inextricably
intertwined with other difficult social conditions, for that is
the case with most social problems. The race problem is rendered particularly difficult *because we not only have a clash of
values between various groups in our society, but frequently
find value conflicts within the same individuals.* Increasingly
there is evidence among whites, even among Southern whites,
that there is growing awareness and sensitivity to some of the
facts about race. Many are finding it more and more difficult to

[8] We have centered our attention on white-Negro relations for two reasons:
(1) A much greater percentage of Americans (some 10 percent) fall into the
"Negro" category than into any other minority group, and (2) prejudice is
more intense and widespread and policies of discrimination more complete than
against any other group. With the possible exception of the Jew, discrimination
against other minority groups is not only less intense, but the discriminatory
practices tend to be more temporary and localized in nature. Few observers
would deny that the Negro problem, for all practical purposes is *the* American
race problem.

reconcile race discrimination with democratic and Christian ideals.

> . . . Even a poor and uneducated white person in some isolated and backward rural region of the Deep South, who is violently prejudiced against the Negro and intent upon depriving him of civic rights and human independence, has also a whole compartment in his valuation sphere housing the entire American Creed of liberty, equality, justice, and fair opportunity for everybody. He is actually also a good Christian and honestly devoted to the ideals of human brotherhood and the Golden Rule. And these more general valuations—more general in the sense that they refer to all human beings—are, to some extent, effective in shaping his behavior. Indeed, it would be impossible to understand why the Negro does not fare worse in some regions of America if it were not constantly kept in mind that behavior is the outcome of a compromise between valuations, among which the equalitarian ideal is one. At the other end, there are few liberals, even in New England, who have not a well-furnished compartment of race prejudice, even if it is usually suppressed from conscious attention.[9]

The conflict of values inherent in race prejudice, on the one hand, with values inherent in the democratic ideology, on the other, cannot, then, be represented simply as the Negro fighting for his democratic rights versus the dominant white group consistently attempting to prevent his getting them. That is only part of the problem. Another important part is the conflict of those same values running through every phase of society, making itself felt increasingly in the conscious and unconscious attitudes of a growing number of people: the basic incompatibility of race discrimination and a democratic way of life. The overt expression of the conflict consists mainly of the attempted overthrow of the caste system by most members of the lower caste and an increasing minority of the upper caste and the resistance to the dissolution of the caste system on the part of a decreasing majority of the upper caste.

In support of the accuracy of Myrdal's analysis that lower-caste members resent most bitterly discrimination of the sixth

[9] Myrdal, *op. cit.*, p. xlviii.

rank (land, credit, jobs, etc.), the most intense value conflicts in the field of race relations center in the Negro's fight for occupational and housing equality. Myrdal's doubts that the "white man is prepared to stick honestly to the rank order" is also apparently substantiated by the intensity with which some members of the upper caste fight to maintain existing inequalities in jobs and housing. It may be, as some observers have contended, that advocates of "white supremacy" suspect that the granting of equality in this sixth rank of discrimination will mean the eventual destruction of the whole caste system.

Fair employment practices. The occupational equality fight has focalized in recent years in the form of legislation under the name of "Fair Employment Practices."

The federal Fair Employment Practice Committee was established in 1941 to insure representation of minority manpower in war industries, but it went out of existence in 1946 with the end of the presidential wartime emergency powers.[10] The federal FEPC owed its existence to the combined effects of the wartime manpower shortage, the existence of the necessary legal mechanisms, and a favorably disposed administration. Filibuster by some Southern senators and other measures have defeated attempts to secure permanent federal legislation requiring employers who hire large numbers of workmen to employ Negroes or other racial groups in approximate proportion to their numbers in the total population of the community from which the industry draws its employees and requiring employers to pay Negroes the same wages which are paid to whites *for the same kind and amount of work.*

At present, eight states, of which New York was the first, have passed Fair Employment Practice laws. Most of the laws are patterned after that of New York, which forbids discrimination in hiring, firing, wages, working conditions, and promotions.

Even if current efforts to secure Fair Employment Practice laws for the nation as a whole are successful, job and wage dis-

[10] For a comprehensive discussion of the federal FEPC and state Fair Employment Practice laws see Louis Ruchames, *Race, Jobs, and Politics,* New York, Columbia University Press, 1953.

crimination against Negroes will not be totally solved. Public opinion in many communities would find ways of circumventing the laws; prejudices against Negroes on the parts of supervisors and fellow workers would still find ways of expressing themselves to the Negro workers' disadvantage; and a number of types of employment would not be covered by the laws. Negro physicians, for example, are often not "invited" to join the staffs of the large, modern hospitals in most communities. Negro lawyers frequently find that prejudice against them on the parts of legal colleagues, judges, and juries renders effective functioning in court very difficult. Although officially Negroes are not prevented from becoming physicians and lawyers and from "freely" practicing in these professions, they are so handicapped in their roles that many Negro citizens feel the need for employing white persons in these professions in order to obtain the best available legal and medical services.

Segregation: Housing. The second large area of value conflict concerns housing segregation, the requirement that Negroes live in areas set aside partly by law and mostly by illegal and unconstitutional tradition as "Negro areas." The battle of the "restricted covenant" (which specifies that only white persons may live in designated real estate) has become a focal point of value clash second only to equality of jobs and wages. Small sections of the community are specified "Negro sections"; the rest of the community, presently occupied and projected into the future, is for "whites only." Not only are large numbers of Negroes crowded into an amount of space that is far too small for decent living, but rents run higher than for comparable white quarters and community facilities—police and fire protection, parks and playgrounds, sanitation provisions, etc.—are almost invariably poorer.

The problem of segregated housing areas for Negroes becomes increasingly acute, for the designated "Negro areas" fail to grow at the same pace as the community as a whole or of the Negro proportion of the population in the large Northern cities (to which there has been heavy Negro migration beginning about 1900). Expansion of Negro sections is vigorously fought

by white persons who live in parts of a city that would be
"taken over." And yet we cannot go on indefinitely packing
Negroes into sections of cities that already house several times
the numbers for which they were originally designed. Either
a peaceful breakdown of "restricted covenants" must be achieved
or we must expect increasing tension and conflict in our large
cities of the type that we have had in Detroit, Chicago, and New
York.

Segregation: Government. In the South the Negro's rights
to vote and hold office are quite directly abridged or prevented
by various expedients such as the poll tax, "grandfather clauses,"
and literacy and "Constitution knowledge" tests (often so administered that the Negro has no chance of passing). In the
North in some cities the Negro's vote is rendered ineffective
by the more subtle method of so arranging districts that white
persons outnumber Negroes and make it difficult or impossible
for a Negro to be elected to an office. The Negro, as a result, is
either unrepresented in city, state, and federal government or
underrepresented in proportion to his percentage of the population. He is thus prevented from using the machinery of government, in any appreciable amount, for the achievement of various
objectives in the direction of reducing caste barriers.

Segregation: Education. Another area of value conflict concerns the segregation of the races in the nation's public schools.
As late as the beginning of 1954 seventeen states and the District
of Columbia had laws requiring racial segregation in their schools
and in four other states racial segregation was permissible. It
was generally held by such states that their citizens would receive
their constitutional guarantee of "equal protection of the laws"
if Negroes and whites were provided with separate school facilities—the so-called "separate-but-equal" doctrine. Many members of both races, however, questioned both the practice of
segregation and the doctrine of "separate but equal." In the
first place, practical application of the doctrine over many years
revealed that the races were certainly separated but that the
schools provided for the Negro were frequently not equal to
those provided whites. The evidence presented in Chapter 14

regarding average expenditure per pupil in Negro and white schools, the amount spent for textbooks, and the like leaves little doubt concerning the general lack of equality of separate schools.

Even more important, however, was the charge that "separate but equal" is an impossibility, logically and otherwise. Can we label equality a situation in which some American citizens are prohibited by law from associating with other citizens in the course of pursuing something that is required by law? Finally, there was the argument that segregation denied the segregated students their chance of exchanging views with some other students and that by its very nature it impaired the personality development of pupils in the lower ranking of the segregated groups.

The clash of values over segregated schools has been disputed legally, editorially, and in other ways for a number of years. On May 17, 1954, the Supreme Court of the United States declared certain legal aspects of the battle over—segregation of the races in public schools is illegal. The following excerpt from the Supreme Court decision indicates some of the reasons on which the decision was based:

> We come then to the question presented: Does segregation of the children in public schools solely on the basis of race, even though the physical facilities and other "tangible" factors may be equal, deprive the children of the minority group of equal educational opportunities? We believe that it does.
>
> Such considerations apply with added force to children in grade and high schools. To separate them from others of similar age and qualifications solely because of their race generates a feeling of inferiority as to their status in the community that may affect their hearts and minds in a way unlikely ever to be undone.
>
> We conclude that in the field of public education the doctrine of "separate but equal" has no place. Separate educational facilities are inherently unequal.[11]

The value issue with regard to segregated schools is certainly not over. Plans are being made for putting the Supreme Court decision into effect at a practical level and some conflicts are

[11] Cited in Public Affairs Pamphlet No. 209, "Segregation and the Schools," New York, Public Affairs Committee, 1954.

arising at this stage. A few Southern states have passed or are proposing legislation that will enable them essentially to by-pass the court decision by "abolishing" public schools for both races. At the time of this writing, the outcome of these attempts is not clear.

Possibilities of amelioration. As we have seen earlier in our discussion, race prejudice tends to be self-perpetuating. Because of our initial prejudice and discrimination, many Negroes are unable to compete successfully in various spheres of life, and our prejudice thus continues to be directed against these "obviously inferior" people. There is evidence of value conflict concerning how to "break into" this vicious circle and ameliorate our race relations problems. One important issue can be phrased, oversimply, "Should we strive to reduce racial prejudice in order eventually to eliminate discrimination or should we legally prohibit discrimination and trust that a reduction in prejudice will follow?"

Reducing prejudice. One common school of thought holds that the soundest approach is one that concentrates on changing the attitudes of the prejudiced. Not until people think and feel differently, it is held, will antidiscriminatory legislation or other measures for improving relations be truly effective. This approach is largely a matter of education, in its broadest sense. Its proponents admit that in the past this process has been slow and will probably continue to be so. The principle on which this approach rests was formulated by the early sociologist Sumner in the assertion that "stateways (laws) cannot change folkways." Proponents further point to the results of national prohibition as evidence that legislation contrary to majority opinion is unsuccessful.

Legislation. An almost diametrically opposed approach is the one that sees antidiscriminatory legislation as the one way of reducing our racial problems. One argument is that the legal elimination of discrimination will allow the Negro to compete educationally, economically, and socially on a more equal level with whites. Following successful competition, it is held, whites will find that their stereotypes and prejudices can no longer be defended. Supporters of this position counter the assertion that the legislative approach "just won't work" by pointing to the only minimum success of almost a hundred years of the "gradual approach." The desire to "move slowly," it is held, may become simply a rationalization for doing nothing!

Recent experiences have shown that people do not always react to "desegregation" in the way they or others anticipate that they will.[12] Fear of loss of sales has sometimes accompanied the employment of Negro sales people; strikes are predicted if Negro workers are to be hired for "white jobs"; and riots or other dire results are forecasted when plans are made to "integrate" Negro and white schools. Most frequently, however, there have been no serious results in any of these cases. Although there is probably insufficient evidence for a broad generalization, certainly there is enough to indicate that perhaps we have been moving slower than necessary in our attempts to reduce racial tensions.

Strength of the democratic ideology. The degree of a person's pessimism regarding the possibilities of bettering the race problem depends, to a considerable extent, on his beliefs concerning the strength of the democratic ideology in American culture. If the white American people can live comfortably by merely paying lip-service to democratic ideals, they are unlikely to make a forceful attack on the race problem because the conflict of values between these ideals and race discrimination is not likely to become sufficiently acute. If on the other hand, the democratic ideology is so powerful and fundamental a set of values in American social life that the dominant white group will be forced again and again to face the conflict of these values with a caste system, considerable amelioration of the race problem must eventually be forthcoming. It may well be that any thoroughgoing reduction of the race problem is dependent, as some observers have contended, upon a fundamental change in the socioeconomic structure. Such a change, if necessary, must undoubtedly come by way of the democratic process, however,

---

[12] For cases of anticipated and actual reaction to FEPC legislation see Ruchames, *op. cit.*, pp. 183-88.

or it is likely that the resulting value conflicts would be as undesirable, or perhaps more undesirable, than the contemporary race problem.

Basis for hope. The situation is not completely disheartening, however. A final quotation from Myrdal seems to be an appropriate conclusion to our analysis of the race problem and the possibilities of its betterment.

> The school, in every community, is likely to be a degree more broad-minded than local opinion. So is the sermon in church. The national labor assembly is prone to decide slightly above the prejudice of the median member. Legislation will, on the whole, be more equitable than the legislators are themselves as private individuals. When the man in the street acts through his orderly collective bodies, he acts more as an American, as a Christian, and as a humanitarian than if he were acting independently. He thus shapes social controls which are going to condition himself.
>
> Through these huge institutional structures, a constant pressure is brought to bear on race prejudice, counteracting the natural tendency for it to spread and become more intense. The same people are acting in the institutions as when manifesting personal prejudice. But they obey different moral valuations on different planes of life. In their institutions they have invested more than their everyday ideas which parallel their actual behavior. They have placed in them their ideals of how the world rightly ought to be. The ideals thereby gain fortifications of power and influence in society. This is the theory of social self-healing that applies to the type of society we call democracy.[13]

▶ SUMMARY

We opened our discussion in Chapter 12 with a consideration of the scientific validity of the concept of "race" and observed that the only usage of the term that could be considered at all legitimate was in reference to a subdivision of mankind based upon hereditary anatomical characteristics. Even this usage, it was pointed out, has led to more confusion than clarity, so that some anthropologists favor the discarding of the concept other than in its employment in the phrase of "the human race."

[13] Myrdal, *op. cit.,* p. 80.

The absence of scientific validity for "race" does not, however, mean that the concept has no social significance. Many people act as if "race" possesses objective reality, and their behavior in relation to the concept thus becomes a *social* reality.

Our next step was to examine the alleged biological, cultural, and psychological "evidence" of racial superiority, especially as it pertained to the "white race," and we concluded that no scientific support for beliefs in such superiority has been established and that, on the basis of existing research findings, none could be expected.

Having examined and rejected the hypothesis that race prejudice is innate in the human organism, we observed the economic and psychological utilities of race prejudice for the dominant white group in our society. We further pointed out that prejudice, once begun, tends to be self-perpetuating and pervades the literature and other media of communication of a culture.

Our next consideration was directed toward the concept of "caste" as it applies to Negro-white relations in our society, and we decided that the use of the word in this connection is permissible if we remember that some caste qualities have already been removed and others are disappearing. The employment of the concept of "caste" assisted us in understanding the degrees of discrimination directed toward the Negro as lower caste by the white upper caste and the inverse rank order of resentment and rebellion against these restrictions by the lower caste.

The essence of the "race problem" in the United States, we proceeded to assert, is the conflict between the values inherent in the caste system and the values inherent in the democratic ideology. The problem is complicated by the fact that these two basically incompatible sets of values are not only held by conflicting groups in our society, but are found lodged, in varying degrees of intensity, in most of the individual members of the society.

Job and wage equality, improvement of housing conditions, and segregation in the schools were discussed as three major focal points of value conflict in contemporary race relations.

Effective action in these and other areas is partially prevented by restrictive measures in relation to the Negro's rights to vote and to hold public office.

Suggestions for the amelioration of the race problem are not without their own value conflicts. One issue concerns whether reduction of racial prejudice or prohibition of discrimination should be the main focus of attack. Dire forecasts of the results of antidiscriminatory action occurring before the people are "ready" have not been borne out. A further observation was made that the degree of pessimism held in regard to the general amelioration of the race problem was related inversely to the degree of faith attached to the democratic process. If the democratic ideology is deeply rooted in the American people, fundamental improvement of the race problem must eventually be worked out in American society.

SUGGESTED READINGS

Ashmore, Harry S., *The Negro and the School*, Chapel Hill, University of North Carolina Press, 1954. A thoroughly objective analysis of school segregation and experiences with desegregation. Quotes facts on school expenditures in white and Negro schools and interprets the recent Supreme Court decision in a succinct and readable manner.

Berger, Monroe, *Equality by Statute*, New York, Columbia University Press, 1952, Chap. 5. A good treatment of the efficacy of law in reducing discrimination and its influences on attitudes. Pertinent research findings complement the theoretical discussion.

Berry, Brewton, *Race Relations*, Boston, Houghton Mifflin Co., 1951. Artfully describes and analyzes the results of contacts between racially and culturally different peoples. Its world-wide, semihistoric approach enables the student to view the current situation with perspective and understanding.

McDonagh, Edward C., and Eugene S. Richards, *Ethnic Relations in the United States*, New York, Appleton-Century-Crofts, 1953. A good basic text. Seven ethnic minority groups are examined in terms of their position in American society and their relations with the majority group.

Rose, Arnold (ed.), *Race Prejudice and Discrimination*, New York, Alfred A. Knopf, 1951. A careful selection of over fifty articles on minority group problems. A handy reference.

Ruchames, Louis, *Race, Jobs, and Politics*, New York, Columbia University Press, 1953. Traces FEPC legislation up to the postwar attempts of states to enact such laws. Good for case materials on anticipated and actual reaction to nondiscriminatory legislation.

Saenger, Gerhart, *The Social Psychology of Prejudice*, New York, Harper & Bros., 1953. A systematic treatment of the subject with emphasis on the prejudiced personality. The possibility of value clashes is apparent in the treatment of the techniques for combatting prejudice and discrimination. A readable and provocative work.

Trager, Helen G., and Marian R. Yarrow, *They Learn What They Live*, New York, Harper & Bros., 1952. This is a report of a field study of prejudice in young children. Investigates how and when prejudices are learned, adult awareness of prejudice in children, and methods of teaching democratic attitudes. A significant study of particular value to parents and teachers.

STUDY QUESTIONS

1. Which criteria are most frequently used to differentiate various races? What types of confusion result when we attempt to classify the world's population on the basis of these criteria?

2. In what sense is race a "myth"? In what sense is it quite "real"?

3. What type of biological, psychological, and cultural evidence is used to disprove the "superiority" of any race?

4. Cite the main line of evidence that seems to disprove the theory that race prejudice is innate.

5. Describe the "vicious circle" involved in the perpetuation of race prejudice. Where would you suggest "breaking into" this "vicious circle"?

6. In what ways are Negro-white relations in the United States "castelike"? In what ways are they not?

7. Why is race discrimination incompatible with a democratic way of life? How is this related to the "Negro problem" in the United States?

8. Describe the basic stipulations of "Fair Employment Practices." What possible desirable effects could such laws have other than strictly economic ones?

9. Why is the concept "separate but equal" considered a logical impossibility? For what other reasons did the Supreme Court rule that segregation in public schools is illegal?

10. Describe the two general approaches to the reduction of prejudice and discrimination. Cite some difficulties with each approach when it is put into practice.

· *13* ·   Old Age

At no time in our history have we had the concern with the problems of the aged that the past several decades have witnessed. Although there are many who do not recognize the problems of old age or do not define the present situation as a "problem," public concern continues to grow. One reason for this increasing interest is that changes in the economy have tended to reduce the usefulness of old people. Another and more impelling cause for concern is the increasing percentage of the population which falls into the old-age category. And, finally, traditional "solutions" to the problems of the aged, which typically involved the older person sharing the home of his son or daughter, no longer seem possible under modern urban conditions nor acceptable to most young and old people. In this chapter, then, we will discuss the factors contributing to the development of the problem of old age and some of the more specific conditions over which value conflicts have arisen. Since concern with this problem is of relatively recent origin, it will be necessary to supply basic information relevant to aging and the aged.

Number and growth of aged. Before we can speak about the number of persons in the population falling into the old-age category, we must have a definition of what constitutes old age. Any chronological age which is selected as the beginning of old age is bound to be artificial. Some people are slow in thought and action, "worn out," at sixty; others proceed vigorously and efficiently with their daily lives at seventy-five. Since there is a growing tendency to retire employed persons at sixty-five, that age is often arbitrarily chosen as the beginning of the old-age period. For statistical purposes, then, we shall accept this customary definition of an aged person as anyone sixty-five years of age or older. We shall, however, take occasion later to discuss less arbitrary and more functional criteria which may be used in describing old age.

The number of persons sixty-five years of age and older has definitely increased. In 1900 there were some 3 million people in this category and by 1930 their numbers had more than doubled. The number of aged had more than doubled again by 1950, at which time there were over 12 million persons in this category.

The number of aged continues to increase at the rate of 300,000 to 400,000 per year; in 1955 they numbered almost 14 million. And we can predict with some accuracy how many aged there will be in the future. All of the people, for example, who will be sixty-five or over in the year 2000 have already been born and are already at least twenty years of age. Barring war or some other mass catastrophe that would affect the death rate of this age group, it can be estimated that there will be between 25 and 26 million people sixty-five and over by A.D. 2000. From 1950 to 2000, then, the number of aged is expected to double once more, regardless of the present and future growth of the rest of the population. Just from the standpoint of the numbers involved, old age becomes an increasingly important matter of social concern.

Table 8. Total Population and Population 65 and Over, 1900-1954 *

Year	Total population	Number of persons 65 and over	Percentage of persons 65 and over
1900	75,994,575	3,080,498	4.1
1910	91,972,266	3,949,524	4.3
1920	105,710,620	4,933,215	4.7
1930	122,775,046	6,333,805	5.4
1940	131,669,275	9,019,314	6.8
1950	150,697,361	12,271,178	8.1
1954	162,400,000	13,700,000	8.4

* Data assembled from reports of the Bureau of the Census. 1954 figures are provisional estimates released to press by Bureau of the Census.

Proportion of aged in total population. The sheer number of old people in a society is important for various reasons. It makes a difference, for example, whether as a society we need to provide for the economic, health, recreation, and other needs of 7 million or 14 million old people. But it is also necessary to know what *proportion* of the population is sixty-five and over and what changes are taking place with regard to the growth of this segment *relative to the growth of the rest of the population.* This is particularly important in a society, such as ours, that seems increasingly willing for economic productivity to cease or definitely be curtailed at age sixty-five.

In 1850 only 2.6 percent of the population were sixty-five or older. In 1900 the percentage was 4.1; in 1930, 5.4; in 1950, 8.1; and in 1955, 8.6. The percentage of old people at some future date obviously is dependent both on how many old people there will be at that time and the total population size. We can be less precise with any prediction dependent on future birth rates.

One population authority has estimated that there will be 175 to 200 million people in the United States by 2000 A.D.[1] Using the highest figure, which assumes a relatively high birth rate, the estimated 25 to 26 million in the sixty-five and over group would constitute almost 13 percent of the population at the turn of the century. If the birth rate is such that our population in 2000 is 175 million, we would still have 25 to 26 million old people, and they would constitute close to 15 percent of the population.

It should be apparent that persons over sixty-five are now, and will continue to be, a "sizable minority." It is not too much to expect, in a democracy, that the wishes of this ever-growing segment of our population will have increasingly more impact on our economic, social, and other policies.

The nature of "old age." Aging is generally a very gradual process. A person is not one day a responsible adult and the next day an irresponsible old man or woman. There is usually a slow transition period from the status of independent adulthood to

[1] Warren S. Thompson, "Our Old People," in T. Lynn Smith, ed., *Problems of America's Aging Population,* Gainesville, University of Florida Press, 1951, Chap. 1.

dependent or partially dependent old age. Various physical, psychological, and sociological traits come to characterize persons who are growing old. No one old person has all of these characteristics, but the traits are found among old people as a group.[2]

Physical old age. Not only are there wide individual differences as to when a particular type of physical decline or deterioration will appear, but there is no one age in any specific individual when all functions begin to show a decline. Often, too, changes in physical functioning occur so slowly in later life that they are difficult to measure except over relatively long periods of time.

Some of the physical changes that will generally occur at some point in the period of old age (providing the person lives long enough for many of these things to occur) are: general decline in physical strength and vitality, increased tendency toward fatigue, and a slowing down in reactions. These are often preceded, accompanied, or followed by some such organic deficiency as a failing in hearing or eyesight. The old person likewise becomes much more susceptible to chronic illnesses or incapacities resulting from specific diseases, falls and broken bones, or gradual failure of internal organs to function properly.

It should be emphasized again that there is considerable individual variation with respect to the presence of these physical marks of aging. Among the physically old will be found men as young as fifty, while others who are years their seniors will in some respects be "younger." And we are not talking about "youthful outlook" nor are we giving support to popular beliefs about maintaining one's youth by "thinking young." It is simply a fact that people exhibit the *physical* symptoms of old age at different chronological ages. From a practical standpoint, then, this means that in addition to earlier existing differences, old people of the same age differ in their physical ability to work,

[2] In this section on the nature of old age the authors have drawn heavily upon material contained in Ruth Cavan, Ernest Burgess, Robert Havighurst, and Herbert Goldhamer, *Personal Adjustment in Old Age*, Chicago, Science Research Associates, 1949. Although no material is quoted, much is paraphrased, and the authors wish to express their indebtedness to this very thorough and careful research.

to read, to play, to drive automobiles, and so on. All too frequently our policies toward the aged ignore these differences.

A given individual, furthermore, does not exhibit each of the various indications of physical old age with the same intensity. His eyesight, for example, may begin to fail earlier or may fail more rapidly than his hearing, or both of these faculties may continue to be "good" long after his cardiovascular system has quite definitely "aged." For an individual, then, this lack in a uniform progression of the aging process may mean that he is "too old" to perform *his* job at sixty-five, sixty, or even younger, but that he is physically capable of performing other jobs. This applies too, of course, to types of recreation and anything else that requires use of one's physical faculties.

Psychological old age. The onset of old age may first become apparent through mental rather than physical decline. Psychological deterioration is much more difficult to measure than physical decline. Criteria are less reliable and valid. Full cooperation of the subject is necessary for successful mental testing, and older people are often less familiar with and interested in psychological measurements than are younger people. Then, too, because of wide individual variations in all age categories, psychological test results would be needed on the same persons over many years in order to give an accurate picture of mental decline. Most tests, in addition, are based on the experiences of children, adolescents, and young adults, and frequently may not be applicable to the experience-world of an older person.

The chief data which are available, therefore, are based on observations, especially of psychiatrists who have older persons as patients, rather than upon systematically and statistically derived samplings of the older population. Presence of many of the following traits in intense form is characteristic of senile dementia. Most older people have a number of these characteristics to some degree, however, without bordering seriously on actual mental illness. The most common psychological deteriorations are loss of memory (especially regarding recent events), inability to concentrate over long periods of time, and difficulty in learning new skills. Other common mental developments are attitudes of suspicion, narrowing of interests, feeling of insecurity, of guilt, and of being unwanted, conservatism and inflexibility, a tendency to relive the past, worry (especially about money and health), garrulity, hoarding, and increased liking of quiescence and dislike of activity.

The standardized tests that have been administered to groups of older people indicate that the various types of mental skills apparently deteriorate at different rates. For example, performance on vocabulary, general information, and verbal comprehension tests has been found to show little or no decline until a very old age, while there is some indication of a more pronounced decline on the "reasoning" and "judgment" tests.[3] Much more research needs to be conducted in this area and with regard to attitudinal changes of the aged.

It should be clear that psychological characteristics of aging, like physical ones, do not occur in all individuals at the same chronological age and do not progress at the same rate for all persons. Some men may find it best to retire from work or to change jobs at sixty, while others may be psychologically equipped to continue their lifetime work to seventy-five or over.

Sociological old age. Sociological old age is characterized by the relinquishment of responsibilities and privileges typical of adulthood and the acceptance of different and (in our culture) lesser roles. For the man, it is often most conspicuously heralded by retirement from full-time employment. Women, often less abruptly, give up household management. The term "retirement" has a middle- and upper-income group tone; old men in the lower economic groups are generally considered old much earlier in life and do not "retire," but are "laid off," "asked to go," or, more simply, "fired." At any rate, at about the time of a man's retirement, or shortly following his termination of employment, there is often a loss of the independent household. Or, in case the woman outlives her husband (as an increasing

---

[3] Wilma T. Donahue, "Psychological Aspects of Aging," in T. Lynn Smith, ed., *Problems of America's Aging Population*, Gainesville, University of Florida Press, 1951, pp. 56-60.

number of women are tending to do), the independent home may be given up shortly following her husband's death.

Large numbers of old people become economically dependent upon their children or society. Formerly independent in their actions, they must now take positions subordinate to adult children, social workers, or supervisors of a nursing or old-people's home.

There is a gradual reduction and contraction of interests, of long-term plans, and of active community and organizational leadership. Old people tend to plan in terms of immediate goals, to confine membership to groups constituted chiefly of other old persons, and to transfer interest from their own lives to those of their children and grandchildren.

Need for subcategories of old age. Much needless confusion has arisen from the common use of terms such as "old age" or "the aged" to refer to all people who have had sixty-five birthdays. But the number of years that people can live beyond sixty-five is too great, and the individual variations in the aging processes are too varied to allow us to expect any real homogeneity in the sixty-five and over group. The serious suggestion for increasing the width of our doorways to enable the ready passage of the wheel chairs of our "aged" may not make much sense to the man who thinks of the aged in terms of his sixty-six-year-old, agile, and quick-witted mother and others like her. Again, the recreational needs of the seventy-one-year-old man who boasts of his ability to command "a day's pay for a day's work" are scarcely the same as those of one who is chronologically his junior but who has "aged" to the extent that residence in a nursing home seems advisable.

In order to avoid the confusion accompanying the use of the term "old age" to describe such a broad and varied period of man's life, one authority has suggested the division of the post-adult years into three periods: early senescence, middle senescence, and later senescence.[4] The periods would be differentiated on the basis of the degree of deviation from adult standards. It

[4] Cavan, *op. cit.*, p. 8.

is not yet possible, however, to measure such deviation precisely, but there would seem to be much merit in the use of subcategories of old age even if based on crude and approximate criteria.

▶ PROBLEMS OF OLD AGE AND VALUE CONFLICTS

Just as the adolescent's value conflicts arise partly from the inconsistency of adult expectations of him as half child and half adult, the difficulties of adjustment of the person who makes the transition from adulthood to old age result from similar causes. While he is considered young enough for some adult activities and responsibilities, he is considered too old for others. Although he is expected to manage his own social affairs, he is often treated like a child by his own children and other associates. He is expected to participate financially and personally in community and organizational affairs, but is criticized for accepting positions of leadership and thus not "giving young people a chance."

Gradually, like the adolescent, the older person passes through the transitional period, achieves the full distinction (such as it is) of being "elderly," and is no longer expected to conform to many adult standards. In the meantime, however, his adjustment to old age may have been rendered psychologically and sociologically much more difficult by conflicts in society's expectation of him.

There are, of course, any number of conditions and situations that constitute "problems" for some or even many of the aged. The ones with which we will be concerned, however, are *social* problems, since added to the objective situation is a conflict of societal values that has helped to bring about the condition, has aggravated it, or perhaps, has just hindered its amelioration. Different studies have shown that many old people list "health" and "money" as their chief worries and that the aged are prone to feelings of "uselessness." This is still another reason for considering problems related to the economic conditions, health, and the social role of the aged.

Economic problems. The Bureau of Labor Statistics, after a study of living costs in thirty-four cities, determined what it would cost an elderly couple to maintain a "modest but adequate" level of living in 1950.[5] The needed yearly "budget," which provided for a one-to-three-room rented dwelling, food, and other goods, but no automobile, ranged between $1,602 and $1,908.

Table 9. Income Distribution of Couples and Individuals 65 and Over, 1952 *

Yearly income	Number of economic units (in millions) †	Percent of all units
No money income	2.4	23
Under $500	2.1	20
$500-$1,999	4.1	40
$2,000-$4,999	1.5	14
$5,000 or more	0.4	3
All units	10.5	100

* Data from *Social Security Bulletin*, Vol. 17 (October 1954), p. 8.
† In 1952 there were about 13 million persons 65 years of age and over. Husbands and wives are considered one "economic unit" and their incomes have been combined.

According to the 1950 Census reports, the income of *half* of the families in which the head was sixty-five years of age or older was less than $1,900, the amount required to live in the "most expensive" of the different cities. Almost 45 percent of such families did not receive enough income to live according to the suggested standards in the "least expensive" cities. Looking at it a bit differently, in 1952 there were some 2.5 million people (or couples, if husband and wife were both over sixty-five and living together) with no money income whatsoever and another 2 million with an income of less than $500 annually.[6] Even when

[5] The following data on living costs are derived from Federal Security Agency, *Fact Book on Aging*, Washington, D. C., U. S. Government Printing Office, 1952, p. 51.
[6] See: *Social Security Bulletin*, Vol. 17 (October 1954), p. 8.

allowance is made for the receipt of money not covered by the definition of "income," [7] it is clear that many of our aged do not receive enough money to maintain an adequate standard of living. It should be apparent that no one measure would "solve" the financial needs of the aged. What would be appropriate for those in early senescence might be unworkable for those in later senescence.

Employment. One obvious way to satisfy the financial needs of some of our aged is to provide jobs for those who are able and who either need or want to work. For the past half a century the proportion of our aged who are gainfully employed has been decreasing. In 1890, for example, 68 percent of men sixty-five or older were in the labor force; in 1952 this had declined to 41 percent. While the employment rate of older women has increased, still only about 10 percent of all women over sixty-five are gainfully employed. It is generally conceded that most of the people over sixty-five (it must be remembered that half of the men over sixty-five are under seventy) are not voluntarily unemployed. One study, for example, found that people over sixty-five were as anxious to continue full-time employment as were those between fifty and sixty-four years of age.[8] Another study, conducted in Pittsburgh and Detroit, discovered that 60 percent of workers eligible for retirement in the auto and steel industries preferred to keep on working.[9] Finally, the Social Security Agency reports that its studies reveal that less than half of the social security beneficiaries voluntarily quit their jobs despite the fact that if they did so they could then obtain Old Age and Survivors Insurance benefits.[10] Compulsory retirement provisions, technological changes, and discriminatory practices of employers, are some of the factors that make it difficult for the able-bodied older worker to find employment. Some, it is true,

[7] Family income as defined by the Census excludes money received from loans, gifts, lump-sum inheritances, and various payments in kind.

[8] Edrita Fried, "Attitudes of the Older Population Groups towards Activity and Inactivity," *Journal of Gerontology*, Vol. 4 (1949), p. 141 ff.

[9] "Old Hands Snub Pensions," *Business Week* (Nov. 18, 1950), p. 124 ff.

[10] Margaret L. Stecker, "Beneficiaries Prefer to Work," *Social Security Bulletin*, Vol. 14 (January 1951), pp. 15-17.

solve this through self-employment, but not everyone has the capital and the ability for this type of venture.

There is evidence, too, that any number of older people are capable of performing some types of work. Placed in the right job, they have been found to have production and absentee records similar to those of younger workers. It is well to note also that employed older people generally have been found to have better personality adjustment than the unemployed.

Table 10. Why Social Security Beneficiaries Stop Work *

Reason for termination of employment	Percent
Lost job	53.2
Quit job to retire	5.5
Quit job for reasons of health	34.9
Quit job for other reasons	6.4

* Based on Margaret L. Stecker, "Beneficiaries Prefer to Work," *Social Security Bulletin*, Vol. 14 (1951), pp. 15-17.

The big issue seems to be, then, whether society is willing and can find ways for its older citizens to make their contribution to its productive efforts. During the economic depression of the 1930's the movement toward earlier retirement gained real impetus. It was felt that somehow it was not "fair" for older people to work while numerous younger men were unemployed. However, during the war years that followed, it was felt that it was not "fair" for older people to remain "idle" when we were in such obvious need of their productive help. And it was the wartime experiences that demonstrated so forcibly how much and how well many older people *could* work.

What should our policy on the employment of older people be in so-called "normal" times? Are our economy and our industrial capacity really such that older workers constitute a threat to the employment of younger men? Must we force one man to retire so that another can be employed, or is there room for both?

On the other hand, can society afford to lose the productive contributions of the older workers? With the growing proportion of aged in our society, it is becoming increasingly more important to answer these and related questions. Most would agree that we must provide for the financial needs of our older citizens. But *how* is the question.

Insurance for old age. It would be entirely unrealistic to expect all older people to provide for their needs through current employment. Although this is true of people of all ages, it is particularly so of those at that stage of life we have called later senescence. Almost by definition persons thus designated are unemployable because of the extent of physical and psychological aging. About one third of all people sixty-five or over are now receiving Old Age and Survivors Insurance benefits. This is the exclusively federal program supported at present by equal contributions from employer and employee. When a person reaches sixty-five and retires, or when he retires thereafter, he is eligible to receive monthly benefits, the amount of which is based on his earnings while he was employed. In 1953 the maximum possible old-age benefits were $85 per month, but the average actually paid was $51 per month.[11]

Old Age and Survivors Insurance as presently constituted cannot in itself meet the financial needs of all people over sixty-five. In the first place, the payments are small, averaging much less than the amount necessary for an adequate standard of living. Secondly, there are some who are not eligible for benefits, although their numbers are decreasing, and, finally, there will always be some older people with needs greater than can be met through such a program. It is a matter of arithmetic to demonstrate what would be needed to finance a program that would provide adequate retirement income for everyone when he reached age sixty-five. Whatever this amount is, it would remain to be determined just how the bill would be met. The various alternatives for financing the program are each fraught with value conflicts. If workers would have to contribute substantially more to the

[11] Floyd A. Bond and others, *Our Needy Aged*, New York, Henry Holt and Co., 1954, p. xvi.

program, many would resent the necessary curtailment of spending during youth and middle age; a sizable increase in employers' share would meet some public disapproval because prices of many goods may increase to absorb the added costs, and so on.

The monthly income derived from most special retirement programs is not sufficient to provide an adequate standard of liv-

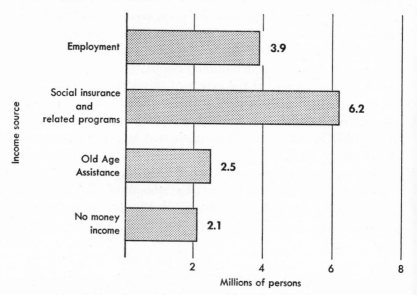

Fig. 12. Income sources of persons 65 and over, 1954. (From *Social Security Bulletin*, Vol. 17, December 1954, pp. 16-18.)

ing. Even in industries which according to today's standards have "liberal" retirement programs many workers choose not to retire partly because they do not wish to take the loss in income that retirement on a company pension would mean. Finally, only a very small portion of the nation's wage earners can afford to purchase an annuity from a commercial concern. A man of thirty, for example, would have to pay about $500 per year, or a total of over $17,000 before he is sixty-five, in order to receive a guaranteed yearly income of $2,000 thereafter.

Old Age Assistance. About one person in five of those over sixty-five is receiving Old Age Assistance, the state-administered program which provides payment to old people who are in financial need.[12] Workers and employers do not contribute directly to this program; the funds are derived partly from the federal and partly from the state governments. Old Age Assistance payments totaled $1.5 billion in 1950, with the average grant per recipient being approximately $50 per month. Although some such program is necessary as long as we have needy older people, it is scarcely realistic to expect everyone over sixty-five to be supported by state and federal tax funds.

Health problems. A part of the aging process, as we have defined it, is the general loss of physical vigor and the decreased functioning of various physiological processes and organs. It is not surprising, then, that "health" should be one of the chief worries of older people. The physical pathology of aging is not in itself a social problem, but health of the aged becomes one if and when there are societal factors that aggravate the problem or interfere with its diminution.

There are various ways of measuring the extent of the health problem of our aged. Using the "symptoms" approach,[13] a study in Michigan discovered that about two thirds of people over sixty had one or more physical or psychological complaints that required medical attention.[14] This was twice the proportion of youths reporting symptoms and in no age group under fifty did as many as half of the people report conditions requiring medical attention. On a given day, about five persons out of a hundred in the general population are unable to perform their regular duties because of a disabling illness, as compared to fourteen out of every hundred persons sixty-five and older.[15] In 1954 a health insurance company collected data concerning the utilization of hospital facilities by its subscribers of different ages. It was discovered that about 20 percent of policyholders sixty-five and

[12] These and the following statistics regarding Old Age Assistance are derived from Bond, *op. cit.*, pp. xiv-xv.

[13] For a fuller description of this method and its application, see Chapter 6.

[14] Charles R. Hoffer and others, *Health Needs and Health Care in Michigan*, East Lansing, Michigan State College Agricultural Experiment Station, 1950, p. 18.

[15] Federal Security Agency, *op. cit.*, p. 3.

over once admitted to a hospital remained there for twenty-two days or longer. Less than 2 percent of younger policyholders remained in the hospital for this length of time. Due to their length of stay in the hospital and the nature of treatment received, the hospital bills of the aged were considerably higher than were those of younger persons.[16]

Older people seem to have difficulty meeting the costs of the medical care that they can be expected to require. As we have already seen, many are operating on an extremely limited income. Coupled to this is the fact that, as a group, they are likely to need more costly medical attention than other age groups. But only one person in four over sixty-five is likely to have some kind of hospitalization insurance, while the ratio for the general population is about one in two. Many profit-making health insurance concerns either charge higher rates for persons over sixty-five or simply refuse to insure those in this "higher risk" category. Since there is strong value conflict concerning proposals that involve some kind of governmental aid in financing the health costs of aged and other low-income groups,[17] it is unlikely that the problem of meeting the costs of medical care will be adequately solved in the immediate future.

Lack of useful roles. Older people frequently complain of a feeling of "uselessness" or express in some other way that there is no purposeful role that they can perform in society. Such complaints cannot be passed over as some kind of delusion of a failing mind or as a mass indulgence in self-pity. Whether we care to admit it or not, there *is* no useful role for many of our aged today. Although it is not in any sense suggested that we can "return to the past," it is well to note that the lack of useful roles for the aged is a relatively recent phenomenon in our society.

About a hundred years ago almost 90 percent of America's population was classified as "rural." With the vast majority of

---

[16] The data on hospitalization utilization were gathered by the central office of a large health insurance concern in order to assess its rates and practices. They were received in a private communication to the authors with the understanding that the company would not be identified.

[17] See Chapter 6.

our older people living on farms there was no lack of "things to do." The operation of a farm and farm home involved the daily performance of many varied tasks. Some required more skill and physical ability than others, but even the slow-moving and weaker hands of the aged could find something that actually needed to be done. Old women could weave, sew, dye, cook, and care for the many children in the large farm families, thus releasing the younger women for more vigorous chores. Old men were helpful in various farm-maintenance activities, in the lighter agricultural functions, and as a source of information and training for the younger men in the various skills involved in a household economy. Retirement from farming was likely to be more gradual than, for example, retirement from a contemporary factory job. As the farmer grew older and less capable of work, he relinquished more and more of his duties to his son or son-in-law or to whomever else would eventually "take over the family place." Even if or when a farmer did "retire" from work altogether, it was more likely to be a matter of choice or at least it was not the same as the worker today who finds that it is the "company policy" to retire him at a given age whether or not he is capable of working, wants to continue working, or has sufficient money on which to live. Finally, our farmer of one hundred years ago was respected for his wisdom and was turned to for advice by younger men. It was not a matter of well-developed "filial piety" or giving "proper respect" to the aged, but simply that the lifetime experiences of the older person served as a valuable guide to the solution of current problems.

Today we are an urban, industrial, rapidly changing society with, quite literally, no place for the older person. He is no longer wanted at the factory, for, rightly or wrongly, it is felt he should not compete with the younger workers for jobs or that he is incapable of performing the job. Many older persons become economically dependent on their children or on social agencies, for government provisions for the aged are inadequate. Children of the aged are often operating on wages or salaries which do not permit them to support their parents in separate establishments and are living in urban residences which will not accommodate the addition of one or more persons. And, even when parents are taken into their children's homes, difficulties often occur both on the side of the supporting family and on the part of the old people as well.

The home life of most old people, then, tends to be an unsatisfactory one. It is a life alone with too little income. Or it is with children in a tense relationship. Or it is in a poor and cheerless old-people's home with other unwanted aged. "Home" brings no sense of security and usefulness to many old people.

Urban life does not encourage the participation of old people in institutional situations other than the family. Dues, assessments, admission prices, expense and difficulties of transportation, the difficulty of replacing old friends with new ones, the feelings of younger adults that old people are "wet blankets," and the general decline of physical strength and energy contribute to the general withdrawal of older people from activities of the community.

In recent years there has been effort on the part of society to provide for the recreational and social needs of older people. Some have labeled the programs "superficial" and the activities "busy work" but, at any rate, there has been a real growth of organizations for and by the aged. In a few localities, civic and other organizations have provided club rooms or game centers where the older person can spend his time at shuffleboard or cards, or, as one such "club" boasts, where checkers, "both regular and Chinese," are available. It is undoubtedly true that some of the aged are able to spend their days more pleasantly and with less concern over "what to do" as a result of the existence of such centers. But life for the aged is still far from being purposeful and useful, and some oldsters complain that it more resembles "playing at living" than living itself. It is no wonder that such a high proportion of workers approach retirement with uneasiness or meet it with disillusionment.

The oldest and most infirm of our aged may be forced to spend their remaining days in some type of "institution." Disguised as they may be with the word "home" in their name, it is difficult to imagine that many regard such places as an adequate substitution for the more usual variety of home. The public-supported institutions usually can furnish only a minimum of care and comfort, and some such "homes" lack basic necessities and have even been called veritable "fire traps." Private institutions usually fare better with respect to physical facilities and equipment, but many old people and their families cannot afford the costs of a private institution, even if some kind of nursing care seems necessary. Basically, institutional provisions for any group in the population tend to be inadequate substitutes for full and useful social functioning. Our society needs to face and find the answer to how it can utilize the citizenship potentialities of at least the healthiest segment of its aged population. Nothing less than *fundamental economic, educational, and recreational alterations* would seem to be necessary for anything approaching an adequate social solution.

The lack of a useful role for our aged, whether in economic spheres, in community life, or in the home, is a very real phenomenon to many of the aged. It is not something, furthermore, which can be remedied by any simple measures, for it is intricately tied up with the other problems of older people. Perhaps the relationship between the problems of the aged will become more evident as we turn to a discussion of suggestions for the amelioration of these problems.

▶ AMELIORATIVE PROGRAMS

As suggested earlier, the problems of the aged have only recently appeared because of the recent increase in the number of old people, and because value conflicts have tended to develop only as our society has become more and more urbanized. This has had the practical result that there are few specific remedies that can be judged and that we are necessarily restricted to broad "plans of attack."

Research. A prerequisite to realistic planning is more extensive research into the sociological, psychological, and physical factors of old age. The research that has been done over the years has forced us to question some of our earlier notions regarding the aged and has indicated the nature and extent of their problems. Now there is need for research directed toward the amelioration of the problems that have been discovered. It has become apparent, for example, that there is lack of a purposeful social role for many of our aged. But what kind of a role can we substitute and how will this new role affect our general economic and social life? We have learned much about the physical processes involved in aging, but there is still much more to learn. What, for instance, are the *meaningful* criteria of physical aging and how can these accurately be measured? When, according to these criteria, does an individual become "too old" for gainful employment, or for *what kind of* gainful employment?

In order to obtain the answers to these and a host of other questions, there has to be a certain relocation of our values. Problems of old age will have to receive a more prominent place in the hierarchy of problems our society wishes to attempt to solve. Geriatrics will have to become as important a field of medical endeavor as pediatrics. Housing programs for the aged may compete with plans for superhighways, parks, or even schools. The value conflicts involved in devoting increasingly more attention to problems of the aged are not to be minimized.

Immediate programs.   Although the need for large-scale planning and research is imminent, there are some things that can be done today to lessen the problems of the present population of older people. Some of these are "stop-gap" measures designed to treat the symptoms of the difficulties rather than remove the difficulties. But to the 14 million old people now living they would represent a real improvement over present conditions. First of all, we could provide better for the financial needs of those older people in need of such assistance. The machinery for doing this is already in existence in the form of Old Age and Survivors Insurance and Old Age Assistance. Most states need to convert their county almshouses into nursing homes, which will take paying old people as well as the indigent. A few states have begun to address themselves to the psychological and social problems of the inhabitants of old people's homes as well as to the improvement of their physical well-being. But much more needs to be done, including the provision of occupational therapists, recreation specialists, and social workers for such homes.

Industry and other employers of large numbers of people can, with little expense, help prepare workers for retirement. Several large concerns already provide counseling and guidance programs that begin five years before retirement, but such programs are not as yet widespread. Finally, communities can provide recreational facilities geared to the capabilities and desires of older people and can add to their social welfare staffs counselors and social workers who are specifically trained to deal with the problems of the aged. Although all of these suggestions require the expenditure of some money, they would not be costly. To put them into effect, however, it is necessary that society recognizes the existence of problems and becomes willing to do something about them.

Attitudinal changes. The chances of securing many of the specific recommendations for temporary relief of problems of the aged as well as the direction of research resources and long-range planning to problems of this age group rest in a large part on the ability of society to develop new attitudes toward old age and its problems. Employers may have to change their minds regarding the employment of older workers, and retirement programs may have to be revamped. Older people themselves are faced with necessary changes in attitudes regarding what constitutes a useful role, and individually they need to prepare for shifts in roles. The rest of society must somehow accept or adjust to these role changes, whatever they may come to be. Such changes in attitudes will not be easy for a society which has defined usefulness as productivity, and in which youth is beauty, the new is perforce better than the old, and economic idleness is somehow indecent if not downright wrong. But various attitudinal changes that cut across our whole scheme of values, nevertheless, are necessary before large-scale ameliorative programs can be instituted. This is a problem which even the most selfish young adults should consider worth solving, for, while they may

fancy themselves as not intimately involved in some social problems, most of them will one day be old people.

▶ SUMMARY

Between 1900 and 1950 the population of the United States
doubled while the number of people sixty-five years of age and
older quadrupled. In 1900 about 4.1 percent of the population
were sixty-five or older; in 1955, the percentage was 8.6; in 2000
it is expected to be between 13 and 15. Because of the growing
percentage of old people in our population, and of the little provision for helping them to be useful in our society under urban
conditions, increasing attention has recently been directed toward the problem of old age.

Any chronological designation of old age is arbitrary, but there
are certain discernible, though relative, physical, psychological,
and sociological criteria of aging. Since the span of quite a few
years can be encompassed in the period called "old age," and
since the individual variations in the aging process are so great,
it has been suggested that the postadult period be subdivided into
early senescence, middle senescence, and later senescence.

The specific problems of the aged selected for analysis were
those relating to the economic and health status of older people
and their lack of a useful role in society. Although it can be
demonstrated that many older people currently do not have
sufficient income to maintain a modest but adequate standard of
living, there is considerable disagreement over how society
should provide for its older citizens. Some older people can be
employed, but younger adults sometimes resent the competition.
As presently constituted, Old Age and Survivors Insurance benefits are not sufficient to provide an adequate standard of living for
all persons sixty-five and over, but to increase such benefits
would be costly. Finally, it is not realistic to expect everyone over
sixty-five to be supported by state and federal tax funds, as
through a program such as Old Age Assistance.

Health is of more concern to the aged than to people of
younger age groups and older people frequently experience dif-

ficulty meeting the costs of the medical care that they can be expected to require. They are less likely to have some kind of hospitalization insurance, partly because of the cost of such insurance and partly because some companies refuse to insure older people.

The lack of a useful role in society is a major complaint of many older people. The shift from a predominantly rural to an increasingly urban and industrial society, compulsory retirement, and lack of economic independence of many older people, have helped to bring about this condition. Some recent attempts have been made to give older people "something to do" with their time, but this is not necessarily the same as a purposeful role in society.

Society can attempt to reduce the problems of old age through research, through immediate relief programs, and by effecting gross changes in attitudes on the part of its members. But conflicting societal values are interfering with ameliorative efforts; there seems to be disagreement concerning whether or not problems actually exist and even those who recognize the problems of old age sometimes radically differ over proposals for reducing them.

SUGGESTED READINGS

American Journal of Sociology, Vol. 59 (January 1954). This entire issue is devoted to studies of aging and retirement.

Breckinridge, Elizabeth L., *Effective Use of Older Workers*, New York, Wilcox and Follet Co., 1953. Retirement practices and preretirement programs are studied in ninety corporations. A good account of what business and industry can do, are doing, or are failing to do for older workers.

Cavan, Ruth, Ernest Burgess, Robert Havighurst, and Herbert Goldhamer, *Personal Adjustment in Old Age*, Chicago, Science Research Associates, 1949. This book presents an excellent summary of much of the information already known about old people, discusses their problems in terms of modern psychological and sociological concepts, and presents the results of some original research conducted by the authors.

Donahue, Wilma (ed.), *Housing the Aging*, Ann Arbor, University of Michigan Press, 1954. Report of the University of Michigan's Fifth Annual Conference on Aging. The delineated area of housing problems is carefully reviewed. Contains excellent case histories of astonishing housing improvisation resorted to by some of our aged.

Federal Security Agency, *Fact Book on Aging*, Washington, D. C., U. S. Government Printing Office, 1952. A brief, clear presentation of statistical data on personal characteristics, income, employment, living arrangements, and health of older people.

Havighurst, Robert J., and Ruth Albrecht, *Older People*, New York, Longmans, Green and Co., 1953. An intensive study of older people in a small Midwest town coupled with a general analysis of problems of old age. A readable work that can be considered a basic text in social gerontology.

Kaplan, Jerome, *A Social Program for Older People*, Minneapolis, The University of Minnesota Press, 1953. Presents guides to group activity for older persons developed from experience with senior citizen organizations. An imposing program for enabling older persons to remain contributing members of the community.

Kaplan, Oscar J., "Psychological Aspects of Aging," *Annals*, Vol. 279 (January 1952), pp. 32-42. Good summary and critique of existing research into mental abilities and other psychological characteristics of aging.

Mathiasen, Geneva (ed.), *Criteria for Retirement*, New York, G. P. Putnam's Sons, 1953. Report of a national conference to investigate what yardsticks, other than chronological age, could be used as a basis for retirement. A good coverage of the problem and introduces some new approaches.

STUDY QUESTIONS

1. Why is it important to know both the *number* and the *proportion* of aged in a society? Illustrate.

2. State as concisely as possible the changes that have taken place or are expected to take place with regard to the number and percentage of aged in the United States between 1900 and 2000.

3. What is physical old age? Give an illustration of the individual variation with respect to physical aging.

4. What is meant by sociological old age? Illustrate how sociological old age could either precede or follow physical old age.

5. Why is it felt that we need subcategories of the period com-

monly called "old age"? What subcategories have been suggested?

6. What is the evidence that many problems of the aged are economic ones? How are economic and health problems related? Illustrate.

7. What are three basic ways of meeting the financial needs of older people and what value clashes are associated with each?

8. Contrast the role of an older person living on a farm one hundred years ago with that of an older urban dweller of today. Is the older person today justified in his feeling of "uselessness"?

9. Outline some needed research in the field of old age. What value conflicts would you anticipate if this suggested research were to compete with research in other areas?

10. What are some attitudinal changes considered necessary for major reform in the area of old age? Illustrate how changes in attitudes would be related to the success of a specific program you consider necessary or desirable for improving some problems of old age.

· 14 ·   Education

Generally speaking Americans are proud of their system of mass education and profess great faith in its eventual contribution to the evolution of a better social world. On a typical school day over 1 million teachers teach some 33 million full-time students. In view of the general consensus regarding the efficacy of education and our high utilization of mass education, it may seem unusual to find "education" included in a discussion of social problems. But there are some strong value conflicts in this area. Most of the societal conflicts tend to center not around whether education itself is good or bad but rather around the *nature of education* and the *kinds of teaching which are desirable.*

There is, to be sure, considerable belief that many American communities are penurious in their expenditures for education and that our loudly voiced respect for education is not very effectively translated into better school buildings, adequate salaries for teachers, and support of educational programs which now are known to be good but somewhat more costly than traditional education. Comparative statistics have from time to time been compiled to show that our "gigantic educational structure" is not as imposing as it might at first seem to be. One statistician points out that the nation spends more money per year for tobacco than it does for education. Others have made similar startling comparisons. It has been pointed out that our expenditures for education are shamefully low; not only do other nations excel us in educational outlay but we, a wealthy nation, could well afford to support education more liberally than we actually do. Nevertheless, as compared to the other nations of the world, the American educational system now touches more people for a longer period of time than any other comparable system.

▶ WHO CONTROLS THE SCHOOLS?

We hear much about the allegedly "free" character of American schools. The student learns in studying American history how the traditions of education were formed during the gradual emancipation of our schools from church and state domination. All too often the incorrect implication is drawn that American education is entirely free, in the sense that no one except the teaching profession dictates what shall be taught or tries to use the school as a propagandizing agency. The truth is, of course, to the contrary.

Pressure groups. Educational administrators are constantly harassed by this group or that which wishes to use the schools for the purpose of indoctrinating children in the community with some point of view regarded as desirable. In Chicago, for example, during "Big Bill" Thompson's regime, political pressure was brought upon the schools to teach American history in such a way as to perpetuate what historians had demonstrated were untruths about our history. Pressure has from time to time been brought to bear by "conservative interests" against the use of certain textbooks. Accusations vary in intensity from the outright charge that the books "strive to inculcate communistic attitudes in children" to the more moderate charges that the books advocate social change of which the complainants disapprove. Controversies over religious and moral questions are likewise numerous. One pressure group attempts to force the schools to disseminate propaganda against consumption of liquor and tobacco; another is devoted to putting pressure upon the schools so that Bible reading may become a required part of the curriculum; a third is currently attempting to encourage the schools to give instruction on problems of marriage, while still another group bitterly opposes such educational training for high-school students.

For what does the school exist? The conflicting demands of these several groups are no mere quibbles over technique or course content: they are fundamental issues vitally affecting the very nature of education itself. The significant question which all of these demands repeatedly pose is: *Should the educational system of the society be the creature or agent of pressure groups or should it be a semiautonomous part of society, free to determine its policies on the basis of the professional judgments of teachers and administrators?* In short, there is reason to doubt whether Americans mean what they say when they praise the "freedom" of American education, for so many of them are members of pressure groups which spend considerable time and money trying to induce the schools *not* to be free and impartial.

Domination of schools and the democratic process. It should not be inferred that the task of maintaining a free school system is an easy one. The problem of domination by extra-educational "interests" inheres in the nature of the American system. If the schools are to be run "democratically," then they ought presumably to implement the wishes of the people. Hence, if the people wish to use their own schools as indoctrinating agencies, it is difficult to rationalize opposing their exercise of democratic rights. On the other hand, it is very doubtful whether the various pressure groups which perennially try to use the schools as indoctrinating agencies represent any significant portion of the total population; on the contrary, they are relatively small but powerfully organized special-interest groups with purposes which are difficult to justify as "in the interest of the public welfare." To be sure, attempts are usually made to "sell" pressure-group-sponsored ideas to the public in the name of "Americanism," "character formation" or "proper respect for God," but closer examination usually reveals that the programs can be reduced to the simple terms of indoctrination in the mundane cause which the sponsoring group represents. This simply shows that the ideals of objectivity, openmindedness, and fair play which the schools have tried to observe on social issues are difficult to maintain in the practical situation.

There are even those persons who contend that it is a mistake for the school system to be neutral on social issues, that the teacher should throw the weight of his prestige and effort in one direction or another for the purpose of guiding the attitudes and ideas of the future citizens of the nation. Such a point of view is tantamount to saying that the school is a creature of the power groups of a society and that it exists as the propaganda agency for such groups.

Are the schools "Communist dominated"? While it may not be as common a complaint as some others, probably the most serious charge against modern educators is that they are purposefully attempting to condition their students for life in a collectivistic type of society. The attacks range all the way from rather loose talk about "socialistic leanings" of school teachers to the out-and-out charge that the schools are "Communist dominated." Generally speaking, the more specific the charge of this nature, the easier it is to demonstrate its utter falsity. It is simply a matter of record, for example, that very, very few teachers, at all levels, have been found to be members of the Communist Party. Two Senate investigating committees, as a matter of fact, were able to discover only a handful of college instructors (42, to be exact, or less than three-hundredths of 1 percent of all college professors and instructors) who declined to affirm that they were not members of the Communist Party.[1] The bulk of these, it appears, were motivated in their refusals to comment by reasons other than their guilt of subversion. The National Education Association, the professional society of elementary and secondary school teachers, has taken a strong stand on Communism. Members of the Communist Party are barred from membership in the N.E.A., and the organization has passed a resolution that members of the Communist Party should not be allowed to teach in public schools. But still the charges persist, and emotionally charged pamphlets filled with unsubstantiated generalizations continue to make their appearance. For example, one such pamphlet titled, "How Red is the Little Red School House?"[2] pic-

[1] Reported in an analysis of the hearings of the House of Representatives Committee on Un-American Activities and the Senate Sub-Committee on Internal Security in *Christian Science Monitor* (July 21, 1953).

[2] Published by Employers Association of Chicago, Chicago, Ill.

tured on its cover a foreign soldier injecting a needle labeled "Organized Communist Propaganda" into the little red school house. Others, by innuendo, suggestion, or downright accusation, link any new idea with political radicalism, political radicalism, in turn, with socialism, and socialism with totalitarian communism to "prove" that a teacher with an up-to-date educational outlook is therefore indoctrinating along Communistic lines!

It is probably little comfort to educators to realize that attacks directed at them are no recent matter. We can go back at least as far as 399 B.C. when the courts found the Athenian teacher, Socrates, guilty of corrupting the youth of his day. And, in a little different framework, another teacher of admittedly "radical" ideas was rewarded with crucifixion. There is even less comfort to be gained from knowing that the present conflict over those with "new ideas" is by no means restricted to educators. Although we have talked of this as a "school problem," in a later chapter it will become obvious that society in general is finding it difficult to agree on the distinction between dissent and disloyalty, or even freedom of speech and subversive propaganda.

What is the purpose of education?   There is a basic theoretical issue of educational philosophy which is implicit in the perennial squabbles over control of the policies of educational institutions. Stated in somewhat extreme form, the present value judgments seem to embody three distinct conceptions:

1. That education should be concerned solely with the *indoctrination of the young into the culture of the group* which controls the educational system—that is, that the schools should teach each new generation to be precisely like its predecessor in as many ways as possible. This we may call the "function of indoctrination."

2. That the function of education is not merely to perpetuate the existing culture without bias, but to *evaluate* it—that is, to analyze it, to raise questions concerning the relative worth of things, and to *consider various proposals for the perpetuation or modification of the society* in which the student lives (more or less as we are doing in this book).

3. That it is the function of education to *direct social change* along lines which appear to be desirable and in the interest of public welfare—that is, the schools should take the initiative in remaking society by shaping the attitudes and skills of children so as to facilitate an emerging but different society. This, too, is a type of indoctrination, but it is a dynamic rather than a static orientation. It warrants the term indoctrination, however, because the emphasis is placed upon teaching people what they ought to think, rather than simply training them to be critical, analytical, and open-minded about social issues.

If one examines carefully his own conception of education, he will probably find that he holds in some measure with all three of these somewhat distinct philosophies. He will probably maintain the school's right to teach reading, writing, and arithmetic, the social graces, and a respect for American traditions and culture. To this extent, then, he wants the schools to indoctrinate with the time-honored ways of thought and action which we have mentioned. But, like most people, he will also claim to desire that children be taught "to think," to analyze new ideas and learn to be critical, to learn not to accept blindly the accumulated errors of the past as if they represented eternal verities. Finally, he will probably doubt that it is possible for the world to remain changeless, will want his children prepared to live in the kind of future world which they are likely to encounter, because he wishes them to adapt as painlessly as possible to the requirements of new times.

So long as we state educational philosophy in such general terms as the above, not much controversy occurs. But when we specifically implement these broad principles, it is easy for controversies to ensue. Imagine the business-class parent who wants his child to "think clearly on social issues" when his son announces during the Christmas holiday that, as a result of his economics studies, he is sympathetic with the cause of labor and has decided to become a union organizer. Had Junior decided to be a corporation lawyer as a result of "viewing all sides of the problem," Father might very well be pleased with the "liberalism" of his son's college. This not-wholly hypothetical anecdote calls attention to the fact that differences in social philosophy and vested interests tend naturally to be carried over into one's educational philosophy, at least for some people in this society at this time.

Schools and society. Perhaps the most important point to our discussion thus far is the demonstration that no institution in our society escapes the tensions and value clashes of the rest of the society. Class issues, racial tensions, and religious ideologies leave no segment of the society unaffected. It appears that democracy is peculiarly well fitted to this diffusion of conflict because, to the extent that people are free to influence their institutions, they accordingly have the power to use their institutions to further whatever points of view they favor. Opposing groups, of course, have the same privilege and seek also to achieve their goals by the same procedures. The result is that economic issues, for example, do not remain merely economic issues: they become religious issues and educational issues as well.

▶ SOME CURRENT ISSUES IN AMERICAN EDUCATION

In the foregoing paragraphs we have discussed what is probably the basic over-all issue of American education—namely, the problem of the relationship of the school to the value conflicts of the time. Pressures are brought upon the school on the one hand to lead the forces of change and on the other hand to exert its influence to buttress the forces of reaction. Meanwhile there are numerous more circumscribed educational problems which in some ways relate to the more basic issue but in many other ways are independent of it. Some of these we shall discuss in the following paragraphs.

Adjusting teaching methods to new technology. Ours is a world of mechanical contrivances and fast-moving activity, but our educational methods have been handed down from a simpler society with a slower pace. Education has traditionally meant book reading, drill, and "the correct" explanation from the teacher. Currently, however, it is doubtful whether one learns as much from reading books as he does from nonreading sources, such as the radio, travel, moving pictures, television, and experimentation with mechanical apparatus found in abundance in almost every home. Within the memory of millions of persons still living, none of these educational sources except travel existed or was deemed possible. Experimental evidence now shows conclusively that many things can more effectively be learned through such media as motion pictures than through the reading of books. Yet traditional attitudes on the part of parents and even on the part of some school administrators and teachers, have often made it difficult for the schools to secure permission from their constituents to move as rapidly as they could in taking advantage of many of the benefits of modern scientific aids to education.

Not only has the new world brought new educational aids; it has also brought new educational problems. The great number and speed of automobiles, for example, makes safety education a more fundamental teaching objective than reading or writing, for the child must learn a complicated pattern of adjustment to the automobile or his very existence is in jeopardy. The radio, television, and moving picture have also brought added educational problems along with commercial recreation. And the schools have not always been quick to make the necessary adjustments in curricula so as to serve youth in the best possible way by teaching how better to live under the conditions of the new existence.

The chief impediment which the schools have encountered has been a tradition-mindedness on the part of parents and other citizens whose conception of education, schools, and teachers is the product of another era so radically different from the present one that the old patterns no longer fit. Gradually the schools are learning that if they are to do an effective job in educating children they must begin with new education for the children's parents. It is unfortunate that the parent education movement began so late, for educational progress has been much retarded by the inertia of parent attitudes of a by-gone day.

Passing of "discipline."   Much of traditional education was concerned with what was known as "discipline." The older philosophy emphasized the importance of "training the mind" of the child so that he would find it easy to do the right things at the right time—the right things and the right time reflecting, of course, the traditional folkways and mores of the society. Much reliance was placed upon such "difficult" subjects as Latin, mathematics, formal English grammar, philosophy, and ancient history because these disciplines were thought to "train the character" in the desired way since they represented "the best that had been thought and said" by the ancient worthies. Modern educational research has largely demonstrated that the assumptions of the older discipline theory are false, that, for example, Greek and mathematics do not train uniquely for character, and that the mere difficulty of educational tasks has little to do with the creation of desirable educational outcomes for the child. We now know that teaching children to march to class like Prussian cadets does not make for obedience any more than reciting the names of the Presidents in order teaches anything vital about the processes of American history.

It is probably true that the same outward manifestations of discipline found in schools years ago are not found as frequently in today's schools. A visitor to the local elementary or high school is more likely to observe an active discussion of a "class project" than he is to see row after row of children sitting with hands neatly folded quietly listening to an authoritarian teacher. But if our visitor remains long enough, he will be forced to admit that the lack of absolute quiet is not synonymous with chaos and that the children are "disciplined" in the sense that they are learning cooperativeness, the respect of the wishes and feelings of others, and the necessity, sometimes, for subordinating individual wishes to those of the group. In part, then, the reality of lack of "discipline" in schools is dependent on what we mean by "discipline."

Neglect of the "fundamentals."   A somewhat related complaint levied against today's schools is that the various "new-fangled" methods have led to a neglect of the "basic subjects."

In almost any community one can find those who in all seriousness claim that children today are not being taught "the three R's." Others, with equal seriousness, simply assert that the typical high school graduate cannot write a decent sentence, or spell, or do something else, depending on the views of his accuser. Still others allege that too much time is spent on such "fads" and "frivolities" as driver training and homemaking.

Not generally known is that the United States Office of Education has on file many comparative studies in which today's children were given tests previously administered to children of their parents' and grandparents' generations. Present-day children have made an excellent showing, generally scoring as well or better than children of other generations. Apparently, present teaching methods and better trained teachers have made it possible for children to learn the traditional school subjects as well as ever in addition to pursuing newer educational goals. From the evidence at hand, then, we are forced to conclude that today's methods not only work, but work fairly well.

It has been a difficult task, however, to win support for newer educational thinking. There are many thousands of parents and citizens who still think in terms of "eternal verities" which modern educational research has demonstrated to be utter nonsense. This precipitates one of the current problems of education— namely, public interpretation of the findings of educational science and the implications for sound educational practice which flow from these findings. So long as there is some measure of democratic control of the school, and so long as the public is unaware of the findings of research and unsympathetic to the new educational techniques, the school will continue to be unable to make the full use of its knowledge. It is still very common to find fairly well-informed adults poking fun at new educational ideas, using as their authority some myth about human behavior which educational experts long ago have exploded. Many of the issues between schools and community can be solved only if and as the community better understands what the schools are undertaking to do and what evidence they have for their current and proposed programs.

Class bias in the school system. Ostensibly the American school system is democratic. Apparently it was the intention, in establishing a free (that is, tax-supported) educational system, to make the benefits of education available to everyone, irrespective of class position, wealth, or income. The compulsory feature in school attendance was intended to further the over-all coverage of educational benefits. With the exception of a relatively few children who attend nonparochial, private schools catering mainly to the wealthy, there is considerable democracy in American schools. But it is a democracy more apparent than real. Studies of the interactions of school children show without doubt that the social-class characteristics of the outside community also operate in the classroom where racial and religious prejudice, cliques, pecuniary rivalries, and other conditions inimical to the operation of true educational democracy are very evident and interfere with the attainment of the best possible educational experience for all of the children. More important, perhaps, in a practical way, is the fact that educational facilities are not used proportionately by the children of different economic levels.

Tables 11 and 12 illustrate a condition which some persons believe is harmful to the best interests of society. They show the loss to the entire society by not using the talents and not developing the mentality of numbers of the children of the less privileged classes. Some persons attempt to explain away these facts by citing the alleged "lack of ambition" among the children of lower economic status, as if the difference could be explained solely in terms of differential ambition. The fact is that there is an important economic basis for the failure of children from the lower-income classes to attend college and even high school proportionately to their numbers in the total population. What is that economic reason?

Our so-called "free" education is not actually free beyond the elementary grades. It is true that often no high school tuition is imposed and that the children of rich and poor are legally equally free to attend, but books and clothes and miscellaneous expenses which must be borne by the parents of the child constitute a

Table 11. *Relation of Intelligence to Educational Opportunity* *

(Record of students with intelligence quotients of 110 or above)

Educational advance	Socio-economic status above average, in percent	Socio-economic status below average, in percent
Dropped school at 8th grade or below	0.7	7.9
Completed 9th, 10th, or 11th grade but did not graduate from high school	6.2	20.2
Graduated from high school but did not attend college	36.3	59.0
Attended college	56.8	12.9

* Data from W. Lloyd Warner, Robert J. Havighurst, Martin B. Loeb, *Who Shall Be Educated?*, New York, Harper & Bros., 1944, p. 52.

Table 12. *Relation of Parental Income to Full-time College Attendance of "Superior" Milwaukee High School Graduates* *

Parental income	Percent in college full time
$8,000 plus	100.0
$5,000-$7,999	92.0
$3,000-$4,999	72.9
$2,000-$2,999	44.4
$1,500-$1,999	28.9
$1,000-$1,499	25.5
$ 500-$ 999	26.8
Under $500	20.4

* Data from W. Lloyd Warner, Robert J. Havighurst, and Martin B. Loeb, *Who Shall Be Educated?*, New York, Harper & Bros., 1944, p. 53.

great, and often an impossible, financial burden for the parents to bear, with the result that high schools and especially colleges are virtually closed to children of low-income families. It is argued, again, that this results in an appreciable loss of talent to a society and that, therefore, "something should be done" to stop it. To this end it is advocated that we develop some form of complete subsidization which would make it possible for all children to get as much educational training as they have the ability to absorb, irrespective of their families' abilities to pay. Obviously this is a costly proposal—at least it can be made to appear so by its opponents.

In another sense, the educational system is class-biased. It is charged that there is insufficient attention to the life needs of the lower-income people. There is said to be insufficient attention given, for example, to the vocational needs of the working classes. To some extent, of course, the vocational school is a step in this direction, but it is thought to be an insufficient step because in many communities there are no vocational schools and those that exist are often not supported by comparable funds and emphasis.

Segregated schools. When we turn to a comparison of schools that are segregated on the basis of race it seems that the quality of our "free" education differs according to the skin color of the students pursuing it. At least that is the inference that can be derived from many of the available objective data. In the South in 1952, for example, school operating expenses for all-Negro schools averaged $116 per pupil as opposed to $180 for each white pupil.[3] Teachers of Negro children averaged a few more pupils in each class than the average of white pupils per teacher. The number of books available in a school library should be one index of a "good" school. In this respect, it was discovered that the number of books available per Negro student was less than half that available for each white student. Finally, nearly twice the proportion of white as Negro children ate in federally aided

[3] These and subsequent statistics reported in "Segregation and the Schools," Public Affairs Pamphlet No. 209, New York, Public Affairs Committee, 1954, pp. 17-18.

school lunchrooms. And, although we would assume their biological needs to be much the same, more money was spent *per pupil* to feed the white children in the lunch program than the Negro.

These and similar statistics lend support to our remarks in Chapter 12 that school systems operating on the "separate-but-equal" doctrine are infrequently equal. And although the Supreme Court has ruled that such practices are unconstitutional, it seems that the segregated school system will, for a time at least, remain in some of the states. This particular issue in American education obviously is more than a "school problem."

Special educational needs. Most educational programs have been set up in terms of the needs of the more or less average child. There is, of course, a wide range of individual variation in the personalities of children, and hence there is considerable maladjustment of many children to the school system or of the school system to the children, whichever way one may care to state it. The child who learns more slowly than the average or who learns more rapidly than the average, the child who is hard of hearing, the child with emotional problems, the child with defective eyesight, and the child with peculiar interests and disinterests—all pose special problems for schools and teachers.

The traditional approach. The older ideology simply attempted to coerce every child into conformity with the general pattern of education, and those who failed to measure up were required to repeat grades and endure humiliations of one sort or another designed to stimulate greater effort—the dunce cap, staying after school, extra "home work," and the like. Those children who were unable to fulfill the requirements of minimum conformity were, after more or less humiliation and concomitant mental-emotional damage, dropped from the educational process somewhere along the line. There are still many people, mostly laymen, who adhere to this conception of education. There is growing recognition, however, that the special needs of children, whether the result of extremes of intelligence, variations of emotional make-up, special abilities, disabilities, interests and apathies, require and deserve somewhat unique kinds of instruction and learning experience.

Special classes. Two educational emphases, quite distinct in character, have grown out of this recognition of the great importance of individual difference. The earlier adjustment consisted of the formation of special schools and special classes for such categories of children as the hard of hearing, the slow learners, the fast learners, and "problem children." The chief difficulty with this segregated form of education is in the highly artificial nature of the educational experience of the child in the "special" class; he tends to lose touch with the larger community of more or less normal people. Thus, participation in these specialized classes fosters and accentuates uniqueness and maladjustment rather than teaching the necessary techniques for adjustment to the world of more nearly normal people in which the child will eventually have to live. Another difficulty with special schools and classes is the realization on the part of children and their parents that they are "different" from other people. In many communities great stigma becomes attached to a child's placement in a special class, particularly when the uniqueness in his personality is not especially conspicuous to the layman, and his assignment to a special group is deeply resented.

Individualized treatment. In order, then, to give such children a more nearly normal educational experience and to protect them from the stigma of low-status placement, considerable emphasis has come to be placed upon an educational system which does not segregate special groups. Instead it adapts itself to specialized needs and disabilities by the somewhat variable treatment of each child. Many educational experts allow greater and greater individual leeway in school work requirements, and justify the wide variations in type and amount of learning experience by mental hygiene criteria rather than by those of formal education.

Considerable public resistance has been encountered to this individualization of educational programs. The critics, better versed in the philosophies and rationalizations of the older education than in the newly discovered mental hygiene needs of children, have attacked the new education. They have cited such arguments as the "depreciation of academic standings," ensuing "lack of discipline," and the "unfortunate" result that many children now seem to enjoy their educational experience rather than to detest it. The implication is all too clear among many critics that, if the children like the new education, if some variation in curriculum for different students is allowed, and if clever and slow-witted students are allowed the same privileges, the system is *per se* "not sound." Many of the issues between professional educators and the communities they serve would be reduced or eliminated if a better job of interpretation of the objectives and values of the new education were diffused among the lay elements of the population. As the matter now stands, disagreements are common because there is often no real meeting of the minds between professional educators and laymen as to the values which the educational system is striving to implement.

Educational services to adult, part-time students. As we have pointed out in innumerable places in this book, ours is a rapidly changing society. Changes occur so frequently and the individual's position in the social web is dependent upon so many different and intricate forces, that more or less continuous education is necessary to enable even the better informed citizen to "keep up" with the ongoing process. Increasing numbers of people seem to understand the need for continuous education, not only to keep them apace of changing events in their professions and occupations but to keep them at least minimally intelligent with respect to the accumulated scientific and other knowledge which is of great practical importance in their daily lives.

The prevailing educational organization and ideologies, however, are not well adjusted to this obvious need. Many people still think of schools in terms of little children, or at least of the relatively young, and it is not at all uncommon to hear even fairly well-informed people define "education" and "life" as though neither had much to do with the other.

Financial problems. Even where there is admitted need on the part of adult members of the population for educational services, it is, as a rule, difficult to obtain financial support for adult education programs. The "extension" programs of many colleges and universities, for instance, set tuition and other fees so that the adult education program will be self-supporting, while setting much lower fees for the full time, more juvenile students who are served. Apparently we are willing to provide more nearly free education at public expense to young people than to the adults who are only able to devote part time to their educational endeavor.

Teaching problems. Not only is the educational system financially maladjusted to extensive adult education but it is also not well suited to making the kinds of adjustment necessary to meet the educational needs of adult students. One of the problems of a large Midwestern university which operates a night school for adults is the selection of a staff suited to the instruction of adults; another is convincing administrative and faculty committees that somewhat different educational procedures for adult students are not *per se* inferior merely because they are different. Some adult students have despaired of their attempt at further education because their instructors persisted in treating them as adolescents and pursued teaching practices better suited to juveniles than to their parents. Some of the more honest and introspective teachers have also been frank to admit that they feel ill at ease with more mature students and frustrated because techniques which are effective with adolescents seem not to be so effective with more adult personalities.

In the area of adult education we again see a familiar and fundamental ideological difficulty which is involved in so many other social problems: *Social change brings about new conditions and new needs for people, but we encounter ideological obstacles when we attempt to meet the new needs.* So often the personalities and the institutions upon whom new responsibilities fall are so bound in old ways and empty traditions that they operate at relatively low efficiency and high degrees of confusion.

New roles for educational personnel. Traditionally the teacher has been thought of as a peculiar kind of virtuous and unreal personality, akin to the clergyman. One wag has said that there are three sexes in America: men, women, and school teachers. In the past the teacher was "to set a good example" to the children and to some extent to all of the community. She was not allowed to participate in many of the more or less tolerated diversions and recreations which other people found pleasant and inviting. Almost everything from her mode of dress and manner of speech to her morals was subject to public censure on the basis of standards of propriety appreciably higher than those to which the rest of the community was required or willing to comply.

Now we are confronted with a growing number of teachers, well-trained and skillful in their handling of children, who refuse to be cowed by the tradition that a teacher is in any significant sense a peculiar personality type. To what extent this new group of teachers is the product of new modes in teacher training, to what extent it is an unconscious reaction to the extreme repressions imposed upon teachers in the past, and to what extent it is simply the extension of secular ideas to the teaching profession, we do not now know. But the fact of change is reasonably clear. Teachers today are permitted far greater personal freedom than in the past. They dress like other people, are free in growing numbers of communities to join unions, and insist on elimination or nonenforcement of those clauses in their contracts restricting personal conduct. Although it might be difficult to prove by strict statistical evidence, the generalization seems defensible that present-day teachers in America from the kindergarten to the university are becoming a much more nearly normal group in appearance, personal conduct, interests, and ambitions.

The lay community has by no means wholly approved this change, but despite the opposition which has occurred, the "new teacher" is as much here to stay as the "new family" or the "new government." He is the product, apparently, of social forces, and there is increasing recognition that the fates which brought him about were probably kind fates after all.

New roles for students. Not only has the role of the teacher changed, but the role of the student has changed as well. It is difficult to describe all of the changes and the true extent of them, but a few can be enumerated. There is growing recognition of the fact that students are human beings. Of course, it was never explicitly denied that children were human beings, but the traditional school tended to treat them as if they were at least some strange order of humankind, to be heard only on permission, to have their wishes and ideas always subject to the superior wisdom and censure of adults, their interests presumed not to be quite trusted, and their knowledge necessarily inferior. By contrast the present educational philosophy allows the student many new roles. Student government, for example, which is permitted to some degree, at least, in many schools and to great degree in a few, illustrates the change. Instead of always being told precisely what to do in the school situation, the modern student, at least from junior high school on, is allowed to make many decisions for himself. In consultation with his fellows he is permitted considerable voice, especially in the conduct of so-called extracurricular affairs and increasingly even in such curricula matters as what shall be studied, for how long, and when.

There seems still to be considerable opposition to the concepts of teacher-student curricular planning and to such practices as student courts for handling infractions of school rules, but both practices are spreading. Probably the chief reason for the opposition of many laymen to new teacher and student roles again grows out of values associated with older educational thinking in which the personal "example" of the teacher and the child's "respect" for the teacher and "discipline" were important concepts. These days we are more concerned with the *outcome* of the educational process, with the mental-emotional make-up which the child acquires and the social ideals which are developed, than we are with the empty luxury of such amenities as "respect" for teachers, formalized "discipline," and "example."

▶ SUMMARY

In this chapter we have first treated the over-all problem of education—namely, the extent to which the educational system is and will be allowed to be free from domination by the rest of the society. Value clashes are frequent with respect both to the facts of the matter and to the desirability of a truly "free" and autonomous educational system. Generally speaking, there is a strong tendency toward trying to make the schools subservient to one cause or another, causes which are tied up conspicuously with the ideologies of various social classes. Apparently the various sides consider it important to win friends for themselves at the juvenile level. Many observers fear that an unfree educational system may already be in the making and are apprehensive about each new evidence that freedom is being lost. Despite the ease with which we can unmistakably demonstrate that very, very few teachers, at all levels, are members of the Communist Party, the charges still persist that the schools are "Communist dominated." Under the guise of "fighting Communism" a few groups have actually fought educational freedom.

Attention was then given to a number of more specific problems of organized education in the United States: the problem of adjusting teaching methods to the new scientific and technological world, the passing of the ideology of discipline, the complaint that today's schools neglect the "fundamentals," the problems of class bias in the school system, racially segregated schools, the problems of meeting the educational needs of special categories of people, the extension of educational services to adult, part-time learners, and the evaluation of new educational roles for both students and teachers. Throughout this discussion it has been emphasized that the crux of our problems is the attempts of many people to meet new situations by the application of outworn and obsolete ideologies and practices, by which we do not necessarily mean that they were unsuited to a by-gone day but that they are incompatible with present-day ideas, values, and material culture.

Throughout this chapter we have implied that the "problems of the school system" are not actually or uniquely the problems of the school system alone; they are, instead, the problems of the whole society *reflected in* the program of the school and in the changing roles of teachers and their students.

SUGGESTED READINGS

Bestor, Arthur E., *Educational Wastelands*, Urbana, University of Illinois Press, 1953. A trenchant reprobation of contemporary education methods and philosophy. More incisive and astute than the usual "attack" on the schools, this work cannot be ignored by the student concerned with value clashes in education.

Hulburd, David, *This Happened in Pasadena*, New York, The Macmillan Co., 1951. A stirring but objective account of how an active minority led an attack against Pasadena's schools and the superintendent. A good illustration of current controversial issues in public education.

Knowles, Malcolm S., "Adult Education in the United States," *Adult Education*, Vol. 5 (Winter 1955), pp. 67-76. This article in the official journal of the Adult Education Association provides a quick review of the history of adult education in America, enrollment trends, and its present scope of program. Other issues of the journal contain material on problems in this area.

Melby, Ernest O., and Morton Puner, *Freedom and Public Education*, New York, Frederick A. Praeger, 1953. Selections by men of great stature in education, by citizens working for good schools, and by the school's critics. A well-balanced account of the perennial struggle to keep educational institutions free from domination by outside groups.

Nesbitt, Marion, *A Public School for Tomorrow*, New York, Harper & Bros., 1953. Teachers, pupils, parents become an imaginative team in one community with the result that the school was completely revamped. The product is not necessarily suggested as a standard but is certain to stir discussion.

Progressive Education, Vol. 29 (January 1952). This issue is entitled, "Meeting the Attacks on Education." Covers a variety of controversial points.

Robbins, Florence G., *Educational Sociology*, New York, Henry Holt and Co., 1953. An excellent text in its field. Parts II and III constitute a good treatment of the modern outlook toward the school and the community approach to education.

Stewart, George R., *The Year of the Oath*, Garden City, N. Y., Doubleday & Co., 1950. A vivid history of the University of California's struggle with academic freedom and the loyalty oath. Forcefully written by a member of the faculty.

STUDY QUESTIONS

1. Cite an example from your own experience of domination of the schools by extra-educational interests. Why is it difficult to determine even at one time and one place who exactly controls the schools?

2. What is the charge regarding "Communist domination" of American schools? What is the factual evidence on this matter?

3. State your own belief regarding the purpose of education in relation to the three distinct conceptions presented in the text.

4. Compare the contemporary school and that of the past with respect to "discipline." How does this relate to the different educational goals of the two types of schools?

5. What is the evidence concerning the charge that today's schools "neglect the fundamentals"? In view of this, why does the charge persist?

6. Cite the evidence used to demonstrate the existence of a class bias in the American school system. What are the chief objections to this condition?

7. What evidence supports the position that in school systems segregated on the basis of race the Negro schools are "unequal"?

8. Contrast the traditional and two newer approaches to meeting the educational needs of special groups. State the logic of each position.

9. Why do you think the idea of education for adults is not fully accepted in many communities? What are the chief problems of adult education?

10. Contrast the emerging new roles for teachers and students with those of earlier times and show how these role changes are related to changing educational goals.

· *15* ·   Recreation and Leisure

Throughout human history probably all men have had some leisure and some men have even had much leisure. But it is indeed a recent phenomenon to find large masses of people with considerable free time after they have attended to the practical necessities of life. There is much evidence that this new-found leisure has been a "mixed blessing." Group vies with group concerning the objectives of leisure-time programs. One group sponsors nebulous, almost spiritual, values as "improving the mind" or "elevating the spirit," while another considers the primary aim of leisure-time pursuits is to keep people, particularly children and adolescents, "off the streets" or "out of trouble." And even within groups that can come to agree on leisure-time objectives, disputes are frequent concerning the methods of achieving them. Underlying values are in sharp conflict, and large sections of the public are concerned. Here indeed we have a modern social problem. How have recreation and leisure come to be a major difficulty in America?

Popular opinion has not always supported the desirability of even the existence of leisure time for the individual. Our Puritan forefathers held that it was "the stuff of the devil." Duty for them was always calling, and for the individual to have leisure— that is, time to do as he *pleased* rather than as he was *obliged*— was an indication of wicked self-indulgence and neglect of duty. Even when no disapproval of leisure time existed in our society, the amount of time most citizens had free from their various responsibilities for sheer recreational activity was decidedly limited. Leisure in any large amount was the privilege of only a very small minority. Not only were the hours spent in remunerative work long and arduous, but the "chores" of the premodern home filled most of the remaining time not occupied in sleep.

Today the tasks of the modern home rest chiefly on one person, the mother-wife. As most of those engaged in remunerative activities, she is said to spend approximately 40 hours a week at required effort. While it is realized that the mother of young children often "works" considerably more than a 40-hour week, actually much less time than this is required in those homes where children are older, where there are no children, or where outside help is employed. Hence, the average of 40-hour week of actual work in the home for the modern woman is probably an overly liberal allowance. Allowing 56 hours a week for sleep, most individuals in contemporary America have about 72 hours a week for leisure-time pursuits. From a quantitative standpoint then, leisure is the most important block of time in the life of the modern adult American, and assumes even larger proportions in the life of children and adolescents!

▶ THE NATURE OF CONTEMPORARY LEISURE-TIME PURSUITS

Having a large amount of leisure time, however, does not necessarily create a "problem." It is from the qualitative approach that we encounter difficulties; an increasing number of Americans have come to be dissatisfied with the way they and their fellow citizens use their leisure. *Values which many American citizens believe should be inherent in their recreation and leisure are apparently not being fulfilled.* "They don't know what to do with themselves." And what "they" do do fails to satisfy certain values deemed important for them as individuals and for society. Here seems to lie the crux of the social problem of recreation and leisure. Let us examine what seem to be the major leisure-time pursuits of the American people and what values apparently are and are not being satisfied by these activities.

Contemporary values to be met by recreation. As we have constantly reiterated throughout this book, values held by individuals and groups vary widely and are often in conflict. Sweeping generalizations about what values the American people "must" achieve through leisure-time activities would be exceedingly unrealistic. Analysis of the contemporary occupational aspects of our culture, however, together with an examination of stresses and strains to which most members of our societies are submitted, may lead us to see some of the values that large numbers of Americans hold which are not satisfied by vocations and hence should be provided by avocations.

Occupation of time. One important occupational aspect of modern American culture has already been mentioned and is repeated so that in its very obviousness it will not be overlooked. We refer to the fact that most people today spend considerably less than half of their waking hours performing required tasks. Accordingly a fundamental value of living that must be met by recreation is *the sheer occupation of time*. This, for any large percentage of a population, is a uniquely modern role of recreation.

Fuller use of mind and body. Another important characteristic of the modern occupational scene is the growing technology. Machines have taken over many of the physical and mental tasks formerly performed by persons and have rendered the vast majority of occupations such that they require very little mental or physical exertion. In short, the minds and bodies of many Americans are only fractionally employed by their work. What leisure existed for earlier generations could often best be used in rest and relaxation; many modern workers have relatively little from which to rest and relax. More active recreation, mentally and physically, is apparently needed. Psychological and manual skills, unmet by many occupations, must be provided by leisure-time pursuits. A second value to be met by recreation in modern society is *the providing of opportunity for a fuller use of mind and body*.

Esthetic creation and appreciation. Closely related to the foregoing are the values of esthetic participation and appreciation. Creation and enjoyment of beauty, though variously defined, are found in every culture and are probably universal needs of mankind. Yet for many Americans, both at their work and in their homes, this value is unfulfilled. A third value, then, which it is thought should be met by recreation in modern society *is the providing of opportunity for esthetic creation and appreciation.*

Intimate group participation. America has become a predominantly urban society. One of the most prominent characteristics of life in the city is its individualistic nature. Primary groups like the neighborhood and family are weakened, and most of the individual's contacts with his fellow citizens are superficial, impersonal, nonintimate. Whether by training or by nature or by a combination of the two, persons desire intimate group experience. The nature of most occupations are such today that this experience is not provided for most individuals in their work. Hence, again, it must be found in their leisure. A fourth value to be met by recreation in modern society is *the providing of opportunity for full, intimate group participation.*

Direct contact with nature. Another characteristic of modern urban living and its occupations is the complete removal of most individuals from direct contact with much of nature. While we shall refrain from any poetic exaggerations about the "beauties of the earth and its flora and fauna," the vacation and holiday treks of urban dwellers to the country, together with the unanimity of philosophical and social thinkers concerning the values to be derived from contact with nature, make legitimate our inclusion of it as a need for many Americans that is currently unsatisfied by urban living. Since the work of most Americans keeps them in the city, this value, too, must be satisfied during their leisure. A fifth value to be met by recreation in modern society is *the providing of opportunity for direct contact with nature.*

We do not contend that these are all the values that must be met by leisure-time activities in modern American society, nor that these values are held by all Americans. They are apparently values held by many Americans, however, that are not satisfied outside their leisure hours, and they may serve as a frame of reference for examining the present status of leisure and recreation in the United States.

Commercial recreation. For the most part people do what is easiest to do in their leisure, and the most universally accessible form of recreation for Americans of all ages is the commercially provided variety. The leading American "amusements" are movies, "beer joints," night clubs, reading, sports, television, and radio, both from the standpoint of amount of time spent and from the standpoint of the percentage of persons participating. Two important characteristics that all of these types of recreation have in common are (1) commercial domination and (2), largely, passiveness of roles. Even with sports, spectators vastly exceed active participants. An important football game, for example, will have upward of thirty-five active participants, some one hundred thousand spectators, and millions of radio listeners and newspaper readers. Similar millions of primary and secondary spectators center around two boxers and a referee. And so on with many other forms of recreation.

"Killing time." How well do commercial activities meet our five recreational values? Certainly they may be credited with successful fulfillment of the value of occupying time. The words and actions of many Americans testify to the point that they would "go crazy" if they were not able to "kill time" via movies, television, the radio, reading, and alcoholic drinking. The frequent use of the phrase, "kill time," gives us a clue to the doubtful satisfaction of many of the other desired values of living by commercial recreation.

"Spectatoritis." The passive-spectator nature of most commercial recreation is evidence of its failure to offer opportunity for "full use of mind and body." Listening to most radio programs, watching most television programs and movies, and reading most of the widest selling literature are little challenge to the intellect and none to the body. The same is true of the sports spectator and the "barfly." Sports participation, from the physical standpoint, is, of course, another matter, and popular sports that are commercially (in part) provided fulfill at least half of this value. For most Americans, however, the time and money

spent in the passive commercial amusements far exceed the amount devoted to the active sports.

Limited value fulfillment. The values of esthetic creation and appreciation and of contact with nature are very limited in the major commercial recreations. The value of group participation is met in part by some of the "amusements," but it is usually of a superficial nature. What Wrenn and Harley state about the social opportunities of commercial recreation for youth applies even more fully often to adults.

> There is, of course, a social element in cabarets, roadhouses, and even soda fountains. Movies, skating rinks, and sometimes bowling alleys and swimming pools are also places to which young people of both sexes may resort. But as a rule boys and girls who associate in these places have paired off beforehand. What young people need and what they really want is some place where they can go to make the acquaintance of other young people of the opposite sex.[1]

Popularity of commercial recreation. If commercial recreation fails so completely to meet important values of the American people, why does it remain so popular? One answer is that in most communities there are either no alternatives or no readily accessible alternatives. The widespread appeal of television is a case in point. Many, many Americans watch television programs every day, sometimes for hours at a time. On the surface it would seem that surely television must be meeting most of the important recreational values of its viewers. But at the same time many people frankly admit that television's chief advantage is that it gives them "*something* to do," some not unpleasant way of passing the time between the end of the workday and bedtime.[2] Thus, various forms of commercial recreation may be resorted to not because of their own positive attraction, but simply because "there is nothing else to do."

[1] From C. Gilbert Wrenn and Dudley L. Harley, *Time On Their Hands*, Washington, D. C., American Council on Education, 1941, p. 57, by permission.

[2] Both the high frequency of television viewing and indications of its passive acceptance were discovered in a recent study of leisure time activities in Columbus, Ohio. See Alfred C. Clarke, *The Use of Leisure and Urban Stratification*, unpublished Ph.D. Dissertation, Department of Sociology and Anthropology, The Ohio State University, 1955, pp. 40-42.

Linked with this is the factor of "created demand"; commercial interests "whip up" appetites for their products by various techniques. Once people are lured into commercial recreational activities by various propaganda devices (and since there is "nothing else to do anyhow"), they tend to continue with them. "Low-level" recreation—that is, recreation failing to satisfy values defined as important by the society—is apparently habit forming. The person who begins attending insipid movies or reading pulp magazines or listening to "soap operas" or having a few "short ones" at the corner bar because "everybody else is doing it" and because there are no readily available alternatives, may soon reach a condition where he no longer consciously desires "anything better." Values must be met in the individual or they tend to be buried. As the psychiatrists have so forcibly instructed us, "buried" values are by no means lost; they "fester in the unconscious mind" of the individual. It is suggested here that many Americans not only unconsciously feel that much of their commercially derived recreation is a "waste of time," but that some of it is definitely wrong (contrary to traditional moral values with which they have been indoctrinated). It seems quite probable that our social problem of recreation is intimately related to our social problem of mental health.

The popularity of commercial recreation continues and grows. A pertinent question to raise is this: What are the probabilities of commercial offerings to meet more adequately important social values?

Likelihood of continuing low-quality offerings. The fundamental reason for the low quality of commercial recreation is profit. The kind of facilities, personnel, and space needed to provide the types of recreation giving opportunity for "full use of mind and body, esthetic creation and appreciation, full and intimate group participation, and contact with nature" are simply not in tune with the ring of the cash register. The probability that commercial offerings will alter appreciably to meet these values with any force is small indeed. Profit lies, to put it bluntly, in a small, low-rent "joint," with admission rates that "fit everybody's purse," and with a sufficiently brief and superficial type of entertainment to allow for a large "turnover."

Another reason for not hoping for commercial satisfaction of additional recreational values is cost. Even if the needed types of recreation could be made profitable, they could become so only by appealing to a wealthy clientele; even with the relatively cheap varieties of commercial recreation available at present, a large minority of our population is not able to afford them or can enjoy them only by the sacrifice of some necessities of living. More valuable recreational services from commercial sources would be no answer for the recreational needs of many Americans.

Present status of private, nonprofit recreational programs. Although the development of noncommercial recreation has been inadequate and much less impressive than the gigantic growth of commercial recreation, many public and private, nonprofit agencies exist whose partial or full-time purpose is to provide leisure-time services. Private organizations recognized and began partially to meet the recreational needs of parts of the population prior to the acceptance of any public responsibility in this field. But their major concern in the recreational field has been with the leisure-time activities of youth.

Complexity of private recreational offerings. It is not easy, however, even to gain a clear understanding of the recreational offerings for youth that are provided by the various private agencies. Some leisure organizations of youth are offshoots of adult organizations, such as youth church groups and youth groups affiliated with fraternal orders. Other youth organizations, although not affiliated with an adult organization, are led by adults. Then again, women's clubs, businessmen's clubs, and other adult organizations sometimes "sponsor" youth organizations by supplying facilities or encouraging the public to supply facilities, although they do not work directly with the young people. Finally, there are some organizations composed entirely of youth, directed by them, and not connected in any way with an adult organization. Some "Teen Clubs" fall into this category. Generally their resources for equipment and facilities are meager and they do not receive much community encouragement, probably because of their lack of adult influence.

The existence of such varied leisure-time youth groups makes for difficulty in assessing the recreational resources of a community. Many youth organizations, even those with recreation as a large part of their programs, tend to de-emphasize their recreational objectives and accent such values as "character building," "personal adjustment," and "leadership training." This further complicates the job of evaluating the community recreational resources available to youth.

The same obscurity of recreational purpose characterizes the complex variety of organizations serving adults. Even lodges, fraternities, luncheon clubs, fellowship societies, athletic clubs, etc., whose most obvious reason for being is the entertainment of their members, profess to high service, spiritual, and other "uplifting" aims and minimize, or even deny, their recreational functions. The idea that recreation in and of itself is a worth-while goal is not widespread. Frequently recreation is rationalized as being necessary to promote health and well-being, to prevent boredom, to enable one to do his best on the job, and so on. For this reason, there are few community organizations with fulfillment of the recreational needs of adults as their avowed primary aim. Could it be that we still cling unconsciously to the notion held by our Puritan ancestors that "fun is sin"?

Inadequacies of privately sponsored recreation. Although the number of private organizations in the United States with varyingly covert recreational aims is large and their claimed memberships impressive, several glaring inadequacies appear in their recreational services. They are, first of all, primarily nonadult. The YMCA and YWCA and the settlement houses are exceptions with their adult recreational programs, but even these groups have activities directed principally toward youth and appeal to only a very small fraction of the adult population. Most of the other private organizations make no pretensions of meeting adult needs. It is not suggested that the emphasis on the needs of youth should be reduced, for, as we shall presently observe, they, too, are inadequately served. We are merely pointing out that one deficiency of the recreational activities of private organizations is the lack of an adult program. (The adult service and fraternal and social orders, in general, have very limited programs for a very limited membership; or, as in the case of the large societies and veterans' organizations, largely duplicate commercial recreational offerings for their members' private consumption.)

In addition to not adequately serving adults, private organizations apparently fail in fulfilling the recreational needs of youth. Although the more than a hundred national youth agencies have a steady and even, for some, an increasing membership, they actually reach but a small proportion of all youth. Apparently a large number of young people are attracted neither by the programs of such organizations nor by the personnel providing the program. Reasons often given by young people themselves for their lack of interest in programs sponsored by many of the private agencies are that "goons"—that is, adults whose personalities are not attractive to the young people—are often in charge; that these same persons dominate the activities in such a way as to make full, intimate participation of the young people themselves unappealing or impossible; and that the activities themselves are designed to meet preconceived adult standards of what the young people "ought" to be interested in rather than what really interests them.

Even if we grant that some of these alleged deficiencies in the recreational programs of private organizations are exaggerated and unfair, it is obvious that we cannot expect these groups sufficiently to expand their programs to meet all of the unfulfilled recreational needs of all the old and young people in our society. For providing an area in which to experiment with new ideas on a small scale, for programs requiring individualized attention, for meeting needs of special groups, and for organizing efforts to secure community-wide recreational facilities, the private agencies are indispensable. But to bring adequate recreation to the whole community, the community must turn to itself.

Present status of public recreational programs. Probably the first act of any government in the United States directed toward providing recreational facilities at public expense was the purchase of Central Park by New York City in 1853. The federal government purchased its first national park (Yellowstone) in 1872; one state had a park system prior to 1900. The public recreation movement is very young, and, considering its age, has reached impressive size.

Growth of public recreation. Beginning with the minimal notion of providing space for children's play and adults' rest, public recreation programs have gradually expanded the quantity and quality of their leisure-time provisions for all age groups in the community.

In 1950 the National Recreation Association received reports of public recreation programs from over 2,000 communities, more communities than ever before reporting.[3] These reports indicate, for example, that the number of playgrounds has increased twelvefold since 1910, and indoor centers have increased thirty-threefold during the same period. In the hundred largest United States cities alone, there are over 240,000 acres of municipal park land, about twice the park land in these same cities in 1926.

In communities with well-developed recreation programs, numerous facilities are available to people of all ages. In addition to the more usual playground and park facilities, some communities operate day camps, shooting ranges, bridle trails, outdoor theaters, and bowling greens. Winter sports and indoor recreation centers are being added as communities attempt to extend their program throughout the year.

At the state level we find increasing concern with recreation. Three states, North Carolina, California, and Vermont, have established separate governmental agencies giving full-time service to recreation and all forty-eight states have some type of recreation agency. Increased appropriations for recreation, making possible the steady acquisition of park lands and the improvement of existing facilities, point to the growth of recreation at the state level.

---

[3] *Recreation and Park Yearbook: Midcentury Edition,* New York, National Recreation Association, 1950.

The federal government, through various of its departments and agencies, has long been interested in recreation. Recently the Federal Inter-Agency Committee on Recreation has been formed to co-ordinate the services of the many federal agencies concerned with recreation, to exchange information, and to do cooperative planning. Some see as the next step a separate federal agency devoted solely to recreation—a Federal Recreation Service.

This growth of public recreation at the community, state, and national levels has been sporadic and by no means easily won. Failure of public opinion to accept recreation as an important and inevitable part of life noted in our discussion of private agencies has been even a greater deterring factor for the development of an adequate public recreation program. "Hard-headed" taxpayers and their representatives have often been difficult to convince of the desirability of expending public funds so that people (especially adults) could "play."

During the period of prolonged mass unemployment in the 1930's considerable impetus was given to the public recreation movement. The federal government is estimated to have spent a billion and a half dollars in constructing and improving recreation facilities during the depression years. Shortly after this "boom" in publicly provided leisure-time facilities got well under way, the defense and war programs intervened to divert both funds and personnel from less essential activities. Not only was further expansion of recreational programs, (except the temporary ones provided servicemen) halted by the war, but existing facilities were permitted to deteriorate. In the early postwar period public recreation facilities and activities remained at a low ebb, while at present, there is evidence of renewed concern with recreation at national, state and local levels. The still widespread belief that recreation is "nonessential" and hence "dispensable," coupled with the lesser held notion that any extension of governmental activities is "dangerous" suggest a note of caution when considering the likelihood of any large growth in public recreational offerings in the immediate future.

Schools. Considerable burden for local recreational leadership and for provision of some of the needed facilities has been placed upon the public schools. An increasing number of educators consider this a legitimate responsibility of the school for two reasons. First, the main activity for which the school needs to educate is the use of leisure. This is true both from the standpoint of the obvious ignorance manifested by many Americans of creative use of leisure and from the standpoint of the large percentage of the individual's life that is now spent in leisure. Secondly, all leisure-time pursuits condition, or educate, the individual; it is to the school's advantage that the curricular and extracurricular types of education to which the individual is subjected be complementary rather than counteractive.

Although the conception of the complementary roles of education and recreation has gradually grown, it has by no means been unanimously adopted and acted upon by the schools. The notions still prevail, in practice if not in theory, that education is "preparation for life," something practical in which students start participating after leaving school, and that recreation is "fun here and now" and hence dispensable as a "frill" or justifiable only as a means of keeping students out of trouble after school hours. So long as these ideas are current in many communities, full cooperation of educators and the public in the use of school facilities and school leadership for recreational programs is not possible.

A related obstacle to the full use of the school in recreational programs is the traditional academic atmosphere that surrounds both its facilities and its personnel. Youngsters and adults alike have constructed the stereotype of teacher and school as something "stuffy" and displeasurable and, hence, not to be sought after in leisure hours. Like many stereotypes, truth is contained therein; many teachers bring to recreational activities a pedantic, instructional, "dignified" approach that is of doubtful value even in the classroom role.

Despite such difficulties as these, however, the schools in most communities have made contributions to recreation at least by encouraging extracurricular activities, by teaching an increasing number of subjects with leisure-time value, and by opening the school recreational facilities to some community-wide activities. A few school systems have organized and operated recreational programs for the whole community.

At the present writing, school systems throughout the nation have reached a severe crisis and are having difficulty, in many instances, of meeting satisfactorily even the most minimum educational requirements. We may not expect the schools to take much additional leadership in leisure activities at present, but ultimately the further blending of recreation and education would seem to be inescapable.

Libraries. Aside from the schools, public libraries are the most universally available source of community recreation in America. Almost all cities over 10,000 population have public libraries as do some smaller cities and towns. Libraries, particularly the larger and better financed ones, have increased their cultural offerings beyond the collection of books and other reading matter. Some have a weekly or more frequent "story telling hour" for children, conduct art exhibits, and have lending collections of art reproductions, films, and phonograph records. Still others seek to extend their services to persons in outlying areas by establishing branch libraries or traveling "bookmobiles." Since reading is probably the most frequent leisure-time activity, it is well that in many communities there is available a ready source of good reading material.

While the important service of the public library to the recreational life of the community is not to be minimized, the public library falls short of its potential service in a number of respects. Somewhere close to one fifth of the nation does not have ready access to libraries, and the libraries available to easily another third are inadequately supplied with books, staff, and other facilities. In the professional world, the poorly paid schoolteacher is ingloriously outshadowed by the poorly paid librarian. Just as the school suffers by failure to attract and hold competent persons for financial reasons, so does the library. While the competent faithfuls who stick by both institutions in the face of near poverty is impressive, a large number of incompetents is understandably found in each place. The skill of the good librarian is more than pulling the proper book off the shelf, just as the skill of the good teacher is more than masterly recitation of the multiplication tables. A competent librarian is one who not only knows books well, but is able to sense the needs and interests of her readers and skillfully guide them through a transition of tastes into new interests and new needs of which they were originally unaware. Such librarians plus an adequate supply of the best books in all fields plus comfortable and pleasant physical surroundings are essentials of a good public library. Such libraries are rare indeed, for most communities have not yet recognized the need to supply the funds that are prerequisite to this type of public educational-recreational service.

State and national recreation. There are many who feel that the total responsibility for public recreation cannot be left to the community alone. Many towns do not have the necessary resources, and in others the co-ordination of services is poor. Then too, there are certain types of facilities, such as extensive park lands, that most towns and cities cannot afford. State operation of recreational services, then, is one solution to the problem that faces the roughly four out of five Americans living in communities without a "reasonably adequate" recreation program.

Space does not permit a very full discussion of recreational services provided by the states and by the federal government. The main function of states at present in the recreational field is the provision of parks and forests. The program in most states was improved by federal assistance provided by the Civilian Conservation Corps during the depression years, but still more lands are required. Another important function now served by a few states is the provision of a state recreation service which assists in appraising community resources, organizing local recreation systems, selecting and training leaders, and in obtaining funds for facilities and personnel.

Most of the extensive activities of the federal government in the field of recreation were temporary depression measures carried out by now deceased agencies like the Works Progress Administration, the Civilian Conservation Corps, and the National

Youth Administration. Some permanent functions, however, continue under various federal auspices. The most notable of these are the National Park Service in the Department of the Interior and the Forest Service of the Department of Agriculture. Both of these services cooperate with local and state governments, schools, and private groups in providing recreational activities such as mountain climbing, pack and saddle trips, camping, fishing, hunting, picnicking, nature study, skiing, etc. Valuable work in assisting and stimulating rural communities to provide adequate recreational opportunities for its population has been and continues to be provided by the Extension Service of the Department of Agriculture.

▶ PLANNING FOR LEISURE

In order to meet effectively the recreational values of the American people, planning is needed at the community, state, and national levels. Planning for recreation, however, cannot be done in isolation; it must be co-ordinated with educational, health, political, economic, and other institutional plans. Haphazard, overlapping, conflicting programs are in operation in all of our institutional functionings as a society, and all plans for one must be made flexibly and with an eye on developments in the others. Some general directions for planning recreation are observable, however, at all three levels of government.

Community planning. Because of the complementary objectives of recreational and educational activities in a community, some sort of merging or co-ordination of these functions, rather than separate administration and policy making, is very much needed in all communities. This can perhaps be best accomplished, as the Educational Policies Committee of the National Education Association suggests, by a Public Education Authority (containing school, library, and public recreation administrations). A Public Education Authority should, for the co-ordination of the community's program, have a strong advisory relationship with private agencies carrying out leisure-time activities; such an advisory relationship should be mutual, with suggestions, assistance, pioneer efforts, and experimentation undertaken by private agencies in the field of leisure pursuits.

State planning. Every state needs a planning agency with state-wide conceptions and authority in order to take a broad view of the leisure-time needs of its people and to see that these needs are met.

Most states have planning boards that could include a more active program of promoting and co-ordinating leisure-time functions and be delegated more authority for and vitalization of other aspects of their program. Essential parts of any state-wide planning for the use of leisure would seem to be the duty of equalizing recreational opportunities, including the granting of financial aid to local governments which are not able to maintain costs themselves of an adequate program; the provision of recreational services of a broader scope than local governments can furnish, including a more adequate park and forest service; and the rendering of advisory and promotion services for local communities.

A reorganization of state departments of education to secure broader and more progressive authority is also a need in most states, together with the co-ordination, through the state planning boards or some other medium, of revitalized educational and recreational programs.

More effective state library extension services could do much to reach persons for whom local public libraries are not now available, to help establish more libraries, and to assist existing local libraries in planning more adequate services in their communities.

And finally, many states are undoubtedly in a sufficiently sound financial position to undertake a re-establishment and expansion of much of the recreational work that federal agencies (especially WPA, NYA, and CCC) performed during the depression.

National planning. Few educational and recreational leaders in our society feel any longer that it is possible to have adequate and fully consistent programs for the nation as a whole without some federal planning, promotion, and financial assistance.

Strong public reaction against what is generally termed "federal interference" has been characteristic of the American people. During the severe economic crisis of the 1930's this resistance to federal participation in many fields was relaxed, but seems to have been restored in some groups in the postwar era. If proper precautions are taken against the granting of unbalanced authority to the federal government, our concern in this direction, as Lindeman points out, would seem to be unfounded.

What has to be taken into account in all planning under a federal system of government is the fact that every step in the growth of national power must be accompanied by a concurrent increase in local power. A federal system may be said to grow when the two foci of authority are convergent. I can see no fundamental inconsistency, for example, in the accelerated development of local recreation programs which are augmented by the national government. On the other hand, it seems to me thoroughly consistent with federal principles to assume that it is the function of a national democratic government to strive for an equalization of all elements comprising a good life. The function of a democratic government is to extend, not restrict privileges and opportunities, to give assurance, *e.g.*, that if cultural leisure is good for the North and the East, it must also be good for the South and West. A government which cannot give such assurances will not long remain democratic.

When I contend for participation of the national government in developing a program for the people's leisure, I am often confronted by critics who insist that they recognize the strategic importance of recreation but they fear that a program such as I am advocating will open the door to politics. There are two appropriate responses to be made to criticism of this type: (*a*) there already exists a great deal of politics in almost every recreation department of every municipality in America; and (*b*) high politics is better than low politics. I have seen enough of low politics in the sphere of poor relief administered wholly by local authorities to know that the political process does not purify itself automatically by merely becoming petty.[4]

Planning on the national level must include research into the leisure-time needs of the whole society, co-ordination of federal,

[4] From Eduard C. Lindeman, *Leisure—A National Issue*, New York, Association Press, 1939, pp. 59-60, by permission.

state, local, and private recreational services, and the promotion and (where necessary) partial financing of needed recreational services throughout the country. While recreation is to be thought of as an essential part of life itself and not as a means of solving problems in other areas of living, it is closely inter-related with many other activities about which government con-cerns itself. Co-ordination at the national level, therefore, should include more than strictly recreational functions and should es-pecially take into account the interfunctioning of recreation with education, health, housing, labor conditions, and similar matters.

▶ SUMMARY

The use of leisure time, for the mass of people, is strictly a modern problem. Most of the population in previous societies and in earlier generations of our own society had little time free from duties. While recreational needs and interests vary widely for individuals in the United States, there are at least five main values that recreation must fulfill for many modern Amer-icans. These values are (1) sheer occupation of time not other-wise filled, which, for most of our citizens, is the largest block of time per week; (2) providing of opportunities for full use of mind and body; (3) providing of opportunities for esthetic creation and appreciation; (4) providing of opportunity for full, intimate group participation; and (5) providing of opportunities for direct contact with nature.

The type of leisure-time activity in which the largest amount of time, energy, and money is spent by the American people is commercial recreation. An examination of commercial offer-ings in the field of recreation clearly indicates that only the first of the five values of recreation are adequately fulfilled (and not even this first value for the large minority of our citizens who cannot afford it except at the risk of sacrificing other essentials of full living).

Even though commercial recreation fails to satisfy the leisure-time values of most Americans, it continues to prosper because of the lack of adequate alternatives and because of its habit-forming nature. Its habit-forming characteristics may have a mentally undesirable effect on some individuals by leading them to suppress important unsatisfied values of living.

One of the currently inadequate alternatives to commercial recreation is the programs offered by private, nonprofit organizations. These groups have done little to meet adult recreational needs, reach relatively few of the nation's youth, make recreation incidental to other purposes, fail to appeal to many young persons by their type of program and personnel, and have resources too limited to do more than supplement publicly sponsored leisure-time programs.

Although public recreational services are very inadequate, considering the recency of public concern with the use of leisure, their growth has been encouraging. The three main functions of local communities in providing public recreational services, in the order of diminishing prevalence, are public schools, public libraries, and public recreation departments. Most state governments have done no more than provide park systems; three states have established separate agencies giving full-time service to recreation and all forty-eight states have some type of recreation agency or planning boards of potential usefulness for recreational services. While the federal government provided tremendous stimulus to the cause of public recreation during the 1930's (especially from 1935 to 1939), defense and war measures cut off most of these services. The chief continuing contributions to the use of leisure by the federal government are through its park and forest services and, for rural dwellers, through the Extension Service of the Department of Agriculture. To co-ordinate the services of the many federal agencies concerned with recreation, there has recently been established a Federal Inter-Agency Committee on Recreation. Some see as the next step a separate federal agency devoted solely to recreation—a Federal Recreation Service.

Full satisfaction of such values of living as the five presented must apparently derive principally from public recreational programs. For these programs to be effective for the whole citizenry, social planning at the local, state, and national levels is essential.

SUGGESTED READINGS

Bahman, Isabel, and others, "Leisure of Adolescents: Constructive or Destructive?", *Progressive Education*, Vol. 31 (May 1954), pp. 219-24. A brief treatment of school recreation programs. Examples of such programs in force throughout the country are presented.

Brightbill, Charles K., and Harold D. Meyer, *Recreation*, New York, Prentice-Hall, 1953. Selected readings on the status, resources, and special problems of contemporary recreation. A convenient source of material on a variety of recreation topics.

Danford, Howard G., *Recreation in the American Community*, New York, Harper & Bros., 1953. This book provides a representative view of the envisioned scope of community recreation. Contains a good treatment of the values to be met by recreation.

Recreation and Park Yearbook: Midcentury Edition, New York, National Recreation Association, 1950. Traces the growth of municipal and county parks from 1900 to 1950. An excellent source for factual data on park facilities, activities, expenditures, and leadership.

Saunders, Dero A., and Sanford S. Parker, "$30 Billion for Fun," *Fortune*, Vol. 10 (June 1954), pp. 115-19 ff. A popular article largely concerned with recreation as a "market." Charts amount of money and proportion of income spent on leisure-time pursuits and discusses future trends.

Staley, Eugene (ed.), *Creating An Industrial Civilization*, New York, Harper & Bros., 1952, Chap. 3, "Leisure and Human Values in Industrial Civilization." Report of a round-table discussion by representatives of the business, labor, government, and academic worlds on the nature and role of leisure. Illustrates the clash of values in this area.

Williams, Arthur, *Recreation for the Aging*, New York, Association Press, 1953. A comprehensive treatment of leisure-time programs for older adults based upon what has already been done in some communities. Interesting from the standpoint of the variety of programs and activities suitable for this particular age group.

STUDY QUESTIONS

1. Why is it that only relatively recently large masses of men have had considerable leisure? State why you think this trend will or will not continue in our society.

2. Describe five values held by many Americans that could be achieved through leisure-time pursuits.

3. Show how commercial recreation contributes or fails to contribute to the fulfillment of the five values isolated in question two.

4. Describe three different types of private youth organizations that are involved with recreation to some extent. Which type do you think is most appealing to adults? To youth?

5. What are the chief inadequacies of privately sponsored recreational groups?

6. Briefly trace the growth of public recreation at the local, state, and national levels. What were and are some of the obstacles in the way of more pronounced growth?

7. Why do you think many adults fail to admit or de-emphasize the recreational nature of many of their activities?

8. Why does the school seem to be a good place around which to build the community's recreational program? What prevents full use of the school for this purpose?

9. Why do some feel that the total responsibility for public recreation cannot be left to the community alone but must be met at the state and national levels?

10. What do you feel would be the strengths and weaknesses of a Federal Recreation Service? What would you imagine the public reaction to be?

· 16 · Marriage and the Family

There are many indications that various family-related phenomena constitute "problems" for contemporary American society. Divorce is both decried as "the greatest social evil" and hailed as a "humane liberator." Some observers, probing a bit deeper, see divorce as but one manifestation of a bigger problem, general unhappiness in marriage. Other phenomena, such as adult and child delinquency, women attempting to escape from the role of childbearing and homemaking, and sexual behavior outside of marriage, are sometimes interpreted as further indications of a fairly widespread dissatisfaction with present-day marriage and family life.

It is, then, not difficult to establish the existence and general recognition of many and fundamental problems in the area of sex, marriage, and the family. It will prove much more difficult, however, to unravel the complex fabric of social relationships for the purposes of isolating significant, basic social problems in this area and of charting the various proposals designed to cope with these problems.

Even were there no other obstacle, the student would experience unusual difficulty in this area of study because of his lack of training in objective thinking along these lines. Our emotions are so deeply invested in our concepts of what marriage is and ought to be, our own personalities have been so strongly fashioned by the kind of family system within which we were nurtured, and the basic components of domestic life are so inextricably interwoven with religious ideologies that objective thinking will encounter numerous and serious emotional blocks. This is usually so not because the proposed changes in the sex, marriage, and family area of life are so radical, but because the allegiance of most people to the stereotypes of the past is so steadfast that even minor alterations in the domestic way of life seem to be difficult, unnecessary—if not even dangerous—and sinful. Thus, if one has had a happy childhood in a family in which the mother devoted her entire time and attention to the care of children and the duties of homemaking, and in which the father "ruled the roost with a firm but gentle hand," it usually proves difficult to grasp quickly the logic of careers for married women and of democracy in family rule. The difficulty is not that we do not wish to be what we call "progressive" or that we do not espouse humanitarian values but that we are so rooted in emotionally buttressed habits of thought and action that different ways seem ill advised, if not impossible of successful observance.

▶ THE AMERICAN FAMILY TRADITION

Before we can thoughtfully consider the nature of present-day family problems and the changes, if any, which are being advocated, it is well to consider the kind of sex, marriage, and family system in which our society had its origins. The roots of the family system in America can be conceived, at the risk of possible over-simplification, largely in terms of three concepts: rurality, patriarchy, and sacredness.

Rurality. As we have pointed out at numerous points in this book, the over-all traditions of America are rural traditions. This nation is only just emerging from a society in which rural occupations, rural ways, and rural thinking constituted the basic motif of "the American way." During the last fifty to seventy-five years the great growth of urban centers has reconverted the basic structure of American life so that now we are predominantly an urban people with city ways gradually but certainly becoming ascendant. But our thinking has not been reconverted as quickly or as completely as our dwellings, our occupations, and our daily schedules.

In traditional rural society the family is the basic, central social unit. The family is the unit of production as well as the unit of consumption. There is work for every member of the family from the incredibly early age at which a child gathers the eggs, feeds the baby chicks, and picks strawberries. No one person makes the family living or spends it. The family's finances are a joint enterprise. Moreover, the farm family produces for itself many of the goods and services which the urban family has to buy. It is not the cost or the buying, however, which constitutes the real difference; the real difference is psychological, the necessary sharing of responsibility among the family members in the production of the goods to supply the family's needs from grandmother with the spinning wheel to grandchild garnering the strawberries. It is not difficult to nurture a "we" feeling when the every activity and every need of everyone are as closely interlaced as they are in the rural farm family.

The farm family was, and to some degree still is, a big family. Not only was the birth rate relatively high, but the household was usually augmented by the presence of a grandparent or two, unmarried brothers or sisters of the parents, and resident hired help.

Patriarchy. The rural family was rooted in the patriarchal tradition. It was taken for granted by virtually everyone that major decisions were to be made by the father and, that although one might disagree with his decisions, there was no escaping from them. One is not to infer that patriarchal rule necessarily meant tyranny because there is no necessary connection between the possession of power and the misuse of it. The point is simply that patriarchal government was the rule. Few doubted seriously that it was the only rule ordained of God, for after all, God too was masculine, a kind of superfather, firm and authoritarian but never unjust or to be questioned.

Sacredness. The traditional family also had a philosophical-religious logic which helped to hold it together and served as the frame of reference for inducting the young into it: First, marriage was "ordained by God in the Garden of Eden." That gave marriage supernatural sanction; it was no man-made institution to be tampered with by mortals, who somehow were not quite to be trusted in such matters anyway. Moreover, Jesus Christ spoke uncompromisingly against divorce. It was said by Him to be a sin, and that was that. Finally, reproduction carried a sacred aura. Except for a few very obvious and elementary facts, the biology and psychology of sex were mostly unknown and tended to be regarded as unknowable. Large families were held in high regard by virtue of the Jewish-Christian tradition that a man should be fruitful so that "his seed might inherit the earth." No one was especially concerned if a woman bore so many children or had them so close together that she died a premature death. She merely "passed on to her reward" earlier; there were some tears, of course, and the mourning husband soon went about finding another mate to take over the responsibilities left unfinished by his deceased spouse. No one talked much— except perhaps the poets—about happiness, whether or not the husband and wife "still loved each other," or whether the mental health of the third eldest son was secure. Somehow such matters were taken for granted. This was the way of life, and it worked *reasonably well most* of the time. If there were many who doubted the all-sufficiency of this scheme of things, they were not very numerous and certainly not very vocal.

▶ MODERN TRENDS

The traditional family system—or at least many salient aspects of it—have largely disappeared from the American scene. Some of the changes are obvious and can be charted in statistical tables or represented by trend lines on graphs.

The trend toward smaller family and household groups, the high divorce rate, the increasing employment of women, both single and married, outside the home, and the shrinking size of the dwelling unit all illustrate these objectively depictable trends.

Other changes cannot be so neatly described. Here we must rely upon such evidence as the testimony of experts, based upon their familiarity with the facts, and derived by other than statistical procedures. There is substantial agreement, however, that

Table 13. Average Number of Persons per Family Household in the United States, 1850-1953 *

Year	Persons per family
1850	5.6
1860	5.3
1870	5.1
1880	5.0
1890	4.9
1900	4.7
1910	4.5
1920	4.3
1930	4.1
1940	3.8
1950	3.5
1953	3.3

* Data assembled from the reports of the Bureau of the Census.

the following have occurred: (1) An increasingly varied and self-centered morality, often called an "emancipated" moral code, seems to be emerging for the unmarried and, to a smaller degree, for married persons. (2) A more democratic treatment of children and women—democracy in family government—is gradually superseding the patriarchal type of rule. (3) Sex is being faced increasingly on a factual instead of a mythical basis; it is being increasingly realized that many problems of living—from childhood through old age—are rooted in the incorrect handling of the sexual side of life.

Finally, there are subtle ideological changes which can be observed among a seemingly growing proportion of people. The traditional and sacred approach to family-related problems which involved, among other things, a seeking after solutions in a religious context and a general disavowal of man's right to alter the nature of marriage and the family, seems to be losing ground to something akin to a scientific and rational approach. Increasingly, at least, men and women are willing to grant that it is the providence of man to apply his intelligence to the solution of family-

related problems. Many now try to analyze causes and to anticipate the possible consequences of the various proposals made
for the improvement of present conditions. Some of us not only
feel that it is our right but also our duty to *improve* the quality
of human life in the realms of sex, marriage, and family living.
We recognize no "sacred cows," so to speak, in this area of culture; we consider anything that promises to help people to be
healthier (physically and mentally), happier, and more useful
to other people and to the groups in which they function. This
does not mean that every "half-baked proposal" which somebody
makes for the alleged improvement of the family ought necessarily to be tried. But it ought at least to be examined for possible merit before it is discarded. Proposals, some of us think,
should be evaluated on the basis of their merits, not on the basis
of our ungoverned prejudices.

Society is not in agreement that the rational, secular evaluation of marriage proposals is a worth-while objective. Value
positions are frequently strong in this area, and prejudices are
subtle and not always distinguishable by the person who holds
them. There are some, for example, who uncompromisingly
would deny man the right to evaluate and analyze divorce because they are already sure that divorce and remarriage after
divorce are morally wrong and that any findings concerning the
increased happiness and better mental health of the persons involved would be irrelevant to the central moral issue. Others,
meanwhile, argue that man should quite definitely investigate
matters such as divorce and initiate new policies based on his most
thorough investigations. Such individuals hold that it is both
manifestly unwise and morally wrong for society to force maladjusted persons to live out their lives in psychological torment
because when they were twenty they made a mistake in judgment one night under the moon. Thus, regarding family-related
problems there is a clash of values concerning whether or not
proposals for the reduction of the problems should even be investigated. But this basic conflict notwithstanding, we shall examine the various proposals which have been formulated for the

conservation of the family or, to put it otherwise, for the treatment of the social problems of sex, marriage, and the family.

▶ PROBLEM AREAS IN THE AMERICAN FAMILY

We have repeatedly pointed out throughout this book that social problems arise out of clashes between the values held by the various persons and groups in a society. What, then, are the value issues over which controversy pertaining to sex, marriage, and the family now rages?

Monogamy and rising divorce. "Whomsoever God hath joined together let no man put asunder," is a familiar line from a standard marriage ceremony. It expresses the value of lasting monogamy. It carries the sanction of the Divine Being and admonishes the mortals to stay married. But let us look at the facts. Currently one marriage out of each four that are contracted ends in divorce. This is somewhat lower than the postwar peak, often quoted, at which time nearer to one out of three marriages resulted in divorce. Few would deny, however, that this rate is "too high."

The folk wisdom which we have inherited from an early age interprets the high divorce rate as simply a reflection of the defects of character and intelligence of the parties to the broken marriages. We are told that if marriage were more difficult to enter into, if people "thought twice," if people "observed the God-given codes," if mates were more "patient" and "less selfish," then the divorce rate would shrink. Young people are currently being reminded that in the good old days when people "took their marriage vows more seriously" divorce was almost nonexistent, the implication being very clear that present divorce rates are high because people do not take their vows seriously. No one knows, of course, whether the seriousness with which people regard their marriage vows is important or unimportant in the high rate of marriage failure, or for that matter whether it is even true that people regard their vows as any less binding than they formerly did.

Table 14. Divorces and Divorce Rate per 100 Marriages from 1925 to 1953 *

Year	Number of divorces	Rate per 100 marriages
1925	175,449	14.8
1930	195,961	17.4
1935	218,000	16.4
1940	264,000	16.5
1945	485,000	30.6
1950	385,144	23.1
1953	390,000	25.4

* Data assembled from reports of the Bureau of the Census and estimates from National Office of Vital Statistics.

Less moralistic interpreters see the problem of marriage instability in the nature of modern marriage rather than in terms of individual character. Modern life is different in its tempo, its objectives, and its needs. Marriage is not a thing apart from the general life, and thus it reflects the insecurities and tensions and rapid change of the whole society. Problems of inadequate income, poor mental health, impaired physical health, ideological difference, race, class, and occupational maladjustment all converge and leave their impact upon the families of the people upon whom the problems impinge. Wars and depressions set forces in motion which remake the family as surely as they remake governments. The impact of social change and problems is complicated further by the deep emotional and sentimental ties which people have toward marriage—ties which are rooted both in the religious heritage and in secular custom. Thus many people expect satisfactions which marriage does not, and possibly cannot, bring. Much strain is brought upon marriage also by unrealistic expectations and naïve underestimation of problems. Love, however important, is not enough to marry on, for example, and even the love which promises great security may be so misunderstood that it becomes a problem itself. All these and other factors are involved, irrespective of the moral integrity of the persons involved; the institution itself imposes the strain upon the person. This is not to imply that character is not important to successful marriage; the point is that character is not enough. Moreover, the forces which encroach upon the person frequently destroy in time the faithful adherence of many to high ideals.

Here we have a basic value clash with respect to the interpretation of the cardinal social fact that a smaller and smaller proportion of the people who get married stay married. One school of thought sees the causes largely in defects of character and other personal traits; the other school sees the chief source as a general societal one, tied up inextricably with the problems and changes of the entire society. There is probably validity to both views of the matter, but it seems certain that more attention must be given to the societal forces which shape the over-all pattern of living.

The role of women. Traditionally women have been homemakers and childbearers. They have largely fulfilled the function of perpetuating the race, finding no doubt much happiness in that role. But now women are said to have become "emancipated," by which is usually meant that they are free to substitute out-of-home occupations for part or all of their working time.

Today about one out of four married women take advantage of this freedom, and, for the first time in our history, there are actually more married than single women in the labor force. And many married women who pass up the opportunity for out-of-home work say that they have done so with much regret, indecision, and ambivalence. If a woman is happier with a career than with the traditional role of mother of a large family, then, say some, why should she not do so? Meanwhile other observers are extremely critical of her for shirking her duties, for mimicking men, and for denying their birthright to her unborn children. Actually the society has not made up its mind as to what the functions of the women should be, not even to the extent of granting to the individual woman the democratic right to make up her mind which way she wants to handle her life.

While she is *legally* free to choose, she is under conflicting *social pressures,* no matter which choice she makes.

Table 15. Married Women Workers, 1900-1954 *

Year	No. of married women workers	Percent of all married women	Percent of all women workers
1900	769,477	5.6	15.4
1910	1,890,661	10.7	24.7
1920	1,920,281	9.0	23.0
1930	3,071,302	11.7	28.9
1940	5,040,000	16.7	36.4
1950	8,550,000	22.8	48.0
1951	9,086,000	25.2	48.8
1952	9,222,000	25.3	49.1
1953	9,588,000	25.8	50.7
1954	9,900,000	26.5	50.3

* Data assembled and computed from reports and estimates of the Bureau of the Census. Data for 1950 to 1954 are for married women over 14 *with spouse present:* previous data are for *all* married women over 14.

Sexual morality. At one time in our history society was fairly well in agreement regarding the rightness and wrongness of sexual intercourse outside of marriage. All such behavior was "taboo" and that was that. Transgressors of the rigid code were found, to be sure, but they were apparently few and from all reports they were dealt with swiftly and severely.

Today, from all indications, society cannot make up its mind on numerous matters of sexual morality. Almost anyone who has grown up in our society recognizes that the "underlying theme" of our sexual code is to relegate sexual intercourse to marriage and marriage alone. Premarital chastity is fostered as an ideal, and well-entrenched in our stated ideals is the idea that it is somehow even more important that a married person engage in sexual relations with no one other than his or her spouse. At the same time, any American who reads his newspaper or merely listens to those around him knows full well that our stated sex codes are rather openly violated. He knows too, that there is a fairly widespread acceptance of the idea that the sexual code is open to discussion and interpretation.

What has emerged, then, is a rather confused morality. The individual is frequently forced to decide many issues for himself, and many find the task anything but easy. The moralistic restraints of the past no longer seem to "square" with his observations, and the older additional restraints of fear of "conception, infection, and detection" do not seem to carry the force that once they did. And even the "modern" emphasis on premarital chastity as a means of helping to assure a happy marriage is dismissed by some as but a more sophisticated kind of threat dressed up in subtle psychological garb.

A large part of the difficulty with the present state of our sexual morality, then, seems to be the divergence between societal ideals and tolerated practices and the general lack of consensus on the morality of premarital and extramarital sexual conduct. Precise facts are hard to get, but what samples and inferences we have seem to show that a wide variety of standards of conduct are currently being followed by substantial numbers of American people. Confusion, indecision, regret, guilt, deception, and disillusionment with both self and others are very common in this confused state of affairs. It is not difficult to find people—even among the philosophers—who will support almost any morality, but the difficulty is that a dozen other moralities which are inconsistent are sanctioned too.

Societal frustrations.   Even after one has decided upon what values he thinks the family ought to foster for him, he frequently finds that serious problems are still faced because of the nature of the society. He may, for example, think that early marriage and large families are good—but if he cannot get a house to live in and cannot secure an income large enough to support even a moderate-sized family, his good judgment in following the ways of his fathers can bring him little but disappointment. If a war interrupts his education for five years, then he must face the fact that he is five years retarded in his plan for the realization of marriage and family living. These five years can be trouble-some years morally, physically, if not even spiritually.

Not only a person's personal virtues but the "high standards" of the society may also frustrate him. For example, America is notorious for its high standard of living. Color advertisements, attractive show windows, and his more opulent friends may stimulate in him a burning desire to participate in the high standard, but other societal realities such as the wage scale in his occupation or his own ability level or his poor fortune may prevent the high standard of living from being anything more than a tantalizing fantasy to him.

There are, of course, other sources of problems in the area of sex, marriage, and the family than those which we have treated, but we have discussed the major ones. In this treatment, emphasis has been placed upon the great diversity of value judgment among the various cultures in our society. We do not know precisely how much of the appalling amount of maladjustment and unhappiness in marriage stems from societal or how much from individual confusion. Very probably the dichotomy of individual and social is a very poor one, since the forces in the individual get there through social experience. Either way one looks at the matter, however, he is impressed with the sharp contrast in judgment concerning almost every objectively describable condition of the family in America. If the pessimists are right that this is a "lost generation," it is not difficult to see how a person could become lost in this morass of value confusion.

▶ PROPOSALS FOR TREATING THE PROBLEMS OF SEX, MARRIAGE, AND THE FAMILY

Legislative approach. Some persons and groups believe that the problems which we have been discussing can be solved by changes in the laws pertaining to marriage and family life. Others believe that the forces creating these problems are inherent in the social system, and that changes in law will have very little to do with the solution of them or may even make the problem conditions much worse than they now are. Meanwhile, there is a third, somewhat middle-of-the-road, school of thought which takes the position that there are certain legal approaches to the problems of marriage and family life which might assist at least some of the people to make better adjustments more of the time than is now the case.

Limitations.   From the objective point of view the weight of accumulated evidence tends to support the somewhat middle-of-the-road position. Our experience with legislative reform in the field of the family indicates that there are serious limitations upon what can be accomplished by the passing of laws, by prohibiting this or that practice, or requiring that something be done under penalty of legal punishment. "You cannot legislate morality" is an adage in which there is considerable scientific truth. It means that even though it is possible to pass laws regulating the intimate conduct of people, it often is difficult, if not impossible, to enforce the laws if the people are not in sympathy. For example, we have laws on the statute books in most American states making it a felony for unmarried persons to indulge in sexual intercourse. It is common knowledge that such laws are frequently and flagrantly violated. Prosecutions of such offenses are almost nonexistent for adults, even though the law-enforcement officers have knowledge of the violations. Numerous states grant divorces for adultery, but in cases where the accused has been found guilty of adultery, or where he admits his guilt, he is not then prosecuted for the felony of "fornication," "illegal cohabitation," or however it is termed in the laws of the state in question. Similarly, in cases of admitted or proved illegal paternity (bastardy), the couple is practically never prosecuted for the legal offense of illicit sex relations as a result of which the illegitimate child is conceived. Legal action is almost always limited to determining the correct paternity and the amount of the man's financial liability for the support of the child.

Of a somewhat different nature are the subterfuges which occur when persons desire strongly to behave in ways contrary to the provisions of law. This occurs thousands of times each year in almost every state in the union with respect to divorce.

The laws stipulate that divorces may be granted when certain conditions, such as adultery, nonsupport, or cruelty have occurred. The injured party may then petition the court to dissolve the marriage, and, if the charges are sustained by the evidence, the court has no recourse but to grant the divorce. It frequently occurs, however, that couples desire divorce simply because they are mismated, no longer "in love," or have incompatible personalities. In other words, they desire divorce but have committed none of the overt acts for which divorces are granted in their state. This leaves the couple to choose from at least three legal subterfuges for securing the divorce anyway. (1) If they have the money, they may migrate to another state and establish a fictional, though technical, residence and secure the divorce there. (2) One mate may charge the other with such legal offense as desertion, even though it has not occurred, and the mate, in order to expedite the divorce, will offer no defense, thus implying his guilt of an act which he never committed. (3) After the couple decides they want a divorce, and it is impossible for financial or other reasons to go to an "easy" state, one or the other may deliberately perform some act such as adultery, for which reason, then, the court grants the other mate a divorce. The latter two procedures constitute, of course, "collusion," and the laws of most states require that if collusion exists the case should be dismissed by the court. Most divorce-court judges realize that collusion, even perjury, exists in the majority of cases which they hear but realize that it is practically futile to dismiss the case, because in most instances it will be brought up again under another pretext.

Role of legal reform. In numerous other ways it could be shown that prohibitory laws, even with strict enforcement, are of little value so long as they do not have the support of the people whose behavior they are intended to regulate. The foregoing is not intended to deny, however, that laws do have their place in the treatment of family problems. Legal reforms do have a legitimate role to play. What is that role? And what guiding principles exist for discharging the legal role? The following suggestions have been repeatedly offered as valid criteria.

1. Marriage and family laws should be democratically based—that is, they should embody the real wishes (values) of the majority of the people. Many existing laws embody the prejudices of some crusading minority who long ago pressured a legislature into enacting legislation which, whatever its virtues at that time, does not now have the respect or support of the majority of the people. The laws centering around marriage, divorce, contraception, and other phases of family life are certainly in need of re-examination in the light of present needs and present wishes of the majority of the people.

2. The enforcement of democratically derived laws should be consistent and as completely effective as possible. Strict law enforcement is essential if any law is to accomplish its purpose. If we are to have laws, for example, which require that no persons under twenty years of age can legally marry, then there should be diligent enforcement at the time of granting licenses so that age falsifications are held to a minimum.

3. Laws should be uniform, or as nearly so as possible. The United States is notoriously vulnerable to criticism in this respect. Within continental United States there are forty-nine separate jurisdictions with forty-nine separate codes of marriage, divorce, and related laws. One student of the problem points out that

> the marital status of a man may change with kaleidoscopic swiftness as he crosses state borders. A present instance is found in three adjoining states; the same man by merely traveling across these states may be a legally married man, a single man, and a bigamist in turn, all within a distance of 15 miles.[1]

Another investigator reports that it is possible for

> an enterprising man not averse to interstate travel, to accumulate by moderate diligence seven wives in as many different states

[1] Ray E. Baber, *Marriage and the Family*, New York, McGraw-Hill Book Co., 1953, p. 75.

of the union . . . without breach of law so as to subject himself to criminal process.[2]

Startling as these revelations may be, they constitute only a beginning. Until recently the state of South Carolina did not allow divorce for any reason whatsoever. Among the forty-eight states divorce may be obtained for reasons which vary in number from one to twenty! [3] Certainly if discrepancies such as these exist, they can contribute only to the cynical conclusion that laws cannot be very rational or important anyway, else they would have to be more consistent.

Some people believe that the solution to the problem of uniformity lies in a federal marriage and divorce law. While such a law would eliminate the confusion caused by the widely differing state laws and the possibilities of law evasion by removal from one state to another, it would create numerous difficulties. In the first place, if Congress did pass such a law—which is very doubtful—it well might be declared unconstitutional by the Supreme Court of the United States on the grounds that authority over marriage and divorce has not been delegated to the federal government by the several states. Secondly, if Congress did pass a uniform marriage and divorce law which was upheld by the Supreme Court, the law would constitute "an artificial *legal* uniformity of practice where there is no natural *social* uniformity of thought and need." [4] In other words, how should the uniform divorce law be written? Should it reflect the philosophy of New York, where adultery is the only recognized reason for divorce, or of Arizona where the law recognizes some nineteen different grounds? How could we possibly be equally fair to the

[2] Robert Grant, "Marriage and Divorce," *Yale Review*, Vol. 14 (January 1925), pp. 223-38. One student suggests that, due to changes in laws, the traveling wife-collector of today might be forced to limit himself to four or five legally acquired spouses.

[3] In New York state, for example, divorce can be granted only for adultery. In Arizona a divorce can be secured for any of the following reasons: adultery, cruelty, desertion, alcoholism, felony conviction, felony before marriage, neglect to provide, pregnancy at marriage, bigamy, separation, indignities, drug addiction, violence, fraudulent contract, crime against nature, husband a vagrant, infamous crime, loathsome disease, or relationship within prohibited degree.

[4] Baber, *op. cit.*, p. 76.

wishes of people of varying viewpoint? To be sure it is probable that the thinking of the rank and file of people of New York and Arizona is not as dissimilar as one might assume from an examination of the laws of these two states, but nevertheless, there are important regional differences in viewpoint. It is thus quite possible that a uniform marriage and divorce law "might increase direct violation, for a law is frequently unenforceable in sections where the prevailing sentiment is strongly against it. The clash would engender bitterness and strife." [5]

Thus, while we recognize the desirability of legal uniformity, we must also recognize the practical difficulties involved in achieving it, especially in the short run. It seems that we must work toward it as an ideal, striving to get individual states whose laws are the extremes to make such modifications as will gradually bring them more in line not only with the thinking of their own people but of their neighboring states as well.

4. Legal machinery should become less formal. Perhaps the best constructive example is provided by the juvenile courts and by the courts of domestic relations in some (too few) cities. Instead of handling domestic relation matters in the forbidding formality of the traditional courtroom with judge, jury, and contentious lawyers, and with galleries filled with curious persons who have no legitimate interest in the case, juvenile and some domestic relations courts are informal. There is a more or less diligent search for solutions which will be equitable rather than merely legal, and the judge has considerable discretionary power. He surrounds himself with technical experts on human behavior, such as psychiatrists and sociologists, who help him to arrive at the kind of decision which will best meet the needs of the persons before him. There is great need for an individualizing of judicial practice so that the law may assist people to work out humane and sound solutions of their marital problems based upon their own peculiar needs and circumstances. We must, it is argued, get away from the idea that a person should have endured a certain uniform accumulation of humiliations and pain before

[5] Baber, *loc. cit.*

he can secure respite from an intolerable marriage; we must emancipate ourselves from the notion that courts are primarily punitive agencies with jurisdiction over shameful wrongdoers. Gradually we have learned that, through the courts, adults and children may receive assistance in solving their problems, provided that the courts have legal freedom to do what is needed and are staffed by people who can recognize human needs and who know how to meet them. We have only begun to make this transition, but the trend is clearly apparent.

Even at best, however, the legal approach leaves the more crucial phase of marriage problems largely untouched. Laws do not make couples incompatible, courts usually do not abuse children, and law-enforcement officers do not cause illicit sex conduct. At best the laws and law-enforcement systems can only serve as regulatory agencies, as umpires, so to speak, of the great enigma. For a more fundamental treatment of solutions which strike deeper at the root of marriage-related problems, we must turn to another approach.

Mental hygiene approaches. We now know, through the use of reliable research procedures, that there is much mental-emotional maladjustment among so-called normal or near-normal people. And, more important for the present discussion, we now have considerable evidence to show that family life has great influence upon mental-emotional health. It would be as accurate, of course, to say that the mental-emotional health of the persons involved has a great deal to do with family life. In other words, persons whose mental hygiene is poor introduce a serious strain on their personal relationships in marriage, with the result that there is much unhappiness and maladjustment and, in many cases, estrangement or divorce. On the other hand, poor mental health grows out of family and especially childhood unhappiness. Here, then, is the vicious cycle: Unhappy families breed maladjusted children; maladjusted children grow up to make unhappy marriages. This is, of course, the general principle—that is, the above statement is true in terms of probabilities in the great majority of cases but may be incorrect so far as some specific case is concerned. Since our purpose in this book is to discuss social problems in the aggregate, we must be concerned primarily with the propositions which are true in general.

How, then, can we break into the vicious cycle of personal-marital maladjustment? It is believed by most specialists in mental hygiene (psychologists, sociologists, psychiatrists, and others) that it is possible, though not easy, to break into the cycle at several crucial points. (1) It is possible to some extent to teach parents, even though they themselves are not entirely well adjusted, enough about practical mental hygiene so that their children will grow up without too serious mental maladjustments. In other words, the amount or degree of maladjustment and unhappiness may be reduced, even though not entirely eliminated, in this way. (2) There is some reason to believe that the proper kind of education in preparation for marriage may have a beneficial effect in increasing the marital adjustment of the marriage partners, thus facilitating their happiness and contributing to the better adjustment of their children. (3) Through the treatment of individual cases by marriage counselors and other clinicians, some degree of improvement in personal adjustment can often be worked out.

Marriage education.   Most colleges and universities now offer some kind of instruction designed to prepare the student for successful marriage and family living. The content of such education varies with the amount and kind of the teacher's professional training, the instructor's freedom to handle such "touchy" questions as sex and contraception, and the amount of time devoted to the course. A few high schools today offer some form of premarriage instruction, and the movement seems to be gaining momentum. YMCA's and YWCA's in some cities give instruction to young men and women whose formal education stopped before college. Likewise, some churches sponsor courses, study groups, and lectures in preparation for marriage.

The effectiveness, if not the very honesty, of these attempts is exceedingly irregular. Probably the chief handicap is a lack of sufficiently trained personnel to serve as teachers, lecturers, and discussion leaders. There is a strong tendency to use "safe" persons—that is, persons who will take sufficiently innocuous positions on most vital issues so that no one will be offended—and the result is that nothing very vital is taught. There is also a tendency to rely too much upon the common-sense qualifications of a teacher or discussion leader instead of insisting upon training in the sciences of human behavior. Eventually we must get rid of the notion that a man who has "set a good example to the community" by avoiding divorce or a woman whose children have escaped suspicion of delinquency can necessarily contribute wise counsel to a group of people seeking guidance in marriage. These achievements no more qualify a person to serve as a marriage authority than a lifetime of good health qualifies a man to serve as a physician. Until this is recognized, many of the people who try to get marriage education from so-called marriage courses will continue to receive the unprofessional instruction which is all too prevalent today.

A second limitation on marriage education, of course, is public apathy and public opposition. In almost every community there are a few powerful persons and minority groups who conceive as their righteous role the prevention of the young from receiving realistic information which might conceivably help to make their marriages more stable and happy. Of course this is not the avowed objective of these "purists." They usually contend that their real motives are to guard the "eternal moralities" and give other high-sounding and sometimes sincere purposes. But their effect is still unfortunate, since they accomplish the dubious purpose of closing the doors of scientific enlightenment to the people who need it most. It seems most unfortunate that the studies which our society makes through costly and time-consuming research are withheld from the people who could use them to make their own lives more happy and their children better-adjusted human beings. Opposition of this sort is fortunately diminishing in most parts of the United States but is still a serious deterrent in many communities.

Parent education.   Most of the principles we have discussed in connection with marriage education apply also to parent education. The need is great. There is growing interest and diminishing community resistance. The serious bottlenecks are the lack of trained personnel and a preoccupation on the part of parents with quick and easy solutions to daily problems instead of with a real and vital concern for the long-run mental health needs of children. Courses are varied in content; probably also in effectiveness. Many of the sources of trouble in the adjustment of children are such that they cannot readily be controlled by parents, however well-informed. In spite of all of these handicaps and limitations, the parent education movement is spreading, and there is some basis for the hope that it may result in an improvement in the mental-emotional health of some children at least.

Marriage counseling. Group education, no matter how thorough, cannot do the entire job for everyone. Individuals, pairs, and families also require special attention from time to time when their marital-adjustment problems become too difficult to handle by their own ingenuity. Often they need professional assistance to find what the problems are. This need has given rise to an emerging profession, known variously as marriage counseling, domestic relation consultation, family guidance, and the like.

Marriage counseling shows great promise but also has its limitations. First, there is an insufficient number of trained persons to serve as counselors. Second, the public, generally speaking, does not know when to consult a marriage counselor and how to distinguish a qualified counselor from a quack. The present-day problems of the marriage-counseling profession are very much like the problems of the medical profession seventy years ago. There is reason to believe, however, that the marriage-counseling profession will improve its qualifications and that the public will soon better understand what the values and limitations of marriage counseling are. The American Association of Marriage Counselors is working on both problems at present, and the outlook is somewhat hopeful.

Other proposals.   There are, of course, other value positions with respect to the conservation of the family. These cover a wide range. There are various movements to "strengthen the economic foundations" of the family by such diverse proce-

dures as consumer cooperatives and efforts to secure more substantial income tax deductions for families with more children.
Other reformers emphasize the need for a "return to religion."
Still others advocate such radical departures from our traditions
as free love and trial marriage. It will be obvious, even to the
casual student, that such sweeping proposals are likely to encounter rabid opposition and to present such practical limitations that they hardly warrant lengthy attention in a book as
general in scope as this one.[6]

▶ SUMMARY

The societal roots of most family problems grow out of the
inconsistencies between our older family traditions which were
based upon rural life, patriarchal rule, and the conception of
marriage as sacred, on the one hand, and the present milieu which
is based upon urbanization, the democratic ideology, and a predominantly secular conception of life, on the other hand. As
we have seen in so many areas of social problems, much of the
difficulty stems from our attempts to maintain values based on a
past social system and to use them in a modern system which
is basically different.

We have discussed the main proposed attacks on the problems of sex, marriage, and the family under two captions: the
legislative approach and the mental hygiene approach. The
legislative approach, in spite of its serious limitations, appears
to have some possibilities of limited scope and value. So long
as forthcoming laws are democratically based, consistently enforced, reasonably uniform, and their application individualized,
at least some amelioration of some of these problems may be anticipated.

Our major emphasis, however, has been upon proposals to improve persons' mental hygiene. This seems justified because of
the close connection between the emotional adjustment of the
person and his ability to function in the various roles which sex,

---

[6] For treatment of some of these, see chapters on "Conflicting Sex Patterns"
and "Conservation of Family Values" in Baber, *op. cit.*

marriage, and family norms require of him. We have examined the cycle of mental ill health as a basic factor in family breakdown and family breakdown as the basic factor in mental ill health, and have pointed out that this cycle is vulnerable to some measure of control through at least three channels: marriage education, parent education, and marriage counseling. We have assayed the strengths and weaknesses of each of these approaches. Together they should at least ameliorate some of the social problems of sex, marriage, and family and might possibly eliminate them.

SUGGESTED READINGS

Cuber, John F., *Marriage Counseling Practice*, New York, Appleton-Century-Crofts, 1948. This book sets forth the basic theory and practices of the marriage-counseling profession. Numerous technical problems are discussed, and the limitations of counseling practice are treated. The movement is appraised sympathetically but critically.

Despert, J. Louise, *Children of Divorce*, Garden City, N. Y., Doubleday & Co., 1953. A leading child psychiatrist takes an objective view of the effects of divorce on the child. Rich in actual case studies.

Harper, Robert A., *Marriage*, New York, Appleton-Century-Crofts, 1949. A textbook designed to supply a "functional" background of information on marriage for the college student. Covers a wide variety of topics. Written in an easy style.

Hill, Reuben, *Families Under Stress*, New York, Harper & Bros., 1949. An important work on the ways in which families adjusted to war separation and reunion. Statistical findings are amply illustrated and supplemented with case histories.

Following are four standard and highly respected treatise-textbooks on the family. None is written primarily around problems of the family, but each contains a great deal of authoritative information on that subject with important interpretative and background data. While each of the books is distinct from the others, the four taken together would provide a comprehensive understanding of the existing knowledge in this field.

Baber, Ray E., *Marriage and the Family*, 2d ed., New York, Mc-Graw-Hill Book Co., 1953.

Burgess, Ernest W., and Harvey Locke, *The Family: From Institution to Companionship*, 2d ed., New York, American Book Co., 1953.

Waller, Willard (revised by Reuben Hill), *The Family: A Dynamic Interpretation*, New York, The Dryden Press, 1951.

Winch, Robert F., *The Modern Family*, New York, Henry Holt and Co., 1952.

STUDY QUESTIONS

1. Why is it desirable to understand the kind of sex, marriage, and family system existing in early American history before considering present-day family problems?

2. What is meant by the "sacredness" of the early American family?

3. What are the chief objective and readily verifiable changes that have taken place in the American family? What other changes have occurred?

4. Cite several family-related problems over which there is a clash of values concerning whether or not the problems should be scientifically investigated. Why is this condition more likely to occur in the area of marraige-family-sex than in some other areas?

5. What is the essential value conflict with regard to the "divorce problem"? What possibility do you see of reaching an agreement or compromise on this issue?

6. State in your own words the societal ideals concerning sexual morality and the practices tolerated by society. What has been the effect of the divergence of the two?

7. What are the "legal subterfuges" frequently practiced with regard to divorce proceedings? Do you see any harmful effects as a result of these practices?

8. What criteria are offered as guides for evaluating legal reform in the sex-marriage-family area? Can you think of any groups that would disagree with one or more of these criteria?

9. What is meant by the "vicious cycle" with regard to the relationship between personal and marital maladjustment? What suggestions are made for breaking into this vicious cycle?

10. Evaluate marriage education at the high school and college levels.

· 17 ·   The City

Nearly everyone identifies such urban phenomena as slums and corrupt government as "problems." Some interpreters have gone so far as to assert that "the city *itself* is the problem," that slums, corrupt government, and many of the problems already discussed, such as residential segregation of Negroes, family instability, and problems of education, are merely indications of the upheaval caused by man's desire to live under such "unnatural conditions" as in cities. But since modern life is predominantly and increasingly urban, the implications of that charge can be dismissed as unrealistic and unproductive. Nevertheless, there is still need for a special focus on the city and upon urban living as a life pattern.

▶ THE NATURE OF THE MODERN CITY

As we have pointed out at numerous points in this book, the modern city is an exceedingly recent phenomenon. The fact that we have had what the historians call "cities" for hundreds of years leads many people to underestimate the many and significant ways in which the present city is unique and probably, therefore, challenging.

At the risk of oversimplification we may point out that the modern city breaks sharply with the historical pattern in at least three important ways: (1) Modern cities are vastly larger than were the so-called "large" cities of London, Rome, and Paris even as recently as 100 years ago. (2) A larger and larger proportion of the total population in the United States resides and works in the city, with the result that we have now reached a stage of development in which city life rather than rural life is the preponderant pattern of living. (3) Great strides in tech-

nological advance in the last half century have revolutionized
life in the city earlier than it has affected life in the country.
These changes, while having useful influences, greatly multiply
the nuisance and danger of living in the city, either as compared
with rural residence now or with urban residence in the recent
past.

Adaptation of rural values. City residence brings with it a
way of life which breaks sharply away from many of the time-
honored and culturally entrenched concepts of a desirable, virtuous, and efficient way of life. Maxims such as "early to bed and
early to rise makes a man healthy, wealthy, and wise" may have
been generally sound common sense in a rural setting, but for the
average resident of an urban center, such a rule of conduct is
either meaningless or in many cases clearly erroneous. The
"proper" time to arise depends not on the time of day but upon
one's work schedule. If a man is employed as an operator of a
movie projector in a theater which runs from 5:00 P.M. to 1:00
A.M., the old adage makes little sense—almost as little as it does
if he works in industry on the "swing shift." Another concept
inherited from our rural antecedents pertained to the virtues of
having large families "so that there will be many little pairs of
hands to help father with the chores." The chores? In a two-bed-
room apartment on the fourth floor? Sentimental little bits like
"every boy should grow up with a dog" would certainly complicate life for the millions of American apartment dwellers with
children who live in the increasingly popular "no-pets-allowed"
housing developments. We might go on and on with illustrations showing how the concepts of proper living which are
deeply rooted in our cultural pattern become either incongruous
or harmful in the urban setting. But we do not give up such
"eternal verities" with ease or with grace.

Occupational modes. City occupations, for the great mass of
urban dwellers, are no less revolutionary in the concepts on
which they are built. Some wag has said that "no one in the city
really makes anything any more," by which he meant that division of labor is so intricate and specialization so universal that no
worker really *makes* automobiles, electric irons, or television

sets. Instead he spends his time and energy screwing bolt number C24W on to nut C42WA for eight long hours of five long days a week for about 300 work days in each year! He hardly knows whether he is working on an automobile or a tricycle, because when the object passes him on the assembly line its final appearance is hard to envisage. Concepts like "pride in workmanship" and the pleasure of foreseeing the satisfaction which another will derive from the use of the products of one's labors become almost meaningless under the conditions of modern production. Whatever subjective satisfactions one gets from his work must of necessity derive from something else than the joy of creation. But from what?

Residential patterns.   The urban dweller typically—though not universally—lives in a neighborhood of comparative strangers who move in and move out, and he scarcely notices their coming and going unless he chances to see the van when it comes to move the furniture. He lives typically in a dwelling unit that is not really his. He may be paying rent, or what is not too different, small monthly amounts which in twenty years will make the dwelling his—that is, if he still lives there, if he is living at all, and if he has been able to make the monthly payments uninterruptedly all that time. Typically, also, these dwelling units are too small—too small, that is, for families of more than one or two children, and frequently too small for comfort and privacy even with that number. Outdoors there is practically no space for children's play, family recreation, gardening, and other kinds of activities which the cultural traditions define as desirable, and which our plethora of advisors on "how to live well and long" so confidently advise.

Government.   No account of the development of the urban way of life would be complete or accurate without giving considerable attention to what is perhaps the most unsavory aspect of urban living, namely, the long history of political ineptness, scandal, corruption, and thorough incompetence in city government. To some degree the extreme conditions obtaining when Lincoln Steffens wrote his famous *Shame of the Cities* have been somewhat mitigated, but enough of the same shady practices persist to make our point still pertinent. It has frequently been pointed out that the lowest ebb of democracy, if by democracy we mean interest in and control of government by the people, is reached in the American city, especially in the larger ones. We do not refer here merely to the occasional scandal or election fraud or outstandingly corrupt political regime which from time to time gets exposed in the public press. We refer, rather, to the largely unexposed and established practices of semiofficial corruption and criminality which occur without public knowledge as part and parcel of city "government." The governmental conscience of the average citizen must indeed be calloused when he permits open and widespread gambling, prostitution, and mismanagement of public funds in his own city to go unchallenged, when each of these is clearly illegal under existing law. Little effective effort is made to bring principle and practice together in such important matters. It is probably natural that in a society in which the dramatic problems appear to be largely national and international, the prime focus of the citizen should be upon the federal government, but that this should result in so complete an abdication of citizenship rights to the lawless forces in the American city strikes many thoughtful Americans as a grievous danger.

Population. The population make-up of the modern city and the trends within that population provide us with much factual information of the extent and effect of urban living. In the first place, more and more people are living in cities. Just seventy-five years ago less than a third of all Americans were urban dwellers; today more than two thirds live in cities. In 1950 there were some 96.5 million people living in cities as opposed to about 3.5 million a hundred years previous.

The ever-growing number and proportion of urban dwellers has been watched carefully by those concerned with the total population growth. For almost all of the past fifty years the urban birth rate has been insufficient to maintain even a stationary population. In very recent years the net reproduction rate of city people has been close to, or above, the rate necessary to keep their numbers stationary, but certainly too low to account for

Table 16. Growth of Urban Population, 1800-1950 *

Year	Number of people in urban areas	Proportion of total population
1800	322,371	6.1
1820	693,255	7.2
1840	1,845,055	10.8
1860	6,216,518	19.8
1880	14,129,735	28.2
1900	30,159,921	39.7
1920	54,157,973	51.2
1940	68,954,823	56.2
1950	96,467,686 †	64.0 †

* Data from U. S. Bureau of Census, *Statistical Abstracts of the U. S.: 1953*, Washington, D. C., U. S. Government Printing Office, 1953, p. 26.

† According to 1950 definition of urban. According to old definition 88,927,464 persons in the U. S. were classified as "urban" in 1950. They represented 59% of total population.

much growth. What this means, then, is that cities have maintained their numbers and grown as a result of migration from rural areas. In a very real sense of the word, cities are, therefore, "parasitic" upon their rural hinterlands. We use the term "parasitic" because the city attracts from the rural area chiefly young adults in whom the rural area has invested considerable sums of money for maintenance and especially for education. Then, when these young people are ready to make their contributions as adults, they desert the communities of their origin and rearing and contribute their work, their taxes, and their leadership to the cities to which they migrate. This process has the effect— though of course not intentional—of giving the city human skills for which it did not pay.

The basic institutions. Even the basic societal institutions are different in the city. Families, as we have pointed out, are smaller on the average. Furthermore they are more impermanent. They move from place to place within the city. In addition, divorce rates among urban populations are generally higher than for rural populations. Many factors are thought to contribute to this, but we do not as yet have sufficient knowledge to permit any dogmatic remarks on the subject. Since higher divorce rates are correlated with occupations which predominate in the city, we cannot be sure whether it is the occupation or the city living

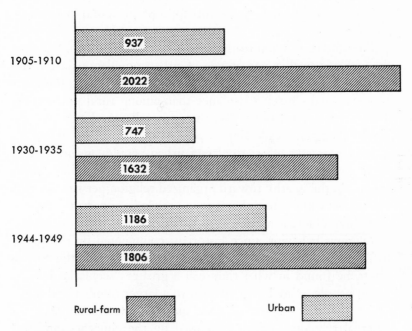

Fig. 13. Net reproduction rate: urban and rural-farm, 1905 to 1949. (Data from Bureau of the Census. A net reproduction rate below 1,000 implies a potentially declining population and a rate above 1,000 a potentially gaining population.)

that is the prime causative factor. It probably makes no practical difference anyway because of the necessary connection between urban living and these occupations.

From what fragmentary evidence we have on the elusive question of "morality," it would seem that the urban family does a less effective job of teaching moral conduct and of controlling the moral behavior of its members than does the rural family. Here again we cannot be completely sure that the difference lies in the family. Perhaps under conditions of urban living the influences which make for behavior contrary to our ideal moral codes are stronger, and, therefore, the families have a much more difficult task before them. Regardless of causation, however, the facts are clear that the behavior of urban populations departs more often and further from the legal and religious precepts which are supposed to prescribe appropriate moral and ethical conduct.

The role of religion to the urbanite is different too. Statistics show that a smaller percentage of urban populations are members of churches, and among those who are members, there is a smaller actual church attendance than among rural populations. This is true in spite of the fact that, generally speaking, the most capable religious leadership is present in the urban setting. In spite of a greater effort to attract urban people, and in spite of what would appear to be intrinsically more attractive church programs, this apathy toward organized religion persists. As with the family, causes are difficult to apprehend. Apparently there is something inherent in the city which makes for these differences in religious behavior, since historians commented on them long before the present era. Some interpreters think that the reasons are to be found in what they call a greater "secularization" of urban people, who, being exposed to a larger number and wider variety of cultural experiences, question more and more the "eternal religious verities" espoused by the churches, and find their life needs met adequately by other activities and experiences. A second factor commonly claimed to explain the difference of religious activity of rural and urban people is the greater competition which the church faces in the urban environment. In the city there are a multitude of competing activities which attract a person almost any hour of the day and any day of the week. Unless the church is able in some way to convince the urbanite that it has a vital service to perform for him, it cannot long count on mere tradition and habit, and the lack of anything else to do, to bring him regularly and dutifully to its doors. In spite of great effort, expense, and probably more efficiency on the part of the personnel devoted to the task, the urban church has not yet been able to draw the active support of as large a percentage of the population of the community as has the country church.

Summary. It would be easy to go on further portraying the urban life pattern, but we seem to have made our point, namely, that the inherent conditions of modern city living are culturally new and revolutionary, not only in superficial detail but in the very essence of living. It should be pointed out, however, that we have not intended to imply that it is necessarily *inferior*. To be sure, many informed people think it is, but that is not the point we are making here. We are solely concerned here with pointing out, and making as vivid as possible, the revolutionary character of modern urban living when viewed in the light of our time-honored habits and cherished traditions.

In this section we have attempted in a broad sweep to point out some of the salient sociological characteristics of the urban community. For convenience sake we have done this largely by comparison with the rural. The obvious advantage of this for descriptive purposes is probably clear. It is always easier to describe something newer by contrasting it with something older than to attempt description without any point of reference. This way of treating the matter, however, often leads to two common errors, both of which should be promptly corrected: (1) the idea that, because the urban way of life breaks markedly with the rural, it is therefore inferior to the rural, and (2) the impression that, while urban life is changing, rural life is changeless. The first of the above erroneous conclusions is at least doubtful because questions of "goodness" and "badness" are sociologically exceedingly difficult to determine. The second is factually wrong. Regardless of what phase is studied—living standards, education, morals, political ideas—the evidence shows clearly that rural ways and rural ideas are becoming increasingly like those of urban people. This is not to deny that differences are still marked in some respects, but the point is that differences are disappearing, and disappearing by the approximation of the rural to the urban, not vice versa.

▶ VALUE CLASHES IN THE AMERICAN CITY

Before discussing specific value clashes which are readily observed in connection with urban social problems, an over-all generalization seems warranted. A large number, possibly most, of
the value clashes pertaining to urban living represent clashes between the survivals of rural culture and the demands of urban
living. We have pointed out that cities are largely populated by
persons directly migrant from farms and villages or one generation removed from the country—American or old world. Consequently urban *dwellers* are to a considerable measure not urban
in culture. They characteristically hold to numerous values,
thought-ways, practices, and modes of life that are normal to
rural living, but that are either impossible or at least inconvenient
for city living. Culturally entrenched values, as a student of
sociology well knows, do not change readily even in the face of
new experiences and of other evidences of their impracticality.
This is due not merely to the fact that values exist as habits in
the person, but perhaps chiefly to the way in which values are
indoctrinated in the person. The person in the course of his
socialization is not taught that getting up early, or saving, or
being kind to animals are merely convenient modes of conduct
which it might be well to observe; he is taught, on the contrary,
that these things are virtuous, are good *per se*, regardless of time,
place, or circumstance. Hence, even though it is convenient or
conducive to one's immediate satisfaction to disobey a value
code, one should not do so because the value represents righteous-
ness, propriety, eternal verity, or the will of God. Thus the individual does not usually adapt readily to the logical demands of a
new environment. Urban dwellers do not stop having pets in the
house—or wanting to have them—merely because urban life is
not well suited to having them. Putting the matter otherwise, our
tendency to cling to our cultural traditions and to pass them on
to our children uncritically may cause us serious difficulties when
we find ourselves in another culture. Many of the problems of
city life result from this attitude. The wag who said, "The

trouble is, we are all hicks under the skin" had apparently glimpsed a profound sociological truth about the modern urban dweller.

Individualism versus the practical demands of communal living. One of the precious values in our pioneer and later rural background was that of "individualism" in the sense that a man's home was his castle, and if he wanted to keep a pig in the parlor, it was no one's concern but his and the pig's. That such an outlook on life was acceptable, in fact necessary, in an earlier day is obvious enough. It is equally obvious that such ideas work havoc when large numbers of people with conflicting ideas have to live close together. When and how loudly one plays his radio, how he disposes of his garbage, where his dog chooses to roam, and where and at what his children play may have a vital influence on his neighbor's health, safety, and convenience, and most assuredly on his temperament. Obviously, a man's freedom of activity and his property rights are conditional upon the effects that they have on neighbors, but numerous problems arise from the practical application of this principle to specific acts and specific neighbors. How much quiet, for example, is it normal and reasonable to expect of children—of one's neighbors' children, that is—the courts have never been able to decide satisfactorily, any more than they have been able to determine what constitutes "unreasonable" barking of a dog or "undue loudness" of a radio.

In spite of the difficulties, however, marked strides have been made in circumventing the cultural tradition that a man's home is his castle and that he can keep a pig in his parlor. The community now reserves the right to quarantine a man in his home for illness and to prevent his being buried by his relatives until a burial certificate has been obtained. In some respects, several observers have already pointed out, we may have gone so far in granting the right to invade each other's lives that unfavorable consequences have resulted. The "no-children-allowed" apartment house may be operated with the landlord's right to rent only to childless couples and to evict them if a child is born. During times of a housing shortage, however, such a property right on the part of the landlord may have an important bearing on social policy, since it is a discouragement to the couple with respect to having children. Childless, they have a home; with a child, who knows?

It seems not overly facetious to generalize that for most urban dwellers the problem of city living resolves itself into how to live *in* the city without being *of* the city. Thus they seek to work out their living arrangements with as much defiance of the logical urban living pattern as their financial condition and ingenuity will allow. Thus, generally speaking, a house is preferred to an apartment of the same size because "the house gives us more freedom and the children like the yard." This urban phenomenon reaches its logical extreme in the case of the suburban dweller who lives as near to the open country as the time and cost of commuting will allow. Thus, in effect, he holds to the advantages of the city occupationally, but escapes from it for most of his, and especially of his family's, actual living. In the more developed suburban areas there are suburban schools, suburban churches, and suburban trading centers, thus providing a whole constellation of institutions which in many ways more nearly resemble a rural community than they do an urban satellite. For many urban dwellers, then, not merely for the suburbanite alone, urban living resolves itself into escaping from the city for living but remaining close enough to the city to secure its occupational and other advantages.

At the other extreme, the cooperative-housing dweller accepts the requirement of close living and works out a pattern of life which maximizes the advantages of such living. Between the suburbanite who solves the problem by escaping it, and the co-operative-housing dweller who solves the problem by capitalizing on it, are the majority of urban dwellers who work out a life pattern consisting of a combination of escapist measures and practical expedients. They capture what measure of solace they can by cultivating a garden ten feet square, with two rose bushes and an elm tree, worrying each day whether Junior or Bowser will create a neighborhood crisis by intruding into "that cranky Mr. Jones's" dahlia garden.

Issues of urban planning and zoning. It has long been obvious to civic leaders as well as to laymen that property owners in the city, even more than in the country, must have their rights somewhat limited by consideration of the rights of those living near by. Although the principle has not been easily or quickly accepted, it is now rather clearly established in the law that only certain uses of land and buildings are appropriate in each part of the city, and that only certain kinds of new construction can be allowed. Thus there are not only residential, industrial, and commercial areas marked off ("zones"), but there are also different classifications within each of these areas. Thus in some residential areas apartment buildings cannot be constructed, and in others only houses of a certain cost, size, and architectural type, can be built.

One of the persistent problems of zoning, however, is that of adjustment to the dynamic character of the city. Suppose that a certain area is set aside as a commercial area. Later the city grows, and the commercial area is inadequate to the needs of the population. The commercial interests wish to expand into areas designated as residential. How can this be done without working a hardship on people who have built homes in these areas on the supposition that they would remain residential? How can the adjustment be made equitably and with a minimum of community conflict?

City planning is a more fundamental concept than mere zoning. City planning comprises a wide variety of aspects including zoning, location and maintenance of parks and playgrounds, financing and organizing welfare services, organizing and modifying traffic plans, establishing parking areas, and so on and on. Most cities of any size have planning commissions under one name or another with more or less power to implement their suggestions in practice. These have often been attacked on the ground that they are undemocratic, that is, that the planning is done in terms of upper- and upper-middle-class needs and values to the total or partial neglect of the working classes, Negroes, and other groups, or that they have served property owners and business groups rather than the community as a whole. Such charges are not difficult to understand in view of the power structure of the community, based as it is so largely upon wealth and those occupations associated with business and commerce. Regardless of these criticisms, many cities have made marked strides in improving their over-all physical plan and activities, and have achieved a working philosophy which balances collective community needs and traditional property rights with reasonable justice and a minimum of community conflict.

Slums.   Although by no means an American invention or monopoly, the slum is a much publicized problem of most of our cities. Physically, slum areas constitute some kind of a low in urban living. Slum housing may be of the multifloored, walk-up, tenement variety, the once private home long since converted into many unbelievably small "housekeeping rooms," or still some other type, but in any case, it accurately fits the census category, "delapidated." Overcrowding abounds, with whole families or even several families sharing a couple of rooms. And it is paradoxical to find in our most up-to-date cities that there are dwellings which lack running water, toilets, and sometimes even electricity.

But the physical conditions of slums are not their only problematic characteristics. It can be readily demonstrated that phenomena such as drug addiction, alcoholism, and certain types of mental disorders are more prevalent in slums than in other areas of the city. The slum has been called the "cradle of gangsters" and the "school of crime." A high infant mortality rate, a high incidence of tuberculosis, and a high venereal disease rate are but a few other distinguishing features of slums. It is difficult indeed to substantiate a precise cause and effect relationship between physical conditions and disease, and it is even more difficult to so relate slum conditions and deviant behavior. There is, of course, a certain amount of "drift" of deviates or near-deviates, the chronic unemployed, and the like, into the slums. It is nevertheless true that from many objective standpoints there is much that is undesirable about slums. And society is fairly well in agreement that the slum conditions of our cities are distasteful. There is little value conflict, then, regarding the definition of slum conditions as a problem. But there is likely to be a rather sharp clash of values and interests when someone proposes to "do something" about the slums that no one wanted in the first place!

On the one hand, there is the individualistic, almost fatalistic attitude toward slum conditions and slum dwellers epitomized by the cliché, "You can get the people out of the slums, but you *can't* get the slum out of the people." Thus, although they dislike the sight of slums and talk of them as a "blight" on our cities, there are some who hold that such conditions are more or less inevitable due to the "sifting and sorting" of people according to their "ambition," "ability," "character," or whatever else the proponent happens to think contributes to what he loosely terms "degeneracy." Such individuals, who are frequently more loquacious than scientific, would strenuously object to spending "good taxpayer's money" on the rehabilitation of slums. Slums are a problem of slum dwellers; they need simply to remove themselves from their environment, and those with the proper "determination" do just that! It scarcely needs to be pointed out that many slum dwellers cannot afford to pay higher rent or, if their skin happens to be a little darker than most, they cannot find another place to live even if they can afford it.

There is, at the same time, the competing idea that slum conditions are a community responsibility and that any amelioration of the problem must take place through the concerted effort of all city dwellers. Without necessarily attaching blame or cause to the conditions, adherents to this philosophy feel that the city as a whole would profit from better and more healthful conditions for all of its citizens. But even within this group there may well be strong disagreements concerning the means and methods of removing slum conditions. Should the city elicit support of the federal government for redevelopment, or is this "too socialistic"? Should the slum housing be removed and municipally owned housing erected on the same sites, or should slum dwellers be relocated in outlying areas? And what about the owners of property classified as "slum"? What are their responsibilities and rights? At whose price should they be reimbursed even if they are willing to sell their property? And so on. These are some of the areas of conflict and disagreement that can harass city officials and citizens bent on "cleaning up" their slums. It is sometimes surprising that actually so much has been done in recent years to alleviate the slum conditions of our cities.

Financing the city government. Under the American system of separate federal, state, and local governments, the city has found it exceedingly difficult to maintain a sound financial base. Traditionally the city has derived its revenues from taxes on real estate. The old theory was that people who owned their own homes and businesses should pay taxes to support the city services such as police and fire protection, maintenance of parks and playgrounds, and education. Persons who lived in rented properties would presumably pay taxes indirectly, since the landlord could shift his tax to the renter. This system worked reasonably well prior to the advent of the automobile and the resulting suburban trend. Now with easy transportation by automobile and bus, larger and larger proportions of the workers in the central city live outside the city. Since they do not live in the central city, a land tax on the property they own or rent does not accrue to the coffers of the central city. And yet the central city has the expense of providing police and fire protection and other services which benefit the worker from the central city. The effect of suburbanization is to increase the burden of taxation for the decreasing percentage of the population of the greater city which still lives in the city limits and pays taxes to the city.

Two devices have been invented in recent years to broaden the base of revenue to the city and relieve the burden to the real estate owner, namely, (1) the city income tax and (2) the city sales or transaction tax.

City income taxes. Although varying from one another in important details, city income taxes usually tax the incomes of all persons who live in or work in the central city, to the extent that the income is earned in activities performed in the central city. The legal basis for such laws is not entirely clear, since the income-tax principle, as we have seen, breaks with some important traditions of taxation. In some states it is unconstitutional to tax the incomes of workers who do not live in the city, and in other states it is unconstitutional for cities to levy income taxes at all. The trend, however, seems clearly in the direction of city income taxes.

City sales or transaction taxes. The logic behind the city sales or transaction tax is essentially the same as that behind the city income tax; in other words, the purpose is to spread the burden of taxation so as to reduce the load on the real estate owner and to increase the burden on the nonresident who benefits from the city's services but does not otherwise pay for these benefits. In general, business interests favor the income tax rather than the sales or transaction tax because they fear that the transaction tax, unless all cities adopt it, will tend to discourage nonresidents from trading in the cities with the taxes. Most tax experts would tend to favor the income tax over the sales tax because it is more clearly based upon the ability-to-pay principle, which is now generally regarded as the soundest fundamental principle in taxation.

The city's financial plight, though alleviated, is not solved by the income tax or the sales tax or any other single expedient. These devices do not solve the problem because they do not get at the root of the trouble, namely, the territorial basis for tax collection. As long as people move very freely over large areas as they do now, and large numbers can therefore live and work in different political jurisdictions, it is relatively easy to escape taxation deliberately or otherwise. The only solution that is theoretically sound would be to place all persons who are functionally a part of the city, regardless of residence, into one political unit, which would provide services to all and tax all. But the practical difficulties in doing this are so great that it appears likely that we shall continue with our present patchwork expedients for a long time to come.

Efficient government and responsible citizenship. The American political system, as everyone knows, is bipartisan, on the theory that the people can best decide vital issues by choosing one or the other of the parties on the basis of what they offer with respect to vital issues. Although this does not result in an entirely responsible government, even on the national level, it works reasonably well there. With respect to the city, however, the theory breaks down completely. A city government does not concern itself, except in very rare and exceptional instances, with policy matters. The government is simply a big business enterprise consisting of important service departments like those for police and fire protection, parks and playgrounds, education, health protection, and the like. There is, obviously, no Republican way or Democratic way of sweeping the streets, controlling disease, regulating traffic, or fighting fires. All that a city needs is an efficient, businesslike handling of these services with a minimum of waste, political patronage, and inefficiency. Accordingly there has arisen a great deal of dissatisfaction with the bipartisan method of selecting officials in city government, and several devices have been invented, presumably to increase the efficiency of the city business enterprise. Among these, the city-manager system, in one form or another, is the most radical departure from our traditions, but it is widespread enough to warrant special treatment.

The city-manager system. The logic of the city-manager plan is as follows. Since the city government is almost exclusively a set of services, it should be run like any business under an executive head who is chosen for his business ability rather than for his party affiliation or skill in vote-getting. Thus, the city manager is hired rather than elected in much the same way as is a superintendent of schools. He is then, presumably, retained or discharged on the basis of the efficiency and honesty with which he handles the city's business.

The high hopes of the early advocates of the city-manager system have not been completely realized, although there is little doubt that city managers have constituted a tremendous improvement in the administration of city governments. In those cases where city managers have not been altogether successful, aside from purely personal considerations, they have failed for the same reason that the traditional city governments have failed—because of some combination of public ignorance and apathy and organized corruption. As we have pointed out previously, corruption in city government is traditional in America. Fortunes have been made by methods more closely resembling those of the racketeer than those of legitimate business, through such devices as overcharging the city and setting up fictitious purchases by the city. The mere replacement of a partisan mayor and council by a city manager cannot automatically guarantee efficiency and honor in the administration of the street-paving department, unless the citizens know and care how their money is being spent. For decades corrupt business practices involving police departments with gambling interests, prostitution, and paving contractors especially, have gone on in many American cities with considerable openness, and with little challenge either from the public press or from any other potentially powerful group. The central problem of city government seems to be one of arousing citizens to a more realistic understanding of the nature of city government and of its relation to their own individual life problems and, then, of exposing the business dealings of the city government and its officials to constant public scrutiny. This is a far cry from present practice, but it appears essential if democratic government in the American city is to be retained.

▶ SUMMARY

Urban living presents to the American citizen a striking counterpart of the modern man who was said to have attempted to propel a racing car by the liberal application of a buggy whip. Viewing the matter sociologically, our hero was no fool; he "knew" that one could secure more activity from a vehicle by the application of a whip. But, alas, the motor-power vehicle did not respond to his cultural skills derived from another mode of life. And so it is with the city. It is new. In a new situation man reacts, almost as if instinctively, to solve problems by the "eternal principles" he has so well learned. But the principles were geared to another cultural machine; in this one the gears do not mesh. Until we learn what kind of gears are needed, the new machine seems likely to give us difficulty. As far as sociological knowledge and evidence are concerned, we cannot say with assurance that urban living is inferior to rural living, but we can say that urban living is different, and that the difference requires cultural skills and values and attitudes and general "know-how" which are different from anything man has yet mastered. Until he masters that new culture, living in the city seems likely to present him with a plethora of knotty problems.

Five areas of value conflict growing out of urban life were discussed: (1) the spirit of individualism versus the demands of communal living; (2) urban planning and zoning; (3) slum conditions; (4) financing the city government; and (5) efficient city government. Since modern life is predominantly urban life, many of the problems discussed in earlier chapters will be readily identified by the student as city problems, even though they were treated in other connections.

SUGGESTED READINGS

Anderson, William, and Edward W. Weidner, *American City Government*, New York, Henry Holt and Co., 1950. A basic, comprehensive text on this subject. Good description and evaluation of forms of municipal government.

Angell, Robert C., "The Moral Integration of American Cities," *American Journal of Sociology*, Vol. 57, No. 1, Part 2 (July 1951). A highly regarded discussion and research report on the differential cohesiveness of cities. Integration scores for forty-three large cities are presented and factors affecting integration are carefully investigated.

Colean, Miles L., *Renewing Our Cities*, New York, The Twentieth Century Fund, 1953. A concise treatment of city problems and efforts made to cope with them. The problems of slums and slum renewal are well handled.

Dahir, James, *Communities for Better Living*, New York, Harper & Bros., 1950. This book calls attention to the social consequences of physical environment, suggests needed improvements, and indicates how they can be accomplished by community members. Contains a general survey of urban community action programs.

Ericksen, E. Gordon, *Urban Behavior*, New York, The Macmillan Co., 1954. A good general text on urban sociology with up-to-date population and other data.

Gallion, Arthur B., *The Urban Pattern*, New York, D. Van Nostrand Co., 1950. An evaluation of attempts at city planning. Defects of past and present cities are strongly portrayed and related to the planning process.

Stein, Clarence S., *Toward New Towns for America*, Chicago, Public Administration Service, 1951. This book describes eleven pre-planned communities. Recounts the planning and research and describes and evaluates the resulting community and its services. Ample photographs and diagrams of the communities.

Woodbury, Coleman (ed.), *The Future of Cities and Urban Redevelopment*, Chicago, The University of Chicago Press, 1953. A group of scholars from different fields discuss the underlying factors in urban growth and planning that have helped to produce city problems. A somewhat advanced work, but rewarding for the serious student.

STUDY QUESTIONS

1. What so-called "rural values" are either incongruous or harmful in the urban setting? Why are such values held and fostered?

2. What proportion of Americans are at present urban dwellers and what changes have occurred in this respect over the last seventy-five years? Why are these changes observed carefully by those concerned with total population growth?

3. What is meant by the statement that even the basic societal institutions are different in the city and rural areas? Illustrate the difference with respect to one institution.

4. Criticize: "Since the urban way of life breaks markedly with the rural, it is therefore inferior to the rural."

5. List various specific areas of life in which the value of individualism must bow to the demand of communal living for urban dwellers.

6. Describe the functions of a city planing commission. What types of difficulties are likely to be encountered in the operation of a planning commission?

7. What is the essential value conflict with regard to the responsibility for urban slum conditions? What other value conflicts frequently occur with respect to slums?

8. Why have cities recently found it difficult to obtain sufficient revenue for their operations? What variations from traditional methods of financing have been utilized in order to remedy this situation?

9. Criticize the bipartisan method of selecting officials in city government.

10. What are the chief advantages of the city-manager system of city government? What are the disadvantages?

·18·   Agriculture and Rural Living

Many of the problem conditions previously discussed are found in rural areas as well as urban. Some, like crime and family instability, seem less pronounced in rural areas but others know no ecological boundaries or even reach a more serious level in rural communities. There are, however, various problems that are unique to agriculture and rural living, and it is these with which we will be concerned in this chapter. In earlier sections of this book we pointed out a number of aspects of rural life which had relevance to the problems being treated. It may be well to review these briefly at the outset.

(1) American society has evolved in the last one hundred years from a predominantly agricultural nation to one in which agriculture is a minority occupation. Only about one employed person out of nine at present is engaged in agriculture as a major occupation. During the past fifty years we have *added* 75 million people to the population yet there are some 4 million *fewer* workers engaged in farming occupations than there were in 1900. The reason is, of course, that the annual output of a farmer has increased phenomenally. This is due to several factors, but chiefly to the great technological changes in agricultural production, chiefly the replacement of manpower and horsepower by machine power, and the application of scientific knowledge to plant and animal culture. A graphic way of presenting this virtual revolution in production is found on page 15 where we showed that in 1820 it required four farmers to support one city person, while in 1954 one farmer can feed himself and fourteen city per-

sons. This represents a fifty-sixfold increase in production. Obviously, if the same proportion of workers were employed in agriculture today as fifty years ago, there would be so great a flood of agricultural products produced that it would be impossible for us to consume them. The farmers who produced them would, of course, go bankrupt. And we would not have the same number of workers in our factories turning out automobiles, refrigerators, televisions, and all of the other products we value.

*Table 17. Workers in Farm and Non-farm Occupations, 1820-1955 **

Year	All gainful workers (millions)	Number of workers in farm occupations (millions)	Percent of all workers in farm occupations
1820	2.9	2.1	71.8
1840	5.4	3.7	68.6
1860	10.5	6.2	58.9
1880	17.4	8.6	49.4
1900	20.1	10.9	37.5
1920	42.4	11.4	27.0
1940	51.7	8.9	17.1
1950	59.0	6.8	11.6
1955	70.7	7.5	10.6

* Data to 1950 from: U. S. Bureau of the Census, *Statistical Abstracts of the United States: 1953*, Washington, D. C., U. S. Government Printing Office, 1953, p. 184. Data for 1955 are estimates derived from *Monthly Labor Review*, Vol. 78 (Oct. 1955), p. 1184.

As this is being written, there is national concern over our farm surpluses. Many agricultural economists are pointing out that there must be further reduction of manpower in agriculture if we are to avoid the creation of even greater surpluses, resulting in further hardship to farmers through lower prices. Meanwhile, our agricultural chemists, agronomists, animal husbandrymen, and horticulturists are continually discovering new and revolutionary ways of increasing the productivity per man and per acre, the net effect of these inventions being, of course, to further and further decrease the percentage of our total working population that can profitably be employed in agricultural pursuits. No one really knows what the ultimate end of this continuous process may be. All that we can now say is that, from all indications, we can maintain an abundant food supply for this country and for export with an ever smaller and smaller percentage of our manpower engaged in farming.

(2) It will also be recalled (as the student probably knows from common sense if not from formal reading) that the stereotyped gross differences between rural and urban life are rapidly disappearing. Farmers are no longer isolated and uneducated, with narrow cultural horizons. Increasing proportions of them attend high school and college, travel extensively, and through use of the automobile have frequent access to the city for business and recreational purposes. Farm homes, although on the average still somewhat below urban homes in the number of modern inventions, are increasingly coming to resemble those of the city. Rural electrification has revolutionized the farm home perhaps even more than it has affected farming as an industry. Even the possession of somewhat stricter moral codes, long thought to be characteristic of rural people, seems not justified by the facts. Studies of smoking and drinking among country girls,[1] for example, and of sexual behavior of both men and women [2] indicate that country people, while they still differ slightly from city people, are rapidly becoming more and more like urbanites. Another student has investigated the results of numerous national public opinion polls conducted over a five-year period.[3] These polls concerned international issues, labor problems, various public issues, and personal beliefs. Rural and urban people responded quite similarly on any number of questions, particularly those

---

[1] Evelyn M. Duvall and Annabelle B. Matz, "Are County Girls So Different?", *Rural Sociology*, Vol. X (September 1945), pp. 263-74.

[2] Alfred Kinsey, *et al.*, *Sexual Behavior in the Human Male*, Philadelphia, W. B. Saunders, 1948; *Sexual Behavior in the Human Female*, Philadelphia, W. B. Saunders, 1953.

[3] Howard W. Beers, "Rural-Urban Differences: Some Evidence from Public Opinion Polls," *Rural Sociology*, Vol. 18 (March 1953), pp. 1-11.

concerning international relations, and the degree of overlapping made it plain that we can scarcely talk about "rural attitudes" versus "urban attitudes." It is only a matter of time, and probably of a short time, before rural-urban differences in standards of living, attitudes, and values, will have entirely disappeared.

The foregoing is, of course, not to be taken as meaning that there do not exist unique and important problems which are distinctly those of the agricultural community and of workers dependent upon agriculture as a means of livelihood. We shall turn our attention in this chapter to the treatment of some of these major problem areas.

▶ SOCIAL AND ECONOMIC PROBLEMS OF AGRICULTURE OF NATIONAL CONCERN

In a highly significant way the problems of the agricultural industry are of vital concern to the entire society and not merely to the 11 percent of Americans gainfully employed in it. Everybody depends for his daily subsistence on the agricultural industry. Although seriously inconvenienced, we could get along without automobiles and radios, and for relatively long periods without new clothing, education, or recreation. But not so with food. Modern science has not yet provided any practical substitute for food produced basically by agriculture.

Public interest in agriculture. Consequently there has long been great concern in national circles for the welfare of the agricultural industry and for the people engaged in it. This is no sentimental concern, but rather one of practicality and expediency. The nation as a whole, being dependent for the maintenance of its life on the quality and quantity of the food produced by farmers, has become interested in the efficiency of that industry, in the quality-standards of the products marketed, in extending scientific knowledge at public expense to the farmer, and, in many other ways, in "interfering" in a sense with his complete freedom to run his enterprise as he pleases.

This general public interest in the agricultural industry has given rise to considerable opposition from some urban groups and even from some farmers. This opposition represents, of course, a clash of values with those implied in the preceding paragraph. Although somewhat less hostile now than fifteen or twenty years ago, there is still considerable opposition on the part of some farmers to the efforts of nonfarming groups to raise the quality of agricultural products. Laws regulating the quality of apples and eggs which can be marketed, requiring accurate labeling and strict quality standards, and applying sanitation rules to dairy products and their handling at the farm, have been attacked as "socialistic interferences" with the right of farmers to conduct their business as they please. In spite of the opposition, however, increasingly the principle has been established that the nonagricultural majority of consumers has a legal, if not also a moral, right to interfere in the agricultural business to the extent of requiring that healthfulness and nutritional quality of the products be maintained at the highest possible levels.

Some urban groups, on the other hand, have opposed public interest in agriculture from the point of view that farmers are increasingly being given undue advantages at the expense of the general taxpayer and consumer who is predominantly a nonagriculturalist. Millions of dollars are spent each year through agricultural extension services and agricultural experiment stations to bring to the farmer, at public expense, the latest information concerning the most improved agricultural practices. The argument that these benefit the consumer in the long run through lower prices and higher quality is to many individualistic people insufficient evidence of the moral right to use public funds to assist one industry.

Farm subsidies. A more fundamental issue has arisen in recent years with respect to farm-subsidy policies of the federal government. In a later part of this chapter we shall attempt to explain the theory underlying the farm-subsidy program. Here it is sufficient to point out that the effect of the farm subsidy is to create artificially high prices for farm products; that is, through the operation of the subsidy, prices of farm products are held higher than they would be if the government took a *laissez-faire* attitude and allowed the forces of supply and demand to operate unchecked. The opponent of subsidies argues that subsidies amount to a hidden bonus taken away from the consumer and paid indirectly to the farmer, that they create an income level for the farmer which is higher than it would be if he had to compete in an open market. The issue of subsidies is a highly complicated one, and our purpose here is not to decide whether the system is sound, or rather, from whose point of view it is sound. We are here merely making the point that the subsidy idea has been adopted by the Congress in response to agricultural pressure groups and to the government's own research experts. This seems to grant the principle, tacitly at least, that the prices of farm products are not solely the problem of agriculture, but rather of the general public.

No doubt there lies behind the subsidy idea another value, however, namely, that of military necessity. In the event of war, food becomes a munition. If the agricultural industry is to be healthy, that is, well supplied with machinery, fertilized soil, good livestock, and so on, so that it can expand quickly in a war emergency, then the farmer must, in a peacetime situation, receive a high enough income to maintain his industry at such a level that he can quickly and efficiently meet the greater demands of a wartime situation. While this military consideration is probably involved in the subsidy plan, it is probably not the prime factor in the establishment and maintenance of farm subsidies as explained previously.

Thus, we see that the agricultural industry is materially affected by its position as a vitally necessary industry in peace time no less than in war. The traditional values of individualism historically associated with the farmer have already been seriously abridged. This has come about slowly but firmly. The principle (value) of societal concern with agriculture seems here to stay. Specific forms of control, and maybe even amounts of control, will probably vary somewhat as the political atmosphere changes. But it is difficult to foresee any reversal of the continued public interest in this industry.

▶ RURAL SOCIAL PROBLEMS

In this section we shall consider three main groups of closely related problems of rural society. Since we cannot treat this topic exhaustively, we shall select typical and important problems for somewhat fuller treatment.

Problems of depopulation. It is obvious from what we have already said that rural communities, with occasional exceptions, are being depleted relative to the total population of the nation. As we have pointed out previously, this takes place chiefly through the migration of relatively young people to the city after they have been reared in the rural communities. Evidence of rural depopulation comes from a wide variety of statistical sources. Census studies reveal, for example, that while the population of the United States as a whole *increased* 23 percent between 1940 and 1954, the number of people living on farms *decreased* 25 percent. In 1954, rural people (both farm and rural nonfarm) made up about one third of the total population, the lowest proportion in the history of our country.

What does a declining population mean to the social life of the rural community? Stated tersely, it means that there is a *rising per-capita cost* of maintaining the basic societal institutions such as schools, churches, and rural government. If the population of a rural community declines, say from one thousand to eight hundred gainfully employed persons, then the eight hundred must assume the burden of supporting the churches, schools, and government which were formerly assumed by the entire one thousand. The faster and more extreme the depopulation, the more marked is the increase of the burden of supporting the basic institutions.

Depopulation may also have a serious qualitative effect on the community, although this point is not entirely clear from the research that has been done. Stated tersely, the question is: "Generally, do the more able or the less able people leave the rural community?" Some studies have found, using intelligence quotients and high school grades as an index, that the superior indi-

Table 18. Proportion of Total Population Living in Rural Areas and on Farms, 1910-1954 *

Year	Proportion of population in rural areas (including on farms)	Proportion of population on farms
1910	54.3	34.7
1920	48.8	29.6
1930	43.8	23.9
1940	43.5	23.9
1950	36.0	16.0
1954	32.4	13.4

* Data to 1950 computed from U. S. Bureau of the Census, *Statistical Abstracts of the United States: 1953*, Washington, D. C., U. S. Government Printing Office, 1953, pp. 13, 26. Percentage of population on farms, 1954, obtained from Census estimate released to press; percentage of population rural, 1954, has been estimated.

viduals by these criteria left the rural communities in greater proportion than did the individuals of lower intelligence and educational success.[4] Other studies have presented evidence based on more exacting criteria of "talent." These studies have shown that, in general, the cities have tended to "drain" persons of talent out of rural communities in great numbers. One method has been to compare the birthplace and childhood rearing with the present residence for persons distinguished enough to be listed in *Who's Who in America* or having other evidence of outstanding success.

The rural community, moreover, is normally forced to bear a disproportionate share of the cost of dependent people—those too young to be gainfully employed and those too old to be efficiently employed. As the following graph indicates, rural farms have a higher proposition of children fifteen years of age and under than do cities. Most of these rural children must mi-

[4] See, for example, C. T. Pihlblad and C. L. Gregory, "Selective Aspects of Migration," *American Sociological Review*, Vol. 19 (June 1954), pp. 314-24.

grate and the majority end up in the city. A study of rural high school graduates in Iowa, for example, revealed that almost 60 percent had left their rural community just one year after completion of high school.[5] Thus the people of the communities largely assumed the cost of rearing and educating the children

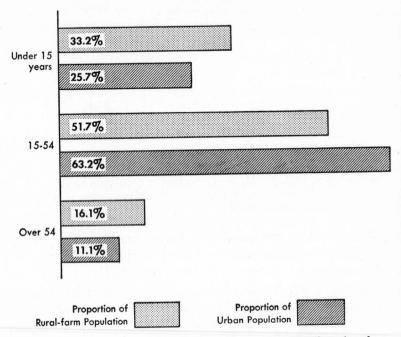

Under 15 years — 33.2% / 25.7%

15-54 — 51.7% / 63.2%

Over 54 — 16.1% / 11.1%

Proportion of Rural-farm Population

Proportion of Urban Population

Fig. 14. Age distribution, urban and rural-farm, 1950. (Based on data from U. S. Bureau of the Census, *Statistical Abstracts of the United States: 1953*, Washington, D. C., U. S. Government Printing Office, 1953, pp. 9, 31.)

but did not receive the services of three fifths of them when they reached the age at which many begin to make contributions to the manpower of the communities. Most rural areas throughout the country exhibit a similar pattern of out-migration of their young people. When one realizes that the average cost of rearing a child, exclusive of college education costs, is upwards of ten

[5] Joe M. Bohlen and Ray E. Wakeley, "Intentions to Migrate and Actual Migration of Rural High School Graduates," *Rural Sociology*, Vol. 15 (December 1950), pp. 328-34.

thousand dollars, and when he then multiplies this per-capita cost by the thousands of young adults who migrate, he can secure some approximate idea of the effect of this parasitism of the city upon the rural community.

Contributing to the same problem is the somewhat less pronounced, but still apparent, tendency for older people to move from the city to the rural areas, especially villages, after their most productive years of urban employment are ended. It is not known what percentage of these people become dependent upon the gainfully employed in the rural communities. Probably an appreciable proportion become wholly or in part dependent upon public relief, charitable relatives and friends, or some combination of the two. Thus the city not only shifts some of the burden of rearing and educating its manpower to the rural community, but it also shifts some of the cost of supporting persons of diminished productivity or of complete dependency due to old age.

It is not known to what extent the lower standards of living characteristic of rural communities may be caused by, or aggravated by, the depopulation process. It is difficult to conclude that long-term depopulation, plus the migration of youth to the city, plus the back-to-the-country migration of aged people, could constitute anything but a depressing influence upon the standard of living enjoyed by rural people. The problem seems to many observers likely to become more serious as the percentage of people gainfully employed in agriculture is further reduced. There is certainly a point below which a rural community cannot operate efficiently if present trends continue. Have we reached that point now? Will we reach it soon? Or will some counter-trend enable us to avoid it?

Price disparity in agriculture. Agricultural economists have long been aware of a condition which they have called "price disparity" with respect to most agricultural products. To explain this concept, it is necessary to delve somewhat more deeply into economic analysis than may seem desirable in a book of this type. Nevertheless, if we are to understand the agricultural occupation in its sociological aspects, we must be familiar with its economic base.

For most of the time during the last one hundred years, there have been two price systems in the American market: (1) agricultural prices, set largely by supply and demand and largely uncontrollable because of dependence on weather conditions, and (2) nonagricultural prices, controlled as a result of protective-tariff policy and of entrepreneurial control over output. Stated tersely, this means that farmers traditionally had to sell their products on a free market without the advantage of tariff protection, but had to buy their nonagricultural products on a somewhat artificial market where the prices were kept high due to tariff and other controls. These two price levels have frequently departed markedly from one another, creating situations such as that during the 1920's when the price level of nonagricultural commodities was relatively high, while agricultural products were fantastically cheap *at the farm.* This was commonly called "overproduction," but the term seems partly misapplied because the condition which brought it about would have prevailed regardless of how much production of agricultural goods there was. To be sure, conditions were worse for the farmer during times when agricultural products were plentiful, but his plight was not caused by the overproduction basically—it was caused by the continual and normal discrepancy between selling on a free market and buying on an artificial one. Hence the term, "price *dis*parity."

To the novice in economics, it might seem relatively easy to correct price disparity. In fact, if one is sufficiently ignorant, he does not even recognize that there is price disparity or that it should present a "problem." To the person somewhat informed on economic matters, it often seems that the problem would be solved by giving the farmer the benefit of tariff protection. This has proved in practice to be practically worthless because we are, for most agricultural products, an exporting nation, not an importing one. It does no good, therefore, to keep foreign products out by a tariff, if none (or few) come in without one.

Beginning in the late 1920's agitation for farm relief, designed to attack the price disparity directly, resulted in Congress twice passing the McNary-Haugen farm relief bill, which both times was vetoed by the president. In the Roosevelt administration the well known and much maligned Agricultural Adjustment Administration was formed. It differed in philosophy from the McNary-Haugen approach, but the purpose was the same—to correct price disparity. In the early days of AAA, under Secretary of Agriculture Henry Wallace, the prevailing theory was an essentially capitalistic one: prices of farm products could be made higher by withholding some products from the market. Thus, production control, long an established practice in industry, was expected to result in higher prices by the simple device of reducing the quantity of stuff on the market.

But how could this objective of production control be implemented in practice? In industry it is relatively easy to regulate output, since there are relatively few producers of a given commodity who make decisions. Moreover, it is not at all uncommon in industry to have "gentlemen's agreements" concerning how many units of some product will be produced in a given year. But in agriculture there are literally millions of independent producers with no means of getting together to make agreements to limit output, and with traditions decidedly hostile to any such procedure.

Before the production-control plan could go into effect, it was concluded, it would be necessary to take from the market those surpluses which were currently depressing prices. Accordingly, the government purchased quantities of wheat and other staples and destroyed them, paid the farmers to plow under certain quantities of corn and cotton, and slaughtered and destroyed quantities of little pigs. As almost anyone who lived through the period will recall, there was violent public opposition to these practices, both among farmers and nonfarmers. Some sacred values were being attacked. Food should never be destroyed, even to increase prices and save an industry. The government should not enter so actively into the affairs of an industry. The Department of Agriculture and the Administration generally were subjected to great ridicule, but it is not known to what extent this fact influenced their future policy.

With immediate surpluses out of the way, the government turned to its acreage-control program, which was designed, as we have already seen, to increase prices by restricting the amount of agricultural products that would be grown. But this practice also broke sharply with American values. Why should the government pay farmers for leaving land idle? Should the farmers not make that decision themselves, and if they so decided, withhold land from cultivation at their own expense, not the government's? Leaving aside the technical economics of the issue, it is certainly clear that most people saw little precedent for the acreage-control program, and for that matter, had little sympathy even with its objectives.

Crop control was regarded then, and is still regarded by some now, as being the incorrect approach because it is thought to be morally wrong to restrict the production of food in order to keep prices up while there are some people who need the food and cannot afford to pay for it at existing prices. The proponents of restricted production point out that this method is consistent with capitalism; that, for example, manufacturers are not expected to flood the market with automobiles and depress the price simply so that needy people may have cars. Why should farmers do otherwise? There is, of course, one difference between the two examples, namely, that the manufacturer does not receive support from the government in return for not producing what might turn out to be a surplus. But, basically, the point seems well taken.

The most recent attack on the problem of price disparity is the so-called "farm-subsidy program," which strives to protect price levels of agricultural products by a different procedure. The agricultural economists in the Department of Agriculture continuously scrutinize the market prices of legally designated basic agricultural products, and when these prices threaten to fall below the point called "parity," the government enters the market as a purchaser and buys sufficient of these products to stimulate an upward price trend. Commodities thus purchased, and termed "surplus," may then be contributed to such presumably worthy causes as school-lunch programs and some kinds of relief. It is important, of course, that the commodities do not return to the market because if they do, the effect of the subsidy would be nullified.

Opposition to subsidies now in effect centers around two arguments, leaving aside the strictly political ones. First, subsidies are said to be unfair to the consumer because, first of all, he pays the bill through taxes when the government buys products to raise the price, and, secondly, he pays more for all of those commodities when he buys them at the new price. There is no doubt, of course, that farm subsidies mean higher prices to consumers. That is precisely what they are supposed to do. The valid issue would seem to be, instead, whether artificial controls upon agricultural prices are desirable.

The root problem, as we have seen, arises from the dual nature of the market system—nonagricultural products being controlled in price by the amount produced, while agricultural products, because of the nature of the industry, are not so readily controllable. The real issue would seem to be whether it would be better to continue subsidies or to take a hands-off policy and let the agriculture industry sink or swim on the basis of its own ingenuity and luck. But further difficulties arise immediately. As we have already seen, during normal times, although especially during war, the nation has a vital interest in the efficiency of the agricultural industry, which efficiency would be seriously impaired if some kind of stabilizing influence were not introduced. Many people do not want to run the risk of a depression in agriculture, threatening our wartime security or our peacetime standard of living.

There is a second factor of broad social policy involved. During periods of agricultural depression (low prices), there are many bankruptcies, especially in certain kinds of agriculture, which means foreclosures of farm mortgages and the eventual ownership of the farms by banks, insurance companies, or wealthy individuals. This increases absentee ownership of farms and accelerates the tendency toward "corporation farming," which is particularly unpalatable to many Americans, both in agriculture and out. In 1933, for example, North Dakota passed a law prohibiting corporations from owning land in that state. This was an extreme instance, to be sure, but typifies the widespread opposition to any departure from the farm-family pattern of agricultural production. Consequently, it is argued, in order to perpetuate the small-farm system—or rather to retard its slow replacement by the corporation type of farm—we need to do everything possible to maintain a financially healthy farm industry along present lines.

Maintenance of an economically healthy farm industry, however, may not require farm subsidies, acreage control, or any specific form of farm relief which we have actually tried. Perhaps there is some kind of device which is now not known, but which can accomplish the objective much better. Moreover, it is entirely possible that, however unpalatable it may be at present, the only eventual solution to the farm price problem may lie with corporation farming, which with unified control would be able without governmental interference to restrict output much as industry now does in order to maintain desired price levels. One thing is obvious, namely, that some of the cherished values will have to be displaced or modified. Which ones, it remains to be seen.

Other kinds of farm relief. Thus far we have limited our discussion of governmental attempts to bring about financial aid to farmers to those which are aimed directly at the price-disparity question. There are, however, other kinds of governmental assistance which should be noted, some of which, by the way, actually work at cross-purposes to subsidy and acreage control because they encourage surpluses by increasing efficiency. *Soil conservation* would be a case in point. Obviously, the nation has an interest in conserving the soil, not only for the present, but also for the future. But as we build the soil, we increase productivity and surpluses. Less directly, *rural electrification* can be so interpreted, through its stimulus to increased efficiency of the farm worker, although the chief gain of electrification would seem to be in the realm of living-standards rather than in production *per se*.

Credit aids to farmers through the Federal Land Banks and also through crop loans find little opposition because Americans rather generally agree with the underlying objective, that is, to encourage the continued existence of the small farm-family unit of production. To be sure, some banking interests do not relish competition by the government in granting more liberal credit to farmers, but that opposition seems not likely to result in any major modification of existing programs.

Dissatisfaction with rural living. Numerous contrasts and inconsistencies among both rural and urban people exist regarding the relative merits of living where they do. Traditionally urban people have tended to look down on farmers as "hicks," "rubes," unschooled and unsophisticated, and have professed hostility toward many aspects of rural values and material culture. Yet these same urban people, as we have seen in the chapter on "The City," manifest many rural "thought-ways" and folkways and go to great pains and inconvenience to preserve many cherished rural practices and ideas. This might mean that urban people reject some aspects of rural culture while accepting others, but even this interpretation leaves many unexplainable contrasts in attitude.

Characteristically, rural people seem to share comparable hostility toward the urban dweller and urban ways. Rural people have from time immemorial regarded living in cities as a substandard mode of life, characterized by dirt and disease, by crime and immorality. Yet these rural people and their children have made up a substantial part of the growing population of the city. Perhaps, to be sure, those who had least objection to the city were the ones who migrated there, but evidence is lacking which would enable us to accept this neat explanation. Moreover, it is entirely possible that the migration of farm people to the city was caused not so much by an attraction to the city as by pressures to leave the farm, such as price disparity, lower wages, longer hours, seasonal employment, and other economic considerations.

It is well to point out that while speculation is rife and tempting, information is only fragmentary on the question of satisfaction of rural and urban people with living in the country or the city *per se*. Many people, probably most, whether in the city or in the country, like some aspects of their situation and dislike others. For example, a city dweller might like his job but dislike living in an apartment and fighting traffic for an hour a day going to and from work. Similarly, a farmer might like his occupation, but dislike being so far removed from the cultural and recreational opportunities of city life. Thus, it seems desirable to turn our attention to those aspects of rural life which are commonly given a low, or negative, value by rural people. While there are, of course, great differences of opinion among rural people about rural life, certain characteristic complaint patterns are evidenced. These may be classified as follows:

Dissatisfaction with agricultural occupations. The long hours, irregular work seasons, and sometimes inconvenient working conditions of agriculture are well known. In spite of the fact that modern technology and modern farming practices have greatly improved working hours and working conditions, there are still many individuals who feel that, in order to make a reasonably good living in agriculture, the individual must work too long and too hard as compared with the urban dweller of comparable ability and similar income.

Perhaps more serious than the foregoing are the occupational problems of the agricultural industry itself. One of the chief of these difficulties is the large amount of capital required for a beginner in agriculture. A responsible official in the Bureau of Agricultural Economics of a Midwestern agricultural college recently said that the minimum capital outlay for a family in farming would be twenty thousand dollars. Such a family, he went on to explain, would be by no means debt-free, but would own the necessary machinery, land, and livestock to proceed with reasonable safety, if the man knew the agricultural business reasonably well. But where can one get the twenty thousand? One current device for meeting the difficulty is for the young man to go into partnership with his father, who is already presumably established, and by the time the father is ready to retire, the son's equity in the business may be sufficient to buy out his father's interest. It is obvious that for many persons this device is not practical—there may be several sons, or the father and son may not be temperamentally suited to business relations with one another, or the son may wish to engage in a type of agricultural production other than that chosen by his father.

Another solution to the problem, which is increasingly common but still unpalatable to many people of rural origin, is to work as a farm laborer in the employ of some individual or corporation farm. This puts the worker in essentially the same position as that of the industrial worker in the city, except that he is less secure because he usually does not have the benefit of union organization and finds considerable seasonal fluctuation in employment.

Limited cultural opportunities. With the coming of the automobile, radio, and television, much of the isolation of the rural population has been reduced, but it is by no means entirely eliminated. Rural youth, particularly, feel "left out" in their desire to participate in the kinds of recreational activities which city youth have at walking distance. Thoughtful rural parents, moreover, who are educated enough to know the difference between quality education of their children and substandard education, frequently voice displeasure with the quality of their schools, teaching equipment, and teachers. Merely being willing to spend more money for teachers' salaries does not solve the problem entirely, for many of the more capable teachers will not serve in rural communities because of the limited cultural and recreational opportunities found there.

This problem is one which does not lend itself readily to solution. Part of the difficulty is that the rural community does not have the financial resources to support an institutional complex equivalent to that of the city, and even if by some miracle it did, the population base would be so small that participation would still seem strange and different as compared to urban patterns.

Substandard medical care. One of the most serious disprivileges of the average person living in the country is the markedly deficient medical service on which he must rely. There are practically no specialists in rural areas, and most of the general practitioners are older, less well trained, and less capable men than those in the cities. Hospital and clinical facilities are, for the most part, unavailable except at considerable distances—and time can be of the essence where a health problem is concerned. Conditions in this respect are much better than they formerly were, but there is no denying that a wide and serious gap still separates the average rural dweller from the best medical facilities of urban society. The Michigan health study referred to in Chapter 6, for example, discovered that about 27 percent of the people living in the "open country" had one or more untreated symptoms of medical disorders, as opposed to about 19 percent of urban people.[6] It further discovered that unmet need for medical care increased directly with distance from a town having a doctor.[7] Other studies have found that as many as *half* of the rural people had unmet medical needs.[8]

Deficiencies in meeting the mental health needs are even more glaring. Thousands of rural counties in the United States, even in the wealthier states, do not have a single resident psychiatrist. A psychiatrist residing as much as a hundred miles away is practically unavailable to the average patient because successful psychiatric treatment in many cases involves somewhat regular care over relatively long periods. Studies have shown that the mental health needs of rural people are about the same as those of urban people, hence one must draw the conclusion that by and large their needs are even more glaringly neglected than are those of the urbanite.

In spite of considerable effort by agricultural extension services and home economics demonstration personnel, by philanthropic bodies like the Kellogg Foundation, and by many un-

[6] Charles R. Hoffer, *et al.*, *Health Needs and Health Care in Michigan*, Special Bulletin 365, East Lansing, Michigan State College Agricultural Experiment Station, 1950, p. 15.

[7] *Ibid.*, p. 21. For a summary of several other studies reaching similar conclusions with regard to distance from a town and unmet medical needs, see Charles P. Loomis and J. Allan Beegle, *Rural Social Systems*, New York, Prentice-Hall, 1950, pp. 723-28.

[8] Selz C. Mayo and Kie Sebastian Fullerton, *Medical Care in Greene County*, Bulletin 363, Raleigh, North Carolina Agricultural Experiment Station, 1948, p. 26.

organized and earnest private individuals and unofficial groups, these cultural contrasts with urban life go on year after year, some of them actually increasing in severity. The reason is that most of the difficulties are irremediable, either because they stem from the unstable economics of the agricultural industry, or because they are inherent in the scattered, small-population pattern of rural life. Perhaps the only solution is the one already well established, namely, the migration of the more acutely dissatisfied ones to communities less culturally restricted. What effect the continuation of this migration will have in the long run upon the biological and cultural quality of the rural population can only be guessed, but observers who are apprehensive about it frequently voice considerable concern.

▶ SUMMARY

In this chapter we have considered the problems of the 11 percent of the nation engaged in the basically important occupation of agriculture. We have sketched historically the development of the nation from one with a predominantly agricultural economy to one with a largely urban economy, and have shown how the economics of the agricultural industry, periodically modified by changing technology, have created numerous problems. We have discussed these problems in terms of depopulation, price disparity, and the cultural disprivileges of rural people. Various solutions to these conditions have been discussed at many points, largely in terms of the clash of values involved.

SUGGESTED READINGS

Anderson, W. A., "High-School Youth and the Values in Rural Living," *Rural Sociology*, Vol. 18 (June 1953), pp. 156-63. A study of the opinions of youth regarding the rural environment as a place in which to live. Summarizes the aspects of rural living most and least valued.

Benedict, Murray R., *Farm Policies of the United States, 1790-1950*, New York, The Twentieth Century Fund, 1953. A comprehensive, historical treatment. Useful in providing background of the area.

Gee, Wilson, *The Social Economics of Agriculture*, New York, The Macmillan Co., 1954. A sociological approach to the study of farming and rural life. Useful for attaining general insight into rural social life and economic policy.

Malone, Carl C., "Appraising Farm Programs and Proposals," *Farm Policy Forum*, Vol. 7 (Winter 1954), pp. 32-36. This brief article outlines the clash of values and disagreement over the goals of a national farm program, the methods for reaching the goals, and the consequences that follow the use of particular methods.

President's Commission on Migratory Labor, *Migratory Labor in American Agriculture*, Washington, D. C., U. S. Government Printing Office, 1951. Deals with agricultural problems not covered in this chapter. A good overview of the social, personal, and economic problems of migratory farm workers.

Schickele, Rainer, *Agricultural Policy*, New York, McGraw-Hill Book Co., 1954. A thorough treatment of economic issues in agriculture. Production and distribution of farm products, farm credit and prices, and the farmers' share of income are carefully appraised.

Smith, T. Lynn, *The Sociology of Rural Life*, 3d ed., New York, Harper & Bros., 1953. A sound text in rural sociology. Although not oriented in terms of rural social problems, it contains much factual information bearing on them.

STUDY QUESTIONS

1. What are some of the important recent changes that have happened with respect to agriculture and rural living?

2. Why are the problems of the agricultural industry of concern to the entire society and not just to farmers? What difficulties have resulted from this situation?

3. Defend the value positions of both the proponents and opponents of the farm subsidy idea. Which position comes closest to your own thinking on the issue?

4. What is meant by the statement that rural depopulation trends may have a qualitative effect on the rural community?

5. Of what concern to the rural areas is the fact that a sizable proportion of their youth migrate to cities? What remedies would you suggest for this situation?

6. Explain what is meant by price disparity with respect to agricultural products.

7. In the 1930's what steps were taken to remove agricultural surpluses from the market? How do you account for the public reaction to this program?

8. What is meant by an acreage-control program? What are the objections of the opponents of such programs?

9. Cite the methods used to meet the need for a large amount of capital for a beginner in agriculture and comment on the feasibility of each method.

10. What is the evidence concerning the substandard medical care in rural areas? Can you think of any economically feasible way to remedy this situation?

·19· Government

In modern society government reaches nearly everywhere and everyone. From one's officially recorded birth to his death and the issuance of a burial permit, the influence of government can scarcely be missed. Government protects our lives and property, provides our schools, conscripts our sons and fathers, regulates our work, our business dealings, and our marriages, and taxes our income. But it was not always so.

In simple cultures, the family is the central institution, containing within itself most of the fundamental behavior patterns of social life. Regulations are chiefly informal, based on custom and tradition.

As a culture grows in size, complexity, and specialization, the family declines in its usefulness as an over-all controlling organ. Educational, religious, welfare, recreational, economic, and other societal activities, which, in so far as they previously existed, were in the hands of the family unit, form new and separate institutional complexes.

The state has become the superinstitution of modern society. It has grown from the "tottering little policeman" that earlier in Western cultural history separated itself from the family to the most powerful of modern institutions. As we have already seen at numerous points in this book, one cannot long consider any problem in American society without taking into account actual or proposed related functions of government. For society to deal with full effectiveness with health, educational, recreational, economic, criminal, racial, and other major social problems, the role of the state must be given weighty consideration. In a sense, then, virtually all modern social problems are, to varying degrees, governmental problems. Some value conflicts, however, concentrate themselves more specifically in the machinery and policies of government. It is to these areas of conflict that we now turn our attention and consider government itself as a modern "social problem."

▶ AMERICAN GOVERNMENT—REAL AND IDEAL

American government cannot be studied realistically without making a rather sharp distinction between its theories and its practices. If a person were to confine his knowledge of our government to information derived from official documents, he would emerge with a highly inaccurate and incomplete conception of how that government functions. He would gather that governmental decision is made according to the will of the people, that abridgement of suffrage privileges and other discriminations are never made because of race or color, that the people elect electors who decide who shall be President and Vice President of the United States, and so on. Yet actual government is largely by political parties, lobbies, and pressure groups; actual government infringes upon, or tolerates infringement upon, the rights of citizens of certain races and colors. *Ideal* American government is "of the people, by the people, and for the people"; *real* American government is a temporary equilibrium among diverse pressure groups fighting for dominance, special privilege, or prestige.

Ideological splits in "one nation indivisible." One source of division in American government is the many major differences in systems of beliefs held by various groups in the population. These differences express themselves along many important lines of governmental action and render government in practice quite different from government in theory. Let us examine examples of significant differences in ideology.

Business, labor, and farmers. As we saw in Chapter 11, big business, organized labor, and farmers strongly differ ideologically regarding what government should do and how it should do it. In general, business is in favor of very limited governmental powers over economic matters, principally because a weak government in the economic sphere probably means continued business dominance. Organized labor, on the other hand, tends to favor strong governmental action in the economic field. The several large farmer organizations, in turn, fight "government interference" or actively plead for governmental action, depending on the current interests of farmers, or, perhaps, the particular type of farmer the organization represents. Thus, each of the "big three" are self-interested groups vying with one another and frequently at odds with the general interest. Since we treated these conflicts of values rather fully in our discussion of pressure groups, we shall do no more here than to remind the student that this is certainly one of the most fundamental problem areas in government today.

Conflicts on military policies. At the time the first edition of this book appeared, two of the sharpest conflicts of values discernible were: (1) how best to maintain the peace (aggressive prevention of Communistic expansion versus a policy of nonintervention in foreign affairs linked with a concentration on domestic problems), and (2) the desirability or undesirability of compulsory military training. On the surface, at least, those issues now seem to be dead. The United States has apparently launched upon a foreign policy which includes full military prevention, when necessary, of Communist aggression, and Selective Service has been reactivated.

Although military preparedness and military action are openly supported, there is a discernible but very quiet undercurrent of discontent. Privately, rather than openly, more citizens seem to be asking whether the road to world peace is patrolled by large armies and are at least musing over the thought that history would seem to bear out the assertion that a nation which launches upon a large military program will soon find itself engaged in a major war. Such thoughts are not frequently articulated because those who dare to do so are suspected of being Communist sympathizers or noble, but ineffectual, pacifists. But perhaps, like the iceberg with but one tenth of its bulk above the surface, this scarcely audible discontent with basic military policies is indicative of a greater submerged rumbling.

There is a quite definite conflict of opinion, however, concerning whether or not war and defense activities are being conducted wisely, economically, and efficiently. Administrative opponents in Congress offer no alternatives in principle to those pursued, but occasionally contend against the time, the degree, and the technique of implementation of military measures. How many and what kind of weapons should we "stockpile," in which countries should we build airfields and station troops, and even which islands should we defend and which should we "evacuate," are issues that are more or less openly debated. Meanwhile, no effective alternative to American rearmament on a large scale has yet been offered by politically influential groups. The major open value conflict situation in this governmental area seems, then, to center around the administration of the program of military preparedness.

To restate our point, there are serious under-the-surface conflicts between the expressed American desire for peace and the present American military program. Since no strong political groups seem to have a workable alternative to the present program, however, this serious conflict of values between peace and militarism expresses itself only indirectly through criticism of the present administrators of the military program rather than against the program itself.

Bureaucracy v. due process of law. Another major point of conflict in government today is between those favoring extension of bureaucratic government and those advocating abolishment or decrease of bureaucracy and a return to government entirely or chiefly by due process of law.

American political tradition is certainly on the side of the supporters of rule by due process of law. Two amendments to the Constitution (Amendments V and XIV) specify that neither the United States nor the states may deprive any person of life, liberty, or property "without due process of law," a legal procedure which means that only the courts can condemn and render judgment and then only after a fair trial.

Practicality, it is often argued, is on the side of the supporters of bureaucratic government. In order for a government to have sufficient power to deal efficiently and immediately with problems, emergencies, and even day-by-day decisions in a modern, complex society, it must have authority to act, to make decisions, and to enforce decisions. For such administration of authority, bodies, boards, commissions, bureaus, etç., are needed. If legal "due process" had to be awaited in any major portion of the activities now being carried out by bureaus, chaos, it is contended, would soon result. Suppose, for example, that public health officers had to await court action to declare by "fair trial" that a person had smallpox and, hence, could be, "by due process of law," deprived of his liberty of movement through quarantine. While litigation was proceeding, the diseased person would have his full freedom to carry smallpox to the entire community! Obviously here is a point where we all desire bureaucratic authority.

During the war, to take another example, what if the Office of Price Administration had had to wait for "due process" in order to deal with "black market" violations? By the time violators had been sent through their constitutionally justified trials and appeals, the war effort could have been irreparably undermined. Here again, bureaus were necessary.

The defenders of bureaucratic government maintain that there are many everyday matters of government comparable to disease and wartime violations that must be dealt with effectively and quickly and that critics have failed to propose any adequate substitute for bureaucracy. It is contended that for such routine occurrences as, say disputes between management and labor, there must be a bureau such as the National Labor Relations Board to make decisions and enforce them. Because our society has become highly complex and is in the process of rapid change, the number of such activities and concomitant bureaus is likely to increase, not decrease.

The foregoing do not exhaust, or even fully represent, the fundamental ideological issues facing the American governmental institution. They will, however, serve us as rather cursory illustrations of one important aspect of government as a modern social problem.

Whom do our representatives represent? The standard answer to this question is, of course, that the "duly elected officials of our government" represent the people of the territorial unit from which they were elected. Most politicians, according to themselves and many high school civics books, represent all the people in their specific district. That is the *myth;* let us look at some *facts.*

"All the people?" We have already observed, first of all, that large groups of people hold sharply conflicting beliefs about the proper courses of action for our government. Not only are there interest groups in every community and every territorial unit maintaining radically different attitudes on fundamental issues such as social class, international policies, and bureaucracy, but on a host of other matters that are of importance, at least, to the individuals who have beliefs about them. How can a representative, even if he wanted to do so, represent veterans, pacifists, prohibitionists, antivivisectionists, Roman Catholics, Negroes, feminists, labor, and the many other interests of his section? The answer is he cannot; he must choose among these many interests the ones he wishes to represent. Sometimes a representative follows the strongest pressures placed upon him; these are not often the groups with the greatest potential votes but the groups that have demonstrated that they have control over a large bloc of votes. Other times a representative will "follow his own convictions," which is to say those interests and values that he has been conditioned to believe most important. In either case, he does not and cannot represent "all the people."

District system of representation. There are other ways in which the people fail to be represented.

A state may have universal suffrage, yet through the manipulation of the boundaries from which representatives in state legislatures and Congress are elected the electoral influence of the voters in certain areas may be minimized. As a result of systematic gerrymandering, large groups may be virtually disfranchised by their being made unable to elect a representative. Short of complete disfranchisement, districts may be so drawn as to reduce representation and, in effect, make a vote in one district count for more than a vote in another district. . . . Dis-

trict lines are seldom drawn so that the representative body reflects the electorate with accuracy, for there is inherent in the
single-member district system of representation a degree of dis-
tortion. At one extreme the strength of a political party, for
example, may be so evenly distributed over the state that it gains
51 percent of the vote in each legislative district and thereby
wins 100 percent of the seats in the legislative body. Because
of the nature of the district system it is virtually impossible to
avoid a degree of underrepresentation or overrepresentation of
some groups in the representative body.

Beyond the inherent limitations of the district system of representation, the boundaries of districts may be deliberately manipu-
lated by either of two methods. (1) Although lip service is paid
to the doctrine that the population of districts should be approximately equal, the boundaries may be drawn so as to create tremendous inequalities in population between districts. In Oklahoma,
to illustrate, one senatorial district a few years ago had a population of 24,108 while another had a population of 187,574. One
vote in the smaller district, when projected into the state senate,
had seven times the strength of one vote in the larger district. Or,
to put it in another way, six out of every seven persons in the
larger district were in effect disfranchised in so far as elections
to the state senate were concerned. (2) Without necessarily involving inequality as between districts, boundaries may be deliberately drawn so as to alter the complexion of the representation
of an area. A strong Republican area, for example, may be divided
and allocated among adjacent Democratic districts in such a fashion that the Republicans will be in the minority in each district.[1]

"Consent of the governed."   Another way in which representatives do not represent "all the people" is that all eligible voters
do not vote and many who do vote apparently do not know for
whom or for what they are voting. One can hardly refer to a
representative government accurately as "the people's choice"
when many people have not participated in the choosing and
many more do not know what it is that they have chosen.

The number of persons voting is always largest during a presidential election and the election of 1952 attracted more voters
than any other in recent years. Nevertheless, about one third of
eligible voters failed to cast a ballot. In 1948, 1944, 1940, and

[1] Reprinted from V. O. Key, Jr., *Politics, Parties, and Pressure Groups,* New
York, Thomas Y. Crowell Co., 1942, pp. 552-54, by permission.

1936, the proportion of eligible voters who actually voted was close to one half. And elections for United States Senators and Representatives usually draw far fewer of the eligible voters.

In addition, many adult citizens, even those who vote, are not politically well informed. Studies have repeatedly shown that a sizable proportion of adults do not know the name of the United States Senators from their own state, cannot name the vice presidential candidate in recent elections, and so on. One study discovered that only 26 percent of those polled could give a "reasonably correct" definition of "bi-partisan foreign policy"; another found that only a third could define "Welfare State." [2] Even the expression, "Universal Military Training" apparently had no or little meaning for one fourth of another group polled. If we have government by the "consent of the governed," it would seem to be both a silent and an ignorant consent!

▶ THE GROWTH AND CENTRALIZATION OF GOVERNMENT

Two of the most obvious facts that appear in any analysis of government are (1) its general growth and (2) an especially increasing centralization of authority in the national government. The growth of government is generally opposed by the business class and by the party out of power. The latter, upon gaining power, however, usually does little or nothing about the reduction of governmental activities for three obvious reasons: (1) most of the increased functions of government, together with the workers and funds necessary to carry them out, are essential for the meeting of values deemed important by most of the vocal voters in our society; (2) unless a governmental activity is extremely distasteful to a highly influential group in the population, once established, it is easier to let it continue; and (3) the party machine pressures the newly elected officials to maintain existing public jobs and, in fact, to create new ones.

Increase in governmental functions. Ogg and Ray have pointed out the relationship of an expanding government to dynamically changing social conditions.

[2] Reported in *Public Opinion Quarterly*, Vol. 14 (June 1950), p. 602.

Whenever one goes, one finds government doing things that nobody a generation ago would have thought of entrusting to it —nay more, things that no one a generation ago had even so much as heard of. William McKinley had no notion of government regulation of aërial transportation; Theodore Roosevelt hardly dreamed of a government that should license radio stations, prescribe their hours of operation, fix their wave-lengths; Herbert Hoover, when in the White House, would hardly have thought it possible that government should tell the farmer how many acres of corn or cotton he might plant. And no end is in sight. Further technical advances, changing ideas on social and economic subjects, hard experience in a score of directions, will go on bringing into play one new governmental activity after another. To be sure, criticism of this inexorable trend is heard every day. Old-line individualists deplore it; people who dislike some particular form of regulation, e.g., the antitrust laws, couch their disapprobation in more or less generalized complaints; so-called "pluralists" seek to relegate government to a place of less importance in comparison with other social institutions. Nothing, however, is more quickly learned from the history of government in all modern countries than that for every form of activity that grows obsolete and is discarded, two or three new ones find places in the ever-lengthening list. Ground once occupied by government is rarely surrendered.[3]

Centralization of power. Whether or not we agree that the growth of government is "inexorable," we must grant that it continues almost unabated. At every step of its expansion there is battle ground of value conflict. Closely related to general governmental growth is the process of centralization of power in the federal government. Just as the "unit-expansionists" are found principally among the business class and the party out of power, "states-rights" advocates are found in the same groups and for similar reasons. The chief argument against increased concentration of authority in the federal government is fear of "loss of freedoms" by the individual citizen and by the local and state governments with which, presumably, he is in closer touch. Some acts of the federal government have given basis for this fear. It is also argued by opponents of further concentra-

[3] Reprinted from Frederic A. Ogg and Perley O. Ray, *Essentials of American Government*, New York, Appleton-Century-Crofts, 1940, pp. 6-7, by permission.

tion of authority in the federal government, that this body has already become "inefficient, top-heavy, and dictatorial." Proponents of governmental centralization argue, on the other hand, that it is the only practicable method of meeting the exigencies of modern social living.

An objective view of centralization. Close examination of both sides of the argument over governmental centralization reveals considerable emotionalism and irrelevancy.

On the one hand, it is contended (1) that the only feasible plan for a land of continental proportions and a people of vast numbers and divergencies is one—such as the makers of our constitution had in mind—which allows a large measure of local and regional autonomy and restricts centralized, uniform, national control over social and economic matters to a minimum; (2) that even if Congress has the constitutional right to extend its regulating activities in certain of the present and proposed directions, it is not wise, or even safe, for it to insist upon going farther than it has already gone, especially in the broad domain of the police power, one supposed to be occupied mainly or entirely by the states; (3) that the national government has already (especially as a result of depression-time and wartime measures) become overgrown, top-heavy, unwieldy, with the people in danger of finding themselves hopelessly weighed down with a vast, professionalized federal bureaucracy, not too careful about the ways of democracy; (4) that in many large domains the state governments are still the more natural and effective agencies of control, because closer to the problems involved and the people concerned; (5) that, in pursuance of this consideration, it is desirable that the states be left wide latitude for serving as "experiment stations"; and (6) that in seeking to enforce uniform standards through an ever-widening network of federal law, backed up by steadily expanding federal administrative machinery, the national government is strangling the states and reducing them to mere local areas charged only with "the neat and humble care of detail in obedience to a nationally determined policy."

In opposition to all this, it is argued (1) that time, inventions, and other forces have so thoroughly nationalized the United States that most fundamental social and economic interests are no longer local, but instead cut across state and sectional boundaries, and are of common concern to the entire country; (2) that along with this great change of conditions has gone a corresponding change of political thought, so that people no longer expect or desire the state or regional autonomy cherished in earlier and simpler days, but, on the contrary, are prepared to see the legalistic *competitive* federalism of the past give way increasingly to the more flexible *cooperative* federalism of the future; (3) that the states have not been so efficient as to have demonstrated their right to be let alone in matters of wide national concern; and (4) that so long as social and economic conditions arise which, if they are to be regulated effectively at all, must be regulated by the national government, it is of no use to say that that government is unfitted to take on more responsibilities, the proper course being, rather, to improve it so as to remedy the deficiency, if it exists.[4]

We may sum up the discussion of the growth and centralization of government in three points: (1) the increase and centralization of governmental power will probably continue to be an important "problem" aspect of American government because of the intense conflicts of value centering in these processes; (2) growth and centralization show every indication of continuing indefinitely; and (3) any *generalized* position for or against growth and centralization *in general* appears unrealistic; each proposal for increase and centralization of governmental power should be examined on its own merits.

Is a large, centralized democracy possible?   There are analysts of our society who would contend that the granting of the three foregoing points is equivalent to admitting that democracy is doomed. A powerful, centralized government, it is argued, is certain to become a totalitarian dictatorship. Once granted power to enter new realms of our social life, government will grow ever more gigantic and powerful until it assumes the arbitrary authority of the dictatorial state.

Other observers maintain, however, that size and centralization are not in themselves threats to democracy. Rather it is a matter of the *areas of our social life* in which we permit our government vast powers.

In our discussion two broad precepts have emerged, the full acceptance of which is essential if democracy is to endure. One is that government should never be suffered to impose its con-

---

[4] Reprinted from Ogg and Ray, *op. cit.*, pp. 80-81, by permission.

trols on the cultural life of the community, to curtail the freedom of men to differ in their faiths and opinions, in their ways of thought and their ways of life, save when in the pursuit of these ways they inflict overt and objectively demonstrable hurt on their fellowmen. The second is a corollary of the first. It is that government should not be entrusted with so exclusive a monopoly over the economic-utilitarian system that the implementation of these functions conveys with it the effective indirect domination of the cultural life. For if the life-chances, the very livelihood, of individuals and groups are at the disposition of government, then the particular values and ideologies of the particular government will inevitably become absolute and will inflexibly impose themselves on the whole community, crushing its free spirit. Only by vigilant adherence to these two precepts can the peoples remain free and still breathe the life-giving air that comes from beyond the realm of government.[5]

More vigorous enforcement of our civil liberties would seem essentially to meet MacIver's first precept for safeguarding our democracy. This can be done only by insisting upon these rights for even those groups and individuals whose programs and principles we dislike or fear and by watching constantly for violations of these liberties.

A method of implementing the second precept is less readily discernible. Government needs enough power in economic-utilitarian realms to prevent domination from other sources, such as business monopoly, but not enough power to dominate "life chances" on its own part. The line between necessary regulation and undemocratic domination at times appears to be thin. Our hope of maintaining the distinction must apparently derive, as in the case of the civil liberties precept, from constant alertness—alertness to the potential significance of each new governmental issue which arises.

▶ THE UNITED STATES IN WORLD POLITICS

The traditional desire of the American people to avoid involvement in "foreign entanglements" has become an increas-

[5] Reprinted from Robert M. MacIver, *The Web of Government*, New York, The Macmillan Co., 1947, pp. 445-46, by permission.

ingly unrealistic one in the modern age. This value has come in conflict with others regarding the kind of world the American people have hoped would emerge. The clash between the value of isolationism and the values that apparently could be achieved or maintained only by intervention in other parts of the world have led to foreign policies marked by vacillation, inconsistency and inefficiency.

A "schizoid" foreign policy. United States government officials seem often to function as if they hope the world in which they live is not the kind of world they know very well it is. During World War II and during the immediate postwar conferences, American representatives acted as if they had never heard that the Soviet Union was governed by a ruthless totalitarian dictatorship. Demobilization was rapidly undertaken, valuable war materials were destroyed or left to rot, war controls on the economy were lifted, and American governmental behavior seemed to be based on absolute assurance that world peace had somehow been magically guaranteed. This was all done in the face of overwhelming public, as well as confidential, information to the contrary. Then, almost overnight, our governmental officials (Republicans, by the way, as well as Democrats) began talking and acting as if the United States were prepared for war at the slightest provocation.

Our government has shown both the shyness and the sudden audacity of a child—and a child it is in the ways of international politics. Our government sat back and watched, for example, the overrunning of the whole of China with hardly token support to the Nationalist government of that country. After the conquest of China by the Communists was an accomplished fact, the American government insisted on functioning as if the Nationalists were still in power by blocking the Chinese Communists from their seat in the United Nations Security Council. Then, with obviously inadequate forethought and preparation, the United States suddenly became the full-fledged defender of South Korea. First we announce to the world a policy of "massive retaliation"; next we assist the Chinese Nationalists in their surrender of the Tachen Islands and try to pass off as a victory the fact that they were able to "evacuate" their territory to the mainland Chinese efficiently and without loss of life. For years while talking about active repression of Communist aggression, we respond with but token assistance in the Indochina affair. To-day the Nationalist-held "off-shore islands" (off the mainland of China, that is) will not be defended from the Chinese Communists; tomorrow perhaps the full weight of the United States war machine will be thrown, if necessary, into the defense of Matsu and Quemoy.

And, in the midst of all these war activities, the government has consistently maintained that "this is the way to avoid war." If this be not a schizoid foreign policy, it is difficult to imagine what could constitute such a policy.

National sovereignty v. world government. The core of American value conflicts in the international area, the real source of our schizoid foreign policy, appears to be our desire for peace, patently obtainable only through real world government, and our fervent wish to hold completely to our national sovereignty. The United Nations as it now exists is quite evidently incapable of maintaining world peace so long as the major nation-states insist upon retaining full national sovereignty. Although it is patriotically popular to place full blame on the Communist countries for the "undermining" of the United Nations, the United States, Great Britain, France, and most of the lesser powers have shown no greater desire to yield any of their actual sovereignty to a world government.

MacIver, among other social scientists, has pointed out that the whole United Nations plan was inadequate even as a beginning step toward world government.

> The whole scheme, setting up a slightly disguised international hegemony of a few great powers, of only three in the last resort, was a retreat from the conception of an international order regulated by international law. No standard of legality, or of international justice, was invoked. The accent was on established power. Although international security was proclaimed as the objective, no system of collective security was established. The maintenance of peace was made to depend solely on the agreement among themselves of the super-power states, unsafeguarded by any bind-

ing procedures of a common law to which they with all the rest were subject. There were no provisions to check the imperialistic designs any one of them might cherish against the others or against the smaller states. The assumption of a permanent will to agree, as existing between three super-powers ideologically far apart and divided by contentions over "spheres of influence," was entirely unreasonable. The further assumption, that the only peril of future war came from the prostrate enemies of the victorious powers and that it would be avoided by devices for keeping the ex-enemies impotent, was a gross rejection of the lessons of history. The constructive idea that collective security required an international system bestowing on all nations, under a common rule of equity, the opportunity to share through cooperative relations in the conditions of a common prosperity, was not implemented.[6]

What of the future?　At the time of this writing, open hostilities in Korea have been over for two years, but few, least of all the South Koreans, are fully satisfied with the armistice terms. The Formosa straits resemble a dynamite keg and sparks with high incendiary potentiality are falling close. Few are content with the latest Communist-non-Communist partitioning, that of Indochina. Russian and American aircraft occasionally engage in what certainly appears like combat and the "trouble spots" in Europe and elsewhere have, if anything, increased in number. And all the while two major world powers continue to stockpile nuclear weapons and to develop more devastating means of destruction. Perhaps total war can still be by-passed on the road to world government and lasting peace. But it is difficult, at times, to engender or encourage a high degree of optimism.

▶ SUMMARY

As American culture has grown in specialization and complexity, only one institution—government—has had sufficient scope and power to keep society functioning more or less as a unit. Government has grown from its earlier "policing" activities to a superinstitution reaching into almost every phase

---

[6] Reprinted from MacIver, *op. cit.*, pp. 394-95, by permission.

of modern life. In some respects, every social problem has become a "governmental problem," but certain difficulties center in government itself.

One of the most important areas of value conflict in American government was treated in the chapter on pressure groups, but other important clashes center about international policies and their domestic accompaniments and bureaucracy versus due process of law. Both of these conflicts rest upon complicated assumptions that are difficult to prove or disprove.

Another problem of contemporary American government arises from the realities of the representative system. Through various inadequacies of the system in operation, minorities rather than "all the people" control the government; representatives represent these various minority groups, not, unless incidentally, the "public welfare."

Two important trends in modern government are growth in size and increase in national centralization of power. Since these tendencies show strong indication of continuing, they are significant problem areas of value conflict. Democracy is probably not incompatible with large, centralized government, providing two safeguards are observed: (1) full preservation of civil liberties and (2) prevention of governmental domination of the "life chances" of individuals and groups.

"Confusions" and "conflicts" over domestic issues are currently overshadowed by crises revolving around the participation of the United States in world politics. In a chaotic world situation where clearsighted American leadership is much needed, the United States shows lack of such. The two most powerful nations, the United States and the Soviet Union, demonstrate equal unwillingness to sacrifice narrow nationalistic interests for principles of strong world government. Because of this unwillingness and because of fundamental defects in its organization, the United Nations does not now appear to be an effective step toward world order. While we would like to view optimistically the prospects for preventing a full-scale world conflict, it is sometimes difficult to do so. The tenor of the actions and utterances of both the United States and the Soviet Union seems to be that of already committed belligerents rather than seekers of a peace. The authors, as patriotic citizens, do and will support the American government. But the authors, as social scientists, see many fallacies in the foreign policies of the United States as well as Russia. The question of "Where do we go from this point to avoid World War III?" is one for which no one, including these authors, seems to have an adequate answer.

SUGGESTED READINGS

American Academy of Political and Social Science, *Annals*, Vol. 282 (July 1952). This issue is entitled "The National Interest—Alone or With Others?" and is devoted to a presentation of various points of view regarding America's proper interest in international affairs and policies to implement this interest.

Ballantine, Joseph W., *Formosa: A Problem of United States Foreign Policy*, Washington, D. C., The Brookings Institution, 1952. Analyzes the development of United States policy toward Formosa, the present situation, and unresolved questions. A specific illustration of the need for sound and consistent foreign policy.

Clark, J. M., "America's Changing Capitalism," in Morroe Berger and others, *Freedom and Control in Modern Society*, New York, D. Van Nostrand Co., 1954. The present interpretation of the fields of government and economics is examined and its development traced. Aptly sets forth one phase of governmental growth and its present role in economic affairs.

Major Problems of United States Foreign Policy, 1954, Washington, D. C., The Brookings Institution, 1954. This is the seventh annual issue of a publication devoted to a summary account of developments and action in the area of foreign policy. Discusses recent international relations and foreign policy affairs and presents a survey of developing problems.

United Nations, *Yearbook of the United Nations, 1953*, New York, International Documents Service, Columbia University Press, 1954. This yearbook contains a detailed account of the work and achievements of the United Nations during the eight years that had passed. Describes also the structure of the United Nations organization and the functions and work of each of the specialized agencies.

STUDY QUESTIONS

1. How do you explain the fact that government is not a "superior institution" in simple cultures? How and by what institution is behavior regulated and controlled in such societies?

2. Distinguish between "ideal" and "real" government. Why is it necessary to make this distinction?

3. What is the major open value conflict with respect to military policies? What possibilities do you see for the reduction or elimination of this conflict?

4. What is included in the area of "quiet discontent" with military policies? Why is discontent in this area "quiet"? Which do you consider the most important value conflict, the open or the inarticulated area?

5. Why has bureaucratic government replaced "due process of law" in some areas? State why you either approve or disapprove of this change.

6. To what extent do we have government by the "consent of the governed"? How would you propose to improve this situation?

7. Explain why there has been a general increase in governmental functions, and a greater centralization of power in the federal government. Why do you agree or disagree that this is an "inexorable" process?

8. Why is American foreign policy described as "schizoid"? Cite examples, other than those given in the text, that would seem to make this an appropriate label.

9. Explain the value conflict between national sovereignty and world government.

10. Do you think the value conflict between national sovereignty and world government would be reduced or intensified following another global war? Explain.

·20· Religion

It is doubtful whether most laymen would include religion among America's more pressing social problems. Nevertheless, when the matter is viewed objectively, it is readily seen that religion in America intensifies, or in some instances creates, value conflicts out of which social problems arise. Partly this is due to the great complexities and diversities of values which are collected under the headings of "religion" and "the church." Some portion of that 60 percent of the population listed as members of some church are claimed by 250 religious denominations with great varieties of beliefs and practices. Other reasons why religion is credited with value conflicts lie in the fact of its espousal of some measures of social change, on the one hand, and its resistance, on the other, to some attempts at social change in the secular society. It is our purpose, therefore, to analyze the value conflicts and problem situations associated with religion rather than to embark on a survey or discussion of theological differences among religions.

▶ THE CHURCH AND THE STATE

Government and religion are more thoroughly separated in the United States than in any other major country. The opening words of the first amendment to the Constitution specify that "Congress shall make no law respecting an establishment of religion, or prohibiting the free exercise thereof." Interpretations of the bearing of the first amendment upon specific laws and practices of government, however, have varied. Some have argued that any law which in *principle* makes possible an interlocking relationship of church and state is unconstitutional and a threat to the religious freedom of the American people. Presidents Grant and Garfield, for example, contended that government should not even aid the church to the extent of exempting its property from taxation because this prevented the divorce of church and state from being absolute.

Many churchmen, on the other hand, demand support of the church by the state far beyond tax-exemption of property. Especially in relation to education, church representatives argue that present policies in state-supported education actually operate to suppress religious liberty and to spread antireligious and atheistic doctrines.

Parochial school issues. The Roman Catholic Church has taken the position that children who attend its parochial schools should be given the same aids that the state provides children who attend the public schools. At the present writing a bill to provide federal aids to public schools is blocked in Congress, in part, by strong Catholic opposition because the bill does not provide similar aids to parochial schools. Non-Catholic opposition is just as strong against including such assistance to church-sponsored schools.

The Catholic position. Catholic spokesmen insist that a democratic state should recognize the right of parochial schools to give a civil education which conforms to legal standards together with a religious education which satisfies the desires of the parents and the church. When public schools only receive state support, it is held, an injustice is done to all nonpublic schools which by the states' own standards perform the same services (in nonreligious areas) for citizens of the state. Separation of church and state is said to require governmental "neutrality" by which is meant that the government should not favor secularized education over that which provides religious training in addition to secular instruction. It is argued that, if the state withholds from these parochial schools privileges which are extended to public schools, it is thus putting pressure on parents to withdraw their children from Catholic schools and to send them to schools where either Protestantism or godlessness is taught.

This Catholic point of view has expressed itself in various

specific issues throughout the country involving free transportation, books, and school lunches. In most of the legal testings of such issues, the courts have upheld the Catholic position. However, in one recent attempt to incorporate a parochial school into the tax-supported educational system of a community (North College Hill, a Cincinnati suburb), the court rebuffed the Catholic majority of the school board who had made this attempt.

The non-Catholic position. Those who oppose state-aided parochial schools argue that such aid would be the first step toward breaking down the barrier between church and state. If the Catholic Church is permitted to obtain public funds for parochial schools, it is contended, it will then proceed to seize more and more power in its movement toward the alleged goal of becoming the one state-supported church. Since the public schools are open to Catholics as well as to non-Catholics, those parents who cannot afford to send their children to parochial schools are still free to indoctrinate their children at home and through the church. Public funds, it is argued, should not be turned over to schools where teaching is under ecclesiastical rather than public control.

The issuance of free textbooks to parochial schools is frequently cited as an example of the practical consequences to the public school system if once state aid to nonpublic schools is begun. In some of the states where free textbooks have been issued to parochial schools, the schools then began to exert pressure to assure that only "proper" textbooks were issued. Again, what may start out as a provision to allow parochial school children transportation on publicly financed school buses along regular routes may end up with the establishment of publicly supported routes designed especially to serve the parochial school children. In other words, once the principle of separation of church and state is violated by allotting *some* public funds to parochial schools, it becomes difficult to determine just where to "draw the line."

Protestant-sponsored religious education. The earliest major attempts to bring about or keep religion in the public schools were largely made by Protestants. These attempts centered around the daily reading of a Bible passage, the singing of hymns, and the recitation of the Lord's Prayer. At the turn of the century and in the early 1900's, court cases in the separation-of-church-and-school area usually involved Catholics and Jews protesting against their children's compulsory attendance at Bible readings in the public schools, compulsory memorization of passages from the King James' version of the Bible, and the like. Nevertheless, there is still some type of Bible reading in the public schools of the majority of our states. Both Catholics and Jews continue to protest on what seems to be the indisputable basis that there is no such thing as a nonsectarian Bible. Passages selected, emphases and interpretations in reading, and other factors would inherently be affected by the prejudices of the teacher.

Another attempt upon the part of Protestants to bring religion into the schools was the released-time educational plan. As it first developed in Gary, Indiana, in 1913, it meant releasing students before the end of the school day to attend religious-education classes in their churches, but numerous variations have developed. It has been estimated that in 1948 (the year of one adverse decision of the Supreme Court) about 2 million children in over 2,000 communities were participating in some type of released-time program for religious instruction. Protestant, Catholic, and Jewish leaders have provided instruction for their groups but, generally, the released-time plan has not been favorably accepted by Catholics and Jews. The reason for Catholic objections is not clear, but the Jewish authorities have been the most consistent of any religious groups in maintaining that religious education is a private matter that is the concern of parents and churches, and that public schools are for secular education exclusively.

Many Protestants further contend that the answer to the conflict over religion in the public schools is to provide a nonsectarian religion in which all the major faiths may find a common meeting ground. This likewise has met with the opposition not only of the nonreligious or nonaffiliated portions of the population, but also of most Catholics and Jews. Advocates of teaching universal religious truths, it is contended, are deluded by strivings toward unity within Protestant churches into believing that unity of the three major faiths is likewise possible. Such teachings, opponents of the nonsectarian program further suggest, would even more thoroughly convey the prejudices of the sponsors of the program than do the Bible-reading procedures.

In two recent cases (*Everson v. Board of Education* and *Mc-Collum v. Board of Education*) the United States Supreme Court has spoken out strongly against the use of public school buildings, facilities, or personnel in the support of any or all religious faiths or sects in the dissemination of their doctrines and ideals. The Court also contended (McCollum case) that such a position could not be legitimately interpreted as hostility to religion, but rather as the conviction that both religion and government flourish best when rigidly separated. A secular public school, according to the Court, is the means of reconciling freedom in general with religious freedom.

Various legal problems remain unsolved, and numerous educational and religious values continue in conflict. Desires upon the part of leaders of churches to strengthen their membership lead them to seek in differing ways the support of the educational institutions. The pursual of this value of greater security and growth for their particular religious beliefs brings them into conflict with the constitutionally embodied value of religious freedom as based on the rigid separation of church and state. All three major faiths have become alarmed in recent decades with the apparent growth of values which they consider unethical and immoral. They have tended to blame such social developments as divorce, crime, delinquency, mental illness, and alcoholism on the "godless public schools." Since their values include, however, varying degrees of disbelief in and distrust of the values of competing faiths, they cannot unite on the common value of getting the "godlessness" out of public-sponsored education.

Other church-state value clashes. It must not be concluded that the only difficulties that have arisen over the principle of separation of church and state have had their locus in the schools.

There are cases on record, although not many in number, in which the putting into practice of religious teachings clearly conflicts with laws of the state. For example, members of some organized religions, such as the Society of Friends, simply cannot continue to practice their religion and comply with legislation that requires them to bear arms. Using a stricter and more literal interpretation of the Commandment "Thou shalt not kill" than other Americans are wont to apply, some men have refused to be taken into military service for, even if they themselves did no killing, membership in the Armed Forces in time of war would seem to involve a certain amount of help and support for those who did kill. This particular issue eventually was resolved in favor of religion. A man who for religious reasons cannot enter military service does not now have to do so, although he is often required to perform some other service, such as serving as a mental hospital attendant, for a similar period of time.

One other example of a basic conflict between the laws of the state and the teachings of a minor-sect religion will perhaps suffice. The Church of Jesus Christ of the Latter Day Saints, or the Mormon Church as it is better known, at one time openly taught that it was right and even good for a man to have more than one wife at the same time. It was not a matter of convenience or personal desire but that, according to this religion, men's and women's chances of reaching the hereafter were substantially increased under such an arrangement and that polygamy was considered right in the eyes of God. Although the major divisions of the Mormon Church no longer encourage their members to practice polygamy, a few small subdivisions do instruct along this line and their members have been discovered putting this religious doctrine into practice.[1] One such group was recently found in Short Creek, Arizona. Although they were living unto themselves in a remote section of the desert, the collective conscience of the rest of the state was sufficiently wounded to suggest that "something be done" about the situation. The re-

[1] In 1890 the President of the Mormon Church issued a formal proclamation to members to refrain from polygamous marriages. From this date to the present the main body of the Mormon Church has upheld monogamous marriage.

sult was that the husbands and fathers were arrested and the children were forcibly separated from their families.[2] Some serious thinking Americans, even though not believing in polygamy themselves, began to ask if this was not an open prohibition of the free exercise of religion.

The cases concerning the religions that teach nonviolence and the Mormon belief in polygamy illustrate that serious difficulties can arise when the principle of the separation of church and state is put into practice. For how indeed can the two remain separate if the teachings of one's religion result in his violation of state laws or if his compliance with legal prescriptions necessitates his falling into disfavor with his church?

▶ RELIGION AND SOCIAL ACTION

Traditionally, religious organizations have aligned themselves with reactionary forces in our society. Churches have often feared that alterations in the *status quo* would remove some of their existing benefits. In addition, strong advocacy of certain social reforms could well bring the withdrawal of financial support of the church by wealthy conservative members. Increasingly in recent decades, however, the leaders of the three major faiths have issued social pronouncements which commit religious organizations to changes in various aspects of the existing order. Many times these social creeds seem to represent a minority conviction attempting to achieve majority status, and many times action fails to follow pronouncement. Very few white parishes, for example, have attempted actually to bring in and fully accept Negroes in all church activities even though officially their churches are on record in favor of complete racial nondiscrimination. Nevertheless, at least from the standpoint of their efforts to educate their own members, many churches may no longer be accused of offering a religion which is the "opiate of the people."

---

[2] This is by no means the strongest attack on the Mormon Church, merely one of the most recent ones. For a report of the conflicts throughout much of the church's history, see Kimball Young. *Isn't One Wife Enough?* New York, Henry Holt and Co., 1954.

Apocalyptic churches. Many of the smaller sects, the new evangelical movements, and fundamentalist divisions in the older denominations continue to preach an otherworldliness which diverts its members from the problems of their society and constitutes an obstacle to social action. The Jehovah's Witnesses, for example, teach that the course of history has been toward degradation, that it is close to its lowest depths, and that nothing in this world is worth attempting to salvage. With divine intervention momentarily expected, it behooves the member of an apocalyptic religion to concentrate on the saving of his own soul and the possible conversion of others to the select minority of the saved and to disregard the evils of the world about him. The financial success of numerous evangelical preachers of many varieties of "old-fashioned religion" is testimony to the continuing escapist appeal of apocalyptic teachings to large sections of the population.

Social Gospel churches. During the past half century, most of the major religious denominations have become more and more concerned with the advancement of social causes. They have reacted against the emotional and personal-salvation values of the apocalyptic faiths and have come to concentrate on social issues such as race relations, crime and delinquency, international relations, and world peace. The Social Gospel advocates have contended that the old type of religion was occupied with "snatching brands from the burning." The church, they insist, must be concerned with the circumstances in which people live and must deal with society as a whole and the basic factors therein which produce sinful living.

World peace. In the interim between the first and second World Wars, strong peace movements were initiated or supported by many of the major churches. During the course of World War II, church leaders led all other educational forces in recommending a study of the terms for peace and the development of a world organization which would maintain the peace. Most of the churches also supported the rights of conscientious objectors to refuse military service and were instrumental in obtaining governmental recognition of these rights in Selective Service legislation.

Many church leaders likewise protested the atomic bombings of Hiroshima and Nagasaki and have worked for international control of atomic bombs and reduction of armaments. Many church leaders and members likewise constitute the core of many movements to bring about world government, and offer their churches as meeting places for peace groups of all kinds.

Although at this writing current efforts toward world peace and world government do not look much more promising than the more naïve peace attempts made between the two World Wars, many of the churches deserve much of the credit for such social action as has been undertaken toward the realization of these values to which most of the population verbally subscribes.

Race relations. While all of the major churches have frequently spoken out against racial discriminations of all types, most of the churches themselves continue to operate along lines of racial segregation. Some of the most liberal churches in the North actually welcome Negroes for worship in predominantly white churches, but the majority merely profess belief in, and fail to practice, such "brotherhood." There is still truth in the assertion that eleven to twelve on Sunday morning is the most segregated time in America.

Not only within their own churches, but for the most part in the rest of the community, the majority of church members are content to let the *status quo* continue in race relations. For the removal of discriminatory practices which have been achieved to date, minority groups owe much more thanks to the courts than to the churches. In an educational way, however, some credit for improvements in the treatment of minority groups should probably be given to religious organizations.

Capital and labor. Although traditionally affiliated with the objectives of business and finance, the three major faiths have issued denouncements of the exploitation of labor by capital. They have asked for controls on speculation and the profit motive, a wider and fairer distribution of wealth, social security, improvement of working conditions and reduction of hours, right of collective bargaining, and abolition of child labor. While the gains of labor in such areas as these may have come more directly from legislative and other pressure-group methods, the support of many of the churches in labor's struggle for social justice has been of educational service. The church's support of some of labor's causes has lent "respectability" to labor's aims. *Crime and delinquency.* The churches have contributed educationally to reforms in various public institutions, including those dealing with criminals and delinquents. Church leaders have often "spearheaded" movements in communities which have changed abuses and injustices in police departments and have aroused the public to demand more adequate criminological and penological practices. Some of the improvements in probation and parole practices and in the development of juvenile courts may be credited to church activity.

It may be argued, on the other hand, that "do-good" activities of church people have actually contributed to the maintenance and spread of some forms of crime and vice. Religious zealots sometimes launch reform actions with little understanding of the problems or the values of the people involved in the problems. The church-sponsored Eighteenth Amendment is the most notable example of crime and vice enhancement by misguided reform. Prostitution, illegitimacy, gambling, homosexuality are often merely diffused and made less subject to enlightened social control by reforming religionists. Social Gospel religion is sometimes no more intelligently directed than apocalyptic religion in bringing about a better society.

Reaction. Direct attack on social evils advocated by the Social Gospel religionists has brought protests and countermovements in most of the denominations. These critics maintain that the proponents of action have, in their attempt to reform society, forgotten that the fundamental purpose of Christian religion is to "save the individual sinner." Some of the critics favor a complete return to the old revivalism, an emotional appeal to the individual sinner to be saved. Others, while favoring greater concentration of the church's attention on the salvation of individual souls, make their main point that the church's social roles should be confined strictly to education rather than including coercive action. They point out that the church is competent to function only in relation to social ideals and motives, and that it should leave social action to government officials, social workers, and others who are presumably better qualified to conduct reforms.

▶ THE MODERN STATUS OF RELIGION

Recently there has been a noticeable increase in membership of most of the organized churches in the United States. But religious leaders of all denominations are not altogether satisfied that the so-called "mid-century spiritual renaissance" is real, sincere, or even lasting. Too many, it is said, are hopefully viewing religion as simply a pragmatic mechanism for accomplishing worldly goals that somehow force and science and politics have been unable to accomplish. If religion works, so much the better; if not, try something else. Others see the recent upsurge in church membership as a reflection of the anxiety-laden atmosphere of our times. Religion is said to have become but a new type of personal therapy overlaid with appropriate scriptural references. Whether or not this "religious revival" is a revival of "real religion" and whether or not participants in it are "sincere" quite obviously depends on how and by whom these terms are defined. And since we are still so close to it, time alone will tell whether the growth in church membership is a temporary or lasting phenomenon. Nevertheless, we can attempt to investigate the more objective evidence concerning the impact of present day churches on the American scene.

Influence of the churches. Just how important is organized religion in contemporary American society? Roughly 60 percent of the population holds membership in a church and probably half of these actively participate in some part of their church's program. If these estimates are correct (and they must be guesses because no fully reliable data are available on either membership or attendance), approximately two Americans out of every three do not directly participate in organized religious activities. A study conducted by one of the authors in a large city showed that a majority of church participants either were not familiar with the religious teachings of their respective churches or did not agree with them. A smaller sample of clergymen showed that they were more likely to know where their churches stood on doctrinal matters, but a majority of them still did not agree with all the doctrinal stands taken by their own denominations.[3]

Recently, Dr. George H. Gallup, director of the American Institute of Public Opinion, conducted a nation-wide poll consisting of ten simple questions on the Bible and religion.[4] The results seem to indicate that many, many Americans, church members included, are completely ignorant of basic religious concepts and have little factual knowledge of either the Old or New Testaments of the Bible. Only about one third of the adults, for example, knew who delivered the Sermon on the Mount, 40 percent only could give a reasonably accurate definition of the Holy Trinity, while just 21 percent could name even *one* prophet mentioned in the Old Testament. All in all, a mere 4 percent of the sample were able to answer nine of the ten questions correctly and only one in a hundred could give correct answers to all of the questions.

Finally, we need no study to document the fact that behavioral standards prescribed by churches are not adhered to by large numbers of persons who consider themselves members. Those in control of the churches know that their prescriptions are ignored or unheeded but retain the erring ones as members in good standing.

Are the churches, then, ineffective? The answer to this question depends, of course, upon what is meant by a church's being effective. We know that no church influences a majority of Americans to follow its chief teachings regarding beliefs, attitudes, and practices. There is likewise strong reason to suspect that most churches do not even so influence a majority of their

---

[3] John Cuber, "Marginal Church Participants," *Sociology and Social Research*, Vol. 25 (September-October 1945), pp. 57-62.

[4] Results released to press by American Institute of Public Opinion on December 19, 1954.

own members. Perhaps it is justifiable to state that the churches are not impressively effective in the realization of their stated objectives. Indirectly, but to a degree very difficult to gauge, churches probably have socially desirable influences upon even some segments of society which never receive their teachings. Some of these positive values are briefly described in the following paragraphs.

Agents of reform. We have already discussed in an earlier portion of the chapter the influence of the Social Gospel churches in achieving reforms along such lines as more humane treatment of criminals, reduction of child labor, improvement of the status of labor in general, education against racial discrimination, and attempts to establish peace and world government. To the churches, too, must go some credit for the abolishment of slavery and the emancipation of women. Even some humanistic reformers who have denounced organized religion have unconsciously borrowed many of their social-justice platforms from representatives of the church. Such basic religious tenets, in addition, as the dignity and worth of the individual have permeated the secular philosophy of democracy. Such influences may not be measurable but are nonetheless significant.

Philanthropic agencies. Until basic social reforms are achieved, individuals and groups who suffer under existing conditions have need of help, and the churches and church-initiated social agencies continue to provide much assistance. Even most of the social security and social assistance programs now sponsored by the government had their beginnings in organized religion. A withdrawal of church financing and church-affiliated personnel from the private social agencies which still do a significant portion of present-day philanthropic work would bring chaos to their activities.

Instruments of social control. Although the conservative influence of the churches has sometimes frustrated scientific inquiry and delayed needed social improvements, it also functions as a barrier to undesirable changes or to transitions that are too rapid for social adjustment. When the pendulums of other aspects of the culture oscillate rapidly, slow-moving religious institutions preserve certain values. At least some of these values will probably be desired by succeeding generations of men to fit somehow into the culture patterns of their times.

Sources of security. It is in this very conservatism of the churches that many people apparently find security. Even though many of the beliefs and practices of a particular religion may not bear rational examination, their relatively unchanging obscurantism in a rapidly changing world which emphasizes rationality brings solace to some individuals. Some future social order may be composed of individuals who need no such comfort, but the absence of such a need seems not to be the nature of at least a sizable minority of contemporary American citizens. And there is reason to suspect that, in times of crises, many Americans who are not affiliated with churches draw comfort from the beliefs and feelings and practices which these churches sponsor.

Prospects for the churches. Religion in America may be considered in a textbook on social problems for three important reasons:

(1) Through the diverse teachings and activities of its many component churches, American religion intensifies and in some instances creates value conflicts out of which social problems arise.

(2) Through its resistance to changes in secular society and its frequent opposition to the spread of new values, a large portion of organized religion may be further credited with intensifying value conflicts and accompanying social problems.

(3) Through its active espousal of other social changes, various reforms in the *status quo*, some portion of organized religion may be credited with further intensification of value conflicts.

Although there is justification for questioning the extent of the influence of the churches in some of their expressed objectives, little question can be raised regarding the significance of religion's influences in the foregoing relationships to the problems of American society.

A further problem that religion has added to American social problems is that of the uncertainty regarding the future
of the churches. While the Catholic Church keeps its own
counsel, representatives of Protestant and Jewish churches have
expressed concern over the prospects for their faiths. The chief
Jewish concerns are (1) the small number of children who are
receiving religious Jewish education in proportion to the number
of Jews in the population, (2) the existence of thousands of
Jewish settlements without congregations, and (3) the trend
toward wide and thin dispersion of Jews into rural areas.

Protestant concern is the reverse of the Jews': overchurch-
ing. Too many denominations, with a multiplicity of inadequate
facilities and inadequate personnel, attempt to serve too few
people, especially in the small communities. Although some efforts toward cooperation of the Protestant denominations have
been successful, the picture is still predominantly one of division,
competition, and adherence to petty theological differences.

Unity between Christian and Jew and between Catholic and
Protestants shows very little prospect of materializing in the
foreseeable future. In short, it would seem probable that organized religion will continue to contribute to problems of
American society rather than provide unified and creative leadership toward the solution or notable alleviation of most of these
problems.

▶ SUMMARY

Religion in American society presents a situation of great diversity. Despite recent popularization of a so-called "mid-
century spiritual renaissance," no more than 60 percent of the
population is church affiliated, and it is doubtful whether more
than half of these actively participate in some part of their
church's program. And those who are affiliated with a church
are divided among over 250 denominations with great varieties of
beliefs and practices.

Government and religion are traditionally separated in the
United States, but both Catholics and Protestants challenge this

separation in different ways. The former seek governmental support for their parochial schools, and the latter wish to sponsor religious programs in the public schools under the dubious cloak of "nonsectarianism."

Two major types of religious influences are observable in relation to social action. One is the apocalyptic or revivalist type of religion which appeals to the emotions of the individual, stresses the importance of religious salvation prior to an imminent judgment, and advocates disregard for the evils of the temporal world. The other is the Social Gospel form of religion, widespread in most of the major denominations at the present time, which advocates action for the improvement of the injustices and evils of contemporary society. Division and conflict exist in many churches between the exponents of these extremes and between them and "moderates" who advocate greater concern for the individual's salvation along with educational influence of the church in improving social conditions.

Apparently the churches reach directly only about one third of the population, and many of this minority indicate ignorance of, or disagreement with, the basic teachings of their churches. This apparent ineffectiveness of the churches in contemporary society may be considered partially counterbalanced, however, by their contributions as agents of reform, as philanthropic agencies, as instruments of social control, and as sources of security even to many members of society who are not affiliated with any religious organization.

Religion may be considered a significant force in conflicts of values and in accompanying social problems. Future prospects for religion would seem to be more in the direction of intimate involvement in clashes of values than in the direction of providing outstanding guidance out of the matrices of conflict.

SUGGESTED READINGS

Blanshard, Paul, *American Freedom and Catholic Power*, Boston, Beacon Press, 1949. This admittedly controversial book largely treats the social power of the Catholic Church although doctrinal issues are discussed as they relate to its alleged power. When read in conjunction with James M. O'Neill's work, cited below, the student will become aware of a value conflict that is more than a "squabble" between two authors.

Braden, Charles S., *These Also Believe*, New York, The Macmillan Co., 1949. An objective but sympathetic study of the beliefs and practices of thirteen minority religious groups in America. Useful for obtaining insights into the sources of value conflict between the cults and the larger society.

O'Neill, James M., *Catholicism and American Freedom*, New York, Harper & Bros., 1952. This volume was avowedly written in defense of American Catholics and their relation to American freedom. Forcefully questions the assumptions, facts, and interpretations in Paul Blanshard's work, cited above, and presents the interpretation of the Catholic layman. The informed citizen will want to read both Blanshard's and O'Neill's treatises.

Thayer, V. T., *The Attack upon the American Secular School*, Boston, Beacon Press, 1951. A thorough discussion of the application of the principle of separation of church and state to the field of public education. Treats early as well as contemporary issues and legal cases in this area.

Tobey, James A., "Public Health and Religious Freedom," *American Journal of Public Health*, Vol. 44 (October 1954), pp. 1293-99. Cites leading court decisions and cases in which it was claimed that the exercise of religious liberty was abridged by public health and other laws. An intriguing but apparently little known area of value conflict in the area of religion.

Yearbook of American Churches, 1955, New York, National Council of the Churches of Christ, 1955. This yearly publication contains the latest factual information on membership, finance, clergy, and the like, of all organized religious bodies in the U. S. Also contains brief description of the religious bodies and lists their officers, affiliated organizations, and official periodicals.

Young, Kimball, *Isn't One Wife Enough?* New York, Henry Holt and Co., 1954. A sociological study of Mormon polygamy. Contains a clear exposition of the practice and its religious significance and a vivid account of the public controversy over Mormon polygamy.

STUDY QUESTIONS

1. State different interpretations of the first amendent to the Constitution relevant to the separation of government and religion. How would you re-word the Constitution to make different interpretations less likely?

2. State in your own words the Catholic and the non-Catholic positions with regard to state aid for parochial schools. Try to discover among your acquaintances how many Catholics adhere to the "Catholic position" and how many non-Catholics to the "non-Catholic position."

3. In what ways could it be said that Protestants have violated the principle of separation of church and school? To what extent do these conditions still exist?

4. Illustrate with specific examples, either from your own knowledge or with the help of a religious leader, what is meant by the statement that there is no such thing as a nonsectarian Bible.

5. State the logic of the religious prohibition against engaging in warfare. How do other religions rationalize the seemingly opposite position?

6. What is an "apocalyptic religion"? Describe several doctrines of such religions.

7. Explain the logic of the Social Gospel advocates. With what social issues have churches following this philosophy been concerned?

8. Illustrate how the churches have intensified or actually created a social problem. Give an illustration of how the churches have helped ameliorate a problematical condition.

9. How important is organized religion in contemporary American society? Cite the evidence and discuss the difficulties involved in answering this question.

10. Discuss the so-called "mid-century spiritual renaissance" from the standpoint of its present significance, its causes, and its lasting effects. What are some of the difficulties involved in studying this matter?

· 21 ·

National Security
and the Tradition
of Civil Liberties

The value clashes to which this chapter is addressed are serious, controversial, and important. The underlying problem that confronts loyal and patriotic Americans is how to safeguard our national security and, at the same time, to protect our civil liberties. When it comes to specific programs to achieve these objectives, however, strong value clashes immediately become evident.

There is, on the one hand, the faction that sees the major threat only to national security and it appears willing to take almost any step to safeguard national security. These groups are little concerned with civil liberties; they hold that certain abridgments and restrictions are necessary in order to safeguard security. There has been talk, too, in recent years that a literal interpretation of our Constitutional freedoms is no longer possible or desirable; "times have changed" and so, we are told by some, must our concepts of liberty and freedom.

There is the sharply opposing view which stresses the "threats to civil liberties" that should be of concern to Americans. Threats to national security, both from without and within, are recognized but are not considered as warranting radical changes in the Constitutional rights of all citizens. It is not that this faction favors protection of individual freedom *over* the safeguard of national security, but rather that it focuses attention where it believes too little attention is given—on keeping our secure nation free while striving to keep our free nation secure.

Before investigating the specific value issues in this area it is necessary to try to take a realistic view of the present American scene in which these value differences are taking place. Our intention is not to alarm nor to overstate the threats either to national security or civil liberties, but merely to furnish as objective as possible a backdrop for the tense drama we are witnessing.

▶ AN AGE OF FEAR AND SUSPICION

There is in the world today a strong revolutionary force that can be judged as a present or potential threat to our democratic way of life. This force has literally millions of loyal and trained adherents and at present it dominates most of Eurasia. It has its "home base" in the only nation that today could challenge us militarily or could match our technical military skills. This revolutionary force presumably seeking world-domination is "Communism"; its cultural center is the U.S.S.R.

Our national leaders have deemed it necessary to get and keep the United States in a state of military preparedness. Military and other experts have helped decide just what preparedness is and what it entails. If the threat to our nation is as great as it is purported to be, and if military preparedness is necessary to counteract this threat, then we must not compromise our defense efforts. This means that we cannot tolerate individuals who will sabotage our defense efforts or who will transmit our military knowledge to our avowed potential enemies.

There is, for example, a certain "surprise component" in new weapons which increases their effectiveness due to the lack of attempted counteraction on the part of the recipients of their force. We must not nullify this surprise component by allowing traitors to pass on to presumed enemies the details of our weapons of war or, for that matter, of our total military strength. Among the most recent weapons are, of course, the various nuclear devices which we and other countries continue to test and perfect.

Although there is no such thing as *an* atomic secret in the sense of a simple key to the whole nuclear puzzle, caution is nevertheless necessary to insure that we do not destroy any interim advantage we may have in this new field of military armament. We must, then, continue to seek out traitors and to some this means "investigations." And it would be to our decided advantage to prevent those intent upon sabotage and espionage from achieving positions in which they could damage our defense efforts, and this means "loyalty checks." Such things as loyalty checks and security investigations are unpopular to many Americans because they seem to smack of the very thing against which we are protecting ourselves. Nevertheless, as long as such precautions are necessary and are administered capably, personal inconveniences bow to national safety.

Thus, there are *real* forces in the world that have been defined as *real* threats to our national security. And as long as this is so there is *real* reason for men to be afraid, for it is no indication of deficient valor for mature men to fear fearful things. But there is also such a thing as a "phobia," which is a fear disproportionate to the actual danger.

There are some indications that present widespread reactions have gone beyond "normal fears" and have taken on the proportions of true phobias. Such indications are difficult to evaluate and must be done so with caution for, taken individually, some may seem to be indicators of nothing at all.

A few years ago, for example, reporters from a Wisconsin newspaper asked 112 people to sign their names to a "pledge." [1] Only *one* person was prepared to do so; the remainder considered the document as too "dangerous" or "subversive." The document was the preamble to the Declaration of Independence!

More recently, public opinion pollers presented a national sample of Americans with a list of organizations and asked which, if any, were on the "Attorney General's list of subversive or 'front' organizations." [2] The Congress of Industrial Organizations

---

[1] Reported in Henry S. Commager, *Freedom, Loyalty, Dissent*, New York, Oxford University Press, 1954, p. 121.

[2] Reported in *Public Opinion Quarterly*, Vol. 18 (Summer 1954), p. 208.

(CIO), the Association of American University Professors, and the Americans for Democratic Action, none of which are actually on the Attorney General's list, were thought to be there by 26 to 41 percent of the people polled. An organization that actually appears on the Attorney General's list, the Civil Rights Congress, was cited only about as frequently as were two organizations that are not so blacklisted. Apparently, Americans become immediately suspicious of any group with words like "America," or "Democracy," or "Peace" in its title, or which seems "too labor oriented" or "too intellectual."

In another context, a statement concerning human rights was read to a committee of the American Congress who agreed that certainly this sounded like "the Communist line." Actually, it was a verbatim reproduction of the official and publicly available writings of two Popes. Finally, there is the recent case of the Girl Scout organization which had to revise its handbook because certain statements did not conform to the American Legion's definition of "Americanism." If the Declaration of Independence, the Pope of Rome, legitimate labor unions, the Girl Scouts, and the Association of American University Professors are met with suspicion, who indeed is next? The popular attitude seems to be, to paraphrase the self-satisfied Quaker, "The whole world is subversive but me and thee, and sometimes I think that even thee are just a *little* subversive."

This growing tendency for Americans to be suspicious of their fellow citizens has had the result that rather than have one's loyalty assumed he must loudly proclaim his lack of disloyalty. This point is aptly illustrated in the following quotation:

> To be a non-communist is hardly enough. It is better to be an ex-communist turned anti-communist than never to have been a communist at all, i.e., to have been a non-communist. The latter can hardly be expected to take the correct attitude toward communism, anti-communism, ex-communism, or pro-communism. The non-communist is suspect because he runs the risk of suffering the defect of being non-anti-communist, or of being pro-non-communist. I have tried to find my own way through this maze of categories and can only conclude that I am a non-anti-pro-non-

communist. The key to the puzzle is to start with the term communist and work backwards through the hyphens.[3]

The foregoing are but a few of the signs that we are indeed living in an age of fear and suspicion. And, as indicated previously, it is also an age marked by what is defined as severe threats to our national security. This is the setting in which the value clashes discussed below are taking place.

▶ CURRENT CIVIL LIBERTIES ISSUES

There can be no doubt but that it is un-American to prevent, or attempt to prevent, a person from exercising those rights and privileges granted him by the Constitution. But yet, in the name of fighting un-Americanism or safeguarding our national security, ideas and practices have come about that would seem to threaten certain Constitutional rights. These and other practices seem also to be contributing to the mass fear and suspicion out of which they have grown.

Congressional investigating committees.   As the schoolboy learns early in life, the three main branches of our government have separate functions and the tripartite set-up allows for a "check" and "balance" among the several branches. Enactment of legislation is the principal function of Congress, or the legislative branch. Although it is not mentioned in the Constitution, it is generally held that Congress has the power to conduct investigations which will enable it better to enact legislation.

The value conflict with regard to Congressional investigating committees is twofold. First, there is the matter of the *subject* of such investigations. Questions have been raised, during particular investigations, concerning the Constitutional right of a Congress to investigate some matters. Determining the legality of Congressional investigations is a highly technical business, and it is here that the "checks and balances" of our government must come into play. Surely there is *some* limit to the subject matter about which legislative investigations can be held. Few would grant,

[3] Reprinted by permission of the publisher, Abelard-Schuman, from *On Education and Freedom* by Harold Taylor, copyright 1954.

for example, that state legislatures have the right to subpoena and question residents under oath concerning their intimate sexual habits in order better to enact marriage laws. So also is there a place where the powers of the federal Congressional investigating committees must bow to the Constitutional rights of the individual to be investigated. It is up to the courts to decide just where this place lies.

Far more concern has been evidenced, particularly in recent years, with *how* Congressional investigating committees operate, rather than in what area they conduct their investigations. On the one hand there is the oft-repeated phrase that "the end justifies the means." By this is usually meant that particularly in its investigations of possible subversion, sabotage, or espionage, it matters not how the committee gathers its information, treats its witnesses, and the like, as long as the investigation is thorough and complete. The end—the uncovering of subversion—is considered so important that the means are largely ignored.

There is the opposing view that holds that we have paid too little attention to the methods and procedures of investigating committees. The crux of the case is that such committees, if left unchecked, can and do overstep their Constitutional powers and infringe on the rights and privileges afforded individuals by the Constitution. Congressional committees are not courts of law, Congressmen are not judges of "guilt" nor administrators of punishment, and witnesses subpoenaed to testify are not on trial. But all too often the proceedings of investigating committees have been said to go beyond those allowed in a court of law. "Professional ex-Communists," for example, parade before the committee and recite their accusations concerning the witness who, in turn, has no right to cross-examine them; the witness is confronted with other "evidence" of his subversive or Communistic proclivities gleaned from confidential documents which remain in the hands of the committee; and, finally, he is questioned at length concerning his past and present activities, views, and associations. It is certainly close to a pronouncement of "guilt" to label a witness a Communist, albeit a "Fifth-Amendment Communist," and witnesses so labeled undoubtedly would agree that they have received punishment in the form of loss of respect, loss of job, humiliation, and the personal expenses involved in being a witness. The innocent as well as those later judged by the courts to be guilty are punished alike, for all too often the mere accusation of disloyalty to one's country spells suspicion, avoidance, and loss of respect by fellow citizens. Sensitive citizens will acclaim that it is a severe personal shock to submit to hours of questioning that seems to have as its avowed aim the substantiation of disloyalty or subversion, even if innocence or guilt is never established in a court of law.

Those who defend the position that Congressional committees need to be restrained in their procedures are aware that subversives may well be in our midst. But the point is not whether the committee witness is or was striving to overthrow the government by force, but whether Congressional committees are the means for determining and acting upon such activities. Is not an American citizen accused of *any* crime guaranteed his "day in Court," with the privilege of counsel and cross-examination of witnesses, the right to refuse to testify "against himself," the weighing of evidence by a jury of his peers, and the meting out of punishment, if found guilty, by an impartial judge in accordance with existing statutes?

And so the clash of basic values continues. No loyal American wants to see the government overthrown by force or changed by unconstitutional means. Some see in the present situation a strong and very real possibility of just such overthrow and eventual submission to a foreign power, and they are willing to take almost any measures to prevent the reckoned possibility from materializing. Others, perhaps defining the danger similarly, are deeply concerned also with the means by which we protect ourselves from it. If Constitutional rights and civil liberties are lost in the fight to guard our Constitutional rights and civil liberties, what really has been won?

The Fifth Amendment.   The clash of values with regard to the meaning, intent, and use of the Fifth Amendment to the Constitution is closely related to the matter of Congressional investigating committees, for it is its use before such committees that has focused so much attention on this Constitutional privilege. The text of the Fifth Amendment pertinent to the issue reads, "No person. . . shall be compelled in any criminal case to be a witness against himself." Thus a person can refuse to testify if it is felt that his testimony would tend to incriminate him. Although it could be interpreted that the Fifth Amendment applies only to defendants in criminal cases, it is generally recognized that it applies also to witnesses in criminal cases and to witnesses before Congressional committees. Congress, at any rate, for the last hundred years has allowed witnesses to refuse to testify before its committees on the grounds of self-incrimination without challenging the Constitutionality of their claim.

There has been a growing tendency to make pleading the Fifth Amendment tantamount to an admission of guilt, particularly when the privilege is invoked at a hearing regarding possible Communistic activities. After all, it is reasoned by some, an "innocent" person has "nothing to hide" and would stand up and verily shout, "No" when he is asked the question, "Are you or have you ever been a member of the Communist Party?" Others simply assert that the Fifth Amendment was intended as a "protection for the innocent" and was never meant to be a Constitutional cloak behind which the guilty could conceal their infamy. Surely, it is reasoned, the founding fathers never intended it to apply to Communists!

It is meaningless to debate whether the privilege against self-incrimination was intended for the innocent or the guilty. By its very nature, it is evident that it was intended for use by the *accused, before* guilt or innocence was determined. It is legitimate, therefore, for an innocent person to refuse to submit testimony that he feels would tend to belie his actual innocence; it is equally legitimate for a guilty person to refuse to furnish testimony to his own guilt. Thus, if an individual "pleads the Fifth" we actually know nothing whatsoever of his guilt or innocence; all we know is that he has been *accused* of something.

Those who uphold the right of all American citizens to invoke the Fifth Amendment when it is legitimate to do so recognize that it will be used by the guilty as well as by the innocent. But this is in accordance with the text of the Amendment and unless, or until, it is revoked it should be made applicable to all citizens. To label a "Fifth-Amendment Communist" someone who invokes a Constitutional privilege tends to make a mockery of the Fifth Amendment. It can be verified that he invoked the Fifth Amendment, but from this evidence alone it is not known whether or not he is a Communist. If a person is guilty of crime, this fact must be discovered and the person must be dealt with swiftly in accordance with the laws of our state. But Constitutional privileges become farcical if by availing oneself of them one is assumed to be guilty of crime.

Thus, there are those among us who have become extremely concerned by what they see as a gradual abridgement of Constitutional guarantees. Loyal Americans are worried lest in striving to maintain our democratic form of government we destroy, in spirit if not in letter, the Constitution on which it is based, and lest in protecting ourselves from totalitarianism we actually encourage it. At the present writing, this particular value issue is far from resolved, for other citizens, who consider themselves equally loyal Americans, continue to equate guilt with invocation of a Constitutional privilege.

Personal guilt v. guilt by association.   Another value clash that manifests itself in the area of national security and civil liberties centers around the concept of "guilt by association." Traditionally, we have sought to adhere to the logically opposite position of personal guilt (although in practice we have not always done so) according to which guilt attaches to an individual because of his own deeds and actions. Guilt by association amounts to punishing a person for what someone else does or says, for belonging to organizations which have been discredited, or even for attending meetings or financially supporting such organizations. In essence, it is giving quasi-legal sanction to the folk belief about birds of a feather.

A major confusion in this area is that between the legal doctrine of conspiracy and the concept of guilt by association. If it can be demonstrated, for example, that three men conspired to rob a bank all three can be punished. And so too in the area of subversion. If a man conspires with others to commit an act leading to the violent overthrow of the government, he is guilty of a crime and can be punished by existing legal statutes. But of what is he guilty if he numbers among his friends or joins organizations some members of which are Communists, or bank robbers, or what have you? Can it really be demonstrated, furthermore, that all present members of the Communist Party are conspiring to commit a crime? And what about those who joined the Party in the mid-thirties or who have been members of groups later listed by the Attorney General as "front organizations"? What have such individuals actually *done* or *conspired to do?* Thus the principle of "guilt by association" knows no bounds. According to its quasi-logic, an organization becomes subversive because some of its members are Communists, and it is next assumed that anyone belonging to such an organization must himself be subversive.

The dragnet of "guilt by association" stretches beyond physical association into the realm of shared ideologies and beliefs. It is becoming unpopular, if not downright foolhardy, to discuss certain political and economic topics simply because Communists also discuss such things. If this at first sounds farfetched, we have but to turn to a pamphlet titled, "How to Spot a Communist" prepared by the First Army.[4] Among other clues to subversion, it lists " a number of specific issues which have been part of the Communist arsenal for a long period of time." It is contended that such issues "are raised not only by Communist appeals to the public but also by the individual Party member or sympathizer who is a product of his Communist environment." Included on the list are:

> "McCarthyism"
> Violation of Civil Rights
> Racial or religious discrimination
> The military budget

[4] The pamphlet in question was used by the Ordinance Corps, Watertown, Massachusetts, as well as by the Continental Air Command. The Army has since withdrawn the pamphlet, however.

Any legislation concerning labor unions
"Peace"

The pamphlet further points out that Communist organizations "frequently seize on any controversial subject from fluoridation of drinking water to 'police brutality' in order to promote their nefarious schemes." Presumably it was not intended to convey the impression that everyone who discusses fluoridation or the military budget is a Communist, but to include such topics in a pamphlet on "How to Spot a Communist," to offer them as "clues" to subversion, is enough to frighten loyal Americans into avoiding their discussion. And certainly there is reason to be cautious when according to the doctrine of guilt by ideological association it is "subversive" to fight violation of Civil Rights or Communistic to favor peace over war! Many would agree that such thinking places us uncomfortably close to the "Big Brother" days of 1984 when "black is white" and "war is peace." [5] Loyal Americans feel no qualms concerning the punishment of criminals for overt actions or conspiracy to commit overt actions. But it is quite another thing to be spied upon by one's fellow citizens and to be met with suspicion because one discusses issues which Communists also discuss.

Loyalty oaths.   At the present writing a number of our states require a "loyalty oath" of educators. The wording of such oaths varies, but generally the incumbent must swear that he is not a member of any organization striving to overthrow the government by violence. The proponents of special loyalty oaths for educators insist that educators are in a peculiarly sensitive position, molding as they do the future adult citizens of the United States. It is not so much that possible disloyal educators would themselves constitute a threat to national security, but rather, it is argued, it is the risk of what exposure to Communist ideology may do to immature minds. Advocates of educators' loyalty oaths further ask, "Why not?" On the surface this sounds simple enough. Why, indeed, should any loyal American object to swearing that he is not disloyal?

[5] We are referring to George Orwell, *Nineteen Eighty-Four*, New York, Harcourt, Brace, and Co., 1949.

If we reverse the question and ask *why* educators should be singled out as a group to stand up and affirm their loyalty, a characteristic that is still assumed of most American citizens, we have the other side of the issue. Forcing a group to affirm its loyalty suggests to some that there is reason to suspect it of disloyalty. For this reason, one group of university professors is reported to have stated that its members would sign oaths that they were not Communists if the Board of Regents, in turn, would swear that they were not homosexuals. The inference is clear in both cases; compelling a person to swear that he is *not* something suggests that there is reason to believe he *might be* just that.

A further difficulty in once initiating loyalty oaths lies in the determination of just how far and to whom to extend them. Suppose, for example, that it became general practice for all educators to be forced to swear that they are not presently members of the Communist Party. Should they, next, be required to add that they have *never* been members? And what about being members of "front organizations" or supporting Henry Wallace who was supported by Communists? In a similar manner, why stop with teachers? Certainly entertainers and fiction writers influence the minds of men. Should not they too be required to take loyalty oaths? Clergymen, lawyers, and union leaders also would seem to be in sensitive positions. It has been suggested that the most economical procedure would be to turn the business over to the Bureau of the Census and require *everyone* to tell the census-taker under oath whether he is, or ever has been, a member of the Communist Party! Thus suspicion once encouraged runs rampant, and it is the threat of encroachment upon the basic liberties of free men that is the concern of those who take a stand against loyalty oaths for special groups.

▶ WHAT OF THE FUTURE?

In the foregoing pages we have pointed out that there are forces in the world and in our own country that are considered to be threats to our national security. We have indicated, too, that there are apparently less recognized threats to our civil liberties. No serious thinking American would recommend that we protect one and sacrifice the other. But it is not easy to draw the line between restrictions required for the safeguard of national security and unnecessary abridgments of civil liberties.

The question that remains is whether we will be able to find our way through this maze of imponderables and emerge both a secure and a free nation. While our democratic form of government itself suggests the highest degree of optimism in answering this question, there is room for pessimism in the fact of an apparent apathy on the part of a sizable segment of the population. Take, for example, popular reaction to the Communist Control Act of 1954 which "outlaws" the Communist Party and strips it of all "rights, privileges, and immunities attendant upon legal bodies." The major effect of this law has been to make it impossible for the Communist Party to offer a slate of candidates on the ballot. The little public reaction to this law seemed mostly favorable. But how does this law look to the free and not-so-free people in the rest of the world? On the one hand, we loudly proclaim the virtues of free elections since we believe that given a free choice at the polls Democracy will triumph over Communism; on the other, Americans themselves are no longer able to exercise this choice!

The merits or necessity for the Communist Control Act are not here under question. Rather, the point is that some find cause for pessimism at the seeming lack of understanding of the implications of this law and, in fact, in the general indifference toward traditional liberties. There is room for optimism, however, in that a reduction of world tensions may remove the tendency to propitiate the god of national security with sacrifices to civil liberties. And it is possible, too, that even if world conditions remain much as they are at present, men will learn that we can protect both our security and our freedom if we truly value each of these concepts.

▶ SUMMARY

Strong value clashes come to fore concerning specific programs for safeguarding our national security while, at the same time, protecting our civil liberties. A realistic view of the present American scene in which the various value clashes are taking place is essential for a thorough understanding of the issues themselves.

Communism, an admittedly strong, world-wide, revolutionary force has been considered to be a threat to our democratic way of life. To the extent that this threat is real, it is entirely appropriate to "fear Communism." There are indications, however, that present-day fear of Communism has gone beyond the bounds of "normal fear" and has led to mass suspicion and anxiety.

Four current issues bearing on civil liberties were investigated: (1) Congressional investigating committees; (2) use of the Fifth Amendment; (3) the concept of guilt by association; and (4) loyalty oaths for educators. These issues bear also on national security. Thus, we are faced with the dual task of keeping our secure nation free while keeping our free nation secure.

The question of the future of the value clashes in the area of national security and civil liberties was investigated and reasons are seen both for optimism and pessimism over the early mitigation of the problems. Security and freedom are not seen as mutually exclusive goals for a nation that truly values both concepts.

SUGGESTED READINGS

Barth, Alan, *Government by Investigation*, New York, The Viking Press, 1955. Investigates investigations forcefully and comprehensively. An eye-opener to many Americans.
——, *The Loyalty of Free Men*, New York, The Viking Press, 1951. A vigorous plea for the maintenance of civil liberties. Numerous records and actual cases are used to document the point that basic freedoms are being surrendered. For verbatim recordings of loyalty investigations see especially Chapter 5, "The Government's Loyalty Program."

Biddle, Francis, *The Fear of Freedom*, Garden City, N. Y., Double-day & Co., 1951. Traces the background of what it sees as a contemporary obsession of fear and anxiety, discusses its present expression and its effect on national security and free American institutions.

The Brookings Institution, *Suggested Standards for Determining Un-American Activities*, Washington, D. C., 1945. Prepared at the request of the Committee on Un-American Activities, this brief manual offers straight-forward guides to a definition of un-Americanism and suggests standards and principles of procedure for investigating committees.

Carr, Robert K., *The House Committee on Un-American Activitites, 1945-1950*, Ithaca, Cornell University Press, 1952. A detailed history of its activities from 1945 to 1950 provides a basis for evaluating its record. An objective, nonpassioned account of a well-known Congressional committee. The thoughtful citizen will appreciate its painstaking compilation and analysis of voluminous records of the Committee.

Commager, Henry Steele, *Freedom, Loyalty, Dissent*, New York, Oxford University Press, 1954. See especially Chap. 5, "Who is Loyal to America?", where loyalty is distinguished from conformity and the effects of the latter on free inquiry and progress are set forth. A series of thought-provoking essays.

Gellhorn, Walter, *Security, Loyalty, and Science*, Ithaca, Cornell University Press, 1950. A case is made that through rigorous controls of scientific research, secrecy, and security requirements, we are purchasing national security at the price of progress. While proper precaution is urged, the constant stress on security is seen to have a deleterious effect on scientific interchange and the recruitment of qualified scientists.

Lasswell, Harold D., *National Security and Individual Freedom*, New York, McGraw-Hill Book Co., 1950, Chap. 3, "The Meaning of National Security Policy." Distinguishes between national security, foreign policy, and defense armament. Sets forth guides to effective maintenance of security.

Taylor, Telford, *Grand Inquest*, New York, Simon and Schuster, 1955. An historical account of Congressional investigations culminating with current loyalty probes. Excellent for the antecedents of a currently controversial problem.

STUDY QUESTIONS

1. State in your own words the basic value conflict underlying the specific problems dealt with in this chapter.

2. What is the evidence that we are living in "an age of fear and suspicion"? Why is it difficult to obtain accurate information in this area?

3. How do you account for the fact that there has been less concern with the subject matter of Congressional investigations than with their procedures? Cite several examples of how the subject of Congressional investigations could constitute a threat to civil liberties.

4. What is the central controversy concerning the procedure of Congressional investigating committees? Cite the specific issues which are said to constitute a threat to traditional liberties.

5. Why is it said to be meaningless to debate whether the Fifth Amendment was intended for the innocent or the guilty? Illustrate with a hypothetical example why an innocent person accused of a crime might wish to avail himself of the Fifth-Amendment privilege.

6. How do you account for the growing tendency to make pleading the Fifth Amendment tantamount to an admission of guilt? What chances do you see for reversing this tendency?

7. Distinguish between the legal doctrine of conspiracy and the concept of guilt by association.

8. Explain what is meant by "guilt by ideological association."

9. State the logic of the position that favors special loyalty oaths for educators. Why do some educators object to such loyalty oaths?

10. Illustrate why it is difficult to determine to whom or to which groups loyalty oaths should be administered. How would you suggest handling this matter?

Part 3

American Ideologies and Values

· 22 ·

The Social
Disorganization
Concept Re-examined

Even a cursory reading of the preceding twenty-one chapters would be enough to convince the student that there are problem conditions in his society. He may have at least entertained the thought that it is not so much that he is living in a society with problems but that his is indeed a "problem society" and, at times, he may have even found himself glibly referring to our present state of "social disorganization." As a sociological concept, "social disorganization" has a certain utility. But is it an appropriate description of modern society? It is our purpose, now, after brief remarks on social *organization*, to examine the concept of social disorganization more fully and especially to investigate the extent to which it is applicable to contemporary American society.

Even in the most primitive state, the human animal is dependent upon others of his kind for survival. As human society becomes more complex, this interdependence of human beings likewise increases. An essential element in the complexity of modern society is an intricate division of labor. This division of labor, in turn, demands an elaborate social organization in order to coordinate the activities of specializing groups and persons. A brief consideration of the specializations upon which our food, clothing, household equipment, and occupational and recreational devices depend is alone sufficient to demonstrate our interdependence and the social organization necessary to make these things available to the individual.

Not only physical objects, but values, sentiments, ideologies, and customs bind us together and make us interdependent. Just as a casual inspection of the materials in our daily enviromnent informs us of the elaborate social organization upon which we as individuals depend, in like manner a stocktaking of our beliefs, attitudes, convictions, manners, morals, and habits will reveal many social sources. All of these sources were opened to us by means of social organization.

▶ THE CONCEPT OF SOCIAL DISORGANIZATION

All societies have some organization, but they differ not only in the content and complexity of their specific institutional configurations but also in the degree to which these parts are integrated into a general pattern which is consistent within itself. It has become a commonplace to refer to American society as "disintegrated" or "disorganized." America, it has frequently been suggested, becomes increasingly a "problem society" because it lacks unifying principles or values, is in a growing state of "social disorganization."

What is meant by social disorganization? The term "disorganization" suggests the disruption of previously existing organization. When traditional behavior patterns no longer prevail and confusion is apparent among the participants in a social situation because of this nonfunctioning of customary patterns, a state of social disorganization is said to exist. If, for example, the instructor of a college class walked into the classroom dressed in boxing tights and began engaging in setting-up exercises, the resulting situation might or might not be one of social disorganization. If he happened to be an instructor of physical education, he would probably be following the behavior patterns considered appropriate to his role; his students would be attitudinally prepared for such behavior and would themselves act in orderly fashion. If, on the other hand, the class were prepared for instruction in, say, political science, the behavior of the instructor would be considered inappropriate for the social situation. Established traditions of conduct relating to a class in political science would have broken down, confusion would undoubtedly result, and a state of social disorganization would be in effect.

Situations more complicated than, but comparable to, our simple classroom illustration are said to exist in many of our basic social institutions in the United States today. Two important institutions among those that are frequently said to be in the process of "breaking down," or passing through progressive stages of social disorganization, are the family and the economic system. We shall, first of all, examine the evidences of disorganization in these two institutions and then critically evaluate the usefulness of the concept of social disorganization as a tool for understanding our problem society.

Is the American family disorganized? A great deal of popular and professional concern about the "disorganization" of the American family has been manifested for several reasons. One of the reasons is the obvious importance of the family situation in molding the personality of the individuals who compose a society. It is in the family that the individual spends most of his time during his most formative years; what he basically becomes as a personality is considerably determined by his early family experiences. If these experiences are of a predominantly "disorganized" type, the results are apt to be "disintegrative" for the individual's personality.

Another reason for the concern of exponents of the disorganization hypothesis is the "sacred" significance attributed to the family in our social traditions. In our early cultural history the family served as a sort of over-all depository of our social heritage, including the most highly prized moral values. The family has been viewed not merely as a secular institution but as a keystone configuration of the most important religious traditions. If the family is "disorganized," by implication some of the most significant traditional meanings of life itself are breaking down.

A third reason for concentrated concern is the intimacy of association and poignancy of experience that the members of our society have with its patterns. Many individuals may have rel-atively little understanding of or disturbance about the "break-down" of due process of law or foreign exchange or legislative procedures, but these same individuals "understand" and are perturbed about such "breakdowns" of family patterns as wives working out of the home, divorce, and childless families.

There can be little doubt that such reasons for concern as the foregoing three have subjectively influenced most of the analyses thus far conducted regarding family "disorganization." As citizens we are quite justifiably "concerned," but as social scientists we are obliged to inquire into the nature of alleged disorganization of the American family in such a way that we do not let our values color our facts.

Some of the changes in family patterns that are often cited as symptoms of disorganization are: (1) the rise in the divorce rate; (2) geographical mobility; (3) decline of parental author-ity over children; (4) decreasing family size, including deliberate childlessness upon the part of an increasing number of couples; (5) increasing number of women with out-of-home careers; (6) increasing "immorality" of both sexes, especially of women; and (7) loss of family functions to other institutions (to the point that the family has little or nothing "left to do"). After a consid-eration of economic "disorganization," we shall return to ex-amine these alleged evidences of a disorganized family institution.

Have we a disorganized economy? Second in sacredness only to the family in American traditions (and perhaps more sacred to many Americans) have been our economic traditions of pri-vate property and free competitive enterprise. The capitalistic economic system has become inextricably intertwined in the thinking of many Americans with the highly prized value of democracy and with the total "American way of life." Small wonder that any achieved or attempted alteration in our eco-nomic institutions has been quickly labeled a symptom of "so-cial disorganization."

Changes in the "free enterprise" of business have come from two major sources: government and organized labor. As labor has organized into unions, it has come increasingly to have a voice in "laying down the rules" under which business will operate. The employer is no longer "free" to do as he pleases in regard to hiring and firing, payment of wages, provision of working conditions and policies. He now must "bargain" with union representatives.

Government has also acted somewhat to curtail the freedom of "free enterprise." This has been done both by the passing of legislation directly designed to curb the employer's liberty to do things deemed contrary to the general welfare and by the passing of legislation assuring workers of their rights to engage in concerted action, to organize in their own way, to bargain collectively, and to receive governmental assistance in the peaceful settlement of labor disputes. While the government has by no means been consistent in passing or enforcing either type of legislation, changes have been marked enough in recent years to alarm many businessmen.

In addition to legislation aiding labor and "restricting" the freedom of business enterprise, government has directly and indirectly engaged in activities considered by some people a serious threat to the concept of private property. One of the most notable examples of "government in business" is the Tennessee Valley Authority, through which electric power and a number of subsidiary services are provided by the federal government. Proposals for additional programs comparable to TVA are currently being considered by the executive and legislative branches of government; various important educational, recreational, insurance, medical, agricultural, and other activities are being increasingly conducted by federal, state, and local governments. We are obviously no longer a simple economy of free competitive enterprise and of private property.

That the many, and in some cases fundamental, economic changes have, like their familial counterparts, caused confusion in American society can scarcely be denied. No one seems quite certain what economically will happen next. He is not sure in which direction or with which group lies the meeting of his own needs or the enhancing of his own interests. This would seem indisputably to be disorganization.

▶ IS SOCIAL DISORGANIZATION A USEFUL CONCEPT?

We have described in the foregoing pages many evidences of alleged disorganization in the family and economic institutions of American society. Similar conditions could be given for all areas of American social life. It is true that our society is in the process of change, some of which is radical, and that a concomitant of this change is, at times, confusion. Since proposed criteria for judging disorganization consist of such conditions as "breakdown of social controls over the behavior of the individual," modifications in social roles, experimentation with new roles, and confusion in the individual's behavior, why show any reluctance about using the term? Stated briefly, the answer to this question is that the term "social disorganization" connotes something temporary and something undesirable. When a society is "disorganized," it is in a "bad" condition, and, because organization is essential to a society, it will have to get "reorganized" in a hurry in order to survive.

Is our society in a temporary, acutely undesirable condition? To answer this question positively or negatively implies that we are fully informed as to the future condition, or at least the next stage, of our social development. Is the American family "breaking down," or are old patterns merely being replaced by new ones? Are the new ones better or worse than the old ones? Many persons think they are worse, but are they not judging in the light of their attachment to the old patterns and their lack of familiarity (and, hence, discomfort) with the new ones? And can any of us be sure of the poorer or better nature of the next stage of development in relation to which the present family patterns may be considered transitory? Is our present economy disorganized or do we merely see some of our old economic values being replaced by other economic values? In our judgments of "social disorganization," how much are we influenced by personal discomforts occasioned by readjustment to new institutional patterns? Let us re-examine the social-disorganization concept more critically with our two examples of economic and familial institutions.

Evaluation of alleged family "disorganization." The most frequently cited symptom of family disorganization, as we have already noted, is the rise in the divorce rate. Divorce is the breakup of *a specific family unit*, but does it necessarily follow that an increase in the number of divorces is a breakdown of *the* family? Within the traditional framework of family values it does follow, for that system of values holds that divorce is a sin. But, looked at differently, the rising divorce rate may be regarded as increased use of legal means to change from one family unit to another. While such change may be personally uncomfortable to some or all of the participants (especially for those who still regard divorce as a sin), it may be considered evidence of social disorganization only if the unalterable truth of a certain system of values (that divorce is an evil) is assumed.

The same reasoning is the basis for citing geographical mobility as evidence of disorganization of the family. In earlier periods in our cultural history many families "stayed put" on the homestead. Traditionally the family has a specific living locus in a specific community. Today many families move from dwelling to dwelling and from city to city. This frequent moving, the reasoning goes, is "bad," unfamilylike evidence of disorganization. Again, although discomforts, inconveniences, and other undesirabilities for individual members of individual families can be demonstrated, do we have a legitimate "symptom of family disorganization"? It would not seem so.

Similarly we find other alleged symptoms of family disorganization undermined when we remove certain *assumptions* about the undesirability of certain conditions for the family. Decline of parental authority is "bad," a symptom of disorganization, from the standpoint of traditional patriarchal family values; it is "good," a symptom of progress, from the standpoint of values advocating the application of democratic values to the family situation; it is neither "good" nor "bad" but merely evidence of change from the standpoint of a social analyst not subscribing to the social disorganization hypothesis. Decreasing family size is evidence of family disorganization if you believe large families are desirable; the increasing number of women with out-of-home careers is "bad," providing you believe that "woman's place is in the home"; a freer sex code is "immoral" if the traditional sex mores were the only inherently "right" ones; and the loss of many functions by the family to other institutions is "disorganization" if you think that the family should have kept them.

In short, what appears at first glance to be an impressive list of symptoms of disorganization in the American family as an institution comes to depend upon our acceptance of previously defined values and of behavior based on these values as the "right," the "organized" status of the institution.

Evaluation of alleged economic "disorganization." Closer inspection of the application of the social-disorganization concept to the American economy brings similar results. Personal discomfort and confusion in the face of changing economic patterns is frequently assumed to be indicative of disorganization of the economic institution. Some observers have suggested, in addition, that much of the confusion is exaggerated and even created by those who are opposed to departures from traditional economic patterns. It is "disorganization" for labor to have an increasing "voice" in management when you believe that traditional lack of such "voice" is the only fully desirable form of economic organization. Increased governmental participation in economic life is inevitably "disorganizing" a system of values that holds *laissez faire* the ideal type of organization for an economy. As we have seen, the breakup of one family unit via divorce does not necessarily signify the breakdown of the family as an institution. In like manner, the confusion in a governmental bureau or the discomfort of a group of businessmen in the face of increased power and recognition for organized labor need not be interpreted as the disorganization of the economic institution.

Economically we have made profound changes as a society and are quite evidently in the process of making many more.

However, to hold that contemporary changes are symptoms of social disorganization is to imply that the formerly established economic patterns were "good" and that the conditions toward which current changes are moving, by virtue of the gifted insight of the analyst, are known to be "bad."

Summary evaluation of the concept. What we have observed regarding the application of the concept of social disorganization to the economic institution and the family can be found in the analysis of religion, government, or any other social institution. The usefulness of social disorganization as an interpretative concept is seriously limited by the fact that specific value judgments underlie its application to any social situation. The term implies disapproval and abnormality, temporary undesirability, a trend which (if unchecked) will lead to institutional dissolution. The use of the social disorganization hypothesis seems often to serve as a shroud for moralizing rather than as a tool for analysis. Instead of stating that the changing sex code is "bad," the exponent of this hypothesis says that departures from the traditional sex standards are a symptom of family disorganization (and—by definition and implication—"disorganization is bad"; hence, we have a moralization once removed but little further insight into existing family conditions). But, to continue with our example, are these increasing departures from the sex mores symptomatic of social disorganization or merely indicative of social change? Confusion, discomfort, inconvenience, longing for the old patterns, and name-calling of the new ways accompanies any marked social change. Yet certainly it is not to be contended that all marked social change is social disorganization.

Our concluding thoughts on this subject, then, are that *social disorganization is a misleading interpretative concept because it (1) contains implications of moralization rather than objectivity and (2) fails to distinguish between "disorganizing" and other types of social change.*

▶CULTURE IN CONTINUOUS CHANGE

It is not necessary to discard entirely the concept of social disorganization. It would seem to be appropriate in times of floods, earthquakes, fires, and the like, for here we have temporary conditions of disruption, agreed upon as undesirable by all sections of a society, and not inextricable parts of any long-time social trends. Here we have the relatively simple process of an existing state of order, the occurrence of disaster (with accompanying disorder or "social disorganization"), and the restoration of orderliness (reorganization). For conditions that arise as parts of general cultural trends, of which the duration and outcome are indefinite or unknown and over which value disagreements occur, the more neutral terms of "social change" or "cultural change" would seem to be more appropriate.

Variations in rate of cultural change. It is a most elementary sociological fact that the rate of change varies in different cultures and at different times in the same culture. At no previous time in American society has the rate of change been so rapid in so many areas of the culture as today. Likewise, never has American culture been so complex. A rapidly changing complexity faces the individual citizen; it is small wonder that he tends to be confused. With the onset of the "atomic age" the speed and complexity of contemporary living will increase, not decrease. Can man adjust to this continuous, rapid, complex cultural change?

When our society was simpler and the rate of change was slower, no single generation had to make radical readjustments in many areas of social living. The colonial had to readjust to a "free" America politically, but an America that proceeded to behave in fundamental economic, religious, educational, familial, and recreational ways like the America of pre-Revolutionary days. The Southern slaveholder had to face some important political and economic readjustments after the Civil War, but (except for the temporary chaos of "Reconstruction") his post-war life had more conditions of institutional familiarity than of fundamental change. Here we have chosen the two most turbulent periods in American history prior to the twentieth century; especially "unchangeful," relative to the contemporary rapidity of change, was the life of those generations not caught by the Revolutionary and Civil wars. Yet the whole of American history is a document of rapid, complex, and profound social change compared with century upon century of history, recorded and unrecorded, of many other societies.

But any point of comparison we wish to take will provide us with sufficient contrast to note the striking rapidity and profundity of contemporary culture change. Family, economic, political, educational, religious, recreational, and other social conditions, as we have seen, are moving in their patterns with such rapidity that no individual in modern American society can fail to feel the impact of these changes. Adjustment of the modern American must include adjustment to rapid change. Any concept of control cannot be based upon "keeping things as they are" but must include guidance of change.

Can we guide the direction of cultural change? At the risk of discouraging the student but in respect for truth, we must answer this question largely in the negative—in light of present knowledge and available methods of social control. Our present knowledge of major social trends is not sufficient to reverse them or make significant alterations in their direction *even if* we could get such programs adopted by the ruling forces in our society. And, furthermore, a realistic analysis of currently available methods of social control must conclude that we are ruled in part by ignorances, prejudices, and interests contrary to the public welfare and in still larger part by intricate interweavings of hardened customs. If, for example, we should have validated data (and we do not) that all governmental centralization is "bad," we would be at a loss as to methods to quickly effect decentralization. We could, probably, slow down the centralizing process somewhat, providing we could convince a majority of the main political forces in our country that this was desirable. But, meantime, tendencies of varying and for the most part unknown strength and relation to the "centralization process" would continue to push toward centralization and would undoubtedly more than counteract our decentralizing efforts.

Suppose, to take another example of the present impossibility of controlling major social trends, we decide current premarital and extramarital sex relations must be stopped. Just how would we proceed? We could make it more difficult for those who engage in such practices so to practice (providing we could get public authorities, hotel managers, tourist-cabin operators, etc., to cooperate with our program), and perhaps we could slow down the rate of change from traditional sex morals. But it is very doubtful that we could reverse the trend toward a freer sex code.

The fact that we do not know enough fundamentally to alter major social trends does not mean that our efforts at social analysis or in the guidance of cultural change need be futile. Our analysis can provide us with ever-increasing knowledge, not only of major trends but of various currents within these trends. And it is the control of these currents that is possible by the application of scientifically derived information to the forming of public policy. Although governmental centralization and increasing governmental authority over all aspects of social life will undoubtedly continue during the next several decades, there are various forms which this centralization and increasing authority may take. Decisions as to the kind of governmental power we desire ought to be made not only on the basis of knowledge derived from the study of governmental trends but in the light of values we hold important as American citizens. If, for example, the American people have genuine faith in democracy, and if they cannot prevent collectivization, *they can see to it that it is a democratically controlled collectivization.* In like manner, we probably cannot prevent or reverse the major trend toward a freer sex code, but we can guide that movement toward greater sex freedom into channels believed to be more in harmony with facts about the way modern Americans behave sexually and with values in harmony with these facts. There are, let us say, principles of behavior that contain respect for the personality of others; such principles may either be followed or ignored in sexual union. Guidance of the trend toward a freer sex code could be made so that this value of respect for human personality would be included.

In concluding this discussion of culture in continuous change, sharp differentiation should be made in the mind of the reader between the use of values in the concept of "social disorganization" and the use of values in the concept of "cultural change" and the possibility of guiding the latter. In the "social disorganization" concept the evaluation of "undesirable" is (implicitly) part of the analysis; in the "cultural-change" concept there is no such evaluation involved in the analysis, but the guidance of cultural change *following the analysis* must of necessity be based upon social values. One cannot advocate or oppose any course of action without proceeding on the basis of a judgment of "good" or "bad." Analysis should be apart from moralizing; guidance or action cannot be.

▶ SUMMARY

American society is frequently referred to as "disorganized." When traditional behavior patterns "break down" and individuals manifest confusion, a state of "social disorganization" is said to exist. Such conditions are said to be widespread in America.

Two institutions most often spoken of as "disorganized" are the family and the economic system. Divorce, mobility, "immorality," and a number of other "symptoms of family disorganization" are frequently cited; and the decline of free enterprise through the activities of government and organized labor are connected with the reputed disorganization of the economic institution. Examination of these "symptoms of disorganization" for both the familial and economic institutions often demonstrates not only the lack of objectivity with which these two institutions are analyzed but also the intrinsic weakness in the whole disorganization concept as a tool for social interpretation. "Disorganization" implies movement away from something presumably desirable (that is, organization) toward something undesirable (change from organization) and fails to distinguish between "disorganizing" and other types of marked social change.

While "social disorganization" as a term seems appropriate for temporary conditions of disruption which are not parts of long-time social trends and about which there is unanimity concerning "undesirability" (such as floods or earthquakes), the more neutral term of "cultural change" seems applicable to conditions arising as parts of general cultural trends.

The rate of cultural change varies during different periods within the same society and from society to society. The rapidity and profundity of cultural change in contemporary American society is not only noteworthy in itself, but raises problems concerning the possibilities of man's adjustment to it and guidance of its direction. It is unlikely that man will soon learn to control the major directions of cultural change, but it does seem possible for him to apply the results of scientific analysis, combined with social values in harmony with major trends thus observed, to guiding some aspects of cultural change. Increased governmental authority over the life of the individual, for example, is probably inevitable, but the kind of governmental authority—that is, democratic or dictatorial—is still subject to social guidance, at least so long as America remains politically as democratic as it now is.

SUGGESTED READINGS

Barnes, Harry E., *Society in Transition*, 2d ed., New York, Prentice-Hall, 1952. The concept of cultural lag is the basic frame of reference of this social problems text. Personal and social disorganization are seen as manifestations of cultural lag and as the immediate bases of most social problems. A good source for historical data on many problematical conditions.

Barnett, H. G., *Innovation: The Basis of Cultural Change*, New York, McGraw-Hill Book Co., 1953. This stimulating book deals with the conception, acceptance, and social consequences of new ideas. Social change in five ethnic groups and a religious cult is studied against the backdrop of the innovation process.

Faris, Robert E. L., *Social Disorganization*, 2d ed., New York, Ronald Press, 1955. This is a standard text written around the social disorganization theme. It is illustrative of how the concept must often be "stretched" to fit various social problems and of the moralizations into which the social disorganization advocate frequently falls. Contains, however, considerable recent factual material.

Ogburn, William F., *Social Change*, rev. ed., New York, Viking Press, 1950. A revision of a classic evaluation of social change with which all advanced students should be familiar. Presents modern social change within a framework of historical comparisons and advances the well-known hypothesis of cultural lag.

—— (ed.), *Technology and International Relations*, Chicago, The University of Chicago Press, 1949. A series of papers examine recent scientific and technological developments as they affect international relations. Atomic energy, aviation, and mass-communication inventions are some of the areas investigated. The social effects of inventions are aptly demonstrated.

STUDY QUESTIONS

1. Explain in your own words what is meant by social organization.

2. Why has there been more concern with the alleged "disorganization" of the family than with other areas?

3. What are the changes in family patterns that are often cited as symptoms of family disorganization?

4. What have been the two major sources of changes in the "free enterprise" of business? Name some specific changes that have taken place.

5. Define social disorganization. Using this definition, *could* divorce be a symptom of social disorganization? Explain.

6. Show how three symptoms of the alleged disorganization of the family could be interpreted as desirable trends. What are your own points of view with regard to these trends? How do you account for them?

7. What changes are frequently cited as symptoms of alleged economic disorganization? Show how these changes could also be interpreted as desirable modifications.

8. For what two reasons is the expression "social disorganization" said to be a misleading interpretative concept? Explain.

9. For what types of conditions is "social disorganization" an

appropriate concept? Analyze one of these conditions in terms of the definition of social disorganization.

10. Distinguish as fully as possible between social change and social disorganization. What do you consider the essential difference between the two concepts?

· 23 · Rational Approach to Our Value Heritage

The core thesis of this book has been that social problems represent conditions over which there is a "clash of values" concerning their nature, their importance or their treatment. It is easy to demonstrate that wide differences of opinion exist concerning every social problem from the quest for national security to the inconsistencies of marriage laws. It remains now to delve somewhat further into the factors that underlie this value diversity and to consider the probabilities that there may be emerging some sort of value agreement which may yet make it possible for the various value adherents to "get together" on some positions at least. Repeatedly it has been asked, by poet and scientist alike, why cannot reasonable, thinking men come to some measure of agreement upon the fundamental value ends of human activity at least within our own society and for our own time? Must we ever resign ourselves to accept divergent opinion and the ill will which it generates as an inherent part of the American way of life? Such questions as these constitute the last chapter of our inquiry into the nature of our problem society.

▶ FACTORS UNDERLYING VALUE DIVERSITY

In so far as it is possible to isolate the factors which appear to be responsible for the present heterogeneity of values in America, we shall list and explain those influences which seem to us to contribute to the current disunity.

Differential vested interest. Throughout this book we have recurrently shown that social problems affect persons of differential social position in greatly varied ways. So great is this variation in effect that conditions which may properly be regarded as problems to people in one social class may not be problems at all to people in other social classes. And even where it can be shown that a given condition is a problem to all strata of the society, it can almost always be readily shown that there are vast differences in the severity of the effect. Finally, and in the extreme, conditions which are deplorable to certain persons and groups may actually be beneficial to the interests of other persons and groups. This latter is illustrated by the disprivilege afforded Negroes, by permitting the payment of less than subsistence wages to certain persons, or by permitting persons to manufacture and sell commodities which are harmful to the physical or mental welfare of the consumers. Under such conditions it is hardly to be expected that agreement could be reached relative to the desirability or undesirability of the condition in question.

Under the existing American value of individuation—the right and the desirability of each person to amass the largest income possible to himself so long as he violates no law thereby—the payer of less than a living wage or the possessor of superior privilege because he is fortunate enough to be white or Gentile or educated or "well bred," can hardly be blamed for failing to see that someone else is being injured or that the system is not a just one. To be sure, idealistically one is expected to be mindful of the needs of other people and sympathetic to their disprivileges, but the point is that it may be asking more magnanimity of him than he is capable of manifesting, after he has been conditioned to the rightness of the individualistic success system. This is not to deny that *some* people are not capable of the degree of identification necessary to understand opposing sides of a value position with comparable vividness, for obviously there are such people. As early as 2,000 years ago, it is written, that at least one socially prominent man had the temerity to give his goods to the poor in an attempt to realize new values which he had come to believe were worthy. And in our time there are more than a few who, while perhaps not going so far as to resign themselves to poverty, more or less consistently take positions on social issues which are antithetical to their own vested interests. But the proportion of such persons seems not now to be large enough to alter the basic condition of personal alignment in terms of vested interest.

Cultural pluralism.   American society has been referred to as a "melting pot" of diverse heritages from most of the rest of the advanced cultures of the world. To some extent this heterogeneous collection of cultures has been assimilated into a unique American culture, but there are evidences of the continued existence of schisms which should not be overlooked. Some nations, whatever their economic differences, have the unifying influence of a single or a predominant religion, such as Italy and Catholicism or England and Anglicanism. But the United States is torn by the ideological conflicts between Catholicism and Protestantism which are, of course, not exclusively matters of religion but vitally affect such matters as birth control, divorce, education, censorship, and many others.

Cultural pluralism, however, seems to affect social problems in other ways than simply providing a source for diversity in viewpoint. It has given us traditions which are incongruous and, therefore, a source of conflict. During the period of high immigration from Europe and Asia, for example, the low social status of the immigrant established patterns of disprivilege which the immigrant groups were forced to accept or tolerate because they were powerless to do otherwise. A more specific example of this is the intolerable slum housing conditions characteristic of the industrial cities in which many immigrants settled. As the immigrant group has lost its identity through assimilation into American culture, first- and second-generation descendants, even though often doing the same kind of work as their immigrant ancestors, have become increasingly unwilling to accept some of the disprivileges which their parents and grandparents had adjusted to. These people are now demanding their "American rights of freedom of opportunity." Meanwhile the more fortunate Americans are attempting to retain the superior privileges which they originally had and deeply resent "the ingratitude" of working-class people of foreign extraction who are pressing for more tangible expression of the equality of opportunity which they have been taught is the essence of America. Sooner or later, apparently, American society will have to make up its mind whether our traditional patterns of differential social privilege will be modified in greater conformity to the democratic ideal of equality of opportunity, or whether we will candidly say that the democratic ideal was a mistake and set about to rationalize a nondemocratic or castelike social system. Whatever may be said for either choice, it would appear that some of our confusion over values would be reduced if our practice became more nearly consistent with our preachment.

Extrarational nature of values. We have referred a number of times to the nonrational or extrarational nature of some specific social form or value. At this point we should perhaps examine the value structure as a whole in order to determine, if possible, whether the traditional and basic values of American society are not inherently extrarational phenomena.

It would probably not be difficult to reach agreement, even among persons of diverse value orientation, that the following values are conspicuous parts of American culture. There would probably be disagreement concerning the relative importance or the acceptance of certain values in the list, but seemingly not upon the existence of the following value ends toward which Americans are oriented.

1. *Monogamous marriage:* that is, one mate at a time, preference for stability and for children to be born within wedlock.
2. *Freedom:* by which is usually meant holding only minimum arbitrary limitations on the will of people to do as they please.
3. *Acquisitiveness:* the desirability of securing as great a proportion as possible of income, wealth and material objects, even far beyond the volume necessary to sustain an abundant physical existence.

4. *Democracy:* There is a somewhat circumscribed application of the equality of opportunity principle—that is, of the belief that almost everyone should have a right to vote and have access to at least some of the "good things" which the society provides, such as the free use of the schools, the highway system, equality before the law, etc.

5. *Education:* There is faith that despite its limitations and its needed modifications, the education of as many people as possible, as much as possible, is a worthy objective, limited to some extent, to be sure, by varying judgments of how much we can afford to spend for this purpose.

6. *Monotheistic religion:* Although regular, weekly participation in organized religion is probably no longer a majority practice in America, adherence to at least some of the traditional tenets of the Christian and Jewish faiths is still taken for granted and taught to children.

7. *Technology and Science:* There is great respect for the specific findings of science and the "miracles" which it has explained. To a vastly lesser degree there is respect for scientific method *per se.* But the chief orientation is toward what science and the man of science can do to help one to achieve desired objectives. Thus it may be more accurate to say that "technology" rather than "science" is held to be the great good, although in the minds of many people the two are inseparably mixed.

What, now, is "extrarational" or nonrational about these seven dominant American value patterns? Is it not self-evident that they are sound, worthy of one's allegiance, important enough, in fact, to die for? The point we are making, however, is not that these values are *ir*rational—that is, contrary to rational judgment—but that they are in themselves judgmental rather than either inherent in human life or objectively demonstrable as representing the greatest possible good. To put our point more simply, such values as democracy, monotheism, science, and so on can be rationalized by intelligent people—that is, can be defended by logical reasoning. The defense is easier, however, to the extent that one is defending the given value to a similarly prejudiced person. If a person, for example, is already a Christian and accepts the admonition that he is his brother's keeper and that all human beings are equal in the sight of God, then it will be easier, probably, to convince him that the freedom-of-opportunity value is an objective worth espousing. In other words, to the extent that the democratic value is similar to or consistent with the Christian value it will appear rational to the Christian.

It is necessary to point out in this connection that antithetical values can both be logically and rationally justified. This can be demonstrated either historically or contemporaneously. At one time slavery was morally right and acceptable in the eyes of God, so far as intelligent people and very Christian people were concerned. Now it seems not to be so. To some contemporaries the practice of birth control is akin to murder and should immediately be ceased, while to others it is a moral imperative that no more children be conceived than can, so far as one can anticipate, be able to participate liberally in the benefits of modern society. Obviously there is a logic and a rationale to both sides, and people of both high and low intelligence can be found who adhere to either of the two opposite positions.

The foregoing, then, is what is meant by the "extrarational" character of values; one cannot prove the validity of a value like democracy or of capitalism or of Christianity in the way that he can prove that the hypotenuse of a right-angle triangle is equal to the square root of the sum of the squares of the other two sides. There is a great element of faith and previous indoctrination which underlies a person's acceptance of any of these value positions. Even science is basically a matter of faith: We believe or hope that, as a result of examining selected phases of the universe by the inductive method, we will uncover laws which will be useful in our lives. Actually we do not know, except by faith, whether we are on the right track. Certainly, up to the present point in the "atomic age," the results of science have been far from an unmixed blessing. But the faith persists that some day, somehow, if the hydrogen bomb does not kill us all, we will be better off for using the scientific method of inquiry as we have.

But people regard their values not only as if they were strictly rational but often even as if they constituted "eternal verities with which man has not the right to tamper." Thus we find in all societies and all times men who have been willing to die for what they have called "principles"; simultaneously on the other side of the ideological or physical battle other men have also been willing to die for the antithesis of the same principles. Possibly, someone has been misinformed, although it is not always easy to determine which one should so be regarded. History is a long record of the coming and going of "eternal" values, of wars and struggles over values, the believers in which apparently ignored the rest of history which shows how relative and temporary most values really are. But the illusion persists that my values are eternal verities and yours, if they differ from mine, simply show that you have been "misguided." So long as individuals and groups persist in these thought ways, agreement as to what to do about specific social problems seems very remote.

Coexistence of inconsistent values. Within a given society, and also within the mind of a given person, two or more opposing values may coexist, even though from a strictly logical point of view they are inconsistent with one another.[1] Thus a man may loudly and sincerely proclaim that he believes in freedom of opportunity for all men but oppose permitting Negro children to attend the same school with his children or, if segregation is operative, refuse to permit his community to spend as much per child on Negro education as upon white education. Or again, while proclaiming his adherence to Christianity and specifically to the Golden Rule, he also proclaims that it "doesn't pay" to be generous to other people "because they take advantage of you," or "in this world it's dog eat dog, and I'm glad I'm a bigger dog."

On the surface it might seem relatively easy for a society, and especially for some one person, to discover such inconsistencies as these, evaluate the two positions, choose one, and discard the other. All this, of course, in the interest of being consistent. But in practice it seems not to be so easy an undertaking. In the first

[1] Read Bain, "Our Schizoid Culture," *Sociology and Social Research,* Vol. 19 (January-February 1935), pp. 266-76.

place, *logical inconsistency may constitute social consistency*—that is, a person whose values seem inconsistent when analyzed by a third party may regard himself to be quite consistent. Both values seem to him to be quite tenable because he can point out other persons in the society as authority for the rightness of each position. There are further complications when an entire society attempts to make up its mind, so to speak, concerning some concrete course of action which involves always some underlying value positions. Requiring people to put governors on their automobiles so that they will run only forty miles per hour, for example, would undoubtedly help to achieve the value of saving some lives, but few people would vote for such a law because other values like saving time and personal freedom would be jeopardized. So the problem persists because we attain one value at the expense of another.

The persistent and very serious problems of income inequality, racial inequality, and inequality between men and women stem in considerable measure from value inconsistency. While we try to apply the equality-of-opportunity value, our other values stand in the way of its complete and direct application to the situation. Along with the democratic ideology we have the traditional white assumptions of the inherent inferiority of the Negro, the social necessity of keeping him "in his place," and an unwillingness to give up the benefits which white exploitation has brought. So solutions to specific problems of race relations are made from time to time within the framework of value conflict, but no clear-cut solution is reached because there is no clear-cut consensus on underlying values.

Thus we have seen that American society, like others, is based upon a number of values which have come down through the past and are *regarded as* eternal principles. The fact that we have pointed this out, of course, or that a relatively small fragment of the population realizes this, does not alter the basic fact that most persons and groups in the society make their decisions *as if* their value positions were self-evidently the right ones. Meanwhile, inconsistencies among values are patent, and much energy is devoted by various groups to indoctrinating as many people as possible with the values which these groups believe are the right ones. There is, however, another factor in the American intellectual climate which is relevant to the relation of values and social problems, namely, what might be called the philosophy of rational examination of values. In the following section we shall examine this philosophy and discuss its relation to the social problem situation in contemporary American society.

▶ RATIONALISM IN THE ANALYSIS OF VALUES

Relatively recently in Western civilization a point of view has emerged which stresses the necessity and the propriety of approaching values rationally, or at least more rationally than has been traditional. There is, to be sure, considerable sociological naïveté in this rational position, in that it tends to overlook the fact that while some people may be capable of manipulating values rationally, many others, probably a majority, are unwilling or unable so to do. Nevertheless, there is considerable evidence of the impact of this so-called rational approach upon social-problems thinking and action.

As this rational philosophy is examined historically and logically, it is apparent that it consists of at least three separable phases.

Identification of values as phenomena. It will probably already be clear that students of society may regard values as distinguishable "things." Of course they are not tangible things, but they may have very tangible results. They are what social theorists term "constructs." The idea of "value" is thus identified as a more or less distinct phase of any society, which for purposes of discussion and analysis we may abstract from the rest of the totality. Having learned, then, to recognize such values as the democratic ideology or Christian ideology or the ideology of science, the student of society, whether theorist or practical man of affairs, has taken a significant step in the direction of greater rationality. Being able automatically to identify values *as data* places a person one step along the way toward "doing something about" his or his society's specific values.

Conception of values as secular elements. Being able to abstract values as distinct phenomena in the total context of a culture will not in itself make for rationality in thinking about values until a second intellectual skill is achieved, namely, the ability to think about values in a secular manner. So long as one identifies values but attributes them to transhuman forces, such as God, the devil, Nature, or some other presumably uncontrollable source, no attempt at value modification would be probable. But to the extent that it becomes apparent, both to the theoretical analyst and to the practical man, that values are man-made, it becomes relatively obvious that man has the power, perhaps the responsibility, to remake, modify, or discard what he has created when it has outgrown its usefulness.

This point of view has been termed "secularism" in contrast to the more "sacred" conception of values which preceded it. Students of social history have indicated that they have reason to believe that one of the most significant over-all trends in human development has been the emergence of a more secularlike ideology in some modern societies.[2] While they do not contend that any existing society is entirely secular, they make a good case for the increasing secularization of the thinking of modern man.

It may be too obvious to mention that secularism is itself a value—the belief that it is good for persons and groups to view their society as a man-made thing subject to more or less modification at his will. We point this out merely to show that there probably is no position which people now take concerning the evaluation of their society which is not, in some measure at least, derived from extrarational value considerations.

Objective evaluation of the values as means. Once we have recognized that values are abstractable phenomena, and have granted the moral rightness of values being subject to the human will, the way becomes open for a scientific testing of at least some of our value positions. We can illustrate this point in numerous ways. On a common-sense level it is implied in Abraham Lincoln's famous clause that "no nation can exist half slave and half

[2] Robert Redfield, "The Folk Society," *American Journal of Sociology*, Vol. 52 (January 1947), pp. 293-309.

free." Factually, of course, Lincoln's statement was incorrect because the United States then was half slave and half free and yet was very much in existence. What Lincoln obviously referred to was the fact that the slavery system and the values which supported it were inconsistent with other values which the American society at that time held. Consequently, he reasoned, either the slavery system would have to go or some other values would have to go. In short, he was applying rationality to the analysis of the social problem of Negro slavery in the society of his time.

But rational value analysis can be, and is now to some extent being, approached in a much more formal manner. Numerous studies have attempted to attain this objective, and some of them at least have yielded results of theoretical and practical importance. The general *modus operandi* of value analysis consists of testing factually any subordinate value which is claimed to have a cause-and-effect relationship. If, for example, it is held that "poverty is good because it makes for better character," then we can study a group of people reared in poverty, compare them with another group reared in comfort, and discover whether the alleged value position holds up under factual analysis or not. At several points in this book attention has been called to research of precisely this sort, but a few additional examples may help to explain the procedure and philosophy.

Character-building agencies such as the Boy Scouts, Camp Fire Girls, YMCA and church groups are, as the term implies, presumed to improve the character of children who come under their influence. Such children become purportedly more honest, more truthful, and more trustworthy. For a long time this was regarded as a self-evident truth until someone conceived the idea of comparing the honesty, truthfulness, and trustworthiness of samples of children who had participated in character-building agencies and others who had not. The findings of these researches have called into sharp question the traditional value assumptions that character-building agencies really develop significantly different character in the persons who participate in their programs.[3]

[3] See, for example, Hugh Hartshorne and Mark May, *Studies in Deceit*, New York, The Macmillan Co., 1928; also their *Studies in Service and Self Con-

Similarly, one of the arguments often advanced against the teaching by schools of "liberal" points of view concerning politics and economics is the assumption that once a person has modified his conservative values in these areas he will also "lose his devotion to religion," "conservative family life," "respect for law and order," and so on. Research has failed to establish the validity of such a point of view. Conservatism in one area of life does not necessarily bring about conservatism in other areas.[4]

One of the most significant over-all studies which attempts by scientific-logical procedures to examine a large sector of American values was discussed at length in the chapter on Race, namely, Myrdal's *An American Dilemma*. Myrdal's analysis, when very simply generalized, is much the same as a number of other analyses which we made throughout this book: it stresses the fact that once a society becomes committed to the democratic ideal of equality of opportunity, it must be expected that such existing inequalities as are found—for example, in race relations, education, income distribution, and health benefits—will become increasingly difficult to rationalize. They would not be difficult to rationalize in a nondemocratic society where differential privilege is either taken for granted or rationalized as a social good. In other words, by a rational examination of the value make-up of a society, it is possible to explain why certain social problems come to the fore rather than others and even in considerable measure to predict what further issues will arise as long as the value structure remains as it is. Thus it is relatively safe to say, for example, that so long as the democratic ideology continues, so long as American technology is capable of producing the abundance of physical goods which it now does, and so long as America remains a sovereign power, we may expect continuing conflict around such conspicuous inequalities as race relations, income distribution, class-biased education, and underrepresentation of certain groups in government. Should, of course, a fascist ideol-

---

trol and *Studies in the Organization of Character*, New York, The Macmillan Co.

[4] See Robert A. Harper, "Is Conformity a General or a Specific Behavior Trait?" *American Sociological Review*, Vol. 12 (February 1947), pp. 82-86.

ogy, for example, supersede the democratic ideology, then presumably such conflicts as these will be reduced because a disfranchised proletariat is hardly in a position to be assertive about its rights—if it can be said to have rights as we know them in contemporary America.

▶ SUMMARY AND CONCLUSION

In the preceding section we have shown, then, that in relatively recent times, in Europe and in the United States at least, a new philosophy pertaining to values has been superimposed upon the older sacred system of extrarational valuation. This new point of view begins with the identification of values as phenomena which can be abstracted from a total social context. Having separated values from the rest of the system, the observer is then in a position to view them secularly—that is, as man-made and man-modifiable conditions. As a basis for possible modification, however, values may be tested to determine whether their cause-and-effect assumptions are valid and what values may coexist with what other values without creating conflict.

Much of the value conflict in American society stems from the crucial inconsistencies between the older nonrational acceptance of value positions and the somewhat rational procedures which we have just discussed. At numerous places in this book we have in one way or another called attention to this important conflict. For instance, some people simply see wage inequalities as the inevitable outgrowth of differences in native ability. It is not uncommon, even, to hear people say that God so ordained the world. At the same time we have the rationalists who point out, by comparing social systems past and present, that there is nothing inevitable about any particular system of income distribution, that any system can appear inherent in the scheme of things, provided one is sufficiently ignorant of other systems or of the nature of the processes involved. The ideological difference between these two positions is no mere quibble over the details of wage rates or the provisions of social security; it is a fundamental and irreconcilable conflict of basic values—either our system of distribution is inherent in nature or God or it is not. We do not mean to imply that there is any simple device for the empiric discovery of the correct answers to such questions as these, because some value positions are still so held that, facts to the contrary notwithstanding, people do not alter their value position in response to factual revelations. We do mean to imply that at least some men can at least some of the time apply their minds to the task of rational analysis of values and that such effort is both proper and practicable.

Our treatment of values and social problems has repeatedly raised, and at no point answered, a fundamental question with respect to man's thinking processes: Undoubtedly man thinks, and apparently values are a conspicuous part of his thinking about social problems, but *how* does he use his thinking processes in relation to values? Does he use his intellect merely to rationalize the values with which he has been indoctrinated before he was able to think critically? Or does his thinking faculty provide him with a somewhat detached point of view which enables him truly to "choose" which values he shall espouse? Putting the issue in still another way: Is it possible for men in our time to formulate a rational system of values or is value formulation inherently a matter of rationalization of extralogical positions? To be sure it does depend upon the individual, and it is apparent that individuals manipulate values differently. But the central problem persists: How rational *can* our society be—how rational does it *want* to be?

SUGGESTED READINGS

Bain, Read, "Our Schizoid Culture," *Sociology and Social Research*, Vol. 19 (January-February 1935), pp. 266-76. This is a widely known and highly regarded article which calls attention to the great number of important inconsistencies in the values of present-day American society. The vigor and color of the writing and the abundant illustrative detail make the study particularly valuable pedagogically.

Index of Names

Index of Subjects

Adolescence: "adolescent rebellion," 213-14; biological v. sociological maturity, 208-9; conditions conducive to trauma in, 210-13; constructive measures in, 221-3; cultural alternatives and trauma in, 211; defined, 208-9; delinquency, 215-16; economic frustration of, 219-20; and educational reform, 222; and free education, 222-3; impersonal relationships and trauma in, 213; indices of difficulty, 215-20; lack of decision-making rationale and trauma in, 211-12; material culture and trauma in, 213; morals in, 217-19; negative conditioning and trauma in, 212; and parent education, 221-2; "peer competition" and trauma in, 212-13; problems generic to society, 223-4; proposed solutions to problems, 220-3; rebellion in, and early child-rearing, 213-14; and recreation, 223; repressive measures in, 220-1; school failures, 216-17; viewed interculturally, 209-10

Adult education, 317-18

Agriculture: and "corporation farming," 403-4; credit aids, 405; crop control, 401-2; dissatisfactions with occupations in, 406-7; McNary-Haugen farm relief bill, 401; price disparity, 399-405; problems of national concern, 393-5; public interest in, 393-4; rural electrification, 392, 404; subsidies, 394-5, 402-3; *see also* Rural life

Agriculture Adjustment Administration, 401-2

Alcoholics Anonymous, 193

Alcoholism: and characteristics of alcoholics, 190-1; compulsive and non-compulsive use of alcohol, 189-90; rate of, 190; value conflicts in control of, 192-3; value conflicts as source of, 191-2

Amelioration v. curative treatment of social problems, 49-51

Amentia, 128, 137-8, 148, 151-2

American Association of Marriage Counselors, 366

American Bankers Association, 235

American Bar Association, 235, 238

American Civil Liberties Union, 228

American Farm Bureau Federation, 235, 244-5

American Federation of Labor, 234, 241

American Legion, 451

American Medical Association, 112, 114-15, 117-18, 238

American Newspaper Publishers Association, 235

American Pharmaceutical Association, 235

American Psychiatric Association, 146

American Short Line Railroad Association, 235

Americans for Democratic Action, 451

Anti-Nicotine League, 28, 29

Anti-Saloon League, 228

Antitrust laws, 239

Anti-Vivisection Society, 228

Anxiety states, 132-3

Association of American University Professors, 451